The Freedom of Lights:
Edmond Jabès and Jewish Philosophy of Modernity

Studies in Jewish History and Memory

Edited by
Lucyna Aleksandrowicz-Pędich

Volume 12

PETER LANG

Przemysław Tacik

The Freedom of Lights:
Edmond Jabès and
Jewish Philosophy of Modernity

Translated by Dr. Patrycja Poniatowska

PETER LANG

Bibliographic Information published by the Deutsche Nationalbibliothek
The Deutsche Nationalbibliothek lists this publication in the Deutsche Nationalbibliografie; detailed bibliographic data is available online at http://dnb.d-nb.de.

Library of Congress Cataloging-in-Publication Data
A CIP catalog record for this book has been applied for at the Library of Congress.

The Publication is founded by Ministry of Science and Higher Education of the Republic of Poland as a part of the National Programme for the Development of the Humanities. This publication reflects the views only of the authors, and the Ministry cannot be held responsible for any use which may be made of the information contained therein.

ISSN 2364-1975
ISBN 978-3-631-67523-6 (Print) · E-ISBN 978-3-653-06891-7 (E-PDF)
E-ISBN 978-3-631-71200-9 (EPUB) · E-ISBN 978-3-631-71201-6 (MOBI)
DOI 10.3726/978-3-653-06891-7

Acknowledgements

With books which take five years to write, as this one has, it is a sheer impossibility to even name, let alone properly thank, all the people to whom such thanks are more than due. The bulky body of writing may seem to grow of its own accord, but it is always made possible by timely help from others. This book makes its way through its writer's life, absorbing the traces of the paths he has walked and challenges he has had to negotiate. It bears witness to these traces by itself while the writer's task is to thank all those who have directly contributed to its making.

My thanks go thus to Professor Agata Bielik-Robson, Professor Marek Drwięga, Professor Rodolphe Gasché, Ireneusz Kania, Professor Krzysztof Kłosiński and Professor Adam Wodnicki, whose invaluable advice and support helped me avoid many mistakes and inspired new interpretive insights.

This book would not be what it is had it not been for the hospitality I gratefully received from the Université de Nice and the State University of New York at Buffalo, which offered me true research comfort. As there are no institutions without people, my special thank-you goes to the SUNY's Professor Stephen Dunnett, Bronisława Karst-Gasché, Professor Ewa Płonowska-Ziarek, Professor Krzysztof Ziarek and Kathy Kubala as well as many other people who kindly helped me in Buffalo.

I would also like to thank Wydawnictwo Austeria, the publisher of this book's Polish version, and in particular Wojciech Ornat, for extraordinary hospitality by the standards of our times.

I am greatly indebted to all those who worked on preparing the English version of this book. The extraordinary translation by Dr. Patrycja Poniatowska combines the highest precision with linguistic elegance. Thanks to her this text, which was already born at the crossroads of a few languages, could get a new life in English. I would also like to express my gratitude to Jan Burzyński, Łukasz Gałecki and Peter Lang Publishing for navigating this text to its publication.

I am grateful to this book's first reader. Olga, this text will forever preserve the trace of your first gaze.

Last but not least, I wish to thank all hidden tsaddikim who helped me in my work although I did not realise how profoundly they contributed to it.

Contents

As whirlwinds in the south pass through;
so it cometh from the desert, from a terrible land.

(Isaiah, 21:1)

Introduction

The time when justifications were given precedence is over, and, clearly, we find ourselves stripped of justifications. "Our sources precede us," insists Edmond Jabès, but at any rate we are not heading from them and towards them; rather, they wane underway, gliding by like shadows, only to dissolve as something one can no longer continue persuading to exist. This is also true of the origins of this book. But if I were to believe that persuasion has a power to create – more even, that persuasion is the only wall between us and nothingness – I would have to say that this book sprouted out of multiple questions following one upon another. The final text has gone a long way from the concern of philosophical interpretation of a modern kabbalist's writings to the question of the status of Jewish philosophy in modernity, to an even broader theme of distinctiveness of modern philosophising as such.

This book's dark prehistory was nurtured by a simple need: a need to interpret Jabès' writings so as to glean a singular philosophy from them. Jabès, a 20th-century poet and kabbalist, the author of scattered and hermetic texts that explode any generic boundaries, has already invited ample research and critical attention. He has been commented on by poets and literary scholars, by writers, such as Paul Auster, by philosophers, such as Jacques Derrida, and Maurice Blanchot, too. Though undoubtedly valuable – and sometimes invaluable – for their minute and yet brilliant insights, all these interpretations fail to face up to the entirety of Jabès' textual production. They do not seek to make a comprehensive connection between myriads of particles that make up the body of his writing. Moreover, they all fall into a trap set by the author of *The Book of Questions*. For, when pondering Jabès, one is easily manoeuvred into following one of two well-trodden paths: one either weaves one's own disjointed and chaotic narrative at the margins of his texts or seeks to come near Jabès writings, interspersing them with a commentary that, as such, ceases to differ from the quoted excerpts. Both approaches bring forth a spectre of Jabès, paler even than it behoves spectres, agonisingly soulless at times and spewing out banalities. By rupturing the writer's signature and textual continuity in order to pour one's own, derivative commentary into the fissures, one adds little to his writing while stripping it of much and flouting its right to be given justice to in its entirety.

Such was the path I wanted to avoid at any cost. From the very beginning, which I can only hold in doubt, it was clear to me that the Jabèsian body of text required powerful thinking capable of entering the lists with other philosophers of the 20th century. It required a very special form of thinking, developed only for this particular occasion and dedicated not so much to explicate the text line by line as to illuminate it from the sidelines. My aim was to surmount the diffusion of his writings and make them yield the underlying structure of thinking that seems to inform them. In other words, besides the typical objectives of a monograph – such as acquainting readers comprehensively with a figure as essential to modern literature as Edmond Jabès, surveying the core motifs of his texts and reviewing his critical interpretations – my goal was also to have philosophy materialise out of his writing.

As Heidegger's example emphatically shows, philosophy that ventures to interpret a literary text is usually blighted with severe blindness. Well, the discourse of philosophy as such is blindness in action. And yet, there is a flicker of chance in this darkness. If skilfully capitalised on, a grand blackout, preposterous as it is, passes over entirely obvious questions, takes no notice of its own status and potency, but for all that it ventures further. For what other philosophical discourse would have the grit to try and quarry the structure of thinking from a poet-kabbalist's writings? Planning this book, I have covertly counted on the value added of philosophical arrogance which digs deeper than other discourses in the humanities because it may forget that depth does not exist. If this design succeeded, the Jabèsian work would see another text arise at a distance – a distance greater than literary studies usually venture to tread – one that could legitimately be referred to as Edmond Jabès' philosophy. Such a Nietzschean gesture of strong interpretation, which shuns no justifiable violence, could help set Jabès apart from his contemporary authors and cleave his work off from the continuum of post-war thinking, demanding a more prominent place for the poet than has been assigned to him. One could also advocate for his position in philosophy, a place he certainly deserves though has never actually been granted.

To carry out this design, I needed a solid footing for thinking of Jabès philosophically. One context offered itself more forcefully than others: the context of modern philosophical re-interpretation of Judaism. In the 20th century – from Hermann Cohen, to Franz Rosenzweig, Walter Benjamin, Emmanuel Lévinas, to Harold Bloom (and further) – the movement invigorated philosophy and other fields of the humanities, infusing them with many fresh ideas, as if purposefully gifted to us for the times that saw metaphysics falling apart. In particular, it renewed the Athens-Jerusalem opposition, binding Greek thought with the declining tradition of Western philosophising and attributing to Jerusalem – a

symbol of anti-idolatrous, writing-focused Jewish thought – the role of replen-
ishing philosophical discourse. The contrast of the two metropolises is focalised
today in the academic doxa of oppositions – of image vs. word, paganism vs.
monotheism, myth vs. faith, immanence vs. Messianism and, finally, the cult of
death vs. vitalism.[1] Embracing the strong opposition of Athens and Jerusalem,
such a context for reading Jabès would be natural insofar as it would fully espouse
the leanings within Judaism that the poet valued highly himself: anti-mythical
tendencies, radical a-theological monotheism, the experience of exile, elaborate
hermeneutical tradition with its special attitude to writing, intertextuality, primacy of word over image, the idea of creation *ex nihilo* and, finally, the messianic
element. It would not pose a serious difficulty to portray Jabès as another Lévinas
or another Blanchot (in his apology of Judaism), all the more so that in many
senses he indeed was both. But in this framework, the poet's thinking would be
reduced to the kind of post-Heideggerian philosophy which vindicates so-far
marginalised or excluded discourses. Jabès would become just another propo-
nent of Jerusalem against Athens, and his work would not inventively stray from
well-trodden paths.

Such an interpretive approach would entail the risk of taking tautology for
a discovery. For Jabès himself contributed to constructing a specific vision of
Judaism in the late 20th-century humanities. No wonder, thus, that the vision
may be re-traced back in his writings. That is why reading his body of work
against academic Judaism would amount to simply explaining *idem per idem*.
Therefore, the context of theses typically propounded as a philosophical re-interpretation of Judaism did not seem a fitting conceptual scaffolding for this book.
Discarding it, I realised, however, that Jabès' thought bears a distressing paradox
that not only prompts one not to read it within Jewish thinking as re-counted by
20th-century philosophy but also compels one to interrogate the legitimacy and
relevance of this very re-counting. The said paradox involves the fact that going
his own way – reading poets rather than philosophers and consistently kindling
the destructive movement of the text he was creating – Jabès arrived where other
20th-century thinkers did even though they had little, or nothing whatsoever, to
do with Judaism: Wittgenstein, Heidegger and Lacan. The latter two have even

---

1   In the Polish humanities, a passionate plea for the relevance and permanence of the
     Athens vs. Jerusalem opposition is to be found in Agata Bielik-Robson's *Erros. Mesjański
     witalizm i filozofia* [*Erros: Messianic vitalism and philosophy*] (Kraków: Universitas,
     2012), which comprehensively discusses the features of Greek and Jewish thinking
     I merely indicate here.

garnered a reputation of paradigmatic, late-time "Greeks." And Jabès' texts are saturated with so deceptively Heideggerian a need to listen for and to age-old silences and absences; and his understanding of reality is so Lacanian in empha- sising non-Totality, which, to be constituted, needs a minimum remnant, an absent fragment. At the same time, however, Jabès suffuses his work with a pro- found subtext of Judaism. He untiringly reaches for various motifs from Jewish tradition to make them part of his argument; more than that, he even proclaims that real meanings of certain concepts of Judaism are fully consonant with his intuitions. A puzzle that presents itself to us is, then, why Jabès entered the path of "Greek" thinking if he walked the "Jewish" way.

This puzzle might be framed slightly differently: Why did the thinker who devoted all his mature works to meditating on Judaism, to contemplating the meaning of revelation and covenant after Auschwitz, and, finally, to pondering the death of God in ways clearly nurtured by Jewish monotheism, come essen- tially so close to Heidegger and Lacan, two heirs to the decaying legacy of "Athens"? Why does he constantly dwell on Nothing, attributing it a Name at the same time? Why is the body of his writing steeped in the death of God – and not only God – instead of in vigorous vitalism? And why is his text subjected to utter simplification, why does it forfeit the richness of content and devastate the nar- rative down to a tatter, reducing itself to a single, ultimate difference? Briefly: Is Jabès "really" of Jerusalem or of Athens? Is he a post-Greek thinker donning Jewish trappings, or is he a Jewish thinker secretly haunted by the nihilism of fallen Athens?

Such questions would probably be raised by the academic humanities with their adamant investment in the permanence of the Athens-vs.-Jerusalem oppo- sition. Nevertheless, such questions are pulverised when clashing against the hard rock of Jabès' writings. What an auspicious coincidence it is that Jabès hails from Cairo. The Athens-vs.-Jerusalem dualism is thus sent into such flutter that it is not only hardly applicable to the author of *The Book of Questions* but also forcefully doomed to dismantling. At the slightest attempt, the carefully culti- vated distinctions between the truly "Jewish" spirit and the intrinsically "Greek" heritage come to resemble a makeshift footbridge over a precipice. Only when an unsettling, excluded position of a "third metropolis" steals into the academic dualism can one look back upon the assumptions underpinning philosophical Greece and philosophical Judaism, and realise how frequently they converge or overlap. Here is one emphatic example: evoking Judaism, 20th-century phi- losophy highlighted an apocalyptic dimension in its re-interpretation of Jewish Messianism. Benjamin and Bloch, major upholders of this stance, hoped for the coming of messianic justice, which would give singularity its due. Yet, doesn't messianic justice, as pictured by 20th-century philosophy, resemble Heidegger's concept of *Gelassenheit*?[2] Is it not informed by similar forces of simplification, seeking ultimate equality devoid of violence? Does the background of messianic justice not harbour a bane of indebtedness to a dark source, which casts a long shadow over modern philosophy, a shadow this philosophy strives to shake off once and for all? Admittedly, the difference between Athens and Jerusalem seems to obtain still – in particular, as regards the way of attaining the ideal of justice – but it remains so closely linked to the movement of simplification that it forces *to look into how this very opposition is implicated in the processes behind transformations in the two tendencies it is eager to set apart.* For why, in two so different traditions, does a similar desire come to the fore whose object is constituted as a deferral?

When the Athens-vs.-Jerusalem opposition is scrutinised carefully, endeavours to separate lastingly one metropolis from the other come to stir increasing doubt. Threads are revealed which stitched the opposition; and it suffices to compare how various thinkers draw the lines between their respective domains to begin to hesitate profoundly whether the outlines of philosophical Judaism may indeed be demarcated in the first place. While Benjamin repudiates guilt, law and fate, which he associates with the myth and views as a residuum of paganism to be eradicated, Kafka follows the opulent kabbalist and Chasidic tradition to see Judaism as wielding a key to law, guilt and judgment. Given this divergence, does the Law belong with Greek or Jewish thought? If the Law was obliterated, and with relief, too, by the apostles of the Greeks, should it be recovered or rather overthrown in philosophical Judaism? And finally, what is actually guilt that comes into being vis-à-vis the Law? Should it be combated, as a vestige of paganism, or should it rather be considered a treasured ethical value?

The path of suspicion guides us far beyond and above the Athens-vs.-Jerusalem opposition. It makes us inquire whether the tectonic changes that re-interpretations of Judaism are subject to in 20th-century philosophy do not, incidentally, ensue from modern thinking as such rather than from Judaism. Isn't this philosophical and academic Jerusalem, by any chance, haunted by, not even the Greek, but the modern spirit? May it not reflect distinctly modern philosophising? In this age of ours, thinking has taken a unique form: it is produced by and of a galaxy of dispersed minds that still

---

2 Cf. Martin Heidegger, *Discourse on Thinking: A Translation of Gelassenheit*, trans. John M. Anderson and E. Hans Freund, with an Introduction by John M. Anderson (New York, Evanston and London: Harper and Row, 1966).

look behind in search of a logic of movement which persistently carries them away in one direction. In this fight for survival, oppositions are valuable, if not outright invaluable, for the one that wants to resist the movement of simplification, but, like anchors, they are part of the drifting ship rather than of the bottom beneath it.

By no means do I wish to suggest here that the Athens-vs.-Jerusalem divide has lost it utility in contemporary thinking. On the contrary, the manner in which 20th-century philosophy vindicates Judaism and contrasts it with the Greek legacy emphatically displays all the peculiarities of modern thought. That is why the meandering path that this book followed started with questions about the feasibility of giving a philosophical account of Jabès' writings and wound up in the exploration of meanings of the links between Judaism and 20th-century thinking, which in themselves hold a mirror up to the phenomenon of modernity. Ultimately, the issues of ethics as implicated in modernity's drive to ultimate simplification proved of great pertinence to me. As a result, to salvage the ethical remnant where all ethics seems overthrown is yet another concern central to this study.

Thus, this book spirals around its pivotal point in ever wider circles: Jabès' work pushes towards the issues of 20th-century philosophical Judaism, which in themselves direct towards the phenomenon of modernity. It is not my aim, then, to abolish the Athens-vs.-Jerusalem opposition (as if oppositions could be abolished in the first place); instead, I want to locate this opposition in the context provided by modern thought. To accomplish this feat, I need a firm foothold of *suspicion*. In this book, the central suspicion is: Is 20th-century philosophical Judaism not just an attempt – beyond justification and non-justification – on the part of modernity's immanent drive towards difference to take advantage of Jewish tradition? And, consequently, is Jerusalem, as portrayed in this philosophy, not just a dummy put up by the modern spirit, which has nothing in common either with Greece or with *Eretz Israel*? Further, is all pre-modern history, as we think it, not this kind of dummy? Or, in other words, does the modern turn not sever us off from the past, forever and decisively, reducing it to the stuff to be utilised in its own constructs? Asking such questions and suspecting that the old oppositions cherished for over twenty centuries may be nothing else or more but a mirage veiling the abyss of the modern shift, we could finally re-think the meanings of the Jewish revival the humanities have orchestrated in the recent decades.

"Pray for the peace of Jerusalem: they shall prosper that love thee," the Scripture says. Love of the philosophical Jerusalem is perhaps the only thing that stands after the Judaism of yore fades away irretrievably in the transparency of pre-modern history. To defend Jerusalem against its opposition to Athens, this is this book's ultimate goal.

Jabès' writings will serve therein as a paradigmatic example of relations between Judaism and 20th-century thought. His work belongs neither to Jewish philosophy nor to Judaism which tends to tailor philosophy to its own needs. It forms an entirely separate realm of its own, where modern forces of thought deploy the historical matter of Jewish tradition. Suspended between the derivatively and selectively absorbed religion and culture of Judaism on the one hand and the intellectual milieu of the 20th century on the other, the position distinctly espoused by Jabès' writing is shared also by other writers and thinkers, their throng including Kafka, Benjamin, Rosenzweig, Buber, Lévinas, and, to a degree, Derrida. How can these relations be explained? Whence does the revival of Judaism in contemporary thinking originate? And, finally, why do the Jewish insights utilised in the 20th century dovetail so closely with philosophy's own conclusions – as if they shared a kind of common inner structure?

To answer such questions, I propose to use a new notion in this book, one of "Jewish philosophy of modernity" which goes beyond the categories of "Jewish philosophy," "modern philosophy," or "modern Jewish philosophy," as applied so far. "Jewish philosophy of modernity" is a notion that, first and foremost, captures the overdetermination characteristic of Judaism-inspired 20th-century concepts, in which one may distinguish several equally valid frameworks of reference: (1) modern philosophy, i.e. philosophy created in the modern era; (2) philosophy of modernity, i.e. all the schools of thought that make modernity an object of reflection; (3) Jewish philosophy, which, as it were, is in and by itself a product of the age of *modernitas*;[3] (4) philosophy that draws on a variety of insights of earlier Jewish, both rabbinical and kabbalist, tradition; (5) philosophy that inquires

---

3   To an extent, I endorse here the position of Michael L. Morgan and Peter Eli Gordon, who insist that the term "philosophy" should be rather selectively applied only to such kinds of thinking which question what is taken for granted, including their own foundations. On this model, pre-modern thought developed within Judaism could be called philosophy only metaphorically, if at all, given its strong rootedness in tradition and subordination to rabbinical control. According to Morgan and Gordon, Jewish philosophy comes into being only when the tradition of Judaism comes to be viewed with detachment and its meanings are interrogated. That is why one of the basic questions pondered by this philosophy is what is actually the criterion of Jewishness. See Michael L. Morgan and Peter Eli Gordon, "Introduction: Modern Jewish Philosophy, Modern Philosophy, and Modern Judaism," in M. L. Morgan, and P. E. Gordon (eds.), *The Cambridge Companion to Modern Jewish Philosophy* (Cambridge et al.: Cambridge UP, 2007), pp. 1–13, on pp. 1–9.

into the meaning of Judaism in the modern era; and finally (6) philosophy that relies on certain trends of Jewish thought in seeking to explain the modern crisis of philosophy. All these threads are tightly knotted, actually beyond any unravelling. Therefore, instead of laboriously distinguishing Jewish philosophy from modern Jewish philosophy and Jewish philosophy from Judaism, I assumed a priori an inner interconnectedness of Judaism and modernity. Conceived in these terms, *"Jewish philosophy of modernity"* is *a complex phenomenon forged in a grid of ongoing reflexive mediations between modern philosophy, thinking about modernity as an epoch, and Jewish tradition.*

It is exactly reflexivity – in its new sense heralded by the Kantian critique – that is distinctive to the position of "Jewish philosophy of modernity." Over centuries, Jewish thought has drawn on innumerable external sources: Greek philosophy, religions of the Near East, Gnosis, Arabic philosophy, Sufism, mediaeval Christian reflection, Protestant tradition, and so forth. Maimonides, the most prominent Jewish rationalist of the Middle Ages, best exemplifies the indebtedness of Jewish thought to Greek, Arabic and Christian philosophies. But "Jewish philosophy of modernity" designates more than just another species of continuing "Jewish philosophy," which in this age derives inspiration from Western thought, just as it was once inspired by Aristotle or Islamic *kalam*. *"Jewish philosophy of modernity"* contemplates the very problem of whether *there actually is a Jewish philosophy as such.* Hardly anything is more typical of contemporary studies of this philosophy than tentative, non-conclusive speculations about what it is that should "really" be called Jewish philosophy.[4] Yet, rather than in

Admittedly, I do not subscribe to Morgan and Gordon's radical coupling of philosophy with (self)reflexivity, but I do believe that this definitional reduction is informed by apt intuitions. *Modern* philosophy is (self)reflexive. That is why modern Jewish philosophy is bred in and from a remoteness into which questioning pushes the tradition of Judaism. I would not say that Maimonides should be denied the name of a philosopher, yet I certainly agree that he clearly differs from modern Jewish philosophers in that he thinks *within* religious tradition while they seek to re-think what has remained of it.

4   See, for example, Adam Lipszyc, *Ślad judaizmu w filozofii XX wieku* [*The trace of Judaism in 20th-century philosophy*] (Warszawa: Fundacja im. Mojżesza Schorra, 2009), pp. 11–21. As Daniel H. Frank aptly observes, history of philosophy comes into being with the onset of the modern period, and "Jewish philosophy" takes no different course, acquiring visibility only with the advent of a modern perspective, which arranges the thinking of past ages into a sequence and looks for its distinctive features. See Daniel H. Frank, "What is Jewish philosophy?" in Daniel H. Frank, and Olivier Leaman (eds.), *History of Jewish Philosophy* (London and New York: Routledge, 1997), pp. 1–8.

finding a sound answer to this question, the problem lies in *the very imperative of raising this question*. In other words, the fact that many authors seem to be compelled to identify the defining criterion of Jewish philosophy speaks to their own philosophical position rather than to the object of their reflection.

Summing up, "Jewish philosophy of modernity" as conceived of in this book is a notion expected to reveal the problematic nature of modern philosophical references to Judaism in their internally overdetermined structure. I believe that a philosophical account of Jabès' thought can help grasp an array of their shared recurrent patterns, more explicitly perhaps than analyses of the philosophical work of Rosenzweig, Benjamin and/or Derrida. Why? There are a few reasons. First, Jabès is not a philosopher; he refers to philosophers very rarely, and his thinking, rather than commenting on traditions already in place, evolves out of and by itself. Curiously, however, his thought tackles the same issues that beleaguer modern philosophy. In this light, Jabès can be assumed to succumb to – besides influences of other authors – a logic that pervades all thinking in modernity. Second, his writings, as I shall seek to show in this book, aggregate into an ongoing meditation on one problem that is getting ever more distilled and simplified, that is, on the question of difference and remnant. That is why Jabès is not only a modern thinker but also an embodiment of the utter simplification and crystallisation of structures that shape an essential part of philosophy of modernity. Third, another author that makes so extensive references to Judaism would be hard to find in the 20th century.[5] When analysis Jabès' writings, there is no evading the question of the status of revision of Jewish tradition. For the trace, the "effect of Jewishness" formed outside the proper discourse of Judaism, as Philippe Boyer writes,[6] is exceptionally pronounced in Jabès. Fourth, Jabès is a thinker who found the reconstruction of Judaism a vital response to the spiritual condition of the contemporary era as well as an effective tool for interpreting it.

Jabès' work displays, and with extraordinary lucidity too, a fusion of two phenomena, i.e. Jewish tradition and modern thought, permeating his texts in the form of a theory of writing and the writer. At the same time, Jabès constantly

---

5   Cf. Miryam Laifer, *Edmond Jabès. Un judaïsme après Dieu* (New York, Berne and Frankfurt am Main: Peter Lang, 1986), p. ix.

6   Philippe Boyer, "Le point de la question," *Change* 22 (février 1975), pp. 41–73, on pp. 41–42.

maintains a minimum difference between the two, insisting that he is not a Jewish writer, but "a Jew and a writer."[7] That is why I believe that the author of *The Book of Questions* best embodies "a Jewish philosopher of modernity," with the term's entire overdetermination. All the influences encapsulated in the term factor in making Jabès' writings a compelling riddle. Hence, like no one else perhaps, he offers a cornerstone on which to develop the concept of Jewish philosophy of modernity.

The argument in this book develops in several interlocking stages. In Chapter One, I begin by formulating the concept of Jewish philosophy of modernity. I focus first on a handful of examples of 20th-century conceptual frameworks that drew on Jewish tradition and attempt to identify the underlying patterns they share. They are later confronted with a portrayal of the turn that ushered in the age of modernity. This will help define what Jewish philosophy of modernity actually is in its overdetermined position between Judaism and modern thought.

Relying on this theoretical framework, I will develop an in-depth account of Jabès' philosophy. To begin with, I will briefly report the author's biography and describe his writings. In the subsequent Chapters, I will address the most pertinent elements of Jabèsian thinking: the idea of *tzimtzum* (Chapter Three), ontology approximating negative theology (Chapters Four and Five), Messianism (Chapter Six), the concept of the Book (Chapter Seven), affinities between Judaism and writing (Chapter Eight) and, finally, ethical issues, therein Jabès' reflection on anti-Semitism and the Holocaust (Chapter Nine) as well as on three para-ethical notions of repetition, resemblance and hospitality (Chapter Ten). Each Chapter has its own conclusion in which its central thematic concerns are related to the concept of Jewish philosophy of modernity. The last Chapter (Eleven) explores the most advanced field of Jabèsian thought: his speculations on the point. It brings together all the previously discussed themes and seeks to grasp the essence of Jewish philosophy of modernity. Key insights into it are comprised in the conclusion to this Chapter while the book's Conclusion recapitulates the findings of the Chapters and revisits the idea of Jewish philosophy of modernity charted at the beginning in an attempt to define what contribution the exploration of Jabès' thought makes to its lore.

In this Introduction, I wish to clarify a few more issues. This book is deeply indebted to such interpreters of Jabès as Jacques Derrida, Gabriel Bounoure, Maurice Blanchot, Rosmarie Waldrop, Beth Hawkins, Warren F. Motte, Didier

---

7 JW, p. 27. Citing Jabès' works, I will use abbreviations explained and documented in Works Cited.

Cahen, Steven Jaron, Marcel Cohen, Mary Ann Caws, Richard Stamelman, Adolfo Fernandez-Zoïla, Llewellyn Brown, François Laruelle, Helena Shillony, William Franke, Stéphane Mosès, Paul Auster and many others. Quotes from and references to their texts speak for themselves, which, however, should not occlude the fact that my project differs considerably from the earlier ways of reading and expounding Jabès and, as such, uses the existing interpretations as props only.

In this book, I had to give up on investigating how the concept of Jewish philosophy of modernity is, or could be, applied to the reading of philosophers other than Jabès. Even though I do think that the concept can be highly effective in interpreting the work of Rosenzweig, Benjamin, Scholem, Lévinas, Celan, Derrida and many other authors, I believe that this must be studied separately. This book only seeks to formulate the concept of Jewish philosophy of modernity and to develop it in a dialectical application to Jabès' work.

Quotes from Jabès' writings are limited to the absolutely indispensable minimum. His writings are specific insofar that although each piece revolves around a particular underlying idea, all the remaining elements of Jabèsian thinking are invariably braided into it. That is why it is impossible exhaustively to cite all passages that convey a given topos without making this book an imitation of Montaigne's *Essays*. Hence, I quote only the excerpts that are most vividly illustrative or open up large interpretive vistas. I view the body of Jabès' writings through the coordinates of a superimposed grid of a philosophical structure, without however commenting on his particular texts step by step.[8] I believe that the notions I propose here are productively applicable to nearly all works of the poet, but I leave these interpretations to my readers.

At this place, I should settle my intellectual debt to two figures whose ghosts persistently haunt this book though they rarely speak in their own voices. These spectral presences are Jacques Derrida and Jacques Lacan. I briefly address a very complex relation between Jabès and Derrida in Chapter Two. Naturally, they share several assumptions and attitudes to interpretation and writing. However,

---

8   Miryam Laifer observed that "the depth of Jabès's writings compels us to believe that studying every or nearly every word is a prerequisite to understanding his work. After several readings, one always feels that a new reading is necessary because the texts seem to elude us." See Laifer, *Edmond Jabès*, p. 104. Indeed, evoking any quote immediately re-directs the course of thinking, as it forces one to go along new paths opened up by the quotation. This pitfall is well exemplified in the existing interpretations of the poet's work. That is why I limit the number of quotations to an absolute minimum, giving more room to the philosophical structure.

my tenet was that, in a book like this one, Jabès must be freed from the shadow of his follower. Consequently, I left aside inquiries into Jabès' influence on Derrida as an entirely separate question which calls for a comprehensive study of its own. Yet, I tried to show that interpretation of the poet's writings yields a fully original philosophy without a recourse to the categories of deconstruction. More than that, some of Jabès' ideas seem to go further than Derrida's suggestions. Should the handling of the former seem to some readers to be beholden to Derridean deconstruction, I must emphasise that it is not because deconstruction informed my interpretation. Jabès walked his own path, but as it nearly dovetailed with Derrida's, *every interpretation of the poet's work begets a new and unique species of deconstruction.* There is no deconstructive reading of Jabès' writings, or rather there is only a meta-deconstructive reading of them, because the core of these texts is formed by the very same mechanisms that fuelled deconstruction. In interpretations of Jabès, deconstruction encounters itself, that is, no one but a modestly intervening difference.

As to the other spectre – Lacan – the matters look rather different. Nothing is basically known about relations between Jabès and Lacan, and even less about their reciprocal influences. Nonetheless, as I mention in the book's Conclusion, they seem to have shared multiple insights. Undoubtedly, the affinity was affected by their common intellectual milieu, that is, post-war French thought. If the interpretations I propose occasionally seem to rely on categories redolent of Lacan's vocabulary, it is not because I put forward a Lacanian reading of the poet. On the contrary, some of Jabès' original formulas come considerably closely to these categories. This conjunction is far more interesting than any Lacanian reading as *the text itself discloses its affinities with this re-interpretation of psychoanalysis, bidding us to inquire what it actually is that underpins these similarities.* I believe that the concept of Jewish philosophy of modernity will help us illuminate this question.

To end with, some technicalities should be explained. Most of Jabès' texts are quoted based on the already canonical translations by Rosmarie Waldrop. Any alterations to them are clearly indicated. Other translations are the joint work of this volume's author and translator. In the footnotes, abbreviations of titles are used, with the full bibliographical data of the editions provided in the Works Cited. Whoever interprets Jabès' writings in a language other than French faces the challenge of striking a balance between a literal translation and a translation that renders the original's poetic depth. In this work, precedence is given to accuracy that conveys the notorious ambiguity of the poet's expressions. Hence, parenthesised original wordings are often provided as otherwise some of the texts' important qualities, therein punning and homophony, would inevitably be emptied out.

Concluding, I should clearly articulate one more assumption which, though obvious, is too essential to be left for casual conjecture. This volume is a very particular and deliberately selective interpretation. Although it is rooted in a very careful reading of Jabès' texts, no interpretation, especially one of a writer like Jabès, can be considered the ultimately right one. In addition, polyvalence, inconsistency and inner dispersal of his writings preclude any interpretive closure. Jabès himself was often tempted to venture into regions that he had earlier repudiated; that is why to look for any consistent mapping of a straightforward trail in his texts is an exercise in futility. To contrive a single interpretation of any book of his, be it one book only, is a sheer impossibility. In such exigencies, there is only one adequate response. As I have mentioned at the beginning of this Introduction, the response involves erecting a philosophical construction *next to* the poet's work so that their mutual correspondences could reveal structural mechanisms un-thought of before. The ramification of such a decision is that responsibility for this chess-playing puppet rests, basically, with me.

1 Jewish Philosophy of Modernity

Because "Jewish philosophy of modernity" serves in this book as the central interpretive notion, I will start my argument from forging it. I will attempt to construct it against a handful of examples of 20th-century thinking, in which Judaism and modernity are conjoined, highlighting at the same time that the interrelation of the two as intimated in these examples is a moot point, indeed. As opposed to the previous incarnations of *Wahlverwandschaften* between Jewish tradition and modern thought, I wish to assume their connectedness explicitly and unambiguously. It is only from such a position that questions about where this connectedness originates and what sense it makes can effectively be asked.

On the Affinities between Modernity and Judaism

Many 20th-century authors revisited the idea of a certain kinship between Jewish tradition and modernity. Both terms are, obviously, very general, but their inconclusiveness corresponds to confusions that envelop this complex issue. In earlier frameworks, "Jewish tradition" meant, for example, modes of interpretation developed within rabbinical Judaism, a distinct Jewish experience (e.g. exile, persecution, the Holocaust, survival of "the remnants of Israel," and so forth), Judaism's ethical ideals, the Jewish take on monotheism, an approach to language and a multitude of other things. Clearly, the theses about an affinity between "Jewish tradition" and "modernity" are predicated on prior, usually latent, preconceptions about what it actually is that lies at the core of the Jewish. "Modernity" is a by no means less vague or less polyvalent moniker which has been used to designate several different directions that philosophy has taken over recent centuries (particularly in the 20th century), contemporary paradigms of literary studies and, also, the conceptual horizons and the spiritual aura of the epoch, including the human condition in the 20th century. Presuppositions about the character of this "modernity" predate ideas about its overlaps with Judaism although particulars, including such apparently basic ones as its time-frame, remain underdefined.

To inventory all such assumptions would take a separate and extensive study of its own. As this is expressly not my goal, in this subchapter I will focus on selected representative examples to demonstrate fundamental insights concerning the affinity of modernity and Judaism. The first of our models is encountered in Gershom Scholem, the most distinguished historian of Jewish mysticism in the 20th century. Admittedly, he ushered into academic research the theme of the Kabbalah, which had earlier been marginalised by the *Wissenschaft des Judentums* movement, yet a vigorous, deeply personal interest in the spiritual legacy of Jewish mystical tradition shines through his objective historical scholarship. Intriguingly, Scholem engaged in the scholarly study of the Kabbalah for distinctly "unscholarly" reasons. He wanted to respond adequately to the formative processes of his age, such as the crisis of Revelation or, even, the withdrawal of God, assimilation, the loss of Judaism's religious heritage and the predicament of the modern man, for whom the world proved an entirely cryptic code. As attested by his famous letter to Salman Schocken,[1] Scholem viewed his endeavours to understand the Kabbalah – over the chasm of time that has passed since its dawn – as part of the toils his contemporary philosophy braved to decipher the enigmatic space in which it found itself.[2] In other words, the expanses of historical oblivion stretching between the Kabbalah and the present moment were the same problem to him as the shrivelling of the world's comprehensibility. That is one reason why Scholem believed that scholarly investigations must strive to give our age a spiritual foothold. If veiled in Scholem's historical studies, such as his classic *Trends in Jewish Mysticism* and articles compiled in the voluminous *Kabbalah*, this aim looms large in his numerous shorter post-war texts and conference papers. Besides philosophising on the condition of modern Judaism, Scholem repeatedly addressed also the preoccupation his contemporary philosophy showed with ideas akin to Judaism. What ideas were they exactly? In one of his conference papers titled "Reflections on Jewish Theology in Our Time," Scholem rehearses quite a repertory of them. Let us look into the following passage:

---

1   See Gershom Scholem, *Le Nom et les symboles de Dieu dans la mystique juive*, trans. Maurice R. Hayoun and Georges Vajda (Paris: Les Éditions du Cerf, 1983), p. 7 ff.

2   As observed by Stéphane Mosès, Scholem found a peculiar aporia in the position the Kabbalah found itself in in his day. On the one hand, the Kabbalah could be viewed as a dead text-corpus good only for a detached historical analysis. On the other hand, as Scholem believed, the Kabbalah was relevant to the present, yet it could be accessed only through a historical study. The aporia lay thus in that the potency of this mysticism could be revealed only when the historical account suspended the text's direct meaning, making the Kabbalah essentially impotent. See Stéphane Mosès, *The Angel of History: Rosenzweig, Benjamin, Scholem*, trans. Barbara Harshav (Stanford, CA: Stanford UP, 2009), pp. 130–1, 163–4. It implies that the Kabbalah's historical situation in the 20th century is in and by itself part of the problem which the Kabbalistic knowledge salvaged from oblivion is expected to solve.

The notion of continuous Creation is connected with an important concept through which the kabbalists have tried to grasp it intellectually by a bold manoeuvre. Since Creation was at the same time a miracle, they sought to render this miracle intelligible through the concept of *tzimtzum* (contraction) – though at a price, that of giving up the concept of the absolute immutability of God. […] The universe of space and time, this living process we call Creation, appeared to the kabbalists to be intelligible only if it constituted an act of God's renunciation, in which He sets Himself a limit. Creation out of nothing, from the void, could be nothing other than creation of the void, that is, of the possibility of thinking anything that was not God. Without such self-limitation, after all, there would be only God – and obviously nothing else. A being that is not God could only become possible and originate by virtue such a contraction, such a paradoxical retreat of God into Himself. By positing a negative factor in Himself, God liberates Creation. This act, however, is not a one-time event; it must constantly repeat itself; again and again a stream streams into the void, a "something" from God. This, to be sure, is the point at which the horrifying experience of God's absence in our world collides irreconcilably and catastrophically with the doctrine of a Creation which renews itself. The radiation of which the mystics speak and which is to attest to the Revelation of God in Creation – that radiation is no longer perceivable by despair. The emptying of the world to a meaningless void not illuminated by any ray of meaning or direction is the experience of him who I would call a pious atheist. The void is the abyss, the chasm or the crack that opens up in all that exists. This is the experience of modern man, surpassingly well depicted in all its desolation by Kafka, for whom nothing has remained of God but the void – in Kafka's sense, to be sure, the void of God.[3]

In this passage, Scholem-the-scholar transfigures into an engaged philosopher. Precise historical references vanish from his considerations; *tzimtzum* is no longer an idea of the Lurianic Kabbalah but a concept of rather indefinite "kabbalists"; and God's contraction becomes indistinguishable from God's modern, post-Nietzschean "death." The nebulous argumentation seems to disguise quite a bold thesis that Scholem seems to posit. Explicitly worded, the thesis would be that modernity, in which the world becomes incomprehensible, devoid of meaning and suffused with nothingness, could be surprisingly aptly captured in the notion of *tzimtzum*, i.e. God's withdrawal. Similarly, the immanent pluralism, if not utter perspectivism, of modern thought is consonant with the Lurianic idea of the world splintered into shards.[4] There is thus a kind of kinship

---

3   Gershom Scholem, "Reflections on Jewish Theology," trans. Gabriela Shalit in Gershom Scholem, *On Jews and Judaism in Crisis: Selected Essays*, ed. Werner J. Dannhauser (Philadelphia, PA: Paul Dry Books, 2012), pp. 261–297, on pp. 282–3.

4   As Moshe Idel emphasises, drawing on Harold Bloom, Scholem was veritably obsessed with "the imagery of catastrophe." See Moshe Idel, *Old Worlds, New Mirrors: On Jewish Mysticism and Twentieth-Century Thought* (Philadelphia PA: University of Pennsylvania Press, 2000), p. 127. The idea of catastrophe recurs both in Scholem's historical research

between the modern "nothingness of Revelation" and the methods of Kabbalistic enquiry, which Kafka's work comes in handy to corroborate,[5] with all its para-doxical parabolic opulence redolent of Jewish mysticism of old and yet making the void its point of reference. Kafka seems thus to seal that recondite coupling of the Kabbalah and modernity.

Another idea espoused by modernity that Scholem evokes is Messianism. "It was better able to stand a reinterpretation into the secular realm than the other ideas," he insists.[6] He is intrigued by the fact that Jewish Messianism, particularly in its apocalyptic version, kindled such interest in the 20th century, engrossing, for example, Ernst Bloch and Walter Benjamin. Scholem seems to assume that the attractiveness of the revolutionary messianic idea echoes the modern world's abysmal collapse, which could be rectified only through an act of profound transfiguration,[7] if not by a radical historical split. This element of Judaic theology serves Bloch and Benjamin as an all-purpose key to modern philosophy (or, to evoke the metaphorical imagery of Benjamin's "Theses on the Philosophy of History," as a little hunchback of theology driving the machinery of contem-porary thought[8]). Both to Bloch and Benjamin themselves and to Scholem as their interpreter, Jewish Messianism is an idea that, in its peculiar way, harmon-ises with the modern condition.

But how? Another curious text by Scholem, sporting the Benjamin-resonant title "Ten Unhistorical Aphorisms on Kabbalah," illuminates this compatibility a bit. It proposes that "[t]he view of the Kabbalists as mystical materialists with a dialectical approach would indeed be completely non-historical, but would not be entirely lacking in meaning."[9] Thesis four argues that an essentially dialecti-cal-materialist mechanism is at work in the thinking of the kabbalists, Luria's successors in particular.[10] If modernity is an age in which dialectics in the strict

(as a patent fascination with the Lurianic Kabbalah and antinomic movements) and in his Gnostic view of the present times.

5 Cf. also Karl Erich Grözinger, *Kafka a Kabała* [Kafka und die Kabbala/Kafka and the Kabbalah], trans. J. Güntner (Kraków: Austeria, 2006).

6 Scholem, "Reflections," p. 284.

7 Cf. *Ibid.*, p. 285.

8 See Walter Benjamin, "Theses on the Philosophy of History," in *Illuminations: Essays and Reflections*, trans. Harry Zohn, ed. Hannah Arendt (New York: Schocken Books, 1969), p. 253.

9 Gershom Scholem, *Another Thing: Chapters in History and Revival II*, ed. Avraham Shapira (Tel Aviv: Am Oved, 1990), p. 34.

10 Also in *Jewish Mysticism*, Scholem clearly preferred the dialectically inflected trends of Kabbalism. For example, he was fascinated with the idea of *Ein-Sof*, a primordial,

sense came into being and spread while the kabbalists indeed reasoned in this way, the affinity of mystical Judaism and modernity would be well grounded. A similar linkage can be glimpsed in Scholem's fascination with Kafka's writings, notably with his parable "Before the Law," which Scholem believed to encapsulate perfectly Jewish theology, "which in its unique dialectic is not destructive, but, on the contrary, radiates powerful inner melancholy."[11] In this optics, Kafka is credited with the founding of the modern Kabbalah since his works deploy Kabbalistic codes and figures to render the modern condition.[12] In Scholem's view, Kafka's point of contact with the Kabbalah proper lies in dialectics, which is both materialist and hopeful for the healing of the broken world.

Scholem's last text that I would like to evoke here is his lecture "Reflections on the Possibility of Jewish Messianism in Our Time,"[13] which serves as a kind of reckoning of many years' worth of research into Messianism. If Scholem's early texts suggested that the present age might be somehow remedied by the historical study of the Kabbalah, this late contribution of 1963 defines such an enterprise

---

boundless form of God that mutates into nothing after creation. This notion makes it possible to reconcile dialectically the radical separateness of God and the world with the dependence of Creation on God. "The creation of the world, that is to say, the creation of something out of nothing, is itself but the external aspect of something that takes place in God Himself. This is also a crisis of the hidden En-Sof who turns from repose to creation, and it is this crisis, creation and Self-Revelation in one which constitutes the great mystery of theosophy and the crucial point for the understanding of the purpose of theosophical speculation. The crisis can be pictured as the break-through of the primordial will, but theosophic Kabbalism frequently employs the bolder metaphor of Nothing. The primary start or wrench in which the introspective God is externalized and the light that shines inwardly made visible, this revolution of perspective transforms En-Sof, the inexpressible fullness, into nothingness." Gershom Scholem, *Major Trends in Jewish Mysticism* (New York: Schocken Books, 1949), p. 213.

11   Greshom Scholem, "On Kafka's *The Trial*," in *On the Possibility of Jewish Mysticism in Our Time & Other Essays*, trans. Jonathan Chipman, ed. Avraham Shapira (Philadelphia, PA & Jerusalem: Jewish Publication Society,1997–5758), p. 193. Scholem perceived his era as drenched in melancholy as a result of a crisis of transcendence. Similarly, he displayed an interest in "Jewish melancholy." Melancholy as a link between the modern condition and the Jewish experience is pondered also by other authors, such as Sergio Quinzio. See Sergio Quinzio, *Hebrajskie korzenie nowożytności* [Radici ebraiche del moderno/Hebraic roots of modernity], trans. M. Bielawski (Kraków: homini, 2005), p. 73.

12   See Mosès, *Angel*, pp. 145–68.

13   Gershom Scholem, "Reflections on the Possibility of Jewish Mysticism in Our Time," in *On the Possibility*, pp. 4–18.

as inexorably aporetic. Scholem argues, namely, that Messianism last flared over two hundred years ago, and in our times its sparks have already dimmed down. Moreover, rather than a contingent phenomenon, it is tightly associated with the contemporary condition of religiosity, in which mystical experiences, if at all existent, remain purely private and do not found mass movements. Additionally, the transmission of tradition has been interrupted. Forms of religiosity have turned anarchic, Scholem insists, while a lack of faith in the God-conferred authority of the Torah – whose ambiguities once spawned ever new interpretations – bars any possibility of a new Kabbalah. Clearly, the modern condition as such is cited as a condition of impossibility of renewing the Kabbalah whereas earlier this very condition was expected to be mended by Jewish mysticism.

To sum up, Scholem's lifetime work bears insights about the affinity of modernity and Judaism (even about the utility of Jewish tradition in interpreting the contemporary universe[14]), but concurrently it addresses time and again the aporetic position of the Kabbalah in the 20th century. Nowhere is the connection between modernity and Jewish mysticism explicitly delineated, and even less philosophically elucidated. It is only through the workings of an abstruse spiritual attraction force that contemporary thinkers are tempted onto the paths trodden by the kabbalist of yore. At the same time, the situation of our epoch remains aporetic to Scholem: the spiritual condition of the present times urges to reach beyond philosophy and into the long-lost past tradition, but the scale and the nature of the loss foreclose the re-creation of the Kabbalah and even more the re-immersion into its flow. What remains is only inconclusive searching, indelibly marked with an imprint of historicity.

Let us move now to our second example. In her influential study *The Slayers of Moses: The Emergence of Rabbinic Interpretation in Modern Literary Theory*, Susan A. Handelman proposes a comprehensive account of contiguities between the development of modern philosophy and literary critique on the one hand and Jewish tradition on the other. Her work stands as a paradigmatic example of the appropriation of Judaism by the (post)deconstructive humanities. It is informed by the idea that, as philosophy's metaphysical load, identified with the legacy of "Athens," dissipated in the 20th century, an opportunity appeared for it to absorb

---

14 Scholem elaborates on the universality of the Jewish experience also in his *On the Kabbalah and Its Symbolism*, where he states that "[i]n the Kabbalah the law of the Torah became a symbol of cosmic law, and the history of the Jewish people a symbol of the cosmic process." See Gershom Scholem, *On the Kabbalah and Its Symbolism*, trans. Ralph Manheim (New York: Schocken Books, 1996), p. 2. In his view, Judaism and modernity are "almost inextricably bound" (*Ibid.*).

the abundant heritage of "Jerusalem." On this model, various threads of Jewish tradition turn out to parallel the ideas developed by philosophy in the 20th century. This mechanism explains why philosophy started to borrow directly from Judaic thought. Handelman analyses "modern Jewish thinkers," such as Freud, Lacan [sic!], Derrida and Bloom, without however defining this parallelism of modernity and Judaism which compels the philosophers who do not endorse Jewish tradition (e.g. Lacan) to gravitate towards it while inclining those who feel affinity with it (e.g. Bloom) to build directly on its formulas.

Let us first scrutinise the line that Handelman draws between Greek and Jewish traditions and then focus on the latter's connections with modernity. According to Handelman, the difference between Athens and Jerusalem is particularly conspicuous in their approaches to textual interpretation. Nowhere else is the division between the "Greek" and the "Jewish" modes of thinking more pronounced than in their divergent premises about the relationship between "words and things," the position of the author, the role of writing and the freedom of interpretation. Clearly indebted to Lévinas and Derrida, Handelman insists that Greek philosophy of the spirit is based on the originary division between words and things.[15] Language is, in her view, a conventional tool for describing things – a transparent medium which helps grasp them. True knowledge, in turn, does not exist in language but resides in ideas, with particular utterances only relating the unchangeable truth.[16] That is why interpretation is an utterly marginal issue and concerns applications of language as a tool but does not infringe on the status of truth. According to Handelman, this presupposition has enduringly impinged on Western philosophy by bringing in the myth of an ideal, abstract language for ideas.[17] It has also effected – through Aristotle's influential pronouncements in *De interpretatione* – a degradation of rhetoric and poetics as "corrupted" with language and, consequently vastly inferior to abstract logic and "true science."[18] It moulded also essentially the Christian take on interpretation, in which textual polysemy is always harnessed by the eternal and immutable "transcendent signifier": "the Incarnate Word" is the ultimate interpretive authority and stabilises the potentially subversive ambiguity of the Scripture. Handelman recognises the primacy of the "Spirit" over the "letter," instituted by Paul of Tarsus, as, basically,

---

15 Susan A. Handelman, *The Slayers of Moses: The Emergence of Rabbinic Interpretation in Modern Literary Theory* (Albany: State University of New York Press, 1982), p. 3 ff.
16 *Ibid.*, p. 11.
17 *Ibid.*, pp. 5–6.
18 *Ibid.*, p. 11.

abolishing the question of interpretation because the allegorical method, which is the major mode of interpretation touted by the Church, helps read the always already presupposed meaning out of every ambiguity.[19] In this way, the abstract meaning is treated as literal, and its metaphorical character is concealed.

In turn, in Jewish tradition, language is inseparable from things. It does not describe objects external to itself but is part of the process in which they come into being. This relationship is symbolised in the already worn-out reference to דבר, *davar*, a Hebrew term that can designate both a word and a thing. This means that "[f]or the Rabbis [...] the primary reality was linguistic; true being was a God who speaks and creates texts [...]."[20] If Greek tradition prioritises the image, which is sensorily available and, as such, constitutes a stable referent, Jewish tradition accords the central position to the spoken or written word, which must still be interpreted.[21] Allegory does not hold sway, nor is there any central agency to fix the text's polysemy. As a result, its interpretations layer up, each in its own right, while commentaries proliferate endlessly. The rabbinical way of reading presupposes intertextuality, shuns universal formulas and emphasises specific links and continuities between particular cases.[22] Interpretation becomes, at the same time, a general method of understanding reality.[23] The linguistic element is enmeshed not only in reading but also in all creation: God Himself creates by uttering words, which proves that they are closely interconnected with things.[24] This thought seeps down so deep that the Talmudic treatise Shabbat describes the Torah as preceding creation.[25]

Quoting Erich Auerbach, Handelman lists dissimilarities of Homeric and biblical narratives to explain the difference between Athens and Jerusalem.[26] Homer renders phenomena in their external, visible and tangible forms as they are established in spatio-temporal relations; nothing remains hidden and unexpressed while events happen in the absolute "now." In the Bible, everything is undetermined and contingent, time and space often remain unspecified, and the protagonists' motives elude expression. There is only the narrative, often residual

---

19 *Ibid.*, pp. 15, 82–90.
20 *Ibid.*, p. 4.
21 *Ibid.*, p. 17.
22 *Ibid.*, pp. 47–50.
23 *Ibid.*, p. 30.
24 *Ibid.*, p. 32.
25 *Ibid.*, p. 36.
26 *Ibid.*, p. 29.

as such; the rest is submerged in darkness. Speech conceals as much as it reveals while the tale is immersed in the layers of history, rather than in the present. Finally, following Hans Jonas, Handelman discusses what she views as ontological differences between the two traditions.[27] In Greek thought, the world is eternal and governed by immutable, universal laws while the Jewish creatio ex nihilo braids contingency and will into the very emergence of the world and makes it dependent on an external power, that is, God. As all things are created, they are, in this sense, ontologically equal. Creation out of nothing emphasises also the particularity of all things created. Unlike in the case of "Athens," singularity is not just a simple derivative of universality, being instead autonomous and irreducible. As Handelman adds later, the difference between God and the world is central to Judaism and precedes the differentiation into the sign and the thing.[28] Hence its anti-mythical and anti-metaphorical tenor; in Judaism, simply, a sign that embodies God cannot exist.[29]

Demarcated in this way, the dividing line between Athens and Jerusalem, as Handelman believes, overlaps largely with the history of relationships between Western philosophy and Judaic thought,[30] at least up until the Reformation. What is it, we might ask, that happens at that point? The answer is: embryonic modern hermeneutics begins to germinate in which there is, admittedly, no "return" to the Jewish take on interpretation, but the text is pushed to the foreground again, and its a-priori given meaning is stripped of primacy.[31] Although Luther relies on the reading of the Scripture for finding a direct divine presence

---

27 *Ibid.*, p. 28 ff.

28 *Ibid.*, p. 104.

29 Starting from the same assumptions, Henri Atlan claimed that the prominent role Judaism awarded to writing was linked to the anti-idolatrous mindset. For writing, as opposed to speech, is always supposed to highlight the distance between the reader and the writer, as a result of which the Torah, a divine text, leaves a chasm between the sign referring to God and God Himself. According to Atlan, writing retains an irreducible component of otherness, a residue of sorts that defies interpretation, which makes God, who reveals Himself through writing, ungraspable in notions that strive to grasp Him. Cf. Henri Atlan, "Niveaux de signification et athéisme de l' écriture," in *La Bible au présent* (Paris: Gallimard, 1982), p. 86.

30 This connection is, of course, far more complicated than the simple Athens-vs.-Jerusalem opposition would seem to imply. The Kabbalah was after all immensely influenced by Gnosticism and Neo-Platonism while the rationalist Jewish philosophy of the Middle Ages found itself under a considerable impact of Aristotelianism. At this moment, however, let us leave such doubts aside and return to them in the following.

31 Handelman, *Slayers*, pp. 123–4.

and a concrete message in it, it is no longer possible to conceal how problematic an issue interpretation is. According to Handelman, Protestant hermeneutics provides a backdrop for the key developmental trajectory of modern philosophy from Schleiermacher to German idealism and Nietzsche, to, finally, Heidegger and Gadamer.[32] As approaches to interpretation radicalise, also due to a historical critique and the concomitant crisis of the Scriptural authority, the "Greek" take on the sign is exposed as limited. At the same time, the progressing assimilation of Jews channels elements of rabbinical thinking into Western philosophy, the trend promoted by the internal dismantling of the legacy of Athens. In this way, as Handelman concludes, the 20th century saw thinkers drawing on both traditions to concoct peculiar philosophical amalgams, with Freud as one of the most notable examples.[33] In the last stage of this history, Lévinas, Derrida and the Yale school make post-Second World War philosophy openly contest the crumbling tradition of Greek thinking and espouse interpretation as developed by Judaism.[34]

Reflecting on Handelman's argument, we could ask what Judaism's peculiar connections to modernity are exactly. She does not give any direct answer, but her book assumes implicitly that it was the decay of the West's metaphysical tradition that steered philosophy and literary studies towards conclusions quite alike those with which Jewish thought had come up centuries earlier. If in the 20th century various ideas cherished by Judaism were revived in a philosophical form, it was because they found fertile ground in this philosophy. But, paradoxically, Handelman's argumentation relies on "Greek" thinking far more extensively than she might wish it to be the case. Handelman builds on the discourses that unveil the West's "metaphysical" history and its termination – the discourses developed, first of all, by Nietzsche, Heidegger and, to a degree, early Derrida. It would not be an excessive simplification to say that Handelman's reasoning proceeds from the assumption of centuries-long "Greek error," which slowly reaches its terminus in modernity and makes room for revived Jewish thought. This insight is commonly found in the academic doxa, which uses the contemporary philosophical reworkings of Judaism. However, the transparency of this historical outline, which seems just to rehearse, one by one, the facts of the history of Western thinking – the initial conquest of the philosophical imagination by the

---

32 *Ibid.*, p. 130.
33 *Ibid.*, p. 126.
34 Cf. *Ibid.*, pp. 164–82.

Greek blueprint of perception, the disintegration of Greek-ridden metaphysics, the ingress of Judaism into the mainstream humanities – is blurred by the premise that depends on "post-Greeks" (such as Heidegger). For it is the very venture of mounting such historical constructs not an offshoot of the thinking that is to be left behind in philosophy's quest toward Judaism? Does it not entail strewing the trappings of Jewish tradition on the mechanisms that derive, strictly, from modern thinking?

Before I try and answer these questions, let me discuss the third example in Harold Bloom's *Kabbalah and Criticism*. The book was driven by an attempt to assemble various Kabbalistic inspirations that Bloom had used earlier to construct his theory of influence and belatedness. He presupposes that the Kabbalah – and in particular the Safed Kabbalah (as developed by Moses Cordovero and Isaac Luria) – offers an elaborate and precise model of relationships among various entities, one easily adaptable to the purposes of literary criticism.[35] According to Bloom, the Safed Kabbalah's unique structure originates in the historical conjuncture where its founders lived in and wrestled with the vast tradition, compelled to develop subtle revisionist techniques of interpreting and opening up the canonical texts.[36] In this way, the Safed Kabbalah can be read as a superb study in the "psychology of belatedness."

More relevant, however, is the structure of relationships among the aspects of Creation (e.g. Cordovero's *behinot*), which Bloom transposes onto relationships within the literary field, showing how the gradual exuding of one aspect by another corresponds to the forming of a new poet in relation to his powerful forerunner.[37] Moreover, in a rather flimsy turn of thought, Bloom suggests that the map of relations of *behinot* or *Sefirot* corresponds to relationships not so much between writers as such as between poems themselves:

> A poem is a deep misprision of a previous poem when we recognize the previous poem as being absent rather than present on the surface of the earlier poem, and yet still being in the earlier poem, implicit or hidden in it, not yet manifest, and yet there.[38]

35 Cf. Harold Bloom, *Kabbalah and Criticism* (New York: The Seabury Press, 1975), p. 33.

36 *Ibid.*, pp. 34, 72.

37 *Ibid.*, p. 67.

38 *Ibid.*, p. 33. Bloom goes on to state that in 19th- and 20th-century discourses, "poem" can be often substituted by "person" or "idea" while the structure describing relations between poems remains applicable to these other entities with equal effectiveness. See *Ibid.*, p. 59.

Refining his theory on the basis of the Lurianic notion of *tzimtzum*,[39] Bloom contends that the interrelations of this structure's particular elements can be comprehended as continued emergence of new entities through the *primal limitation* of their antecedents.[40] The links and traces that come into being as a result of this reduction are identified with literary tropes by Bloom, who suggests that mental defences theorised by psychoanalysis can also be described through this power structure.[41]

Here, we arrive at those of Bloom's insights that are central to our argument in this Chapter. According to Bloom, the structure of relationships among aspects (i.e. poets, poems, tropes, defences, and so forth) borrowed from the Safed kabbalists best suits the post-Miltonic model of Western poetry, and Romantic poetry in particular.[42] Bloom's theoretical sources, i.e. Nietzsche's and Freud's writings, also argue that the *tzimtzum*-based model of thinking and creative work is best applicable to modern developments. Bloom himself observes that the Kabbalah can be regarded as modernism *ante litteram*.[43] In other words, Bloom's theoretical construct seems to be a borrowing based not on one or another superficial similarity but *on a certain latent shared structure* that underpins both the Kabbalah and modernity. The text itself leaves these questions largely underspecified.[44] Symptomatically, Bloom does not draw a clear line between the Kabbalah "as such" and the Safed thought though he takes the latter as his fundamental framework of reference.

That is why *Kabbalah and Criticism* describes a kind of alignment between the (Safed) Kabbalah and modernity which consists in that at least some modern

---

39 *Tzimtzum* (both Isaac Luria's original notion and a version of it developed by Edmond Jabès) will be discussed in Chapter Three. At this point, it is enough just to explain that the notion envisions the primal withdrawal of God, who leaves a void in which the world can only be created. In *tzimtzum*, it is thus assumed that creation of the world takes place in the realm marked by God's contraction.

40 See also Harold Bloom, *A Map of Misreading* (New York: Oxford UP, 1975), pp. 3–4.

41 See Bloom, *Kabbalah*, p. 74 ff.

42 *Ibid.*, p. 88 ff.

43 *Ibid.*, p. 79.

44 In *A Map of Misreading*, Bloom draws on Ernst Robert Curtius to observe that literature after Goethe is not yet properly assessable. The late Enlightenment, Romanticism, Modernism and Post-Modernism are parts of the same phenomenon, whose continuity or discontinuity in regard to the prior tradition, as Bloom contends, cannot be established yet (*Map*, p. 33). Consequently, the indefiniteness of connections between modernity and the Kabbalah results, partly at least, from the fact that we still fall under the historical influence of the phenomenon we set out to analyse.

acts of creation (poems, thoughts, and so forth) are propped by the same structure as creation in Luria's notion, that is, by the mechanisms of originary reduction (*tzimtzum*). Like in Safed's revisionist thought, interpretation in modernity
turns out to be an inevitable, veritably ontological misreading of the past.
Bloom's argumentation is entangled in an essential double bind; namely, in his
view, Cordovero and Luria implicitly found the "theory of belatedness" because
they are themselves belated vis-à-vis Kabbalism's legacy. In other words, their
own revisionism impresses itself on the structure of the concepts they develop.
This means that Luria can think *tzimtzum* as a cosmic event because he performs *tzimtzum* on the existing Kabbalah himself. On another level, he learns
about what he does. At any rate, in Bloom's rhetoric, the fact that he recognised
this affinity is, in turn, an outcome of his own misreading. So the kinship of the
Kabbalah and modernity is explained through the identity of the structure that
results from the historical positioning relative to the existing tradition, which
structure, as such, does not seem to have anything either *par excellence* Jewish or
modern about it.

My fourth and last example comes from Maurice Blanchot's "Being Jewish,"
reprinted in *The Infinite Conversation*.[45] "Being Jewish" is not the only essay in
which Blanchot muses on Judaism as an inspiration of modern thought, yet a
handful of suggestions expressed in it are representative of Blanchot's other writings. First of all, he views Judaism as a tradition that is distinctively nomadic and,
therefore, perceives the world as changeable, uncertain and defying one truth:

> If Judaism is destined to take on meaning for us, it is indeed by showing that, at whatever
> time, one must be ready to set out, because to go out (to step outside) is the exigency
> from which one cannot escape if one wants to maintain a possibility of a just relation.
> The exigency of uprooting; the affirmation of nomadic truth. In this Judaism stands in
> contrast to paganism (all paganism). To be pagan is to be fixed, to plant oneself in the
> earth, as it were, to establish oneself through a pact with the permanence that autho-
> rizes sojourn and is certified by certainty in the land. Nomadism answers to a relation
> that possession cannot satisfy. Each time Jewish man makes a sign to us across his-
> tory it is by the summons of a movement. Happily established in Sumerian civilization,
> Abraham at a certain point breaks with that civilization and renounces dwelling there.
> Later, the Jewish people become a people through the exodus. And where does this
> night of exodus, renewed from year to year, each time lead them? To a place that is not
> a place and where it is not possible to reside. The desert makes of the slaves of Egypt a
> people, but a people without a land and bound by a word. Later, the exodus becomes

---

45 Maurice Blanchot, "Being Jewish," in *The Infinite Conversation*, trans. Susan Hanson
    (Minneapolis: University of Minnesota Press, 2003), pp. 123–30.

the exile that is accompanied by all the trials of a hunted existence, establishing in each heart anxiety, insecurity, affliction, and hope. But this exile, heavy as it is, is not only recognized as being an incomprehensible malediction. There is a truth of exile and there is a vocation of exile; and if being Jewish is being destined to dispersion – just as it is a call to a sojourn without place, just as it ruins every fixed relation of force with *one* individual, *one* group, or *one* state – it is because dispersion, faced with the exigency of the whole, also clears the way for a different exigency and finally forbids the temptation of Unity-Identity.[46]

Given the fact that Blanchot goes to great lengths to dispel the illusion of unity, identity, certainty and unambiguousness, he seems to consider Judaism as his natural ally. More than that – an ally also of all modern thought that demystifies the idols of permanent truths, eternal places and unchangeable ideas. In other words, he assumes a kind of affinity between the strong Jewish anti-mythical tradition and modernity.[47] This interconnection reverberates in his apology of nomadism as a voluntary acceptance of life without enduring guidelines.[48]

Blanchot continues this line of reasoning to assert that – as distinct from Greco-Christian thought – Judaism does not disown "this world"[49] and affirms

---

46 *Ibid.*, pp. 125–6.
47 To be sure, this kind of relationship is not Blanchot's exclusive invention. Rosenzweig, Benjamin and, finally, Lévinas were all inspired by Judaism's anti-idolatrous investment. The Talmud's Megillah states that "whoever repudiates idolatry is accounted a Jew" (see Abraham Cohen, *Everyman's Talmud: The Major Teachings of Rabbinic Sages* [New York: Schocken Books, 1995], p. 6). However, it was only in the 20th century that the Jewish movement against idolatry found philosophical applications. For example, Lévinas insists that "Judaism has decharmed the world, contesting the notion that religions apparently evolved out of enthusiasm and the Sacred. […] Jewish monotheism does not exalt a sacred power. […] Here, Judaism feels very close to the West, by which I mean philosophy. […] Human existence […] is the true place in which the divine word encounters the intellect and loses the rest of its supposedly mystical virtues." Emmanuel Lévinas, "A Religion for Adults," in *Difficult Freedom: Essays on Judaism*, trans. Seán Hand (Baltimore: Johns Hopkins UP, 1997), pp. 11–23, on pp. 14–15.
48 This is another point where Blanchot is close to Lévinas. See also, Quinzio, *Hebrajskie*, pp. 66–9.
49 Blanchot, "Being Jewish," p. 128. Also this idea has had a long interpretive history. The Gemara explains: " 'What purpose did your God have in speaking with Moses from the midst of a bush?' […] 'To teach that there is no place void of the Divine Presence, not even so lowly a thing as a bush' " (see Cohen, *Everyman's Talmud*, p. 9). It is in this sense that Lévinas concludes that "Judaism has always been free with regard to place" (Emmanuel Lévinas, "Heidegger, Gagarin and Us," in *Difficult Freedom*, pp. 231–4, on p. 233), i.e. it has treated the world as a unity with no permanent, demarcated sacred sites.

life instead of denigrating it. This clearly ties in with the Nietzschean re-appraisal of philosophy. However, another trait of Judaism that Blanchot discovers as akin and valuable to modernity calls for more scrutiny. This trait is Jewish monotheism, whose most seminal legacy, rather than in the revelation of personal God, lies in "the revelation of speech as the place where men hold themselves in relation with what excludes all relation: the infinitely Distant, the absolutely Foreign."[50] Blanchot makes two assumptions here: first, he believes that Judaism recognises a dimension that is radically external to our world, and, second, that this outside imprints itself on speech in one way or another. What Blanchot offers is, thus, a thorough re-interpretation of monotheism. Judaism's monotheistic legacy of old, as Blanchot claims, makes it possible to think contact with the absolutely exterior and, thereby, lays ground for relating to the Other in ways that eschew subjugation. This is another point where creation out of nothing by personal God seems to tie in with Judaism's special approach to the particular.

So, for Blanchot, Judaism is a tradition of thinking whose mode of world-perception seems precious for modernity first of all because it discards an idolatrous version of transcendence. The radicalism of the outside and the endorsement of "this-worldliness" as the human life-world rather than as an illusion from which to flee bring Jewish thinking closer to the epoch in which the "Greek" tenets fall apart. Nonetheless, Blanchot does not delve into the reasons for this confluence. On the contrary, a certain vagueness of his musings suggests that he would also be inclined to accept the Nietzschean-Heideggerian model of the "Greek error,"

Scholem, in turn, insists that God's omnipotence, omnipresence and oneness all suggest that reality is a pulsating unity that, subsumed in one spirit, mutates beyond and above the laws of nature; cf. Scholem, *Kabbalah and Its Symbolism*, pp. 94–5. In these interpretations, reality as perceived by Judaism is not split into the defective world of earthly life and the ideal afterlife; nor are there any delimited places of the sacred. Rather, reality is a unity of equal elements that stand before God. That is why Jewish Messianism, unlike Christian one, does not presuppose spiritual "inner transformations," tending rather to regard Messiah's work as a real event in the external world. Cf. Gerhom Scholem, *The Messianic Idea in Judaism* (New York: Schocken Books, 1995), pp. 1–2, 17. Jacob Taubes took issue with this division in his "The Price of Messianism," in *From Cult to Culture. Fragments Toward a Critique of Historical Reason*, eds. Charlotte E. Fonrobert and Amir Engel (Stanford, CA: Stanford UP, 2010), p. 3 ff. Izaak Cylkow seems to have shared the same ideas in his commentary on the first verse of *Bereshit*. Cylkow insisted that it implied "the unity of the world and an absolute solidarity of all its components." *Tora* [Torah], trans. I. Cylkow (Kraków: Austeria, 2010), p. 3.

50 Blanchot, "Being Jewish," p. 127.

which eventually recedes in the 20th century, while Jewish thought, so far im-
mune to it, is coming in handy to revaluate philosophy.

The four examples surveyed above can be usefully concluded with the voice
of Sergio Quinzio, who, in spite of the naive character of his simplifying discourse, captures the reasons for the rise of modern philosophical interest in
Jewish tradition:

> Relics of the Greek and pagan worlds promote understanding of meaning as an all-
> encompassing fullness, as a wondrously all-explaining Logos. As a result, we could
> not but comprehend historical time as uniform continuity, as stairs solidly erected
> on stable ground and, hence, reliably leading up and up; and we could never think of
> time, experiencing each moment in it, as – in Benjamin's description – a small doorway
> through which the Messiah could enter. In reality, however, the humans of today, who
> on the one hand are not certain whether the age-old necessity indeed exists and, on the
> other, have been acutely disappointed with modern, secularised Messianism, experi-
> ence empty time which, devoid of hope, tumbles into nothing. "Meaning" that could
> arise from such an experience cannot be a resumption of some perfect wholeness, of the
> triumphant Logos. The modern age, entirely unconsciously seizing Biblical categories,
> has drawn a circle, as a result of which the entire world experiences an ultimate risk of
> time, of reality which is not rational, a hope that comes through the abyss of Egypt and
> Babylon, through the night of Gethsemane, through the cross and through Auschwitz,
> through all darkness and decomposition that go with apocalyptic times. Meaning is only
> a modest possibility, paradoxical and feeble, and yet full of delicacy and mercy as it
> emerges from the awareness of death and nothingness [...].[51]

My argument above was, by necessity, a bare outline only. I believe, however,
that it encapsulated the fundamental ways of conceptualising affinities between
Judaism and modernity. Below, I will seek to interrogate these conceptualisations.

The Problematic Connectedness between
Judaism and Modern Thought

Despite all their differences, the four examples discussed above display some
common patterns in their conceptualisations of the relationship between
Judaism and modernity. Let us first scrutinise these patterns and, then, define
problems that haunt them. First of all, all our examples presuppose that Judaism
and modernity share, among others, fundamental "ontological" outlooks on the
world, notions of the human condition and attitudes to text, truth and interpretation. All of them also propound similarities between the two which, though

---

51 Quinzio, *Hebrajskie*, pp. 186–7.

rather undefined, concern entirely fundamental philosophical propositions. Second, in each case the assumption of similarity lingers in a kind of penumbra. Seldom proclaimed explicitly, it does not tend to be analytically inspected. And third, the concealment of this assumption is enveloped in two different ratiocinative strategies. In one of them, the alignment of Jewish and modern thinking is framed as a contingent similarity (which is what Bloom basically does in viewing the connection between the Safed Kabbalah and modern poetry as originating in their analogous relations to their respective superfluous traditions). In this case, the problematic tenet of connectedness can be passed over since the comparison involves two phenomena which display certain similar properties only as a result of contingent historical factors.

In the other strategy, the premise of alignment is built into a certain historical pattern which in itself tends to be essentially affected by the very legacy of modern philosophy. This seems to have been the path that Scholem chose to go. Despite the elliptical character of his pronouncements, he can easily be inferred to have treated (at least in his early years) the secrets of the Kabbalah as singularly linked to the modern condition. Interestingly, such a solution can also be detected in Susan Handelman's reasoning, which is worlds apart from Scholem's modernist ideas. Ostensibly, her argument does not posit any noncontingent patterns in the history of thinking. It could after all be assumed that 20th-century philosophy was affected by Judaism through great thinkers (e.g. Rosenzweig, Benjamin, Lévinas, Derrida) who just happened to build on such inspirations. But, curiously, Handelman's reasoning – just like that of the "contingent" researchers of philosophical Judaism – heads towards quasi-historiosophical premises. Unlike in Bloom, modern thought is not envisaged as contingently similar to Jewish thinking. On the contrary, the likeness is an outcome of awakening from the "Greek dream," of discarding the Hellenistic paradigm of thinking, which results in philosophy's confluence with Judaism. It is not coincidental that the Tertullian formula of "Athens or Jerusalem" is reborn in the 20th century and outside Christianity, for it suggests that philosophy has only two options to choose from. If "Greek thought" has naturally reached its limit, there is solely "Jewish thought" to turn to. Of course, not all the authors referred to above endorse as extreme a version of this idea as, for example, Lev Shestov does.[52] However, all of them – not excepting Derrida, who problematises the

---

52 Shestov was perhaps the first thinker to insist adamantly that the Greek truth had colonised the Jewish one thoroughly and that the process was bound to have disastrous consequences. Cf. Lev Shestov, *Athens and Jerusalem*, trans. Bernard Martin (Athens, OH: Ohio UP, 1966), particularly pp. 343 ff.

issue most – consider *the modernity-triggered historical crisis of Western philosophy* to *have catalysed its confrontation with so-far marginalised Jewish thought.* Let us now look closer at this connection by scrutinising "Violence and Metaphysics," an essay that young Derrida wrote about Lévinas. The text opens with a quotation from Matthew Arnold which ushers in the optics of the Athens-vs.-Jerusalem opposition.[53] The first issue that Derrida addresses is the modern crisis of philosophy, which essentially has already suffered an inner death:

> That philosophy died yesterday, since Hegel or Marx, Nietzsche, or Heidegger – and philosophy should wander toward the meaning of its death – or that it has always lived knowing itself to be dying (as is silently confessed in the shadow of the very discourse which *declared philosophia perennis*); that philosophy died *one day, within* history, or that it has always fed on its own agony, on the violent way it opens history by opposing itself to nonphilosophy, which is its past and its concern, its death and wellspring; that beyond the death, or dying nature, of philosophy, perhaps even because of it, thought still has a future, or even, as is said today, is still entirely to come because of what philosophy has held in store; or, more strangely still, that the future itself has a future – all these are unanswerable questions. By right of birth, and for one time at least, these are problems put to philosophy as problems philosophy cannot resolve.[54]

The resurgence of the Athens-vs.-Jerusalem opposition would thus be involved, without doubt, in philosophy's movement towards self-transcendence observable in "Hegel, Marx, Nietzsche and Heidegger," philosophers and anti-philosophers at once. Why? Derrida toys with the following answer: perhaps it is only philosophy's inner depletion, its spectral, posthumous lingering that *unveils the nonphilosophical ground from which it arose and which it has kept hidden.* This fundamental crisis would thus expose questions that philosophy itself is unable to tackle as they pertain to its own construction.

In the face of the crisis, "two great voices" of 20th-century philosophy – Husserl and Heidegger – Derrida continues,[55] plunge into tradition, looking to Greece, to find the roots of their thinking there. For Husserl and Heidegger, the decay of Western philosophy is bound up with its Greek origins, which delimit "the

---

53 "Hebraism and Hellenism – between these two points of influence moves our world. At one time it feels more powerfully the attraction of one of them, at another time of the other; and it ought to be, though it never is, evenly and happily balanced between them." In Jacques Derrida, "Violence and Metaphysics: An Essay on the Thought of Emmanuel Lévinas," trans. Alan Bass, in *Writing and Difference* (London and New York: Routledge, 2005), pp. 97–192, on p. 97.

54 *Ibid.*, pp. 97–8.

55 *Ibid.*, pp. 100–101.

possibility of our language" and "the nexus of our world."[56] What surfaces here is not so much a new philosophical problem as the problem of the grounding of philosophy as such. This is where Jewish thought enters the stage:

It is at this level that the thought of Emmanuel Lévinas can make us tremble. At the heart of the desert, in the growing wasteland, this thought, which fundamentally no longer seeks to be a thought of Being and phenomenality, makes us dream of an inconceivable process of dismantling and dispossession [...]. In Greek, in our language, in a language rich with all the alluvia of its history – [...] in a language that admits to its powers of seduction while playing on them unceasingly, this thought summons us to a dislocation of the Greek logos, to a dislocation of our identity, and perhaps of identity in general; it summons us to depart from the Greek site and perhaps from every site in general, and to move toward what is no longer a source or a site, [...] but toward an *exhalation*, toward a prophetic speech already emitted not only nearer to the source than Plato or pre-Socratics, but inside the Greek origin, close to the other of the Greek [...]. In question, therefore, is a powerful will to explication of the history of Greek speech.[57]

What do Derrida's suggestions imply? Their implication is that *Judaism's advance into modern thought is another stage of philosophy's own movement to reach even deeper after the failure of its reflection on "the Greek origin."* This insight is informed by several assumptions. First, philosophy in the 20th century is driven by a sense of deep dependence on particular conditions which it cannot penetrate by itself. This dependence is associated with a sense of crisis, and its persistence produces an impression that philosophy, while *essentially dead*, is sustained by the sheer force of inertia. This results in "posthumous" mobilisations of philosophy to explore the determinants that weigh on it, even at the potential price of abolishing philosophy as we know it. Second, the mobilisations are governed by the following logic: "dismantling and dispossession" surpass *actual* deadness and appearances. In this way, the movement of "philosophy's self-accusation" is propelled, which compels it to confront a dimension it has not known so far. This dimension – the mysterious "exhalation," as Derrida puts it – seems to be philosophy's precondition even beyond the "Greek origin." It does not instil any new philosophical *content* (new identities, sites, and so forth) but forms the *fundamental structure of the movement of philosophy* (hence "exhalation"). And third, Jewish thought is better equipped than Greek concepts to apprehend this precondition. Therefore, philosophy must reach out to Jewish thought to think through both the crisis in which it has found itself and its own structure as such.

---

56 *Ibid.*, p. 101.
57 *Ibid.*, pp. 101–102.

Thus, Jewish thought appears at the horizon of modern philosophy as a source of inspiration potentially enabling this philosophy to fathom its baseline, contentless, structural precondition, which Derrida calls "exhalation." If we recall that Luria's *tzimtzum* connotes "holding-in-of-the-breath," Derrida's metaphorical language will not seem coincidental. Why the authors cited above are captivated with the idea of *tzimtzum* will also become clear: namely, *tzimtzum can be interpreted as constituting a boundary between philosophy and the outside that determines it and that it endeavours to explore.* Derrida sees in Lévinas a searcher of "exhalation" *from before* philosophy, and, likewise, Scholem views the Lurianic Kabbalah as a model of modernity that has grown dependent on the dimension it cannot decipher.

Looking into Derrida, we could thus ask why inquiry into the affinity of Judaism and modernity so readily marshals quasi-historiosophical arguments. As we have seen, Jewish tradition is easily aligned with "nonphilosophy," supposedly overshadowed by philosophy over the ages of "Athenian" ascendancy. Thus, the nestling of Judaic elements in 20th-century philosophy could be interpreted as a harbinger of philosophy's stepping beyond itself and toward its "nonphilosophical" grounds. Such assumption entails that the idea of convergence of Judaism and modern philosophy – an idea restricted only to *similarities in the content* of two different conceptual traditions – is expanded to include an additional dimension, i.e. *a relationship between this content and the historical site and tradition in which it was formed.* In other words, the dovetailing of Judaic thought and modern thought acquires one more, irreducible component – namely the confluence of Judaism and modernity as such. What is at stake is no longer merely a contingent similitude of ideas, but rather a far more complicated bond between the epochs. We should notice that even when one seeks – like Bloom does – to treat this alignment as contingent and to ignore historical explanations, *history still hovers as an irremovable trace.* Willy-nilly, Bloom had to define a cut-off one way or another – to identify the point where the Safed Kabbalah began to correspond to poetry or philosophy. Once he chose poetry after Milton as this point, on another occasion poetry after Wordsworth; he also located orientation points for philosophy in Nietzsche or in Freud. In Bloom's theory the assumption of the historical shift, the onset of a new epoch in which *tzimtzum* becomes a valid model of creation, lingers unarticulated.

If at the beginning of this subchapter we distinguished two ways of interpreting the confluence of Judaism and modern thought (i.e. either in terms of contingency or in terms of a historical schema), now we can conclude that, in a deeper sense, *both these ways refer to history* and differ only in the explicitness of this reference.

How can these interconnections be accounted for? Where does the irremovable trace of historicity in reflection on the relationships between Judaism and modern philosophy come from?

Before I attempt to answer this, I will ask three more detailed questions invited by the above problematisation of ideas about connectedness between Judaism and modernity.

First, as already mentioned, 20th-century philosophy's movement toward Judaism is associated with philosophy's inner crisis. Derrida observes that – because of "Hegel, Marx, Nietzsche and Heidegger" – philosophy has suffered an inner death, which produces "a desert," a place where it encounters Jewish thought. One thing to ask about is thus *when the hiatus took place that caused the crisis of philosophy and what this hiatus involved.*

Second, there is a problem of the latent determining structure that philosophy has long striven to explore through recourse to Judaism. The question concerns the Derridean "exhalation" and is: *What structure is it and how does it work?*

Third, if Judaism appears within the horizon of modern thought as a result of this thought's own movement, does Western philosophy really open to its as-yet marginalised "Other," or does it rather employ ideas of Judaism in its own field? In other words, is Judaism not just a construct like Nietzsche's or Heidegger's "Greeks" or Hegel's "Christianity"? Is it not, by any chance, a model fabricated by modern thought? If so, is this model actually "modern" rather than "Jewish"?

The Universe of Modernity I: The Historical Hiatus

Let us start from the first of these problems, i.e. the historical hiatus that triggered a crisis of philosophy.

Already quoted, Derrida linked the ripeness of this crisis to post-war thought (and the aftermath of the let-down of Husserl's and Heidegger's inquiries) but saw it mellowing incrementally in the philosophy of "Hegel, Marx, Nietzsche and Heidegger." Therefore, if we were to locate the historical rift, it would have to fall before Hegel. Can a genuine breakthrough be identified in the recent few ages of philosophy to explain why philosophy should suddenly "die" and go on existing only in an incessant return to that event?

In this book, my answer to this question would be: a tectonic change in the workings of knowledge that involved also a breakthrough in philosophy took place in the 18th century. Naturally, this answer is grounded in insights of Michel Foucault, who throughout his oeuvre consistently revisited the turning point positioned towards the end of the 18th century. Because where this point exactly fell and what it entailed precisely tended to fluctuate in Foucault's prolific writings, a certain caveat is in order: I will build on his conclusions in *The Order of Things*.[58] Very briefly, the conclusions are as follows: (1) the transformation we are discussing occurred in the paradigm of knowledge as such, with philosophy and, for that matter, also economy and medicine, only displaying its effects; (2) as such, the transformation cannot be accounted for by positing one or another novel philosophical insight since the very possibility of such an insight results from the shift itself; (3) this transformation concerns the way in which knowledge constitutes reality. In Foucault's view, how does the shift manifest itself? It produces sequent effects. First, the classical order of representation collapses,[59] with signs no longer comprehensively and transparently referring to what is represented. Concomitantly, it becomes imperative to think of a certain deeper level of reality that transcends the directly visible phenomena, which heralds preoccupation with the concept of "the source."[60] There are two modes of reasoning which become particularly relevant: exegesis (of what is hidden) and hermeneutics (necessitated as language has ceased to be a transparent tool and gained depth).[61] Besides, historicity acquires a double relevance as the gap between the compass of cognition and what slips outside it[62] breeds not only the perception of knowledge as historical but also the idea of this unknowable dimension as a "source" that determines knowing.

If Foucault does not err in his conclusions, the crisis of philosophy we are exploring can be directly associated with the peculiar upheaval of the 18th century. For the sake of terminological consistency, I will refer to the age that follows it as "modernity." To scrutinise its imprint on philosophy, we need to specify its properties.

Modernity as conceived here is not simply an "age," that is, one of several periods within continuous history. *The very possibility and necessity to set it apart seems to result from the dimension of historicity that it has opened up.* Modernity would thus designate both: (1) a historically located epoch; and (2) a basic condition that necessitates looking for its historical locatedness in the first place. Consequently, modernity is an overdetermined phenomenon as it is in and by

---

58 Cf. Michel Foucault, *The Order of Things: An Archaeology of Human Sciences*, trans. (London and New York: Routledge, 2005).

59 *Ibid.*, pp. 72–3, 123–4

60 Cf. *Ibid.*, p. 249

61 Cf. Michel Foucault, "Les Mots et les Choses", in *Dits et écrits I. 1954–1975* (Paris: Gallimard, 2001), p. 528.

62 Cf. Foucault, *Order*, pp. 400–401.

itself an answer to the question that it poses. What this pattern specifically means will be seen in particular examples below.

Let us now depict briefly how modernity as defined here informs philosophy or, strictly speaking, the thought of Kant and Hegel, who best serve as a representative case in point. Analysing the structure of Kant's *Critique of Pure Reason*, one notices easily that its model of epistemology *responds to the diagnosis of the crisis*. In his Preface to the *Critique's* first edition, Kant dwells on the need to deal conclusively with reason's specious claims known as "metaphysics."[63] Rather than ahistorical and general, this becomes urgent only when metaphysics has revealed its own inadequacy, as Kant insists. This is a strictly history-specific event that comes to pass when dogmatism is no longer capable of defending metaphysics against scepticism:

> Now after all paths (as we persuade ourselves) have been tried in vain, what rules is tedium and complete indifferentism, the mother of chaos and night in the sciences, but at the same time also the origin, or at least the prelude, of their incipient transformation and enlightenment, when through ill-applied effort they have become obscure, confused, and useless.[64]

Kant goes on to aver that his times "will no longer be put off with illusory knowledge"[65] but will demand that "eternal and unchangeable laws" be pronounced by "the court of justice" – the tribunal of the critique of pure reason.[66] And in the Preface to the second edition, Kant suggests that philosophy's calling is to divest speculative reason of "its hitherto imagined possessions."[67]

The upheaval of modernity features in Kant's thinking in a double role. First, it is, to Kant, a crisis of knowledge that *has already come to pass*: metaphysics has ultimately disclosed its lack of legitimacy and cannot be sustained any longer. Philosophy is now challenged to respond fittingly to the crisis. Such a response can be found in critique. The structure at work here seems to be the same one that I outlined in the previous subchapter, following Derrida: philosophy discerns its own, previously unknown precondition that makes its existing form dead and compels it to move beyond its former paradigm. In other words, to salvage itself, philosophy must venture into the territories it has not trodden yet.

---

63 Immanuel Kant, *Critique of Pure Reason*, trans. Paul Guyer and Allen W. Wood (Cambridge: Cambridge UP, 1998), pp. 99–100.
64 *Ibid.*, p. 100.
65 *Ibid.*, pp. 100–101.
66 *Ibid.*, p. 101.
67 *Ibid.*, p. 117.

Second, modernity in Kant designates also a new age that commences as critique is undertaken. In this age, all previous endeavours of philosophy are revealed as a series of dogmatic attempts from which thinking was decisively disjoined. Philosophy can *inspect* these attempts, but it can no longer *consider them true*. Hence, modernity's relationship to the past is quite specific. *The same crisis that severed off modernity's direct contact with the past makes it possible to produce a detached account of this past*. That is why modernity boasts both a sense of historical ungroundedness and a capacity to scrutinise history that precedes it.

In Hegel's philosophy, the shift of modernity seems to be even more pronounced. *The Phenomenology of Mind*, Hegel's first mature work, offers a structure of reasoning analogous to the *Critique of Pure Reason*. Namely, it opens with a diagnosis of a crisis to which philosophy must respond in an appropriate manner. The crisis, again, lies in that a certain model of thinking has run its course and is dead now. In the Preface, Hegel briefly outlines the genealogy of the crisis:

> Time was when man had a heaven, decked and fitted out with endless wealth of thoughts and pictures. The significance of all that is lay in the thread of light by which it was attached to heaven; instead of dwelling in the present as it is here and now, the eye glanced away over the present to the Divine, away, so to say, to a present that lies beyond. The mind's gaze had to be directed under compulsion to what is earthly and kept fixed there; and it has needed a long time to introduce that clearness, which only celestial realities had, into the crassness and confusion shrouding the essence of things earthly, and to make the attention to the immediate presence as such, which was called Experience, of interest and value. Now we have apparently the need for the opposite of all this: man's mind and interest are so deeply rooted in the earthly that we require a like power to have them raised above that level. His spirit shows such poverty of nature that it seems to long for the mere pitiful feeling of the divine in the abstract, and to get refreshment from that, like a wanderer in the desert craving for the merest mouthful of water. By the little which can thus satisfy the needs of the human spirit *we can measure the extent of its loss* [emphasis added].[68]

Hegel views his times as an age of utter deprivation, in which – in the aftermath of an undefined *event of loss* – thought has forfeited its one-time abundance. Like in Kant, dogmatic (in Hegel "rationalising") philosophy still grinds on and denies this fact, pretending that nothing of that kind has happened. And, like Kant, Hegel believes that true philosophy must first of all acknowledge the relevance of the shift and re-think its hitherto development incisively. "Our epoch is a

---

68 Georg Wilhelm Friedrich Hegel, *The Phenomenology of Mind*, trans. J. B. Baillie (Mineola, NY: Dover Publications, 2003), p. 5.

birth-time, and a period of transition," Hegel contends.[69] The historical threshold is so remote that it de-legitimises even such apparently well-entrenched disciplines as logic and enjoins constructing them anew.[70] How does Hegel envisage philosophy's response to the crisis? It is pithily sketched in the Inaugural address delivered at the University of Berlin in 1818. Hegel insists that after the upheaval of modernity philosophy must: (1) renounce its former opulence, that is, not only acknowledge loss but also consciously bring it to completion; (2) find itself in the solitude of pure thinking; and (3) only with its help *reconstruct* the lost content. As Hegel put it:

> *The decision to philosophise means plunging into pure thinking* (– thinking is alone with itself), as into a *boundless ocean*; all vivid colours, all mainstays have vanished, all friendly lights have faded. Only *one* star shines still, *the inner star* of spirit. It is a *lodestar*. It is natural that Spirit, alone with itself, *is beset by terror. One does not know yet where to head and whence one comes*; there is many a thing amongst what has vanished that one would be loath to forfeit, not even for the world, but they *have not been reinstated* yet in this aloneness and one is doubtful that they will ever be retrieved or recovered. [...] *thinking that finds its origin in itself* knows *the same answers only* in their *unfolding necessity*, and it would be *an unbecoming impatience* that *answers its own questions forthwith* to expect to *arrive home presently at the very beginning. The Spirit must not be afeared to lose that in which it holds a true interest*; that on which what emerges for it in *philosophy* rests is its... This is why philosophy will restore to it *everything* that is true in the representations which *the instinct of reason* first brought forth; but...[71]

This implies that, in the wake of the modern crisis, philosophy must find "its origin in itself" and, only by *reasserting itself in it*, reclaim what was true in the

---

69 *Ibid.*, p. 6.
70 In the Preface to his *Science of Logic*, Hegel insists: "The complete transformation which philosophical thought in Germany has undergone in the last twenty-five years and the higher standpoint reached by spirit in its awareness of itself, have had but little influence as yet on the structure of logic [...] That which, prior to this period, was called metaphysics has been, so to speak, extirpated root and branch and has vanished from the ranks of the sciences. [...] The fact is that there no longer exists any interest either in the form or the content of metaphysics or in both together. [...]
    Healthy common sense has so much lost its respect for the school which claims possession of such laws of truth and still busies itself with them that it ridicules its laws and regards anyone as insufferable who can utter truths in accordance with such laws: the plant is – a plant, science is – science." Georg Wilhelm Friedrich Hegel, *Hegel's Science of Logic*, trans. Arnold V. Miller (New York: Humanity Books, 1998), pp. 25, 38.
71 Georg Wilhelm Friedrich Hegel, *Enzyklopädie der philosophischen Wissenschaften im Grundrisse*, http://www.hegel.de/werke_frei/hw108174.htm.

lost legacy. Hegel's philosophical programme involves thus choosing a contentless, formal foothold, made possible only by the crisis, from which to start reconstructing the content. This movement involves the following stages: (1) identification of the traces of an incomprehensible loss; (2) acceptance of the loss; (3) deliberate pruning of all content of philosophy away to leave only a vestige of pure thinking, a formal point (called "an inner star of spirit" by Hegel); (4) revisiting the past to reproduce its content based on this point. Apparently, ever since the modern shift, philosophy has split into two – into *content* and *pure movement of thinking*. Hegel advocates analysing the movement alone (which in his case produces a dialectical structure) and using it to re-establish the residual "dead" content ("positive content," as he put it elsewhere).

Analysis of the historical shift suggests the following conclusions. The movement of philosophy toward recreating its "outside" through the encounter with Jewish thought seems to ensue not so much from the 20th-century crisis as from a far earlier one that marked the threshold of modernity. As implied by Foucault's findings and Kant's and Hegel's insights, its consequences were analogous to those visible in 20th-century recourses to Judaism. They include: (1) the sense that the hitherto mode of thinking has been emptied out and is "essentially" dead; (2) the imperative that philosophy work through the event that inexplicably determined it; (3) philosophy's need to step beyond its earlier categories in order to find a buried structure that conditions it; (4) re-thinking the content of the past based on a new foothold possibly attained through the fathoming of this structure. Should these analogies be correct, a significant portion of 20th-century thinking on the alignment of Judaism and contemporary philosophy *would be conditioned by the same modern mechanism of crisis whose puzzle German idealism sought to sort out*.

Now we can proceed to the second of the problems formulated above and ask what particular structure of thinking it is that philosophy in modernity hinges on and strives to capture in transcending itself.

The Universe of Modernity II: The Structure that Conditions Thinking

If 20th-century thought and German idealism were indeed driven by the shared mechanism of modern crisis, the structure we are trying to identify would be graspable already in Kant's philosophy. With this assumption in mind, I shall first try to establish what it was that changed in the very "mechanics" of philosophy after the modern breakthrough. This will help us construct a model of this structure.

The basic change in philosophy whose paradigm was instituted by the Kantian critique concerns the relationship between knowing and the object of knowledge, and, consequently, the adopted model of being. The transformation can easily be grasped by comparing Aristotle's classic ontology with Kant's ontological framework.

Aristotle's central notion is *ousia*, that is, following the Latin translation, "substance." The term is commonly known to have more than one meaning in the Stagirite, with *The Metaphysics* alone describing it, among others, as "the essence," "the universal," "the genus" or "the substratum."[72] Nonetheless, all approaches to *ousia* are informed by two crucial considerations: (1) *ousia* is ontologically and notionally primary as well as autonomous; as Aristotle puts it, "that which is primarily, i.e. not in a qualified sense but without qualification, must be substance";[73] (2) *ousia* is inherent in bodies (for example, animals, plants and other physical entities) in which it is present "most obviously."[74] Inferably, *ousia* as a notion renders a physical body "at hand" which is, at the same time, a fundamental source of knowledge. Consequently, although to capture *ousia* may be challenging (hence ways of concluding about it are multiple), *there is no epistemological barrier as such between* ousia *and knowledge*. They belong to one and the same realm. In Aristotle's ontology, the model of being presupposes that *the differentiation of substances and their qualities are primally given and independent of knowledge*. Moreover, knowledge does not change anything in "being as such." This model of relationship between being and knowing seems to permeate all pre-modern thought.

The Kantian critique produces an upheaval in which a new model is forged. The Aristotelian *ousia* no longer constitutes a unity and the olden substance is dispersed into two aspects: the object, that is, "a thing for us" formed a priori by the mechanisms of cognition, and "a thing in itself," that is, an irreducible vestige which *we must assume to remain beyond the whole system of knowledge*. In Kant, then, knowledge is no longer neutral vis-à-vis its object. On the contrary, the object that is available to us is always already predetermined by knowledge. Intertwined with this is the necessity to presuppose "a thing in itself" that constitutes the outside of knowledge. If in Aristotle there was one universe of substances that existed in an originary way, in Kant the universe must be split

---

72 Aristotle, *Metaphysics*, Book VII, trans. William D. Ross (Oxford: Oxford University Press Reprints, 1924).

73 *Ibid.*, 1028 a.

74 *Ibid.*, 1028 b.

into two realms: knowledge, all of whose elements hinge on the same system of conditions, and an exterior remnant. Why does this remainder come into being? Because whatever is subsumed into the system of knowledge, *becomes primally limited*. Without looking into details of Kant's reasoning, as this lies beyond the scope of these considerations, let us ascertain that in order to connect (that is, to know) phenomena in the first place, their originary differentiation must be reduced so that they could be imagined side by side with each other, forming one series. Kant identifies this series with time.[75] Two conclusions follow thence: the knowable world is determined by an elementary plane of continuity (time), and we must presuppose "a thing in itself" as that which has not yet become limited – *something that does not fall under a continuous, temporal series* and, thus, is not imaginable as an ordinarily "abiding" object. Hence, Kantian philosophy structurally harbours the problem of a boundary between the continuous series and what lies beyond it. For Kant himself, the problem is the source of the famous antinomies of pure reason.[76] But in later philosophers (Hegel and Nietzsche, to name but two), it will morph into the question of the relationship between the radically singular and the system within which it would be knowable.

We can therefore say that the Kantian critique thoroughly transforms the structure of fundamental propositions which form the very framework of philosophical thinking. Naturally, not all post-Kantian philosophy is fully enclosed in this framework, and many schools of thought repudiate the critical legacy. This, however, does not mean that it remains merely a source of inspiration. On the contrary, I would argue that *the Kantian critique is implicated in the very manner in which the modern shift re-cast the operations of knowledge*. In other words, structural resolutions of the same problems that Kant raised do not necessarily result from drawing on him directly. They may as well ensue from the fact that these questions are inscribed in the very construction of modern thinking. This insight explains why thinkers who do not refer to Kant at all – Jabès being one of the throng – walk the same paths that he trod. I propose, in this work, to group all the concepts that, whether deliberately or not, replicate the blueprint of Kantian problems under the umbrella term of *modern philosophy*.[77]

---

75 See Kant, *Critique of Pure Reason*, pp. 162–164/178–182.

76 Cf. *Ibid.*, Vol. II, pp. 459–60.

77 Consequently, "modern philosophy," as used in this book, rather than designating all philosophy practised over the last few centuries (depending on where exactly the threshold of modernity is located) will denote only those of its forms which: (1) embody the structure of the modern breakthrough, and through that (2) dwell on problems that surfaced first in Kant's critique

As this thesis calls for a more specific substantiation, we should find out which issues outlined in the Kantian critique have since resurfaced regularly in philosophy labelled modern in this book. For one, there is a tension between the finite, limited field of knowledge and the unrenderable residue that persists beyond its bounds. The term "tension" implies that it is not all about a simple and definitive separation of two areas of the universe. The very act of such separation is in itself entangled in this division as it lies within the compass of knowledge. Already in Kant, it proved a challenge to distinguish phenomena from noumena, which were, on the one hand, a fiction of pure reason and, on the other, its indispensable premise. The structure of the tension between knowledge and its remnant was spelled out only by Hegel, who viewed "a thing in itself" as an irremovable vestige of the originary limitation performed by understanding, the first form of knowing.[78]

One would be hard pressed to find another Kantian problem of equal impact on later philosophical developments. In Nietzsche, it was re-cast into perspectivism, that is, the idea that there are multiple limited forms of knowledge, each of them conditioned in ways it cannot fathom itself.[79] This re-casting has

---

78   In the celebrated passage in *The Phenomenology of Mind*, Hegel addresses "the thing in itself" in the following way: "It is manifest that behind the so-called curtain, which is to hide the inner world, there is nothing to be seen unless we ourselves go behind there, as much in order that we may thereby see, as that there may be something behind there that can be seen. But it is clear at the same time that we cannot without more ado go straightway behind there. For this knowledge of what is the truth of the idea of the realm of appearance and of its inner being, is itself only a result arrived at after a long and devious process, in the course of which the modes of consciousness, 'meaning,' 'perception' and 'understanding' disappear." Hegel, *Phenomenology*, p. 96. For the primary limitation introduced by understanding, see *Ibid.* pp. 40–1; and Slavoj Žižek, *The Ticklish Subject: The Absent Center of Political Ontology* (New York and London: Verso, 2008), pp. 28–35.

79   The structure of relationships between the known and its inaccessible condition is repeatedly addressed by Nietzsche in a variety of forms and throughout his philosophical career. The related insights concern, for example: (1) the relation between language and the "mysterious" X to which it refers – "the thing in itself" (see Friedrich Nietzsche, *On Truth and Lies in a Nonmoral Sense*, trans. Daniel Brazeale [Create Space Independent Publishing Platform, 2005], pp. 12–16); (2) the relation between the meaning of a text and its inner rhythm (see Friedrich Nietzsche, *Daybreak: Thoughts on the Prejudices of Morality*, trans. R. J. Hollingdale, eds. Maudemarie Clark and Brian Leiter [Cambridge: Cambridge UP, 2003], p. 5); (3) the relation between interpretation and the interpreted (see Friedrich Nietzsche, "The Antichrist," trans. H. L. Mencken, § 52, in Anthony Uyl (ed.), *Writings of Nietzsche. Volume I* [Woodstock, ON: Devoted Publishing, 2016], p. 144; Friedrich Nietzsche, *The Will to Power*, trans.

moulded a considerable part of postmodern philosophy,[80] having earlier affected Heidegger's reflection on the finitude of *Dasein*.[81] The Kantian articulation of these problems may have been thoroughly reworked since the time of his critique, but the basic structure set by him has endured. Its axis is the relationship between finite *systems* of knowledge (in more recent formulations: symbolic systems or perspectives) and a certain remnant that eludes them, yet determines them all the same. When we look at recent philosophical currents, we can find this relationship both in Lacan (involving the symbolic and the real) and in Derrida (involving metaphysical oppositions and what he describes as their underlying infrastructures[82]).

A second characteristic trait of Kant-derived philosophy is that it rejects the notion of transcendent God. The point thereof is by no means any simple atheism. Rather, as a result of the re-drawing of relations between knowledge and being, which I sketched juxtaposing Aristotle and Kant, pre-modern concepts of God have become barely tenable. God as the supremely perfect being, a source and a foundation of all other beings, is no longer viable since the very notion of being has been split into "an object" and "a thing in itself" (to use Kant's terminology). If God were an object, as defined by Kant, he would have to be part of the causal sequence, but as such he could not be *the beginning* of this series, for objects are its elements and not its origin. The principle of continuity consistently espoused by Kant stipulates that, as all the empirically available reality is subjected to one system of causes, *its origin cannot belong to this system*. Can God then be comprehended beyond this system? Kant answers:

Walter Kaufmann and R. J. Hollingdale [New York: Vintage Books, 1968], § 481, p. 267); (4) the relation between a value-judgment and the life that makes it possible (see Friedrich Nietzsche, *Twilight of the Idols*, in *The Portable Nietzsche*, trans. W. Kaufmann. New York: Viking Penguin Press, 1977, pp. 485–86); (5) the relation between attitudes to and interpretations of the world and the physiological powers of the interpreter (Friedrich Nietzsche, *Beyond Good and Evil: Prelude to a Philosophy of the Future*, trans. Judith Norman, eds. Rolf-Peter Horstmann and Judith Norman [Cambridge et al.: Cambridge UP, 2003], § 20, p. 20).

80 See Michał Paweł Markowski, *Nietzsche. Filozofia interpretacji* [Nietzsche: Philosophy of Interpretation] (Kraków: Universitas, 2001).

81 See Martin Heidegger, *Kant and the Problem of Metaphysics. Fifth Edition, Enlarged*, trans. Richard Taft (Bloomington and Indianapolis Indiana UP, 1997), pp.18–25.

82 See Rodolphe Gasché, *The Tain of the Mirror: Derrida and the Philosophy of Reflection* (Cambridge, MA: Harvard UP, 1986).

For as far as concerns the void that one might think of outside of the field of possible experience (the world), this does not belong to the jurisdiction of the mere understanding, which only decides about questions concerning the use of given appearances for empirical cognition, and it is a problem for ideal reason, which goes beyond the sphere of a possible experience and would judge about what surrounds and bounds this [...].[83]

Whereas Thomas Aquinas, for one, could conceive of God as a cause in a single chain of causes leading up to the world as we know it, Kant could only see the notion of God as concerning solely the *field fully exterior to the causal sequence* and, therefore, perhaps as an experientially unauthorised idea of pure reason. The God-concept is thus postulative, and his existence cannot possibly be proved as logical thinking has no access to him.

Consequently, after the Kantian critique, the knowable reality becomes ontologically atheistic in being a single, continuous plane devoid of transcendence. If the concept of God is allowable after the critique, it can only be cast in a new role that structurally corresponds to "the thing in itself." In terms of former philosophy, it is a metaphorical usage with "God" referring to a particular structural principle of atheistic reality. This transmutation is patent in several post-Kantian philosophers. Hegel's radically atheistic thought frames God as a representational rendition of a particular moment in the movement of the Absolute. Lacan, in turn, identifies the concept of God with the great Other, which is "really" no transcendent being but an entity produced by the operations of language.[84] Finally, Slavoj Žižek associates divinity with the pure force of negativity which ruptures the unity of the atheistic world and drives its inner movement.[85] The Kantian critique could be said to *unsettle the previous notion of God and clear the way to identifying him not with the stable, transcendent being but with an empty vestige that persists in the reality stripped of transcendence.*

The third and last issue I wish to discuss is the subverting of the status of philosophy precipitated by the Kantian breakthrough. It results from the changes in the relationship between cognition and being, addressed above. Philosophy, namely, ceases to be neutral vis-à-vis its object and no longer provides general, theoretical knowledge of being, independent of the knowing subject. On the

83 Kant, *Critique of Pure Reason*, p. 330.
84 Cf. Jacques Lacan, *The Seminar of Jacques Lacan. Book XX: On Femininne Sexuality. The Limits of Love and Knowledge. 1972–1972 (Encore)*, trans. Bruce Fink, ed. Jacques-Alain Miller (New York and London: W.W. Norton & Company, 1999), pp. 45–6.
85 See Slavoj Žižek, *Less Than Nothing: Hegel and the Shadow of Dialectical Materialism* (London and New York: Verso, 2012), p. 264.

contrary, *philosophy as such is predicated upon the structure that it ponders*. In Kant, this informs the idea that reason analyses its own boundaries rather than any being beyond it. This critical tenet makes Kant-inspired philosophy self-reflexive in erecting its edifice on the very movement of thinking.

Inviting two different appraisals, this feature of modern philosophy indeed propelled two different tendencies. One of them, epitomised by Hegel, edifies philosophy into a universal and fundamental science, with its self-reflexivity acclaimed as a virtue. It is admitted that philosophy as such is dependent on the structure it explores, but self-reflexivity makes it possible to *first detect this structure within philosophy itself* and, then, to apply the mechanism identified in this way in interpreting the "positive content." This reasoning appeared also in the previous subchapter, where I quoted Hegel's claim that philosophy re-establishes what perished in the modern shift and, moreover, in doing so it finds a foothold in itself. This tendency assumes, thus, that because all reality is grounded in the same structure, philosophy's role is to find this structure in its "pure" version (in Hegel, dialectics is knowledge about it) and, subsequently, to use it to re-interpret phenomena.

The other tendency takes the opposite direction. It assumes that since philosophy is unable to offer knowledge neutral of its object and it shares the same underlying structure with its object, *it must be transcended and this transcendence is attainable only in and through a practical act*. An embryo of this approach was already inscribed in Kant's concept of practical reason, radicalised by Fichte,[86] while it was hatched into a full-fledged form by none other than Marx.

Still, crucial to our analysis is that in the philosophy of the 19th and the 20th centuries the two lines of thought usually co-exist in a dialectical tension. As a rule, this coupling is underpinned by the following argumentation:

(1) philosophy has so far been fraught with the error of failing to recognise its own precondition;
(2) that philosophy has persisted in its hitherto form is, as such, an outcome of this error;
(3) still, philosophy has a potential to recognise and explain it;
(4) this recognition is bound up with a practical act that makes real change (in life, society, and so forth);

---

86 Cf. Johann Gottlieb Fichte, *The Science of Knowledge: With the First and the Second Introductions*, trans. Peter Heath and John Lachs (Cambridge et al.: Cambridge UP, 2013), pp. 6–10.

(5) as a result, philosophy itself will be deeply transformed or, in many cases, replaced by an entirely new practice.

Thus, philosophy's position and the need to transcend it turn out to represent two facets of the same problem. Attempts at purification, supposed to yield a pure structure of thought, are analogous to strivings to oust theory for the sake of a pure act of practice. In both cases, that which is must be obliterated to unveil philosophy's aphilosophical determinants.

However abstract it may be, this pattern is palpable in several key modern philosophers associated with various traditions. For example, Nietzsche considers philosophy as practised so far to have been error-haunted since Socrates in that its false attitude to life produces, in Nietzsche's own age, nihilism. At the same time, it is philosophy that must see through this error. The "great noontide" of new, incipient philosophy heralds first and foremost an active and affirmative attitude to life and unfolding of things. What is accomplished in this practical act is, actually, breaking with the former philosophy, although the very category of philosophy is still retained by Nietzsche. Heidegger, similarly, views Western philosophy as moulded by the forgetfulness of Being. This fallacy can be recognised only in a new, liminal form of philosophy which, abandoning its former paradigm, will be replaced by deeper-penetrating, non-theoretical and non-aggregating "thinking" (*Denken*). This kind of thinking, listening to Being and the effort of "emplacing" (Heidegger's *Erörterung*) are closer to a practical act than to philosophy as exercised so far. This model is also discernible within Jewish philosophy itself. Franz Rosenzweig, for one, proposes to replace philosophy – based on the illusory knowledge of "the All" and deliberate obliviousness to death[87]– with the "new thinking" that abandons the edifice of theory, as a result of which "it opens into life."[88] Inspired by Rosenzweig, Lévinas strives to overcome Western philosophy's prioritisation of ontology by foregrounding ethics, a predominantly practical domain, as the new "first philosophy."

Clearly, disclosed by Kant, philosophy's ensnarement in its own object breeds, primarily, endeavours to surmount philosophy and, then, make it catalyse the transformation to be accomplished by fathoming the very structure that

---

87 Franz Rosenzweig, *The Star of Redemption*, trans. Barbara E. Galli (Madison: Wisconsin UP, 2005), pp. 9–11.
88 Cf. *Ibid.*, p. 447.

conditions philosophy as such. The surmounting of philosophy is, thereby, associated with a practical act.

Now we can try and answer the central question of this subchapter: What does the structure involve that determines philosophy which seeks it in self-transcendence? The answer is that *the structure involves an irreducible, particular remnant opposed to a perspectival, finite whole.* I believe that this structure underlies all three problems of modern philosophy analysed in this subchapter. First, it is to be found in reiterated transformations of "the thing in itself" and in modern perspectivism. Besides, the residue-structure serves as a cornerstone of a new notion of God's position. The identification of God with emptiness, interval, central lack, force of negativity, and so forth, in so many modern "theologies" implies that this remnant plays a crucial role in modern philosophy. Finally, the remnant-structure answers also to the last of our issues, that is the surmounting of philosophy. How so? Namely, the remnant-structure is not only *an object* of philosophy but also its construction principle. Modern philosophy searches for a determinant that lies beyond it and opposes its limited knowledge. Hence philosophy's self-overcoming movement, its cancellation in a practical act, is an attempt to remove the boundary between itself and the remnant that conditions it. That is why modern philosophy (as defined above) perceives reality as determined by the residual structure and, at the same time, is subject to this very structure, due to which it futilely strives to transcend itself in search of its own abolishment.

If this reasoning is apt, we should perhaps re-calibrate our perspective on all the discourses which frame Judaism as a tradition which, though forgotten, is "more truthful" than the Greek one and discovered only after the latter has disintegrated. Therefore, I would posit that *vis-à-vis modern philosophy Judaism functions as the vestige constituted by philosophy itself in an attempt to continue its movement through self-transcendence.*

The Universe of Modernity III: The Problem of Philosophical Account of Judaism

With this thesis, we can proceed to our last question, that is whether the position of Judaism in 20th-century philosophy is something unique. Is this newly discovered Judaism not just a construct produced by modern philosophy as part of its own movement? If it were the case, we should find also other conceptual traditions that this philosophy utilises in a similar way. And, indeed, it turns out that mechanisms of re-interpreting traditions, particularly religious ones – exterior to philosophy – are detectable at the threshold of modernity, that is, in Kant. Still identifying himself with Lutheranism, Kant professed that "historical faith 'is dead being alone.'"[89] In the modern optics, it is founded on a doubtful and contingent historical narrative.[90] The impact of the modern shift addressed above is evident here: the continuity of tradition perishes. Despite that, Kant does not advocate discarding religion. Rather, he insists that it should be *reconstructed* based on "the principle of the pure religion of reason, as a revelation (though not empirical one) permanently taking place within all human beings."[91] In other words, the critique of pure reason enables philosophy to establish a new basis for religion and to invest the old beliefs with new meanings. Kant's reasoning proceeds in the following stages: (1) the crisis of faith is undeniable; (2) philosophy overcomes the crisis through critique; (3) that is why the principles of reason it finds *now* can found faith in a new shape; (4) when religion is grounded in the philosophical *structure*, its *content* will be imbued with new meaning. As a consequence, *religion is turned into an external source permanently disjoined from current thinking by the crisis of modernity. This source is subject to reconstruction effected by self-grounded thinking.*[92]

The same mechanism reappears in Hegel. He revives Christian religion smothered by Enlightenment's rationalism,[93] but does so only through reinterpretation based on philosophical solutions. Unlike the detractors of religion, he believes that religion's "positive content" can – and should – be re-created whereby philosophy's advantage lies in its capacity for such a reconstruction.[94] What would that involve? It would involve a *proper understanding* of the content of faith obscured by representations before. Although the formation of a given content predates this understanding by many centuries, Hegel avers that this understanding completes Christianity and is its key moment. Clearly, the

---

89 Immanuel Kant, *Religion within the Boundaries of Mere Reason and Other Writings*, trans. Allen Wood and George di Giovanni (Cambridge: Cambridge UP, 2003), p. 119.

90 Cf. *Ibid.*, pp. 117–22.

91 *Ibid.*, p. 128.

92 Here, Kant reproduces Luther's reasoning in which religion is rebuilt based on the irreducible and fundamental act of faith, with the function of this act re-assigned henceforth to the philosophical critique of reason. Kant can thus profess that "we have reason to say […] that 'the Kingdom of God has come into us'" (*Ibid.*, p. 128). Philosophy's triumph over religion is manifest in that the "Kingdom of God" is an era of reason that by itself reconstructs religion.

93 Cf. Georg Wilhelm Friedrich Hegel, *Lectures on the Philosophy of Religion. Together with a Work on the Proofs of the Existence of God.* Vol. I, trans. E. B. Speirs, B.D., and J. Burdon Sanderson (London: Kegan Paul, Trench, Trübnner & Co. 1895), pp. 36–7.

94 Cf. *Ibid.*, p. 32.

new legitimisation of religion by philosophy[95] involves, essentially, philosophy's employment of an external, prior matter *through which philosophy seems to arrive at its own primal condition.* What it in fact does, however, is insert its own mechanism in the past content and proclaim to have just found it there.

These examples of Kant and Hegel show that the movement of reconstructing religion is intimately implicated in the workings of modern philosophy which seeks its own exterior remnant. "Dead" for philosophy, faith's content functions here as an objectively existing, past matter that philosophy ostensibly relies on while actually reconstructing it.

Western philosophy of the 19th and the 20th centuries repeatedly revisits traditions that lie outside it and deploys them in this exact way. Therein, it crucially insists on describing them as "nonphilosophies," to use Derrida's coinage, which *earlier* fathomed the condition that philosophy has failed to recognise. This is how Schopenhauer viewed the Hinduism of the Upanishads, how Nietzsche saw his abstract "Greeks," how Heidegger framed pre-Socratics and German poets (e.g. Hölderlin and Trakl), how Bataille positioned Gnosticism,[96] and how Kojève, Lacan and Žižek, following Hegel, viewed Christianity. Evidently, not just religion but rather multiple discourses from beyond philosophy are used as such points of reference. *Their content is selected and configured consistently with the logic of modern philosophy which utilises them.* In being re-invented, some of their own tenets that contravene the spirit of modern philosophy are discarded (e.g. this is what happens to transcendent God's real existence in Hegel's version of Christianity) while other ones, though by no means given any eminence within these traditions themselves, are accorded the pivotal status through and in their philosophical reconstruction. In Hegel, this pattern is exposed in that he locates Christianity's uniqueness in Christ's dialectical nature,[97] which is, of

---

95   See *Ibid.*, p. 364.

96   In his "Base Materialism and Gnosticism," Bataille argues that the Gnostics developed an understanding of the matter that approximates present-day dialectical materialism. In this way he presents his own version of the "Hellenistic error" whose dominion over Western philosophy seems to subside. See Georges Bataille, "Base Materialism and Gnosticism," trans. Allan Stoekl, with Carl R. Lovitt and Donald M. Leslie, Jr., in Fred Botting and Scott Wilson (eds.), *The Bataille Reader* (Oxford and Malden, MA: Blackwell, 1997), pp. 160–4. I owe this insight to Professor Rodolphe Gasché.

97   See Georg Wilhelm Friedrich Hegel, *Lectures on the Philosophy of Religion: Volume III. Conusummate Religion*, trans. R. F. Brown, P. C. Hodgson and J. M. Stewart, ed. Peter C. Hodgson (Oxford: Clarendon Press, 2006), pp. 314–6.

course, hardly the religion's fundamental idea but dovetails conveniently with Hegel's own philosophy.

We could say that the forms of modern philosophy referred to above "descry" in past traditions the very structures they want to descry and prove. By the same token, they disguise the fact that these structures are intrinsically modern because, framed in such ways, the structures come across as ahistorical since existing already in the doctrines of old. It could thus be posited that *modern philosophy has a distinct tendency to transform its own structures into oppositions that are supposed to govern the entire history of thought.* This suggests an answer to the question posed at the beginning of this subchapter. Namely, the position of Judaism in 20th-century thought may result from the structural patterning of modern philosophy. The Athens-vs.-Jerusalem opposition seems a veritably paradigmatic outcome of the projection of this philosophy's inner movement onto the whole of history. Judaism is consigned to the position of an external "nonphilosophy," accessible *only now.* The line between philosophy as known so far and the searched-for "nonphilosophy" is extrapolated as the Athens-vs.-Jerusalem opposition and, in this shape, seems to hold sway over the historical vistas of Western thinking. As can easily be noticed, this opposition structurally mirrors similar pairings produced by modern philosophy also much earlier. "Jerusalem" mimics the function attributed to "Christianity" in Kant, Hegel, Lacan and Žižek, to "Greeks" in Nietzsche, and to "pre-Socratics" in Heidegger.[98]

Concluding, for modern philosophy, Judaism is one of the many external discourses that it institutes in the position of its own remnant and deploys in its own movement. This is evinced in a characteristic selectiveness with which it sifts Judaism's vast legacy for aspects of which to avail itself. As I will show in this book (resorting chiefly to the example of Jabès), in making a recourse to Jewish tradition 20th-century thought is happy to reduce it to a few properties (e.g. antimythical inclinations, radical monotheism and Messianism) that are akin to its own premises. In this way, a modern construct is generated and transposed onto

---

98 The paradox inherent in the use philosophy makes of these external discourses is exposed in that the mythical construct of the "Greeks" can function both as a "nonphilosophy" sought by philosophy (e.g. in Nietzsche and Heidegger) and as the philosophical error to be repudiated (as is the case in the Athens-vs.-Jerusalem opposition). Of course, "Athens" is concocted in different ways each time. What is more, in Nietzsche and Heidegger, the very construct of Greek philosophy is split into two parts: the "error" (e.g. post-Socratic philosophy) and the looked-for nonphilosophy (e.g. pre-Socratics).

the expanses of history, with its modern origins carefully erased. This, however, does not change the simple fact that it is in discovering its "nonphilosophies" that modern philosophy feels most at home.

The Concept of Jewish Philosophy of Modernity

With these insights, we can formulate the concept of Jewish philosophy of modernity. As the reasoning above implies, modernity is more than just another historical period. Rather, it is a new site where historicity is produced and perceived. It is an epoch which itself crafts the frameworks that make it into an epoch. A considerable portion of concepts it contrives are overdetermined as they rely at the same time on many various points of reference which, in fact, were formed in advanced by the modern structure. Also Judaism finds itself drawn amidst a grid of interconnections configured in this way and devoid of an Archimedean point. Side by side with religious Jewish studies (spared the strong impact of the modern shift), a broad and varied tendency developed, particularly in the 20th century, to employ Jewish elements in philosophy and literature. As the argument above shows, this tendency is laden with patterns of modern thinking. Therefore, I propose, at least within this book, to abandon the simple idea of Judaism's "influence" on philosophy and, instead, adopt a construct which intrinsically reflects the complexity of relationships among philosophy, modernity and Judaism.

This is the theoretical nucleus of "Jewish philosophy of modernity." Now its model must be fleshed out to compound its typologically distinct patterns discussed in the foregoing. Bringing them together does not mean, of course, that they must all be stamped on the thought of every author that drew on Judaism in the 20th century. Rather, amassed, they add up to a certain ideal type on which to base any more detailed analysis. On this model, Jewish philosophy of modernity would have the following attributes:

(1) an identifiable trace of the modern hiatus manifest in
     (a) recognition of a crisis in contemporary thinking;
     (b) dissociation from the tradition of Judaic thought, perceived as more or less lost in its earlier shape;[99]

---

99 This, admittedly, requires a clarification. Many thinkers whom I associate with Jewish philosophy of modernity did profess Judaism (e.g. Rosenzweig, Taubes and Lévinas) but believed that some of its tenets needed a contemporary re-interpretation. Others, such as Kafka, Scholem, Celan and Jabès himself, were exposed to more or less rudimentary Jewish religious education as children, but were isolated from the continuity

(c) reference to a singular, originary event of loss, formative of the current age – hence popularity of the Lurianic *tzimtzum*;

(d) a chasm between the (apparently lost or "dead") content of thinking and its structure;

(e) conspicuous historicity, i.e. attempts to inscribe the contemporary era within a broader historical narrative;

(2) a more or less pronounced presence of characteristically modern premises outlined already in the Kantian critique, such as:

(a) the division of reality into two realms: one knowable, continuous and dependent on an a priori structure and the other unknowable, radically singular, external and, at the same time, forming a possibility condition of the former;

(b) a tension between the continuity of the series and its ungraspable limit;

(c) primal limitation of knowledge, including also perspectivism;

(d) marking of the finite world by the infinite outside;

(e) dismissal of the notion of transcendent God;

(f) a new concept of Divinity as connoting a remnant, a central lack, a pure negativity;

(3) positing the residual structure not only as philosophy's object but also as its construction principle. As a result, philosophy is perceived as dependent on an ensemble of nonphilosophical conditions that determine the *movement* of thinking rather than its *content*. This dependence causes a crisis of philosophy that can be overcome only if philosophy self-transcends towards the as-yet unknown outside;

(4) framing Judaism as a particular "nonphilosophy," that is, "knowledge" whose structure conditions philosophy. Hence, elements of Jewish thinking are supposed to foster a new, post-crisis form of philosophy (if it is to go by this name in the first place);

(5) linking the "discovery" of Judaism for Western thought to fundamental transformations the latter underwent at the onset of modernity. In this perspective, Judaism seems to have known the "truth" *for long* while philosophy arrives at it only now;

---

of Judaism and did not practise it (at least not in an orthodox form). Their visions of Judaism are thus reconstructions of the lost tradition. Still others (e.g. Blanchot) were never involved in Judaic worship and did not attempt conversion, with Jewish religion being just their philosophical inspiration. The differences between these three groups of thinkers notwithstanding, the continuity of Judaic tradition was rather problematic to all of them both philosophically and personally.

(6) pairing the movement towards Judaism not only with cognition but also with a practical act (e.g. affirmation of life or superiority of ethical action to ontology). The coupling of the two components, i.e.
   (a) philosophy's attempt at self-transcendence through Judaism and
   (b) a practical act, breeds Messianic tendencies within philosophy;

(7) inscription of the tension between philosophy-in-crisis and the "nonphilosophy" sought by it within cross-historical binaries, in particular within the Athens-vs.-Jerusalem opposition, but also within the "paganism"-vs.-"monotheism" dichotomy.

(8) crafting a selective vision of Judaism in which its alleged fundamental premises are those that align with modern philosophy, i.e. radical monotheism,[100] anti-idolatry, primacy of the word over the image, intertextuality, dismissal of one dogmatic truth for the sake of interpretive multiplicity, desacralisation of the world, positive appraisal of "life as such," Messianism, prioritisation of a practical act (ethics) over ontology, embracement of insecurity brought by the happening of things and the nomadic condition;

(9) deployment of this construct of Judaism as a basis for re-interpreting the *content* of philosophy and re-appraising it.

Thus, the tradition of Judaism would stand for something more than just a source of inspiration for Jewish philosophy of modernity. Judaism embodies the goal of its own movement. It seems to harbour the "nonphilosophical" truth about philosophy and, as such, to explain also its structural crisis. *These conclusions imply that the relationship of philosophy and Judaism is thoroughly organised by modern structures.* In other words, that philosophy seeks to absorb elements of Jewish thinking and how it chooses and constructs them reveals more about modern philosophy than about Judaism.

With this theoretical footing, we can now produce an account of Edmond Jabès' philosophy. I shall attempt to show how his work can be interpreted in terms of Jewish philosophy of modernity and, subsequently, formulate further conclusions that will augment the concept outlined above.

To conclude, Jabès as a "Jewish philosopher of modernity" is a rather specific author. Like Celan, he does not set out from philosophy, but from literature.

---

100 Why should radical monotheism be so convergent with modern philosophy if I have stated that modern philosophy perceives reality as one, continuous atheistic space without transcendence? The answer is that radical monotheism, unlike the "Greek" idolatrous one, offers a structure that describes an uncrossable and ubiquitous transcendental line between reality and its "thing in itself."

Nevertheless, his movement towards Judaism produces the same outcomes as in thinkers of a strictly philosophical mindset. This is certainly thought-provoking. For it may as well be that the phenomenon which I labelled "Jewish philosophy of modernity" is, in fact, broader and extends over all modern thinking as such, not only philosophy. Perhaps, the movement of simplifying and processing the external content into a redeeming remnant has a far wider compass than philosophy. If it is indeed the case, Jabès' thought, albeit essentially devoid of any direct philosophical references and focused on the very structure of movement that motivates it, could tell us more about Jewish philosophy of modernity than concepts entangled in internal philosophical disputes are possibly capable of doing.

2 Edmond Jabès: Life and Writing

It is time to step into the universe of Edmond Jabès' thought. To pave the way, I will first discuss his biography and writings. They are so tightly interwoven, at any rate,[1] that without knowing certain facts of his life, one is bound to have only a very cursory understanding of Jabès' texts. The following account is guided by the idea of dual and simultaneous, though unequal, inspirations behind the poet's work, which was nurtured by modern thinking and Jewish tradition. Like Kafka, Benjamin and Derrida, Jabès is neither a Jewish philosopher nor a religious Jew who practised philosophy. Severed from the immediacy of Jewish religion, he re-interprets his Judaism in the intellectual environment indelibly stamped by modernity.

This chapter consists of two parts. The first part is biographical, though not very classically so, as it does not merely recount Jabès' biography but, in a broader view, dwells first of all on the events that he himself regarded as crucial to his life, himself interpreted and himself drew general conclusions from. With this approach, the biographical narrative serves at the same time as an introduction to the universe of the writer's thinking. The second part discusses Jabès' texts. Rather than just bibliographically enumerating his works, it analyses the mode of his writing as well, which is, by the way, one of a kind. In this Chapter, I will also survey literary scholars' commentaries to outline the horizon within which interpreters have addressed the poet's work so far. In conclusion, I will consider Jabès' position on the map of Modernism, Late Modernism and Postmodernism.

Life

Edmond Jabès was born in Cairo on 16 April 1912.[2]

Yet in the case of such a writer, nothing can be as simple and clear. When his birthdate was officially recorded, 14 April was written down in the register by mistake. As Jabès stated, in this way "the first manifestation of my existence was an absence that bore my name."[3] He lived for two days only on paper, so to speak, in a purely symbolic sense, without actually existing as a living human being.

---

1 See DB, p. 9.
2 Cf. the timeline of Jabès' life in DB, pp. 117–118; see also Didier Cahen, *Edmond Jabès* (Paris: Editions Pierre Belfond, 1991), pp. 305–41.
3 DB, p. 5.

Throughout his lifetime, that event haunted him as an idea he never ceased to ponder: "As with the book, as with God in the world, the first manifestation of my existence was an absence that bore my name,"[4] he would repeat time and again. Giving a universal tenor to this seemingly trifling event, Jabès adds that "the real death precedes life given that the other death at least leaves traces."[5] The statement exudes Jabès' characteristic dialectics of the symbolic order and real life. Like in Blanchot, the order gives a living being a name and, thereby, marks his life with an imprint of death, of the named and never present. "Then being named would mean accepting the destiny of life *from the hands of death* [emphasis added],"[6] says the writer, assuming that living in language bears an inexpungible aspect of death, which is the price for the visibility of this life. "Lost," though never really there, the two days made Jabès particularly sensitive, as he professed himself, to emptiness, death and contingency,[7] which envelop life and grant it comprehensibility.

What traces framed Jabès' life? He hailed from a Jewish family that had long been settled in Egypt. Despite the family's Sephardic background and Near-East milieu, its fortunes mimicked those of Judaism in Western Europe, incrementally shrinking down to a purely formal sign of identity.[8] Edmond himself ultimately gave up on any form of religious Jewish worship. Jabès' family was an heir to the opulent cosmopolitan Egyptian culture of the 19th and 20th centuries, permeated by predominantly French influences.[9] The life of a Jewish family in a country where despite the Western influences the population were mostly Muslims always involved difficulties and a serious risk of religious and ethnic persecutions. For this reason, Jabès' grandfather requested Italian citizenship[10] when the Urabi Revolt of 1882 turned against minorities inhabiting Egypt.[11] Even though in this way the family became – as the writer himself puts it – Italian "all of a sudden,"[12] the impact of Francophone culture by no means

---

4   BQ II, p. 178.
5   DB, p. 5.
6   BR II, p. 77.
7   DB, p. 6.
8   IEJ, p. 10.
9   Aimée Israel-Pelletier, "Edmond Jabès, Jacques Hassoun, and Melancholy: The Second Exodus in the Shadow of the Shoah," *MLN*, 123/4 (September 2008) (French issue), pp. 797–818, on pp. 801–802.
10 Cf. DB, p. 21.
11 Cahen, *Edmond Jabès*, p. 305.
12 DB, p. 21.

subsided. Moreover, as at the time there were no Italian schools in Egypt, Jabès' father attended a French school, and French was also his first language.[13] One would indeed be hard pressed to envision a more complex cultural and linguistic melting pot than that in which the poet was growing up. Born and raised in Egypt, a Francophone Italian citizen of Jewish descent who spoke also English, Italian and Arabic[14] – none of these many descriptors furnished Jabès with a rock-hard cornerstone to found his identity on. Instead, their mutual tensions made him a perennial outsider. By the same token, Judaism was for him more of a trace of the past than a basis of self-identification.

Jabès' life was essentially affected by three personal disasters, each of which shaped the series of his *Books* as he continued to interpret them over and over again. Let us look into these momentous events one by one to understand how he made sense of them in retrospect.

The first disaster, and the pivotal event of Jabès' childhood, was the death of his older sister Marcelle, with whom he was very close and who was his first guide in the realm of literature.[15] For a twelve-year-old child he was then, the death meant infinitely more than just a "cruel loss." As he stresses himself, it was tantamount to the trauma of a second birth: "If we admit that certain events mark us indelibly, causing important mutations in our personality, then I would be tempted, in my case, to speak of a second birth, or simply of birth."[16]

It is likely no coincidence, especially if viewed through a psychoanalytical lens, that Jabès associated the experience of writing with death so closely. It was not only a dead person that opened the path to reading and writing for him; it was also when she was dying that he realised the nearly surrealistic power of language which grapples with the inexpressible. This is suggested by Jabès' description of the moment of his sister's death, written in the spirit of Blanchot:

---

13 *Ibid.* p. 22.
14 Admittedly, Jabès was raised in a milieu saturated with French colonial influences, yet the impact of Arabic culture and poetics should not be neglected and, actually, would deserve a separate study. Typical of Arabic literature is the prevalence of the poetic element (cf. Jamel Eddine Bencheikh, *Poétique arabe* [Paris: Gallimard, 1989], pp. 1–2), which is conspicuous also in Jabès' mature, non-poetic works. Similarly, the desert motifs endemic to Arabic poetry (e.g. in Al-Sharif al-Radi) reverberate in Jabès' ubiquitous desert metaphor. See Laifer, *Edmond Jabès*, pp. 8–9.
15 DB, p. 6.
16 *Ibid.*

My sister died practically in my arms. I was alone at her deathbed. I remember having told her something like "You can't die. It's not possible." To which she replied with exactly these words: "Don't think about death. Don't cry. One cannot escape one's destiny." That day I understood that there is a language for death, just as there is a language for life. One doesn't speak to a dying person the way one speaks to a living being. And the dying person doesn't answer you either as he or she might have done only a few moments earlier. Their speech is different. It has nearly reached self-oblivion. Later, I would come across it in the desert: the ultimate reflection, one could say, of a broken mirror. It is a speaking with the impress of great distance, like a dimension added to everyday words. This tone, this distance have never left me; nor has the meaning of her last words which I interpreted thus: destiny is inscribed in death. One never leaves death.[17]

At this moment, we could usefully digress from our biographical narrative to clarify this passage as it will weigh heavily on the analyses to follow. Interpreted in the light of Jabès' lifetime work (as autobiographical reflection is here inextricable from conclusions from his other writings), it suggests that the language of the dying is in a sense truer than everyday language since it does not evade the inexorable. Common language serves to sustain communication among people rather than to express the truth. Although it seems to describe reality, it essentially shelters against reality. When confronted with what is referred to as an inevitable event, which is death, the illusory power of this language is exposed. This language closes itself off from reality and dismisses what it refuses to acknowledge. The language of the dying is different as it speaks in constant tension with that which determines it, that is, with death. In this way, the language of the dying conveys not only its own meaning but also this external determinant: it is death that speaks through it. For this reason, the language of the dying unties itself from the speaking person and becomes the voice of an impersonal truth rather than of an individual agent. Consequently, the language discloses the *trace* it bears.[18]

His sister's death is thus, in a sense, a primal disaster that Jabès' thought must confront and that moulds his future perception of reality.[19] Death demands that

---

17 *Ibid.*, p. 7.
18 In this, Jabès resembles not only Blanchot but first of all insights of high Modernism, in particular of Rilke, who perceived death as the other facet of life and inseparable from it. In Rilke's view, if life is to be fully grasped, the dark light of this covered facet must be restored. See Edith Wyschogrod, *Spirit in Ashes: Hegel, Heidegger, and Man-Made Mass Death* (New Haven, CT, and London: Yale UP, 1985), pp. 6–7.
19 This obviously invites thinking in terms of Freud's idea in "Mourning and Melancholia" that melancholia ensues from a loss that has not been worked through and consists in the lost object being absorbed within the "self" in order to avoid the recognition of

language always tell the truth, that besides the message as such it always refer to death itself.[20] Jabès will strive to meet this demand throughout his mature work.[21] *It will bear an imprint of an irremovable trace of emptiness and, thus, come across as constantly referring to an originary calamity.*

Jabès' adolescence was fraught with fatalism bred from powerlessness vis-à-vis the fate and with incessant rebellion against injustice manifest, first of all, in death.[22] This split not only shaped his books to come[23] but also helped him, years later, re-connect with Judaism, which, as the writer put it, "has made the passivity-rebellion duality its very dwelling place."[24] The young Jabès, admittedly, rather early abandoned the formal Judaic worship – unpropped, after all, by any

---

the loss. Cf. Sigmund Freud, "Mourning and Melancholia," in *The Standard Edition of the Complete Psychological Works of Sigmund Freud*, ed. James Strachey, *Volume XIV (1914–1916): On the History of Psycho-Analytic Movement, Papers on Metapsychology and Other Works* (London: The Hogarth Press and The Institute of Psycho-Analysis), pp. 243–58. Language that refuses to work loss through cannot shake off the burden of the past and activate immediate meanings. But, on the other hand, this language, though dysfunctional for the subject, is paradoxically "truer" as it articulates what remains hidden to the normal sight. Philosophically speaking, thus, it is more valuable than the correctly working language of the subject who has successfully gone through mourning.

Aimée Israel-Pelletier offers an interpretation that Jabès' primary object of loss was Egypt, a homeland where, through the melancholic incorporation within the self, he belongs more deeply than when he was physically there. See Israel-Pelletier, "Edmond Jabès."

20 Cf. DB, p. 8. The difference between Blanchot's and Jabès' attitudes to language is palpable here. Blanchot theorises language in relation to the primary loss of an object which is replaced with a word; literature cannot persist in the negation of loss and, thus, works with an essentially dysfunctional language. Cf. e.g. Maurice Blanchot, "Literature and the Right to Death," trans. Lydia Davis, in Maurice Blanchot, *The Work of Fire* (Stanford, CA: Stanford UP, 1995), pp. 300–44.

For Jabès, every experience, including the loss of an object, takes place in language. Death does not entail the loss of "a real object" and replacing it with a word. On the contrary, this object, formed in language as it is, has its own speech. "There is a language for death just as there is a language for life," the poet concludes. Thus the experience of catastrophe is not a transition from reality to language, but a passage from one form of language to another – one that is truer and earnest since it articulates that which limits it from beyond.

21 Cf. Jabès' own words in QDLB, p. 227.

22 DB, p. 8.

23 *Ibid.*

24 *Ibid.*

specifically Jewish education[25]– but for years continued to participate in important Jewish holidays, cultivated bonds with the Jewish community and saw to the synagogue named after his grandfather, who had committed himself and his descendants to taking care of it.[26] Like Kafka, Scholem and Benjamin, Jabès was disconnected from Judaism by his assimilation-promoting culture, though in his case it was, additionally, a colonial culture radiating from the then "centre" of the empire to the "periphery" of Egypt. French modernism was, as a matter of fact, a far more powerful influence on the young poet than his Jewish heritage, which he did not view favourably.[27]

If in his later works Jabès undertook to re-think Judaism, he did not set out to do it by returning to the faith professed of old. On the contrary, his personal experiences and reflections stirred him to re-construct Judaism out of individually selected items of Jewish tradition.[28] In doing this, Jabès always focused on what appealed to his personal feeling of exile and his rebellion against death. Jabès' re-invention of Judaism is so profound that even when evoking childhood memories, he picks up only one Jewish element – synagogal singing – and invests it immediately with the meaning he wishes to see in it himself, that of complaint against the historical fate. Of Jewish religious services, he remembers first of all:

the long monotonous chords of the traditional chants with their insistent repetitions, rather like wailing. As they unfolded, they slowly awakened a dark past of suffering to which I felt related in spite of myself. [...] As infinite modulation of the word, the Jewish chant has remained glued to the text. It remains very foreign to the Western conception of the chant whose main object is to exalt, to magnify religious feeling. The chant has, in a way, become a work of art that rises towards God, while in the synagogue it is the very words of the sacred, immutable text that let their chant be heard, allowing nothing other to be heard or seen than the word, the infinity of the letter.

It may be of interest to recall here that in the biblical text the inventor of music is given as Jubal, a descendant of Cain. Music therefore appears at its origins as the expression of an unhappy consciousness, of a battered being. It is the very scream of an unbearable suffering stuck, one could say, to the word. These chants carry something like a reproach addressed to God as well as an appeal to his mercifulness – the dazzled awakening of the wounded soul to the sonorities of the Creation.[29]

---

25 IEJ, p. 10.
26 DB, pp. 19–20.
27 Steven Jaron, *Edmond Jabès: The Hazard of Exile* (Oxford: Legenda, 2003), pp. 41–2.
28 Emphatically, "Judaism" is not just a religious designation to Jabès; rather, it denotes all things Jewish.
29 DB, pp. 20–1.

Judaism, thus, is to Jabès not a particular religion, one amidst many others, but a storehouse of tradition where the bonds of the entire Creation are preserved. Attachment to the immutable text makes Judaism reveal the universal interconnectedness of word, letter, scream and being, which is exposed to death and inexorably fraught with unbearable suffering. Jabès, therefore, feels Jewish not through any formal religious membership but through the experience of Creation impressed in Judaism. This is also the meaning he ascribes to Jewishness in his writings. Still, this is, unmistakably, a re-invented species of Judaism, and rather produced than reproduced in its re-inventedness. Jabès re-interprets Judaism's legacy beyond its bounds in search of its universal aspect.[30]

Throughout the 1930's, Jabès alternated between Egypt and France, where he enrolled at the Sorbonne in 1929[31] and developed casual ties with the Surrealist movement. To him, France stood for the intellectual and literary centre. This period saw his first mature literary works – poetry and plays[32]– published in Paris and Cairo. His first volume, *Illusions sentimentales*, modelled on Lamartine, Vigny and Mousset, appeared in 1930[33] and was followed by *Je t'attends* (1931), *Maman* (1932), *Les pieds en l'air* (1934) and *Arrhes poétiques* (1935), playing with allusions to the poet-broker profession.[34] In 1936, his most Surrealism-inflected

---

30 That is why controversy about the "Jewish" status of Jabès' work is rife in literary studies. Joseph Guglielmi denies Jabès any Jewishness because, in his view, the poet is permanently disjoined from Judaism and remains an atheist while his references to the Kabbalah concern "fabricated sources, landmarks abolished by the work of the book and deserted cultural sites scattered by the movement of negation." See Joseph Guglielmi, *La ressemblance impossible: Edmond Jabès* (Paris: Editeurs Français Réunis, 1978), p. 23. Laifer, on the contrary, regards fundamental motifs of Jabès' works as Jewish based on their plentiful similarities to Judaic concerns. For the discussion, see Laifer, *Edmond Jabès*; see also Jean Starobinski's position in "Out of this violated mineral night…," trans. Rosmarie Waldrop, in Eric Gould (ed.), *The Sin of the Book: Edmond Jabès* (Lincoln and London: University of Nebraska Press, 1985), pp. 41–2, on p. 41. I believe this is a somewhat contrived dispute. Jabès' work deploys a plethora of motifs found in Judaism but is so isolated from Judaism that some of its Jewish elements are a pure re-construction. Hence, both parties to the controversy are essentially right.

31 Jaron, *Edmond Jabès*, p. 21.

32 Jabès wrote plays from adolescence to early emigration; see Cahen, *Edmond Jabès*, p. 306 ff. The dialogical passages of *The Book of Questions* seem to owe much to this dramaturgical experience.

33 Jaron, *Edmond Jabès*, p. 23.

34 *Ibid.* p. 37.

collection, *L'obscurité potable*, was released.[35] Unlike his later, barely classifiable writings, these texts are beyond doubt poems. As Jabès himself said in a conversation with Philippe de Saint Cheron, the verses continued the line of great French poetry represented by Mallarmé, Baudelaire, Rimbaud and the Surrealists,[36] though, importantly, Mallarmé became a truly relevant influence only when Jabès adopted his obsession with the total book,[37] that is, no earlier than when working on *The Book of Questions*. Steven Jaron emphasises that the literary atmosphere of Egypt's belated Romanticism was an essential point of reference to the young poet.[38] Besides, his early poetry reverberates with other modernist readings, such as Kafka and Joyce,[39] as well as bears a vital impact of Max Jacob.[40] Jabès met Jacob when the latter grew more and more estranged from his contemporary Surrealists and sought religious and mystical meditation in poetry.[41] Jacob was instrumental to Jabès' development in two ways. First, he

---

35 DB, p. 117.

36 EEJ, p. 65.

37 DB, p. 10.

38 Jaron, *Edmond Jabès*, p. 83.

39 *Ibid.*, p. 28.

40 Lingering on the periphery of the Surrealist mainstream, always singular and personal, Jacob was relevant to Jabès also in that he always brought the Surrealist-forged language back to reality. Anticipating, in a way, Celan's mineralogy and geography, he surrounded himself with things – rocks and pebbles – while writing in order to anchor the language in the all too overly real (DB, p. 12). As Gabriel Bounoure insightfully observers, what an uninitiated reader could regard as pretty and sometimes amusing wordplay in Jacob's poetry conceals a depth spawned by fear; see Gabriel Bounoure, *Edmond Jabès. La demeure et le livre* (Montpellier: Fata Morgana, 1984), p. 19. According to Bounoure, Jabès "loved these verses which by means of fake words find amusement in making the absence of truth cruelly palpable, truth which can be guessed to inhabit the depths of waters, the depths of soul" (*Ibid.*).

Jabès' recognition of this double dimension of the word – which, besides its own meaning, reveals also its background, i.e. nothingness – was triggered by the same conjuncture that affected Celan's poetry, namely by reading a culture's central text at its outskirts. Poems read in Paris have their simple points of reference, but when read in Egypt they are divested of such clarity and reveal themselves in their reality, unblurred by preunderstandings. They speak all the more directly about what is absent from them and highlight the distance between the place of writing and the place of reading. Hence, as Bounoure writes, "Jabès read Jacob in the ennui of the black sun, the burden of whose nothingness Nerval felt only when he travelled to the East" (*Ibid.*, p. 20).

41 See also Matthew Del Nevo, "Edmond Jabès and the Question of Death," in Tod Linafelt (ed.), *Strange Fire: Reading the Bible after the Holocaust* (New York: New York UP, 2000), pp. 121–34, on p. 129 ff.

encouraged the young poet to search for his own language[42] and, second, he re-defined the role of the poetic text which is clearly recognisable in *The Book of Questions*. Spanning over several years, the correspondence of the two writers was terminated by Jacob's death in the Drancy internment camp, another Shoah wound in Jabès' life.

Jabès' pre-war poetry heralds, by the writer's own account, his work to come in later years,[43] bordering on apophatic philosophy rather than on literature. If the poems as such are still embedded in the tradition of Mallarmé, Baudelaire and Rimbaud[44] (mediated through Jacob, Éluard and Michaux), their aphoristic parts epitomise, in Jabès' view, the first, semi-conscious application of the method that will go into the making of *The Book of Questions*.[45] The affinity with the Surrealist diction cannot disguise the Cairo works' distinct interrogatory rhythm, Jabès' trademark. In the long retrospect, after the publication in the 1980's of *Le Seuil Le Sable* – his collected verse, including the juvenilia – Jabès saw his earliest poetry in the following way:

> However, read today, after *The Book of Questions*, they show that they are something completely different [than Surrealism]. There is *a certain voice* [emphasis added] speaking in them, and besides, there is also interrogation of the text through aphorism. The Surrealists used aphorism, Breton did in particular, but it was a different thing. Central to my poetry was the question "What is this?" But that "What is this?" was not simply asking out of curiosity but made up part of the poem because images kept wrecking my meaning by multiplying it. I needed to destroy, destroy and, once again, destroy, to try to simplify only in order to hear the voice that was in the poem, a unique voice of the text. Hence, I believe, the book belongs [to Surrealism] but at the same time eludes [its] tradition.[46]

Flirting with Surrealism in his writings, Jabès tended to discover that which wanted to express itself indirectly in script (that "voice from behind" – *voix*

---

42 Jabès and Jacob had a profound and deeply personal relationship. Jaron suggests that the protagonist of *The Book of Questions* called Yukel Serafi is modelled on Jacob. "Yukel" is a version of Jacob, and his surname means "my seraph" in Hebrew, which may be a reference to Jacob's role in Jabès' life. See Jaron, *Edmond Jabès*, p. 88. On Jacob's role, see also Cahen, *Edmond Jabès*, pp. 309–11.

43 DEJ, p. 301.

44 According to Carola Erbertz, Rimbaud's influences are particularly conspicuous in the volume of *Je bâtis ma demeure*. Cf. Carola Erbertz, *Zur Poetik des Buches bei Edmond Jabès: exiliertes Schreiben im Zeichen von Auschwitz* (Tübingen: Gunter Narr, 2000), pp. 23–4.

45 DEJ, p. 301.

46 EEJ, p. 66.

derrière) rather than declared himself part of the Surrealist movement or shared its goals.[47] In his superb study, Jaron has actually showed that elements which could seem offshoots of Surrealism resulted, in Jabès, from his own evolution, in which he approximated the Surrealist diction yet never embraced its penchant for literary game.[48]

Still, Surrealism helped Jabès acquire experience in formal experimentation, which channelled that hidden voice into a more distinct expression. Even without the liaison with Surrealism, Jabès could have discovered, sooner or later, the same process of destruction and simplification that guided him form early poetry to *The Book of Questions* and further on – that unmistakably modern negativity shared by minds so different as Hegel, Mallarmé, Freud and Heidegger.[49] But, likely, the process would have been less self-aware, less rapid and, for all that, less harmonious. For, as observed by Marcel Cohen, Jabès' language displays "exemplary intransigent classicism [which] seems to be in flagrant contradiction with the exploded form."[50] In other words, the classical language and the exploded form are yoked together to produce tension. Starting with *The Book of Questions*, the formal demolition was not an aim in and by itself but rather served to explore the movement of simplification that represented the withdrawal of God. Perhaps the lessons of Surrealism prevented Jabès from experimenting with form for the sake of form, from indulging in language that forfeits its chance to think of reality.[51]

Tenuous as it had been before, Jabès' connection with Surrealism[52] was ultimately severed by the events of the 1930's and the 1940's. As he recalled years later, in 1936, by which time Jewish refugees from Europe had already appeared

---

47 See Cahen, *Edmond Jabès*, p. 312.
48 Jaron, *Edmond Jabès*.
49 Cf. Julia Kristeva, *La révolution du langage poétique* (Paris: Éditions du Seuil, 1974). For the English translation (abridged), see Julia Kristeva, *Revolution in Poetic Language*, trans. Margaret Waller (New York: Columbia UP, 1984).
50 DB, p. 44.
51 Marcel Cohen highlights this when he writes that Jabès cherished Max Jacob's insight that "Writing for the sake of writing does nothing but show contempt." So, if Jabès, as Cohen has it, "purifies the books of their contents, empties the traditional genres of their specificity (thereby borrowing from all), states only to negate all the more effectively, multiplies styles so skilfully that none seems his own to him, asks only to reject any tentative answer," he does so because this is what the profound and uncompromising questioning requires. Marcel Cohen, "Dix anamnèses," *Europe*, 86/954 (October 2008), pp. 268–275, on p. 275.
52 See IEJ, p. 9.

in Egypt, his French Surrealist friends refused to believe their accounts: "all these allegedly revolutionary groups wallowed in excess, loves and machines while war was already at the gates."[53] Unlike the Surrealists, Jabès actively opposed the progressing spread of Fascism and anti-Semitism.[54] The experience of war and the Shoah affected him powerfully. In 1942, when Rommel's troops were nearing Egypt, he was evacuated by the British to Jerusalem and avoided the Shoah.[55] Till the end of his life he considered himself a Shoah survivor.[56]

Undoubtedly, this was the second (following his sister's death) crucial event that proved formative of his writing. Admittedly, a long time was to pass before that disaster found expression in his texts. However, it was evident to Jabès that in the aftermath of the war and the Shoah the previous lightness of writing was out of the question. Already in 1943, he renounced everything he had written before.[57] He gradually realised the magnitude of the challenge to be confronted by a writer who did not want to fall silent after Auschwitz and was compelled to speak where all normal speaking had become impossible.

Against Adorno's famous thesis of the sheer impossibility to write poetry in the wake of the Shoah, an imperative to write after Auschwitz is evident in Jabès, as Beth Hawkins observes.[58] Writing, however, must re-invent itself and commune with what is expressed in utter despair and inarticulate scream in order to tackle the impossible and absorb it.[59] This laborious

---

53 EEJ, p. 67.
54 Actually, engagement against all nationalisms and chauvinisms and defence of the oppressed, the excluded and immigrants occupied him till the end of his life. Two years before his death, he published a volume titled *Un étranger avec, sous le bras, un livre de petit format* (*A Foreigner Carrying in the Crook of His Arm a Tiny Book*) – a fervent plea for *les sans papiers*, in which he argues that otherness is a common inner condition of the human being. The work has had some role in debates on migration policy in France.
55 Cahen, *Edmond Jabès*, p. 313.
56 DB, pp. 48, 61.
57 *Ibid.*, p. 118.
58 Beth Hawkins, *Reluctant Theologians: Franz Kafka, Paul Celan, Edmond Jabès* (New York: Fordham UP, 2003), p. 156; see also Berel Lang, "Writing-the-Holocaust: Jabès and the Measure of History," in *The Sin of the Book*, pp. 191–206, on p. 193.
59 Berel Lang calls this change a transition from "writing about the Holocaust" to "writing the Holocaust"; *Ibid.*, p. 196.

process, the effects of which surfaced in Celan just after the war, took Jabès more time.[60] In the late 1940's and early 1950's, Jabès was still searching for a language of his own and published Surrealist-tinted poetry in the volumes of *Chansons pour le repas de l'ogre* (1947), *La Voix d'encre* (1949), *La Clef de voûte* (1950) and *L'Écorce du monde* (1955).[61] The first of them was more of "an attempt to revisit childhood while death was rampant all around"[62] than an effort to put in words what had actually happened. If Jabès used the language inherited from the Surrealists, he entertained no doubt that the war and the Shoah had put the motives fuelling Surrealist writing, as well as all its social and societal entanglements, to a definitive end, and that "a language for death" in the face of which the playful writing of old was sinfully blind, to say the least, had to be forged anew. Jabès did not simply think that the Surrealist taste for the shocking had become impotent after Europe's catastrophe, as Adorno suggested.[63] He focused first of all on the ethical injunction to understand what it actually was that had come to pass:

> Had I retained the slightest inclination to adhere to Surrealism after the war, I would have been kept from doing so by an exhibition organized in Cairo in 1947 by the Egyptian Surrealist group, echoing the one that had just taken place in Paris. It contained, among other things, disemboweled dressmakers' dummies stained with red ink. Coming right after the discovery of the horror of the extermination camps, this represented an unacceptable indecency.[64]

In Jabès' view, if Surrealism resolved to continue its pre-war modes as if nothing had happened, it would be lying in the face of the truth of nothingness, which called for urgent and incisive re-thinking. Worse still, its insensitivity would even make this nothingness present. If earlier it had dissociated itself from its imaginary reality and lingered in the void of sustained negative reference to it, after the war it became clear how close to nothingness reality itself had wandered. Surrealism opposed convention as a stable organisation of being. As soon as convention itself turned out to be a tool of annihilation, Surrealism became impossible as it failed to comprehend and was outdone by "Realism," which it

---

60 Basically, the possibility of writing after the Shoah is first confronted only in *The Book of Questions*, which, according to Erbertz, institutes "an Auschwitz-stamped poetics"; Erbertz, *Poetik des Buches*, p. 20.

61 Warren F. Motte, "Hospitable Poetry," *l'Esprit Créateur*, 49/2 (Summer 2009), pp. 34–45, on p. 34.

62 EEJ, p. 67.

63 In Erbertz, *Poetik des Buches*, p. 23.

64 DB, p. 13.

had declared to surpass.[65] Still, the collapse of Surrealism can be posited as an opportunity that Jabès seized and turned to his advantage. Surrealists, namely, had left behind a language furnished with vehicles of negativity, which after the war could be used not to break conventions or contest the existing literature but to render what had happened to reality itself. This is what Jabès did, salvaging the Surrealist devices for thinking beyond Surrealism. In this perspective, Surrealism seems to have offered an opportunity to include nothingness in language, which was seminal to Jabès' apophatics.[66]

In the aftermath of the war, Jabès seems to have found himself in a limbo of sorts. This did not mean inactivity, though. He continued to publish and started to collaborate on a regular basis with French journals (e.g. *Mercure de France, Les Lettres Nouvelles, La Nouvelle Revue Française*) and Egyptian magazines (therein *La Part du Sable*, a literary survey he co-founded). He also had his part in releasing, in Cairo, *Le Chemin des Sources*, a series comprised of the works of such authors as Jean Grenier, Gabriel Bounoure and René Char.[67] He made a living as a broker and, apparently very successful at his profession, was promoted to one of the most important posts at the Cairo Exchange. Yet it took one more event, a third disaster, for Jabès to find his own language and a path to the work that would bring out what had remained latent so far. This shattering personal experience was exile. This is how Israel-Pelletier sketches its historical context:

> This multicultural experience came to an end more or less abruptly and catastrophically when tens of thousands of Jews and foreign nationals were expelled from Egypt in a period of a few months, from November to March, following the 1956 Suez Canal War. Harassment of non-Muslim and particularly Jewish minorities was not new to Egypt. There were blood libel accusations resulting in persecutions during the last decades of the nineteenth century; persecutions continued prior to World War I and in the mid-1930s, with the rise of fascism in Europe and the right-wing Muslim Brotherhood in Egypt; Hitler's rise to power and Egyptian King Farouk's support of the Nazi regime were accompanied by growing anti-Jewish exclusionary acts that struck fear in the community; there were Jewish deaths, large riots, and destruction of Jewish-owned property

---

65 See also Maurice Blanchot, "Reflections on Surrealism," trans. Charlotte Mandell, in *The Work of Fire*, pp. 85–97.

66 In this context, it seems interesting that Celan during his short stay in Bucharest after the war associated with a group of Surrealists; see Edouard Roditi, "Paul Celan and the Cult of Personality," *World Literature Today*, 66/1 (Winter 1992), pp. 11–20, on p. 13. Far less engaged with Surrealism than Jabès, Celan also relinquished its influences on moving to Paris.

67 DB, p. 119.

during the period 1946–1948 when Jews, many very young, girls and boys alike, were imprisoned and expelled after being accused of Zionist activity on behalf of Israel. In 1957, Jabès was a successful poet and stockbroker. As a member of the Stock Exchange Commission he played an important role in stabilizing the chaotic and falling Egyptian stock market. As with other men who held consequential positions in the economy, in education, business, and industry the government kept Jabès in Cairo only long enough to train others to replace him. Threats, intimidation, and humiliation were the strategies used to make men comply.[68]

His connections with France saw Jabès placed in home detention when the Suez Canal War broke out.[69] Ultimately, aged forty-four, he was expelled from Egypt with his family never to return there again. Still, he did not make Aliyah but, regarding himself as a writer of the French language[70] and wishing for "his books to come home,"[71] he left for Paris, where he had already made friends and garnered some reputation as a poet. Despite that, exile turned out to be a disaster to him,[72] and, additionally, revived and made palpably present his earlier experiences of the death of his sister and the flight from the Shoah. It was also the first time, as he claimed himself, that he had been forced to "*live*" his Jewishness and make it central to his life.[73] Whereas earlier, to rely on Paul Auster's account, Jabès had viewed his descent merely as a contingent cultural fact, he suddenly came to feel it as the only reason for being persecuted and recognised as the Other.[74]

By losing everything[75] and, consequently, having nothing more to lose, Jabès eventually started heading towards the work quintessentially focused on exile as

---

68 Israel-Pelletier, "Edmond Jabès," pp. 802–804.

69 Cahen, *Edmond Jabès*, p. 320.

70 DB, p. 29.

71 QJQW, p. 16.

72 EEJ, p. 67.

73 Q JQW, p. 16.

74 IEJ, p. 4.

75 Leaving Egypt, Jabès had to abandon most of his library collected by several generations of his family. He lost many original editions of religious, mystical and world literature classics. "No doubt that loss has contributed to reinforcing in me the idea that my uprootedness affected my culture in its most ancient ties," he insisted later (DB, p. 35). Marcel Cohen lists the volumes that Jabès bought again in France. Kafka and Proust seem to have been his priorities. He managed to get *Ulysses* out of Egypt. Besides, he bought first of all works of his fellow and younger poets; Marcel Cohen, "Anamnezy" [Anamneses] in Edmond Jabès, *Aeli*, trans. A. Wodnicki (Kraków: Austeria, 2006), p. 197. Though its significance should not be overestimated, this biographical detail

an ontological and cosmological state.[76] "Intellectually and materially I felt ready for a totally new adventure, though I had as yet not the slightest inkling what it would be,"[77] he reminisced in conversations with Marcel Cohen. As Adolfo Fernandez-Zoïla concludes,

> the propensity for reflection, meditation and interiority that shines through his verse and aphorisms published before 1957 undergoes a genuine transformation as a result of exile and matures in a process in which the work of self-questioning parallels the composing of *The Book of Questions*, the first volume of a triptych, which triptych announced itself from the very first moment of writing.[78]

The exile from Egypt, as Gary D. Mole emphasises,[79] ultimately puts Jabès' earlier poetic mode to an end. The poet definitely closes this chapter in *Je bâtis ma demeure*, a volume compiling his existing verse, encouraged by Albert Camus and published in 1959. This cut opens the way to a new form, one more suited to the radical, philosophical rather than poetic questioning. Jabès intentionally discards the category of the poet and abandons earlier conventions. Each movement of writing becomes self-questioning for him, a dialogue with that which the just-written content has excluded and which has negatively enabled it in this way. The events of his life made exile the central notion in Jabès' mature work, not only existentially but also ontologically. Thereby, Jabès summons the ancient Jewish idea of *galut*. Exile affects also the shape of the poet's reflection, which relies on distance and retrospection. As Marcel Cohen observers, while Egypt does not feature in any of the poems in *Je bâtis ma demeure*, it recurs constantly in *The Book of Questions* series.[80] Jabès himself comments:

---

intimates something about the poet's interest in contemporary and modernist literature and, for older works, in Jewish mysticism and Talmudic studies.

76 Christophe Wall-Romana calls the work of Jabès and, as a matter of fact, the entire school of French poetry he influenced, *exilique et exscriptif*. Christophe Wall-Romana, "Dure poésie générale," *L'Esprit Créateur*, 49/2 (Summer 2009), pp. 1–8, on p. 4. The latter term, borrowed as it is from Jean-Marie Gleize, plays both on Derrida's concept of inscription and on the Lacanian coinage of "extimate." In relation to Jabès, it aptly highlights the central idea of writing down in the Book as a foundation of being (cf. Chapter Eight).

77 DB, p. 36.

78 Adolfo Fernandez-Zoïla, *Le Livre, recherche autre d'Edmond Jabès* (Paris: J.-M. Place, 1978), p. 25.

79 Gary D. Mole, *Lévinas, Blanchot, Jabès: Figures of Estrangement* (Gainesville, FL: University Press of Florida, 1997), p. 10.

80 DB, p. 30.

That is the problem every writer faces: we cannot behold things without taking a step back. We are crushed by them. One needs to give writing time to take full possession of things. The writer, like the historian lends meaning to the past, but contrary to the latter, he destroys the past by giving it form. The writer does not try to be the witness. He is only there listening to the words that trace his future.[81]

The personal experience of exile induced Jabès' characteristic belief about the magnitude of irreversible damage caused by time. This is the horizon within which the writer's duty is defined, not in terms of reproducing "the truth about the past" but in terms of revealing the absoluteness of the loss of the object described. That is why, for Jabès (a Jew actually pining for Mizraim!), Egypt is a land salvaged solely through writing. It was only in France that Jabès was able to grasp the traces his birthplace had left in him and to work them through reflectively in his texts. Conspicuously, "Egypt" seems to have the same status as "Judaism," that is, the status of re-construction, of a placeholder for the object proper of loss.

The lost legacy of Egypt is usefully illuminated by Jabès' comments on the vital experiences he associated with this country and considered foundational for his thinking. One of them was certainly the experience of the Egyptian landscape resounding with nearly Heideggerian overtones:

The flat landscape of the plain, punctuated by tall palms shooting up to the sky, opens mind to a perception of time infinitely vaster than ours. Nowhere is there an interruption, everything goes on forever. The pharaohs barely belonged to the past.
Over there, time is artificial. Something artificial laid over something real. The real is made up of patiently repeated gestures. The peasant is its surest guarantor. His gestures simultaneously limit and "illimit" him [le limitent et «l'illimitent»]. True to himself, he plants what he has always planted and will continue to plant, in the heart of the seasons. He has inherited his faith from his ancestors and will transmit it to his descendants. That faith is a lighter, a larger breath, an indefinable blue in the motionless blue of the sky. God commands. Life is but incalculable goings and comings along a familiar road. Fatality liberates the peasant from the anguish of death. His words are the wisdom of millennia drawn from the desert – they are the words of the sand, as vast as NOTHINGNESS. That's because the desert assigns its own slow rhythm – a rhythm from beyond silence, from beyond life [d'outre-silence, d'outre-vie] – to the smallest gesture, the most insignificant word.[82]

The Egypt that Jabès re-creates after exile is equally a distance-enhanced experience brought out from memory and the work of the writer's own reflection.[83] To

---

81 Ibid.
82 Ibid., p. 16.
83 Cf. Ibid., p. 26.

him, Egypt stands for continuity where things are never apart while time, instead of a linear chain of units, approximates pure duration. Somewhat against cultural clichés, Jabès does not associate Egypt with the land of immanence and life-in-chains but with the desert – a source of sober freedom sensitive to silence. One could say that ontology itself differs there from the model developed by Western metaphysics. The landscape, the sky, the time and human life correspond to one another; beings do not have strong, discrete existence of their own but are rather manifestations of one, enduring whole. An individual life cannot be interpreted without its foundational context of infinity. Being is caught up in a constant relationship with infinity that weighs upon it. Besides its own existence, it is also a placeholder for infinity itself, at which it invariably gestures. In other words, it is an ontology of the context, where being can never be permanently dissociated either from its continuation or from its negation.[84]

One should remember, however, that the passage exemplifies only one of the Jabèsian paths. In his writings, the poet was never consistent and, hence, statements that we intuitively associate with Jewish thought are interlaced with speculations of a nearly Heideggerian flavour. As the Tanakh accommodates both the Shemot, which restates the Law, and the Ecclesiastes, which offers an utterly havelistic – nay, nearly *Greek* – interpretation of life as essentially dead and futile, so Jabès' writing hosts two contradictory tendencies. As such, it is

---

84 An irresistible question that offers itself is why actually the writer so heavily reliant on Jewish tradition refers to Egypt as his homeland without mobilising the contexts which Judaism associates with Egypt, such as slavery, subjection and idolatry. Does Jabès' voice echo the complaint of the sceptical among the Israelites who, unequal to the hardships of wandering in the desert, accused Moses of leading them to certain death? Does he by any chance miss the land which, though devoid of freedom, still offered some certainty of life? These and similar questions could be raised by the adherents of philosophical Judaism of the belligerent and rebellious variety that boldly plunges itself into the desert if only freedom is to be found there. How can such questions be answered? First, Jabès indeed views the desert as a space of freedom, but things more terrifying than such freedom, which comes at the price of the permanent risk of death, are few and far between. The preachers of the desert often have no idea how monstrous a choice they champion. Second, in Jabès' memories, Egypt is primarily a desert and not a city, which the poet sought to flee. In this way, the opposition of Cairo and the surrounding desert is more relevant than the opposition of Egypt and Sinai. Jabès recalls the Egypt of the desert and not urban Egypt. Third, what kind of creature would it have to be to have a heart that never looked back to the place where everything had been left behind? In the desert, one is a naked being; deliberately to forget what one has been means *to fail to understand the choice and, in fact, not to make any choice at all.*

useful in exploring the meaning and potency of the alleged difference between Jerusalem and Athens. Similar conclusions concern the second of Jabès' formative experiences. Meant here is the desert, which was so relevant as to become one of the central metaphors of his writing. Let us make a detour from the biographical narrative to scrutinise the desert in more detail. The poet's two personal memories cited below reflect the trajectory of transformation of the desert from experience into a metaphor:

> For me, the desert was the privileged place of my depersonalisation. In Cairo I felt a prisoner of the social game [...] In those days, the mainly European quarter where I lived and worked – the commercial and business quarter – was barely the size of the Opéra quarter in Paris. In such a confined atmosphere, the texts I published were considered, at best, a kind of intellectual entertainment. Writing was more prestigious than golf or tennis, but was as inconsequential. I rankled deeply to be considered merely an amateur writer.
>
> Hence the desert, which started at the very city limits, was a life-saving break for me. It fulfilled an urgent need of both body and mind, and I would venture into it with quite contradictory desires: to lose myself, so that, one day, I may find myself.
>
> So the place of the desert in my books is not a simple metaphor. I wasn't really aware – given that I continued to write poems heavily marked by Surrealism, in which image was of course central – that the place was eating away at me, undermining me. Only a few aphorisms written at that time testify to it. Anyway, that undermining, which will take on all its importance after my split with Egypt, will find itself at the core of my writings.
>
> I would often stay for forty-eight hours all alone in the desert. I wouldn't take any books, only a blanket. A silence of that order makes you feel the nearness of death so deeply that it becomes difficult to bear any more of it. Only the nomads can withstand being squeezed in such a vice, because they were born in the desert.
>
> We just cannot imagine ourselves outside of time, outside of an event. The whole of our culture brings us back to allotments of time. Look at the anchorites: they are more dead than alive, literally burned by the silence. Only nomads know how to transform this shattering silence into a life force. [85]
>
> [In my writings] there was a wish to destroy image for the very sake of destroying it, for image disturbed me as contradictory to the experience of the desert. I was looking for a world of absolute bareness. Hence the desire to destroy, the desire to tear down and blast the obstacle – as if images were an obstacle to overcome – that interfered with [finding] absolute bareness.[86]

---

85 DB, pp. 13–14.
86 Mary Ann Caws, "Edmond Jabès: Sill and Sand," *L'Esprit Créateur*, 32/2 (1992), pp. 11–18, on p. 11.

Weaving together his memories, description and reflection, Jabès characteristically linked the experience of the desert to the work of destruction, which helped him strip his writing of all redundancies and open it up to the voice of pure nothingness.[87] Only then could he, in hindsight, aptly capture the experience of the desert. The desert turns out to be a place of "true speaking," too, the speech that Jabès, in recollecting his sister's death, recognised as a language for death. It stands in contrast to game both as a social convention and as an intellectual entertainment.[88] The import of a text resides not in the social acclaim it garners but in its relationship to truth, which is bred only by the experience of nothingness. Although the experience of the desert apparently should bring Jabès closer to the Heideggerian *Eigentlichkeit* (also through the awe of death), its goal is not authentic life; it is rather an annihilating experience than an enriching one. Only the nomads, as the writer insists, are capable of deriving a vital power from it while for others the desert might be a place of respite but not of life in its immediate sense.[89] The desert, which memory carries out from Egypt, is thus

---

87 The desert is the central metaphor that captures both Jabès' writing and his ontology. Guglielmi writes: "The poet turned his fascination [with the desert] into his impossible dwelling place, a site of tragic uncertainty that, from book to book, provides a basic bond, a system of particular signs invigorated by a pluralising, dispersing force that gives the work its structure [...]"; Joseph Guglielmi, "Edmond Jabès ou la fascination du désert", *Critique*, 28/296 (janvier 1972), pp. 32–52, on p. 33. The desert recurs in Jabès' writings so frequently and in so multiple settings that it makes more sense to discuss them separately as related to particular motifs. Still, even at this point, it seems obvious that the desert is, first of all, a place to him: a place that extends where individual beings, therein the author and God, cease to exist. The desert is what goes on and "does not come to the end of ending" (BQ II, p. 129), which is why it has survived after the withdrawal of God.

88 Agnès Chalier encapsulates Jabès' search for the desert: "Jabès' meditation in the desert was becoming urgently indispensable for him just in order to breathe, [...] to celebrate thought." Agnès Chalier, "Le désert jabésien et la notion de vide dans la philosophie classique chinoise," in Richard Stamelman and Mary Ann Caws (eds.), *Écrire le livre autour d'Edmond Jabès. Colloque de Cerisy* (Seyssel: Champ Vallon, 1989), p. 194.

89 As Rosie Pinhas-Delpeuch aptly points out, Western culture has often interpreted the desert in the Torah as, solely, a symbol, thereby missing on its literal sense whereas the desert was a punishment, an ordeal, an experience but never a permanent dwelling place unless for the nomads. A similar obliviousness to the actual experience of the desert may distort the reception of Jabès. The Jabèsian desert of reality must not be viewed simply as a spectacular symbol loaned from Jewish tradition. Rather, it is a place of real agony and irremovable horror of death. Rosie Pinhas-Delpeuch, "Dans la double dépendance du désert," in *Écrire le livre*, pp. 181–90, on p. 181.

something more than just a metaphor to Jabès. It is a live and operative meta-phor for negativity, bolstered all the more by the loss of unmediated experience. As observed by Marcel Cohen, in the Jabès' work the desert accrues at least three meanings: of personal experience, of metaphor of the void and of a biblical al-lusion to Jewish history.[90] David Jasper, in turn, locates Jabès in the context of centuries-long desert mysticism of both religious and literary-poetic varieties.[91] Jabès himself explains:

> The experience of the desert has been crucial for me. Between sky and sand, between All and Nothing, burns the question. It burns without being consumed. It burns for itself, in a void. The experience of the desert is also one of listening, extreme listening. Not only do you hear what you could not hear elsewhere, true silence, cruel and painful because it seems to reproach the heart for beating. But also, as you lie in the sand, for example, a strange noise may suddenly intrigue you, a noise as of a man or animal walking, coming closer every minute or moving away, or seeming to move away while following his path. A long while after, if you are in the right direction, the man or beast announced by your ears appears on the horizon. A nomad could have identified this "living thing" immedi-ately, before seeing it, just by ear. Of course, the desert is his natural habitat. [...] The desert is much more than the practice of silence and listening. It is an eternal open-ness. The openness of all writing, which it is the writer's job to persevere. Openness of all openness.[92]
>
> As far as the word *desert* is concerned, what fascinates me is to see how far the metaphor of the void, from being used so much, has permeated the whole word. The word itself has become a metaphor. To give it back its strength, one has therefore to return to the real desert which is indeed exemplary emptiness – but an emptiness with its own, very real dust.[93]

The first passage describes the desert as a place of all openness. This is because no depiction can contain the whole of the desert; rather, all depiction is already in the desert and, hence, cannot possibly encompass it. The desert has neither land-marks nor signposts, and all its directions seem of equal value and validity. As

---

90 DB, pp. 14–15.

91 "Like the Christian Fathers of old, he crossed the ecological boundary between the city and the desert, so that later as a writer – a poet, philosopher, and perhaps even theologian – the desert functioned at many complex levels as a metaphor in his poetry. Perhaps even more than that: for Jabès book and desert, sand and letter become abso-lutely inseparable, the desert and its truth reconstituted each word of the text." David Jasper, *The Sacred Desert: Religion, Literature, Art, and Culture* (Oxford: Blackwell, 2004), p. 82.

92 BR, pp. 45–6.

93 DB, p. 15.

Claude Nahon writes, the desert has no centre and resembles a ring with a centre both within and without it.[94] To us, the fabric of the desert – sand and rocks – does not form singular beings but rather part of an all-embracing whole. And if a thing that does not belong to the desert, such as a wanderer, finds itself there, it will stand out conspicuously. The desert provides a backdrop for discrete beings that have wound up there one way or another. This is of utmost relevance to Jabès' thought (which I will dwell on in more detail later) because the desert helps us discern how being looms against nothingness.[95] In the desert, we acutely experience our own existence: "as if the desert reproached the heart for beating." Life in the desert is an alien and astounding thing; the blood runs through the body just beneath the boundary that divides it from the perpetual, arid motionlessness. This experience is not so much anti-vital as rather indicative of a startling power of life that has been selected for sentience – if not for bearing witness – from amongst so many particles of lifeless and forgotten matter around. In the desert, being reveals itself in the radical and inexplicable solitude of its being there, a solitude which remains imperceptible when being makes part of the meaningful human world.[96] The desert, finally, is a place of specific perception. In the desert, one does not listen to something; rather, one listens-for, intently focusing attention not on one source of sound but on the entire space in which the sound resonates.[97] One does not listen in order to find out *what being is like*; one listens in order *to ascertain that being is there*, that it leaves traces, that it approaches or departs. In the desert, we rather hear being's voices from afar than witness its full revelation; its traces and echoes are more frequent than its presence.

---

94   Claude Nahon, "La question de l'origine et l'œuvre d'Edmond Jabès," in *La Question de l'Origine* (Nice: Z'éditions, 1987), p. 64.

95   A passage from the Zohar cited by Ireneusz Kania in his essay on Jabès may be illuminating here: "And so we, too, have abandoned the world of men for the harsh desert in order to study Torah there and confound the Other Side [*Sitra Achra*, i.e. Evil]. And also because only there are the words of Torah fully clear […]"; Ireneusz Kania, "Jabès, czyli o składaniu rozsypanego Tekstu" ["Jabès, or on assembling a scattered Text'], in *Edmond Jabès, Powrót do Księgi*, trans. Andrzej Wodnicki (Kraków: Austeria, 2005), p. 129. Undoubtedly, Jabès shares the Zohar's idea of words "being clear" in the desert, the difference being that, in Jabès, words are not only the words of the Torah, but words as such.

96   That is why Jabès can say: "Desert, transparent universe" (BR III, p. 80).

97   *Le Parcours* tells us: "[…] the desert [is] a desolate land of silence and listening; a land propitious to silence and infinite listening, where silence gets intoxicated with its echoes, and listening with the sounds caught at the heart of silence" (P, p. 82).

The second passage quoted above exemplifies the capacity of words to absorb and condense all experiences they have been used to convey, a capacity Jabès was so preoccupied with analysing. When "the desert" is no longer really accessible to us, its metaphorical sense of emptiness is enhanced since it *subsumes that which it no longer is*. If enduring in time destroys both beings and the memories of them, the power of the desert as a metaphor only consolidates in time just like erosion of the already decayed landscape in the real desert only fosters further desertification.

After this detour traversing Jabès' experiences in Egypt, let us resume our journey through his biography. France failed to become his real homeland, and manifestations of anti-Semitism in the country further exacerbated his sense of exile. His life revolved around writing, which, as Jaron suggest, was a homeland for a man without a homeland.[98] Writing, stripped of acquired forms and emptied out of overtones of the literary game that reverberated in it in Cairo, becomes a domain of the pure questioning, verging on philosophy rather than on literature. Therefore, exile granted Jabès, as he insisted himself, a relief or, more specifically, "the revelation of [his] deepest destiny: the confirmation also of the collective Jewish destiny."[99]

It was only at this moment that Judaism re-opened to him as a tradition. Jabès started to read the Jerusalem Talmud he had inherited from his father and never even looked into before.[100] He studied also Kabbalistic texts, commentaries and works by "most of the Jewish spiritual masters."[101] As he claimed himself, the Kabbalah had influenced him primarily as "the shape of the thinking, [...] spiritual depth, particular logic and inventiveness."[102] All these readings served him not so much as any concrete inspiration but rather as a way to "stimulate [his] own questioning [...] to prolong it into an immemorial past."[103] Jabès did not borrow from the Kabbalah, but his thought developed in parallel to it,[104] which

---

98   Jaron, *Edmond Jabès*, p. 2.
99   DB, p. 25.
100 EEJ, p. 70; DB, p. 72.
101 DB, p. 48.
102 *Ibid.*
103 *Ibid.*
104 Even when the Jewish legacy had been "reclaimed" for his work, Jabès' attitude to Judaism remained rather complicated. Consistently atheistic, he would not be confined in any fixed form of worship though, admittedly, towards the end of his life, he was glad to have his texts read out in synagogues. His Judaism was, clearly, a personal construct, so to speak, into which certain elements of tradition were incorporated when and where they were useful. In an interview with Benjamin Taylor, the poet

has been shown conclusively by Jaron. Namely, the early parts of *The Book of Questions* were inspired not by the Kabbalistic sources but by Hamann's biblical meditations.[105] Jabès himself admitted that he had begun to discover the texts of Jewish tradition only when, in the wake of the publication of his first *Books*, he realised their affinity with Jewish literary forms of old. In a degree, thus, the Kabbalistic "origins" of the *Books* are just a retrospective fiction.

It was not only Jewish literature that fuelled Jabès' intellectual life after he had settled in France. As his exile coincided with halcyon days of French thought, bonds of friendship and common readings connected him to many prominent personages of the day. In Paris, he re-connected with Roger Caillois and Jean Grenier, whom he had met earlier; he grew close with René Char, Henri Michaux and Michel Leiris.[106] Similarly, he felt friends with Maurice Blanchot, with whom he never got acquainted in person but corresponded abundantly and whose books he always cherished.[107] Blanchot's well-known post-war aversion to public appearances and close contacts aside, their friendship, as Jabès insists,[108] could only be impaired if they had actually met as it would have lost its cornerstone of silence. Without a doubt, however, Blanchot's influence on Jabès was seminal. Jaron's research implies that it commenced already in the early 1950's. In some of his later texts, Jabès even employs Blanchot's notion of *neutre*.[109]

Their relationship was certainly anything but one-directional as in his later work Blanchot clearly drew on Jabès; for example, *The Writing of the Disaster* seems to be heavily indebted to the author of the *Books*.[110] Besides, Jabès had a

---

stressed that he spoke only of "the singular and eccentric Judaism that is my own," "bound up – identified, even – with *écriture*" (QJQW, p. 16). The attitude of fascination with and resistance to Judaism undoubtedly affected Derrida's likewise complex, though less intensely manifested, relation with the Jewish legacy. Cf. Henry Sussman, "Pulsations of Respect, or Winged Impossibility: Literature with Deconstruction," *diacritics*, 38/1–2 (Spring-Summer 2008), pp. 44–63, on p. 50.

105 Jaron, *Edmond Jabès*, p. 10.
106 DB, pp. 37–8.
107 *Ibid.*, p. 38.
108 *Ibid.*
109 See, for example, BM, p. 13 ff.
110 Cf. Maurice Blanchot, *The Writing of the Disaster*, trans. Ann Smock (Lincoln and London: Nebraska UP, 1986), p. 2. Emphatically, Blanchot was reluctant to speak about Jabès' works in the belief that "discretion" was the best way of approaching them. See Maurice Blanchot, "Interruptions," trans. Rosmarie Waldrop and Paul Auster, in *The Sin of the Book*, pp. 43–54, on pp. 47–8.

warm relationship with and reciprocated admiration for Lévinas[111] and believed they had plenty in common despite disagreeing on some essential points. For example, their attitudes to Jewish religion were very different, if not polar opposites. While Lévinas continued to practise it alongside re-interpreting it, Jabès viewed it as an impediment to the consistent and ultimate questioning.[112] Finally, friendship and tacit community of the Jewish fate bound him to Paul Celan, against the cultural differences between the Sephardic and Ashkenazi varieties of Judaism.[113] They may not have fully understood each other's respective poetics but were, undoubtedly, captivated by them. John Felstiner claims that Celan thought of translating *The Book of Questions* into German.[114]

Celan seems to have taken issue with Jabès' universalisation of the Shoah – as suggested by the "Nein!" he scribbled down in one of *The Book*'s passages[115]– yet they continued close friends and kept in touch regularly in 1966–1970.[116] That Jabès had a special relationship with Blanchot, Lévinas and Celan is evinced by the fact that he devoted separate texts to them, which were later included in *The Book of Margins*.[117]

Jabès' distinct relationship with Derrida deserves separate attention. Derrida was one of Jabès' earliest readers, and two of his essays: "Edmond Jabès and the Question of the Book" and "Ellipsis," included eventually in *Writing and Difference*, bear witness to his involvement. Jabès' significant influence on Derrida showed in the 1960's, when the two indulged in long discussions.[118] The theme deserves, as a matter of fact, a study of its own: it is after all not for no reason that "Ellipsis" concludes one of the pivotal philosophical books of the period. Derrida's famous dictum that in the last ten years nothing has been written in France that does not have its antecedent in Jabès' texts dates from 1973.[119] Arguably, in the 1970's Jabès' impact on Derrida started to subside, but, for that, the vector of inspiration seems to have turned around. Jabès not only read Derrida but also, in the "Letter to Jacques Derrida on the Question of the Book" included in *The Book of*

---

111 EEJ, p. 72.
112 *Ibid.*
113 *Ibid.*, p. 74 ff.
114 John Felstiner, *Paul Celan: Poet. Survivor. Jew* (New Haven, CT: Yale UP, 2001), p. 233.
115 *Ibid.*
116 EEJ, p. 74.
117 They are "There Is No Trace But in the Desert (*With Emmanuel Lévinas*)," "The Unconditional (*Maurice Blanchot*)," parts I and II, and "Memory of Paul Celan."
118 Cahen, *Edmond Jabès*, p. 324.
119 Cf. IEJ, p. 3.

Margins, tried to think along with him and elaborate on the Derridean concepts in his own language. Although these issues would require extensive research, it seems legitimate to assume that the later parts of *The Book of Questions* and *The Book of Resemblances* took shape in the mutual intellectual exchange between Jabès and Derrida.

Derrida must thus seem a permanently hovering spectre to the readers of Jabès.[120] This notwithstanding, Jabès ultimately stood apart as a solitary and singular figure despite all the bonds of friendship and intellectual kinship. His work is so unique, so one of a kind, that explicit influences are difficult to trace down in it. Any inspirations that might have lain at its origins are allowed into his sovereign writing based on its own rules. Jabès' texts on Blanchot, Lévinas or Derrida are an excellent case in point. Not polemical as such, they anyway carry on Jabès' own reflection – its tenets, pace and conclusions – and inquire, in parallel, into issues these thinkers addressed. In this sense, Jabès evades also the notion of "influence" as he does not borrow ideas directly from other authors, with his entire oeuvre, nevertheless, betraying "elective affinities" to Benjamin, Kafka, Blanchot, Celan, Beckett[121] and, even, late Heidegger.[122]

In 1963, Gallimard releases *The Book of Questions,* which, in hindsight, serves as a prelude to the vast expanses of writing produced by Jabès till his death on 2 January 1991. It is in *The Book of Questions,* as Carola Erbertz insists,[123] that the poet's distinct mode of writing comes forth for the first time. The moment of

---

120 In this book I will not tackle the complexities of relations between Jabès and Derrida. For one, this all too broad theme deserves a study of its own. Besides, juxtaposing the two thinkers could produce a misleading impression, which readers of Derrida anyway tend to be deceived by, that Jabès is, at best, his "literary source of inspiration." This book's focus is Jabès' work as philosophy in its own right. Moreover, many explicit intuitions in *The Book of Questions* precede Derrida's ideas of deconstruction. That is why Jabès and Derrida should only be compared in a separate study when Jabès himself steps out of his powerful successor's shadow. In this book, Derrida will be fundamentally just one of the commenting voices.

121 In an interview with Paul Auster, Jabès said that he subscribed to the notion that his concept of writing could be summed up in Beckett's maxim that "To be an artist is to fail as no other dare fail." Cf. Josh Cohen, "Desertions: Paul Auster, Edmond Jabès, and the Writing of Auschwitz," *The Journal of the Midwest Modern Language Association,* 33/3 and 34/1 (Autumn 2000 – Winter 2001), pp. 95–102, on p. 102.

122 Gabriel Bounoure lists three sources of Jabès' work: Kabbalistic Platonism, Romanticism of the "Tübingen trio" (Hölderlin, Hegel and Schelling) and the Jewish faith in the value of word and letter. Cf. Bounoure, *Edmond Jabès,* p. 69.

123 Erbertz, *Poetik des Buches,* pp. 14–16.

its coming – predating the onset of Post-Structuralism – proves that it evolved autonomously and prefigured Post-Structuralist thought soon to come. It is at this point that the history of Jabès as a Jewish philosopher of modernity commences. Before I focus on his writing, I should add that this central, though late, work garnered particular acclaim expressed in the Critics' Award (1970), the Award for Arts, Humanities and Sciences of the French Judaism Foundation (1982) and the Grand National Prize for Poetry (1987). In time, Jabès was made a Knight of the Legion of Honour (1986), became a member of the French Academy's section of Arts and Humanities (1988) and had an exhibition devoted to him put up by the National Centre of Literature (1989). In the 1960's and 1970's, he travelled widely at the invitation of multiple universities, among others, to the US, Israel, Italy, Scandinavia, Germany and Spain. His texts even started to be used in synagogue recitations and be counted among the modern classics of Jewish literature.[124]

What an utterly ironic twist of fate for the thinker of the desert!

Writing

Let us now pass to the second part of this introductory chapter and delve into the characteristic features of Jabès' texts. As Evgen Bavčar states, no greater injustice could be done to Jabès than discussing him as a writer in the traditional sense of the term as this would entail selecting a form or a cliché (copious in literary theory), with the question of Edmond Jabès analysed and sealed before it were really opened up.[125] A similar urgency of opening is suggested by Ammiel Alcalay:

> Simply put, no ready-made slot exists in which to place an Arab Jew, someone who was both a Levantine heir to Rimbaud and French poetry read through the filter of Egypt, and a European re-reader – through the filter of exile in France – of the Kabbalah, Arabic poetic and Auschwitz.[126]

Indeed, given these intricacies, it would be an utmost challenge – if not a sheer impossibility – to try and come up with an overall label for Jabès. He seems to have opted for a modern, dispersed space of thinking as his work simply refuses

---

124 Cf. Gil Anidjar, "Literary History and Hebrew Modernity," *Comparative Literature Studies*, 42/2 (2005), pp. 277–96, on p. 289.

125 Evgen Bavčar, "Mots pour Jabès," *Change*, 22 (février 1975), p. 216.

126 Ammiel Alcalay, "Desert Solitaire: On Edmond Jabès," in Ammiel Alcalay, *Memories of Our Future: Selected Essays 1982–1999* (San Francisco: City Light Books, 1999), pp. 55–9, on p. 56.

to be covered by any single appellation. With such terms lacking, writing as such seems to offer itself as a purely material category whose advantage lies in that it does not impose any specific meanings. Let us, then, scrutinise Jabès' writing in an attempt to find an opening to his "question."

The body of Jabès' writings clearly falls into two parts: the Cairo part (poetic) and the Paris part (series of *Books*). The former comes to a culmination and an end in 1959 with the publication of *Je bâtis ma demeure*, a collection of verse from 1943–1957, the only poetic book of his by his own admission.[127]

The volume with addition of some later short texts (in the late 1970's and 1980's, Jabès wrote three more short poetic cycles *Récit, La Mémoire et la Main* and *L'appel*) was the basis of the ultimate collection of his poems published as *Le Seuil Le Sable* in 1991.[128] I will only seldom refer to this poetic part of his work, wherever the aphoristic form and ideas anticipate or approximate the Parisian work.[129] And how can Jabès' Parisian work be described? It defies any simple

---

127 LSLS, p. 399.

128 The volume consists of two parts. The first one, titled *Le Seuil*, contains the earlier *Je bâtis ma demeure*, and the second, titled *Le Sable*, includes late verse. The volume's meticulously spelled-out chronology shows a lengthy gap between 1957 and the second half of the 1970's, connected with the work on the *Books*. *Le Seuil Le Sable* seems to comprise that which appears before the threshold of the *Books* and after they are abandoned – that is to say, sand. The titles are not merely metaphorical. On the contrary, *The Book of Questions* is, in fact, an epistemological threshold to Jabès: the issues it sounds, resonant with the form in which it is written, radically break up with his earlier texts. *The Book of Questions* heralds the entry into the space of profound and consistent apophatic thinking. At the same time, it discards verse as a form and discovers the space of writing which, always surrounded by whiteness, configures itself in various groupings undefined by dictates of poetics. Hence, the poetry composed after the *Books* series has an altogether different shape: it is diffused, freed from the form, internally pulverised by whiteness – with sand as its metaphorical rendering. But the difference between the "threshold" and the "sand" is also philosophically potent as it signals a transition from a reality based on the Law, unknown though it may be (as in Scholem and Benjamin's famous debate on Kafka), the threshold of which we seek to cross, to a reality devoid of any single organisational principle, deprived of the Law, and made up of a space of fragmented meanings which, like grains of sand, co-exist in the desert. So, indeed, as Derrida had it, *The Book* re-directs the reading of *Je bâtis ma demeure*; the writer's life produces a chasm that divides the threshold from the sand. Cf. Jacques Derrida, "Edmond Jabès and the Question of the Book," in *Writing and Difference*, trans. Alan Bass (London and New York: Routledge, 2005), pp. 77–96.

129 Critics tend to neglect Jabès' Cairo works as, allegedly, unconnected to the Paris writings. However, Steven Jaron in his insightful *Edmond Jabès: The Hazard of Exile* shows

designation. Some critics have coined the notion of "Jabèstext,"[130] which in a way suggests in how far the category of writing overrides the sense of the text.

As already mentioned, Jabès' Parisian work begins with *The Book of Questions*. It already bears Jabès' trademark tensions between the ending of the book and its continuation. *The Book of Questions* is certainly a separate text in its own right and does not seem to imply any further extension; and yet Jabès from the very beginning had a trilogy in mind.[131] An oscillation between the ending and the extension, the ultimate idea and the thought that comes after it anyway, was highly relevant to him. That is why Jabès' *Books* always arrange themselves in cycles, which were not pre-planned in advance.[132] Besides the first text from which it derived its name (*Le Livre des Questions*), the trilogy of *The Book of Questions* includes also *The Book of Yukel* (*Le Livre de Yukel*) of 1964 and *Return to the Book* (*Le retour au livre*) of 1965. Two years later, *Yaël* is published, again first as an autonomous text which is, nonetheless, soon continued in *Elya* (1969) and *Aely* (1972). In this way, a second trilogy comes into being, initially separate from *The Book of Questions* series. It is only in 1973, when Jabès publishes • (*El, or the Last Book*) (• [*El, ou le dernier livre*]),[133] that the two trilogies are, retrospectively, combined and, at the same time, given an ending. In this way, from 1973 on, *The Book of Questions* is a heptalogy.

In the 1970's and 1980's, Jabès writes two other cycles: the *Book of Resemblances* trilogy (*Le Livre des Ressemblances*), comprised of the likewise titled work (1976) and the volumes of *Intimations The Desert* (*Le Soupçon le Désert*) (1978) and *The Ineffaceable The Unperceived* (*L'Ineffaçable l'Inaperçu*) (1980); and *The Book of Limits* tetralogy (*Le livre des limites*), incorporating, retrospectively again, *The Little Book of Unsuspected Subversion* (*Le Petit Livre de la subversion hors du soupçon*) (1982), *The Book of Dialogue* (*Le Livre du Dialogue*) (1984), *Le Parcours*

that this is an ungrounded assumption. The Parisian works, albeit formally different in abandoning verse, are thematically linked to the Cairo texts.

130 Ulrike Schneider, *Der poetische Aphorismus bei Edmond Jabès, Henri Michaux und René Char: zu Grundfragen einer Poetik* (Stuttgart: Franz Steiner Verlag, 1998), p. 54.

131 DB, pp. 53–4.

132 For a comprehensive bibliography of Jabès' works, see Roger Eliot Stoddard, *Edmond Jabès in Bibliography: "Du blanc des mots et du noir des signes": A Record of the Printed Books* (Paris and Caen: Lettres modernes Minard, 2001).

133 This text's proper title is a dot, one that Jabès emphatically wanted to be (and Gallimard's original edition took care to make) red. The subtitle was a compromise with the publisher refusing to have a book with a dot alone as a title. I will discuss the symbolism behind it in Chapter Eleven.

[*The Journey*] (1985) and *The Book of Shares* (*Le Livre du Partage*) (1987). Besides the three cycles, Jabès published also a handful of other texts (partly based on re-editions), to which I will also refer in the following. They are *It Goes Its Way* (*Ça suit son cours*) (1975) and *Doubly Dependent on the Said* (*Dans la double dépendance du dit*) (1984), both combined in *The Book of Margins* (*Le Livre des Marges*) (1987), and, finally, *A Foreigner Carrying in the Crook of His Arm a Tiny Book* (*Un Étranger avec, sous les bras, un livre de petit format*) (1989). Important are also Jabès' conversations with Marcel Cohen, published as *From the Desert to the Book* (*Du désert au livre*, 1981; extended edition, 1990), in which many of the writer's thoughts are formulated more straightforwardly than in other works. Finally, his last book, relevant to the interpretation of his oeuvre, is the posthumously published *Le Livre de l'Hospitalité* [*Book of Hospitality*] (1991).

With this brief overview of Jabès' published works, we can now focus on the characteristics of his mature writing. Without a doubt, these writings are distinctly heterogeneous and remarkably fragmented.[134] Despite that, Jabès' texts display a specific and paradoxical continuity. In these texts, the structure of thinking is so profoundly fractured that they articulate an abiding tension of questioning rather than a transition from a thesis to a conclusion, and in this sense, the work is infused with an internal unity by this very tension. If there is any evolution from text to text (at it is a big if), it consists in exacerbating the experience of nothingness and gradual erasure aimed not to extract a single final thesis but rather to bring thinking closer to duration itself. Therein the structure of the Jabèsian text resembles Heidegger's *Contributions to Philosophy*. Each of its passages seems to confront an ultimate question of its own and, as such, is not continuous with other ones in terms of the content, but carries on invariable questioning.

With this observation, we can decide how best to go about interpreting the poet's writings. We can safely assume that in discussing Jabès' thoughts most excerpts from various books can be cited in parallel since questions forsaken in one book resurface in another, producing a back and forth movement, as the writer himself puts it.[135] However, there are also parts of the text that seek

---

134 The aphoristic form of *The Book of Questions* owes a lot to the manner in which it was being written. Jabès composed it on the underground, commuting to work, as it was the only spare time he had. See Cahen, *Edmond Jabès*, p. 322. This is also how Nietzsche wrote, after all, "reaching [his] thoughts by walking" and excelling in aphorism (See F. Nietzsche, *Twilight of the Idols*, "Maxims and Arrows," No. 34, in *The Portable Nietzsche*, trans. W. Kaufmann, New York: Viking Penguin Press, 1977, p. 471).

135 EEJ, p. 72.

to fathom the same issue but filter it through their own, unique notions. For example, *The Book of Resemblances* "questions by means of resemblance."[136] Besides, Jabès' work contains also parts in which the tension of questioning is so amplified that it sets them apart from the remaining ones more rigorously than is usually the case. A hermeneutical interpreter of Jabès would thus be well advised to, alongside the "main line" of reflection that can be viewed as tolerably homogeneous,[137] attend also to Jabès' special notions, such as repetition or writing, and to passages that represent the intensifying erasure, the withdrawal of God (featuring particularly in • *[El]*). Yet the specific character of Jabès' work makes it impossible to divide his themes into separate threads. It seems that each of them articulates the same concern but from a different perspective; consequently, each of them could serve as a whole work. Jabès' writing enacts a continuous description that at any given moment endeavours to encompass the totality of unified reality. This is one reason why it resembles incessant forgetting and remembering of things gone by – the meaning dissolving in the past and reverberating again in the present, reminiscing on and recognising a likeness to the old splinters.[138] The work's external framework is provided not by a sustained, sound plan, but by time, to which writing gives itself over unreservedly, letting itself forget and live through memories again.

Let us have a closer look at the form of this writing. Critical attention is more often than not engrossed by its enormous heterogeneity and generic elusiveness,[139] deliberately designed to explode any categories one might be tempted to superimpose on it. Warren F. Motte depicts Jabès' writing in the following way:

---

136 *Ibid.*
137 The homogeneity does not mean that there is no difference between the early parts of *The Book of Questions* and its last texts. Jabès' thought was evolving slowly, affected also by other authors. As already mentioned, Derrida's essay most likely induced the writer to deconstruct the quasi-notion of the Book (for more details, see Susan Handelman, "'Torments of an Ancient Word': Edmond Jabès and the Rabbinic Tradition," in *The Sin of the Book*, pp. 55–91, on pp. 71–2. But at the core of the *Books* lies the very tension of questioning, which time only enhances. There might be readings in which a differentiation of Jabès' concepts over his lifetime would be attempted, yet this is not the goal of the present volume.
138 Cf. Warren F. Motte, Jr., *Questioning Edmond Jabès* (Lincoln & London: University of Nebraska Press, 1990), p. x.
139 On the predicament of classifying Jabès' work faced by literary critics, see Henri Raczymow, "Qui est Edmond Jabès?" *Les Cahiers Obsidiane*, no. 5 – *Edmond Jabès* (Paris: Capitales/Obsidiane, 1982), pp. 158–67.

The language is a curious hybrid of discursive norms. Lyric moments confront patently prosaic ones; dialogical passages play out the theatricality of the text; lapidary essays and prose meditations of various sorts are interpolated here and there; aphorisms abound. These texts teem with voices, some of them located in identifiable characters, some of them emanating from unidentifiable sources. Time shifts without warning in these worlds, ranging from a problematic present to a biblical – and largely hypothetical – past. So too does space, whether it be a question of a shaded Parisian street, a concentration camp or a boundless desert. The page that Jabès constructs resembles no other: words wander thereupon with disconcerting mobility, staging themselves in different ways – flush left, flush right, centered, in roman typeface and in italics, cast within quotation marks or parentheses, or suspended in sibylline ellipses.[140]

And Walter A. Strauss highlights the formal allusions to Jewish tradition:

The form of writing, undoubtedly, came in first: the pairing of lyrical and narrative passages and aphorisms, all constantly monitored by imaginary rabbis. It is a writing that resembles all forms of the Old Testament, the Talmud, exegeses of the Torah and the Kabbalah, commentaries, interpretations and mythology, and that seeks to re-new Jewish tradition in the Diaspora, to transform the sacred tradition in the settings of remoteness and exile. As The Book of Questions develops, the language is beset by a restlessness which looks for its centre in questions about Word and about God – or, rather, in the questioning of the language devised to re-create the lost names of God and Word, given in the beginning to the Jewish people and imposing on it the lot of writing-in-exile.[141]

The process of the modern shattering of perspective, the evolution of 20th-century poetics heading towards dispersal and silence and, finally, the wealth of Jewish tradition re-readthrough the Shoah and exile amalgamate at the level of the form itself. It is from this form alone that the image emanates of a world "constantly in peril, in which simple axioms of language are no more,"[142] as Shillony writes. Consequently, no generic categories can accommodate a writing that only lends itself to being described by this very word, purely material as it is. Marcel Cohen points out that

Neither title page nor cover [of The Book of Questions] give any indication of the genre. But, most importantly, one cannot uncover a plan, a procedure [le procédé] underlying the writing. At first glance the sentences appear on the white page as if they were the

---

140 Motte, "Hospitable Poetry," p. 34. Interestingly, in using various text layouts on the page, Jabès patently follows in the footsteps of his powerful precursor Mallarmé in *Un coup de dés jamais n'abolira le hasard*.

141 Walter A. Strauss, *"Le Livre des questions* de Jabès et la question du livre," in *Écrire le livre*, p. 295.

142 Helena Shillony, *Edmond Jabès: une rhétorique de la subversion* (Paris: Lettres Modernes, 1991), p. 3.

reflection of a profound chaos, a kind of weighty, immemorial interior night, as if there was no will to shape the form. In fact, the opposite is true: your major concern seems to be to keep the book from finding its form, thereby keeping it from becoming fixed. It thus becomes clear from the start that it is not a question of a simple refusal of traditional genres but of a "perversion," an "insurrection" at the very core of writing.[143]

Symptomatically, this form of reflection is not a purely literary device but parallels the reality that it sets out to depict – a reality stamped by a disaster, shattered and dispersed.[144] According to Hawkins,

> Jabès constructs a new method of writing that represents the breakdown of language accompanying the collapse of human values. Writing comes to signify a wholly new existential condition, bringing with it a set of wholly new choices.
>
> The movement that Jabès promotes is embraced by the phenomenological method and the strategy of hermeneutics suitable to this method. In much the same way as Kafka does, Jabès incorporates the text-based strategies of Midrash into the ontology of mystical Judaism – particularly Lurianic Kabbalah.[145]

Apparently, Jabès' new language, rather than a species of formal experimentation, is a befitting response to the world it is supposed to render. As Kristjana Gunnars observes,[146] the fragmentation of Jabès' language results from the fact that the perception of reality as such is fragmentary; we never grasp the whole, but always, moment by moment, we reconstruct the totality from tiny particles.[147] "Fragmented" writing is necessitated by the fragmentation of the reality that it seeks to capture.

---

143 DB, p. 42.
144 The structure of the text itself seems to link the *Books* series with the Lurianic Kabbalah and its idea of split. Jabès' predecessor in this is Nachman of Breslov, a 19th-century Judaic mystic, who inferred from *tzimtzum* that Hebraic letters were sacred still – as tradition had them – but because of the breaking of the vessels did not come together in correct forms anymore. That is why, Nachman insisted, the linearity of time and the logical, i.e. natural, course of language should be abandoned as, resulting from a catastrophe, they obscured the real kinship of letters. Language's real structure must be found, which could be achieved only in new modes of writing. Consequently, Nachman relinquished the classical Kabbalistic treatise form and took to writing tales and fables; Benjamin Gross, *L'aventure du langage. L'alliance de la parole dans la pensée juive* (Paris: Albin Michel, 2003), p. 131. Similarly, Jabès' writing in its specificity is a response to his idea of *tzimtzum*.
145 Hawkins, *Reluctant Theologians*, p. 156.
146 Kristjana Gunnars, *Stranger at the Door: Writers and the Act of Writing* (Waterloo, Ontario: Wilfrid Laurier UP, 2004), p. 83.
147 Cf. also IEJ, pp. 20–21.

Jabès' language challenges the reader from the very beginning. Elliptical, laconic and dense, veritably naked, as Richard Stamelman has it, self-aware and self-reflexive, it neither represents nor creates poetic images.[148] It is a threshold at which one must pause in order to, first of all, break one's own thinking. For, in Jabès, there is no new ontology without a new language and a corollary new mode of perception. The poet's work, as Joan Brandt puts it, "accentuates on the most basic structural level the problematical nature of language itself."[149] Gary D. Mole highlights another property of the "Jabèstext":

> The unusual typographical disposition of these books is their most immediately striking feature and contributes to the disorientation the reader experiences in first encountering them. But their predominant characteristic is the melancholic tone of suffering, loss, and death, revealed to Jabès at the age of twelve with the death of his elder sister.[150]

This tone saturates the work's specific form, which Fernandez-Zoïla labels *structure éclatée* – an exploded structure, a term suggested by the poet himself.[151] The phrase connotes a glare, a sudden illumination, the revelation of the whole in a piece. In this formulation, the fragmentation in Jabès' writing exposes its potential for thinking. It is, according to Fernandez-Zoïla, mystical thinking, but its mysticism remains materialist[152] and fundamentally anti-metaphysical (in the Heideggerian take on metaphysics).[153] It is "mysticism, if mysticism is conceived as any attempt at delving into oneself which, in fact, means *stepping beyond oneself* to head towards the concealed, the undiscovered places of one's own self."[154] Besides, it would be mysticism "whose core liturgy lay in the practice of reading and writing."[155] Yet Fernandez-Zoïla's analysis of the relationship between the form of writing and its role does not stop at spotlighting its mystical potential. It also shows how closely connected the "Jabèstext" is to inner dissolution that has

---

148 Richard Stamelman, "The Strangeness of the Other and the Otherness of the Stranger: Edmond Jabès," *Yale French Studies*, 82/1 (1993), pp. 118–34, on p. 124.

149 Joan Elizabeth Brandt, *Geopoetics: The Politics of Mimesis in Poststructuralist French Poetry and Theory* (Stanford, CA: Stanford UP, 1997), p. 172.

150 Mole, *Lévinas, Blanchot, Jabès*, p. 11.

151 Fernandez-Zoïla, *Livre*, p. 12. Jabès describes his writing as *récit éclaté* in an interview with Paul Auster; IEJ, p. 14. Cf. also Gunnars, *Stranger*, p. 83.

152 Fernandez-Zoïla, *Livre*, p. 13.

153 Although she refuses to call Jabès himself a mystic, Rosmarie Waldrop agrees that he knows "mysticism of the book"; Rosmarie Waldrop, "Miroirs et paradoxes," *Change*, 22 (février, 1975), pp. 193–204, on p. 194.

154 Fernandez-Zoïla, *Livre*, p. 13.

155 *Ibid.*

unremittingly plagued philosophy, literature, arts and music since the early 20th century.[156] In this context, *The Book of Questions*, like Nietzsche's thought, the texts of Artaud, Leiris, Bataille and Blanchot, the works of Picasso and Klee and, finally, Mahler's music, is not a neutral description of the disintegration but a testimony delivered from within the process.[157] The term "testimony" presupposes that writing actively plunges into the process of unravelling and endeavours to experience what is going on, eventually, to offer a first-hand report of it:

> The substance of these books is intertwined with their functionalities because no content could be extracted from them and attributed to an "outside," located beyond the written form subordinated to the sources that produced it in an utterly material and real history.[158]

In this sense, Jabès' writing is not just a distanced account of the unfolding phenomena but attests to them, incapable of shaking off its object's impact. The interrelation of form and thought is mirrored in Jabès also in the graphic layout of writing. As Ulrike Schneider reminds,

> The multiplicity of literary forms includes also specific pagination and the dramaturgical use of typography in some books, which makes them unambiguously recognisable as Jabès'.
> [...] italics – with frequent self-reflexive passages – places the text every now and then in a kind of *mise en abyme* of self-commentary; the fragment appears the only possible form of utterance which subjects itself to questioning and remains incomplete. Because what has been said once can be relativised, if not retracted entirely, in the very next sentence, speaking [*das Sprechen*] knows no end.[159]

The breaking of the form is thus the only possibility to radically actualise the questioning that targets itself as well. As the layers of commentary proliferate, writing comes to mean, so to speak, incessant crossing of meta-levels of successive utterances. In Jabès, commentary is not meant to exhaust the commented-on: commentary passes and itself becomes an object of commentary before even having a chance to materialise. Hence, each sentence remains a trace of an unfinished possibility that could not come about because writing is happening all the time and no act of writing could put writing to an end.

Discussing parallels between Jabès' thought and the form of his writing, one must not neglect the role of oppositions ubiquitous in it. All and Nothing, One

---

156 *Ibid.*, p. 39.
157 *Ibid.*, pp. 39–46.
158 *Ibid.*, p. 108.
159 Schneider, *Poetische Aphorismus*, pp. 59–60.

and Infinity, life and death grapple with each other invariably in these texts. The series of oppositions, as Stéphane Mosès emphasises, reveal the "perpetual dialectics" that keeps Jabès' writing in tension.[160] It is in this way that writing constantly endeavours to grasp the other side of meaning and interact with it explicitly. Besides, Jabès frequently resorts in his writing to chiasmi, underscoring the aporias around which they are constructed.[161] Another signature feature of Jabès' writing is reiteration of key words. Jabès himself foregrounds the basic notions of his thinking: God, Jew, Law, Eye, Name and Book.[162] Motte extends the list, adding desert, abode (*demeure*), sand, void, margin, scream, word (*mot*), speech (*parole*), vocable and *verbe*, which – polysemous and untranslatable – covers the semantic field ranging from "verb" to "word" and "foreword."[163] Eric Gould throws in, further, "silence," "center" and "absence."[164]

Jabès' key words do not build any pre-planned meaning. Meaning emerges only as a short-lived constellation of their aspect as captured at a particular moment. Because this aspect, rather than curtailing the polysemy of words, only highlights it by its own fleeting and fragmentary character, the entire utterance becomes momentary and atomised. In Jabès, thus, an utterance remains secondary to words and is made possible by their current state in the process of evolution. Meaning does not endure in time; rather, it perishes, leaving behind merely a slight displacement within the semantic fields of key words.

Surveying the development of Jabès' writing, one easily notices that key words tend to be paired in oppositions. Still, the oppositions do not last: sometimes they are used only within one book, and on other occasions they disappear to resurface only in another work. For example, in *The Book of Resemblances* "oblivion" and "likeness" bump into each other even though, at first sight, they have nothing in common and, certainly, are no antonyms. However, Jabès incrementally brings them closer together sentence by sentence, binds them first only by an external suggestion and, at last, decisively re-casts their denotative fields to couple them. In this way, the manner in which Jabès works upon words mirrors the Hegelian "dissolution," used already by Mallarmé.[165]

---

160 Mosès, "Edmond Jabès," in *Écrire le livre*, p. 48.
161 Helena Shillony, "Edmond Jabès: une rhétorique de la subversion et de l' harmonie," *Romance Notes*, XXVI/1 (1985), pp. 3–11, on pp. 3–4.
162 BR II, p. 70.
163 Shillony, *Edmond Jabès*, p. 14
164 Gould, "Introduction," in *The Sin of the Book*, p. xiv.
165 Cf. Kristeva, *La révolution*, pp. 101–116 (*Revolution in poetic language*, pp. 107–126).

If Jabès himself insisted that his books were varieties of essentially the same questioning filtered through different words each time, it could be added that the questioning usually is effected through their oppositions. The difference apprehended in a given opposition for a brief moment embodies the fundamental difference, recurring constantly and motivating the questioning as such. Hélène Trivouss-Haïk proposes a similar conclusion,[166] observing that Jabès time and again plots "an association grid," a net of words in which to comprise the entire reality. In other words, Jabès shows how various grids of terms render the same recurring structure. This is the essence of his questioning carried on across his texts.

Conclusion: Jabès' Supercooled Modernism

Concluding, we could ask: Who was Edmond Jabès after all? His biography, specific though it is, binds him to a group of similar authors: Lévinas, Derrida, Blanchot and Celan. Born and bred on the peripheries, they were all, to a lesser or greater degree, formed by the cultural and intellectual centre of Paris. The ideological environment in which Jabès grew up was not unique to him, either. Many were affected by the twilight of Modernism, which was on the lookout for new paths and wrestled with the horrors of the Shoah.

Jabès' Cairo poetry amply shows that already in the 1930's he found himself treading the path that Western philosophy and literature were turning. The young poet's verses ooze the belief that the place of truth remains concealed – truth shines through but is forever inaccessible.[167] This modernist axiom will later transmute profoundly in Jabès, with truth's one place transfiguring into a myriad delusively oscillating enigmas, underpinned by a shared structure. Jabès is not alone in this evolution, which largely charts the trajectory from Modernism to Postmodernism. Another prominent motif of the Cairo verse – inhabiting, abode, settling – undergoes an analogous transformation. In Jabès' Paris texts, it will morph into meditations on exile, unbelongingness and lack of definable identity. Thus, while the poet's pre-war themes sound Heideggerian, his postwar pivots radicalise in an effort to find a new response to the Shoah. Finally, the very appearance of the text evolves from pre-war, Surrealist-indebted solutions to ultra-fragmentation and disintegration of the narrative in the Parisian *Books*.

---

166 Trivouss-Haïk, "Désirer lire la mise en acte de l'écrit," in *Écrire le livre*, pp. 271–6, on
    p. 271.
167 Jaron, *Edmond Jabès*, p. 118.

This notwithstanding, a continuity with the Cairo poems shows in Jabès' fondness for experimenting with the graphic layout.

Still, while there is no clear rift between Postmodernism and Modernism (on the contrary, high modernist texts are *almost-already* postmodernist), Jabès remains profoundly modernist, at the same time anticipating the shift of the late 1960's. The belatedness of Egypt's late Romanticism made Jabès enter late Modernism already with a delay. That is why he ultimately evades any simple categorisation, for he is not, either, a late modernist who consciously reverted to Modernism after the turn that problematised the movement. Therefore, I propose a new term – *supercooled Modernism* – to label Jabès' work. In chemistry, a supercooled liquid is one in which temperature has dropped below the freezing level, but the state of matter has not changed because the pure solution contains no condensation-triggering pollutants. There is no stimulus to initiate solidification of this liquid, which, theoretically speaking, should not be liquid anymore. If any foreign particle gets into the solution, a chain reaction is set off in which the liquid congeals, returning to the freezing temperature exceeded before without turning into a solid. A similar process is detectable in the Jabèsian Modernism: in the course of the arch-modernist procedures of purification, refining and distilment of the text, a crystal-clear writing is produced which, formally, is and comes across as postmodernist even though it continues to behave like a modernist *state of matter*. It crosses the boundary between epochs and, as modernist, is already belated: formally it mimics its environment though its pellucidity binds it to the times past. It is through this clarity that it both opens a new epoch for itself and, in fact, prevents itself submerging fully into it as it preserves a strictly modernist enclave within its Postmodernism. Compellingly, for all his awareness of the new paths – of fragmentation, truncatedness and intertextuality – Jabès imbued his writing with a signature modernist tension. It certainly looks like any slight admixture to this chiselled poetics could immediately trigger a chain reaction in which the entire modernist energy would be radiated out and writing pushed to undergo a shift it missed on its unique way of belatedness. That which remained after such a collapse would constitute a postmodernist, tension-free body of writing.

It seems, thus, that Jabès – for all the singularity of his path – partly emulates the evolution of 20th-century philosophy and literature. Hence, his solitude and his affinity with other authors are inseparable. There is one more element to be added to the landscape of solstitial Modernism, namely the re-invention of Judaism, which provided Jabès with intellectual forms to develop (particularly in the further volumes of *The Book of Questions* and later texts). This is also where the poet joins Lévinas and Derrida, yet his own interpretation of Judaism seems more comprehensive, more innovative and more radical, though at the same time utterly impoverished in its innovation.

In this perspective, Jabès seems to be a paradigmatic modern thinker, one severed from religious tradition, damaged by war and exile, consistently expanding his questioning and, finally, re-inventing Judaism on the basis of his personal experiences. Meet Edmond Jabès, a Jewish philosopher of modernity.

3 *Tzimtzum:* Jabès and Luria

Let us now focus on Jabès' thought. Its most conspicuous feature is probably that it concerns an utterly dispersed and scattered reality, as a result of which the text itself is fragmented to the utmost. This pervasive fragmentation deserves to be discussed first. A pertinent question is, of course, what caused this disintegration. Jabès himself does not shun the question. His texts reiterate the idea of a primordial catastrophe, a drastic event of the beginning. Most commentators agree to view this as analogous to the Lurianic concept of *tzimtzum*. In this Chapter, I will however show that the Jabèsian version of *tzimtzum* is far more akin to modern Western philosophy than it appears to be.[1]

To start with, I will consider whether, in Jabès' view, the initial catastrophe is knowable in the first place. Subsequently, I will focus on the disaster's consequences for the world that it gave rise to. Taking stock of these sequent effects will help me not only fathom the nature of the catastrophe itself but also identify Jabès' fundamental philosophical tenets. Based on this, I will attempt to describe the mechanism of his *tzimtzum*. To do so, I will first recount the poet's insights as worded by him and, then, outline a more abstract, philosophical model of that event and, additionally, depict the act of writing, which Jabès construes as a model of creation. To conclude, I will compare Luria's and Jabès' notions of *tzimtzum* to bring out the modern character of the latter.

Inaccessibility of the Origins

The first thing to be noted about the idea of a discontinuous beginning is that, according to Jabès, it is not knowable directly and can be accessed only through a kind of fiction:

"Commencement, *'beginning'*: comment se ment? *How does the beginning lie to itself in order to compel recognition as beginning? How does it, in lying to itself, lie to us and*

---

1 Before we proceed any further, it must be clearly stated that Jabès never directly speaks of the concept of *tzimtzum*. Still he refers time and again to the idea of the withdrawal of God leaving emptiness behind. He also repeatedly plays on associations with "inhalation" and "exhalation," which are supposed to be at the core of the act of creation. Such connotations explicitly evoke the Lurianic *tzimtzum* (which I will describe below). That is why, following some commentators, I will refer to "the Jabèsian *tzimtzum*," distilling a notion analogical to Luria's from the poet's writings. Emphatically, however, this formulation remains just an interpretive construct.

establish its lie so firmly it makes us believe we begin with it [que nous commençons avec lui]"?[2]

The passage implies that any idea of the beginning which we are tempted to place at the origin of continuous history as a discontinuous event, is a "lie." A lie, in this context, is meant not so much as a negation of truth but as a patent fiction that offers itself as the inaccessible origin. "Beginning is a human invention, an anguished speculation about origins."[3] The beginning would thus be that which we are compelled to think instead of thinking an event that, radically strange to us, defies any description since description as such is made possible by it in the first place:

> We are unable to think origins. It's the origins, one after another [*successivement*], that think us.[4]
> Thinking about the beginning is impossible for no other reason than that the beginning

itself makes thinking possible (and, in this sense, it "thinks us"). Jabès insists that we are perpetually dependent on an originary event which is identifiable only in retrospect.[5] Still, the plural number in the quote implies something else, too. Namely, the beginning is not reducible to one primal catastrophe that brought forth the entire reality. On the contrary, there are several beginnings which, importantly, succeed one another. That reality is sustained at all results, thus, from the subsequent, unfounded beginnings, each of them giving rise to a certain form of the world and appearing to it as its own originary void.

Effects of the Catastrophe

What follows is that the primal disaster can only be rendered in an explicitly fictional account spun from its effects backwards. Therefore, before focusing on the nature of that catastrophe, we must scrutinise the consequences it caused.

---

2   BR II, p. 22.
3   *Ibid.*, p. 21.
4   LH, p. 21.
5   Similarly, the Haggadah in Talmud's Chagigah explains: "Why does the story of Creation begin with the letter *beth* [in the *Bereshit*]? … In the same manner that the letter *beth* is closed on all sides and only open in front [ב], similarly you are not permitted to inquire into what is before or what is behind, but only from the actual time of Creation." Abraham Cohen, *Everyman's Talmud,* p. 27. As Scholem points out, the Kabbalah revived mythical speculations about Creation, but precisely as patent myths occluding the inaccessible beginning. See Scholem, *Kabbalah and Its Symbolism,* p. 101.

The first effect is the discontinuity of time. Here are Jabès' central formulations that provide us with interpretive guidelines:

> There is no continuity in time.[6]
> *Stability of beings, things, the world – you are but a scant time of respite between two escapes; imperceptible time we rely on which became illusory: our indigent time.*[7]
> […] time means separation, and we live in time.[8]

These three passages are only seemingly contradictory. In fact, they convey a rather complex structure of time posited by Jabès as he actually seems to presuppose two kinds of time. Time as expressed in the first excerpt could be called "real"[9] and is a pure, repeated discontinuity – a chain of entirely discrete moments. Time as rendered in the second excerpt is an illusory "human" time that guarantees an ostensible stability of beings. According to Jabès, we live in a kind of protective "indigent time," which breaks down the radicalism of change ushered in by the real time into separate, measurable moments. This illusory time is delimited by "two escapes," standing, we might think, for manifestations of the real time, which it flees and to which it eventually returns. In this light, the third passage could be construed as indicating that *the time in which we live essentially isolates us from the real time.* Inferably, what the disaster brought about is a lack of any objective time that passes uniformly for the entire reality. Instead, there is the real time as a sequence of radical discontinuities – inconceivable to us and separated from the illusory time, in which beings can continue, though it is only a seeming duration. For, inextricable from the illusory time, the real time affects us even when the illusion prevents us from recognising its workings.

This is evidenced by the second effect of the catastrophe, that is, by the impermanence of a sentence's validity in time:

> […] *If only our thought were longer than a moment, we would get a foretaste of eternity.*[10]
> […] You write. But doesn't what you write hold for the moment?

---

6   LR I, p. 97.
7   LR I, p. 111.
8   BQ II, p. 40.
9   Jabès uses the phrase "real time" in *The Ineffaceable The Unperceived* to describe a time in which eternity looks into itself and realises its own nature (BR III, p. 63). Here, I extend this term to include all the cases in which Jabès ponders the time of infinity itself.
10   LR I, p. 33.

The infinite excludes all improvisations of the finite, just as eternity crosses out, with one unbounded pen-stroke, the moment expressed in all that it expresses and valid only at and for the moment it occurs.[11]

Jabès does not believe that an utterance could possibly hold past a certain defined time. The articulated thought is so tightly bound to the moment in which it emerged – or, more precisely, to the configuration of conditions that made it possible – that it can by no means survive the passage of time. In other words, each utterance is inscribed in its own origin, which passes and is replaced by another one. Its ostensible stability is but an effect of the illusory time. Temporality is conceived here so radically that it affects also the most general conceptual frameworks, which also perish. What Hegel and Nietzsche discovered as putting the entire prior thinking about truth and history to the test is the very starting point in Jabès. Importantly, Jabès is not tempted to opt simply for relativism, in which each thought would be equally irrelevant. On the contrary, he assumes that, all the reservations notwithstanding, a thought, on emerging, has a relevance of its own. How to reconcile the idea of the thought's relevance with its radical temporality poses an entirely new challenge to philosophy.

Third, the foregoing suggests that, as a result of the catastrophe, meaning is not reproducible in time. The passage of the real time seems to destroy the comprehensibility of an utterance irreversibly. That is why an alleged reproduction of it in later reading is only illusory as it rather entails producing a new thought that veils what has been lost:

One reads only one's own reading.[12]

Factual truth means only that others (and we ourselves) accept our interpretation of an event.[13]

...facing the text, the writer is in the same position as the eventual reader, the text always opening up to the degree that we *are able* to read it. It is each time the *text of our reading*, that is to say, a new text.[14]

That new text is by no means an arbitrary variation on the prior one as it is shaped *through and by* the experience of loss. The quotations above imply two conclusions. First, the very nature of time in Jabès makes the text take on two different forms: a material form that persists in the real time and is inaccessible to us as soon as it is written down, and a fractional interpretation that emerges

---

11 BR II, p. 26.
12 LH, p. 62.
13 BQ II, p. 66.
14 BM, p. 124.

from reading and inevitably differs with every passing moment. Any hermeneutics as apperception of the original meaning is precluded a priori. Second, in
the epistemology that ensues thereof, the very catastrophe makes it impossible
to grasp a catastrophe as an event that marks the beginning of time because the
catastrophe ruptured the continuity of time. Third, in effect, there is no common
measure that, by accommodating simultaneously the moment of the beginning
and the moment of thinking, could make comparing them possible.[15] Even sup-
posing that the meaning of the catastrophe was discovered, it would not survive
beyond the moment of being forged. In this sense, the catastrophe still continues
and affects reality moment by moment.

Fourth, the catastrophe also shattered truth. As time was split into the illusory and the real one, truth falls apart into two as well. What we actually have is
a perspectival truth,[16] holding for a brief moment within which it is capable of
sustaining its validity in time. This truth – or, rather, these truths – can be ver-
balised in language. But because they emerge as a result of disowning transience,
as a result of disguising their own perspectivism, they do not convey *the truth of
the whole*. The latter is described by Jabès only as a negative liminal point, a fiction reflexively crafted by perspectivism. Since all articulation and all meaning
are perspectival, the truth of the whole cannot possibly be articulated. In this
sense, Jabès can propose that "truth is the void"[17] and its voice is a "[f]atal call of
the void."[18] Also, these insights apophatically bring us closer to truth, but insofar
as they are part of a perspective, they are not truth. "For truth is a mirage of a
summit which our mountains point toward,"[19] *Yaël* insists. Truth is a mobilisation which, though unreachable as such, can be indicated by truths of individual
perspectives in their temporary mobilisations (hence the "mountains").

The interrelation of the two forms of truth is represented in Jabès' notori-
ously ambiguous assertion that *"la verité est en poussière."*[20] One of its meanings
is that "the truth lies in dust": there is no unified, universal truth as the disaster
made it impossible. *"Truth is incessant invention since it contradicts itself, since*

---

15 Clearly, this represents the same problem of continuity and limit of a continuous series
    that Kant grappled with (particularly in his antinomies). Cf. Chapter One.
16 Admittedly, Jabès does not use the words "perspective" or "perspectival," but given
    the utility of these concepts, boosted by post-Nietzschean perspectivism of Western
    philosophy, I will employ them in further interpretations.
17 BQ I, p. 117.
18 BQ II, p. 60.
19 *Ibid.*, p. 60
20 LH, s. 41.

only the provisional is true, only what can be shared.[21] What is more, each of the dispersed, fleeting particles preserves a moment of common truth, just like the Lurianic spark does. "What you call *Truth*," *The Book of Shares* proclaims, "is truth in shreds. To each his own. Once ripped from the Whole, this miserable shred has no reality except its misery."[22] This is how the immanent Jabèsian perspectivism, highlighted by Waldrop, manifests itself.[23] The particles of truth are separated by a discontinuity, *a space of pure nothingness*, in the same way that specks of dust are separated by empty space. The catastrophe means a raid of that pure nothingness into the universe and causing the originary truth to disintegrate into perspectives. The present tense of the sentence ascertains that this is the current state of affairs, and any disaster we could possibly imagine to have happened in the past – likewise the primal total truth the disaster could destroy – remains our fiction at best, cloaking the inaccessible.

The sentence can also be construed to mean something else. "The truth *is* in the dust" – it is the fragmentation that is the truth, and the truth can be read out from its entirety.[24] This is the "truth of the void" evoked above. "The truth is in the dust" can be also taken to imply that truth can be found in that which is most useless and pointless, in the remnants left over after the dissolution. In this sense, the truth would be what has *persisted beyond disintegration, what survives successive catastrophes because it is nothing but dust*. Dust is utterly pulverised matter, matter that has been eroding for so long that it has reached the very end of destruction, and erosion cannot affect it anymore. In the philosophical parlance, Jabès claims that truth can be found only in that which has been purified in consecutive disasters and utterly evacuated of meaning, refusing to accrue any new meaning in subsequent perspectives – that whose essence is duration itself.

Fifth, the catastrophe also brought about writing as Jabès conceived of it. Writing issues from a basic incommensurability between the meaning that we give to the word as it is being written down and the processes that the word

---

21 BQ I, p. 175.
22 BS, p. 18.
23 Rosmarie Waldrop, *Lavish Absence: Recalling and Rereading Edmond Jabès* (Middletown, CT: 2002), p. 17. In an interview with Benjamin Taylor, Jabès explains that his texts profusely feature statements attributed to various invented characters (predominantly rabbis) to underscore that while all of them have their own respective alleged truths, their truths neither add up to a whole nor can be conclusively regarded as final (QJQW, p. 17). The writer employs multiple characters to convey perspectivism through them.
24 See also IEJ, p. 19.

undergoes later. The incommensurability is easily perceived when compared with the functions of a memory prop and a speech supplement that Western metaphysics ascribes to writing.[25] The basic assumption of this functional attribution is that the relation between writing and meaning remains essentially the same from inscription to reading. Of course, misreadings cannot be ruled out as the past written down can become so estranged as to resist simple reading; nevertheless, both the writing-down and the reading are events located within the same temporal sequence. In Jabès, the word written down parts ways with the meaning that was there while writing. A *fundamental quasi-ontological displacement* happens because the meaning perishes alongside the perspective that produced it whereas writing itself still carries on. In this way, writing becomes autonomous vis-à-vis the meaning it was supposed to preserve.

> Any word which eludes the meaning bent on fixing it is free in terms of an absence which is its freedom to live and die, towards which it has always gravitated;
> [...] *Words lose their transparency in being read.*[26]

This loss of transparency implies that the word holds something more than the meaning it seems to bear. Writing down the meaning makes it possible to see it pass in the real time exactly because the word that it leaves behind becomes opaque. Writing does not serve to prop memory; more than that, it *exposes the discontinuity within memory* by explicitly pointing out the absence of the lost meaning. In this sense, for Jabès, writing is not a space of perpetuated and legible signs; rather, it is a radically apophatic dimension which, moment by moment, shows us the finitude and perspectivism of any meaning.

Sixth, another effect of the disaster is what we can call "the solipsism of the present moment," for the first time identified as part of Western philosophy by

---

25 This issue was comprehensively discussed by Derrida in *Of Grammatology*, where he cites, for example, Rousseau and Plato. Rousseau viewed writing as "a supplement to the spoken word" and fully subsumed in the logic of the supplement. See Jacques Derrida, *Of Grammatology*, trans. Gayatri Chakravorty Spivak (Baltimore: Johns Hopkins UP, 1997), p. 7 ff. The role of the sign makes for a central philosophical difference between Athens and Jerusalem. Gross reminds that in the Biblical tradition the word was not considered distinct from the meaning that it conveyed, with this idea being part of the Greek legacy. See Gross, *L'aventure*, pp. 79–83. In this optics, Jabès, in whom the message is tightly intertwined with the word and autonomous language is irreducible to a mere tool, follows in the footsteps of Jewish thinkers.

26 BQ II, p. 250.

David Hume.[27] It refers to the fact that, if the very possibility of a meaningful utterance depends on certain conditions of possibility bound up with a given moment in time, the utterances about the past and the future have no universal grounding. There is no universal history because there are no enunciations that could possibly retain validity across it. In a sense, our knowledge is a knowledge of the present moment only; a proper knowledge about the future must be the knowledge of this very future and, as such, it requires a passage of time.

> How can I know who I am if only the past can teach me that? Tomorrow can't be questioned.[28]

That is why the human identity is not continuous, either. This is another point in which Jabès seems to share Hume's position:

> To delve deep into ourselves in search of identity, what an illusion! There is no continuity in being. Everything within us is laid waste, O layers upon layers of ashes![29]

But if in Hume the self was simply an outcome of impressions,[30] in Jabès the self is comprised of "ashes" – that is, of *failed attempts at establishing a proper identity*. Hume neither suggests anything beyond a sequence of simple impressions nor posits any human need to derive identity from them. Jabès, however, seems to claim that such a vision is unacceptable to us. We strive to establish an identity, to enclose life in meaning, though it ends up, essentially, in ruin. That is why "we" are "layers upon layers of ashes" rather than a sequence of sensations.

Because of this "solipsism of the present moment," meaning parts ways with life comprehended as duration of a living being in time. Related in the previous Chapter, the mistake while registering his birth date helped Jabès express this pattern vividly: according to him, to be (physically) born is one thing and to

---

27 Hume's "solipsism of the present moment" ensues from the dualism the philosopher adopts. He distinguishes between present sensory perceptions with their legitimacy claims from illegitimate statements about the past that depend on former impressions preserved by memory. See David Hume, *A Treatise on Human Nature* (Mineola, NY: Dover Publications, 2003) p. 61. In fact, the link between different moments in time is provided by memory only and has no objective existence. "[...] there appears not, throughout all nature, any one instance of connection which is conceivable by us. All events seem entirely loose and separate. One event follows another; but we never can observe any tie between them." David Hume, *An Enquiry Concerning Human Understanding*, ed. Charles W. Hendel (Pearson, 1995), p. 47.

28 P, p. 21.

29 BR II, p. 14.

30 See Hume, *Treatise*, p. 180.

come to the world another. This difference holds everything that distinguishes a human being – as a symbolic entity – from the purely corporeal life.[31] The divergence of life and meaning surfaces also in thinking about death:

> "When death comes, he won't see me.
> In this way, he won't know whether he fell behind the schedule or maybe I was ahead of my fate," a sage wrote.[32]
> Death does not come at the end of eternity but out of the moment [de l'instant].[33]

The duration of a living being terminated in death cannot be inscribed in meaning; it exceeds meaning. One can think of death, imagine it and place it in the future as an end of the imaginary chain of events starting this very moment. But death will always come too late or too early compared to where one has placed it ("the schedule"), and for this reason we are unable to think death meaningfully. It will come "out of the moment." At this point, Jabès' thought resembles the insights of Giorgio Agamben, who shows the parting of meaningfulness and "bare life" defined as a duration to which meaning does not apply.[34] The death that we ponder has essentially nothing in common with real death, which belongs to the order of pure duration and is entirely exterior to knowledge. Real death is an end that disrupts duration and automatically terminates meaning, remaining as alien to it as bare life is. "Death is the gratuitous act *par excellence*,"[35] writes Jabès. He thus clearly dissociates death as a figure of thought employed by himself and used in philosophy by, for example, Hegel, Heidegger and Blanchot, from real death, which is alien to meaning.[36]

Therefore, what the disaster produced is complete incommensurability of pure duration and meaning in which we wish to frame it. No utterance can possibly invest duration with a permanent meaning without it being always already exceeded. In trying to describe duration, meaning only exposes itself to its own transience:

> There is no goal that, at the very moment it is reached, is not already surpassed.[37]

---

31 Cf. Ddier Cahen, "Jalons," *Europe*, 954 (Octobre 2008), pp. 263–7, on p. 263.
32 LH, p. 19.
33 *Ibid.*, p. 33.
34 Cf., for example, Giorgio Agamben, *Homo Sacer: Sovereign Power and Bare Life*, trans. Daniel Heller-Roazen (Stanford, CA: Stanford UP, 1998).
35 BQ II, p. 33.
36 This is what is meant in *It Goes Its Way*: "Impossible to give a name to death" (BM, p. 66).
37 DB, p. xiv.

[…] to create means only to show the birth and death of an object. We speak, we write but for the moment. Duration is not for us.[38]

The sentence dies the moment it is put together. The words survive it.[39]

This brief survey of the consequences of the catastrophe implies that its fundamental effect is discontinuity, which makes various perspective, various moments in time, writing and meaning as well as life and meaning incompatible. Because this discontinuity is all-encompassing, the entire reality gets pulverised and each resulting particle is incommensurable with all the other ones even though all of them re-enact the same atomisation. In this sense, reality is utterly dispersed but, paradoxically, homogeneous in its incessant discontinuity as it is re-enacted ubiquitously all over again. Hence, the desert is Jabès' central metaphor for reality because in the desert everything finds itself ultimately fragmented and, yet, because of it, appears unified.

The Jabèsian *Tzimtzum*: An Outline

Having sketched the general "mechanics" of the catastrophe, we can focus on the vision of the originary event that initiated it. As elucidated above, the vision is an explicitly self-proclaimed myth and an imaginary rendition of the event.[40] For Jabès, thus, describing the disaster is not part of either theology or metaphysics since this kind of disaster invalidates theology and metaphysics as such because thinking about the disaster *re-enacts it* rather than *refers to it*. Therefore, the description of the primordial catastrophe can be regarded as nothing other than one of Jabès' innumerable descriptions of the present catastrophe.

Let us assemble the bits and pieces left over from this fictional cosmo-theogony. Jabès' texts put forward a new version of the Lurianic idea of *tzimtzum* – the

---

38 BM, p. 172.

39 LSLS, p. 163.

40 *The Return to the Book* recounts: "And one morning shortly after dawn, Elohim died of the death of His people. The desert counted its wrinkles; eagle and falcon rushed to spread the news. Since then every day is twelve hours of mourning for the day" (BQ I, p. 321). If Jabès first seems to describe an event bound to a particular moment ("one morning"), towards the end of the passage, the event turns out to be a fiction only as it presupposes day, night and, consequently, also that morning. The originary event already assumes that which made it possible and, as such, it is just an imaginary rendering. By the way, the excerpt interestingly plays with the Nietzschean motif of God's death and animals from *Zarathustra*.

withdrawal of God in the act of Creation.[41] The first point they make is the eva-
nescence and perishment of God, who existed once in one way or another, but
now only the void remains after him.

[…] God will die in a conflagration.[42]

Nobody has seen God, but the stages of His death are visible to all of us.[43]

---

41 Briefly speaking, Luria's concept of *tzimtzum* explains the preliminary stage of
     Creation in which the primordial, undifferentiated pleroma of Divine light (or, more
     precisely, *Ein-Sof*) must transform to make room for creation. Discussing Luria's ideas,
     Chaim Vital explains that before creation there was no empty place (מוקם פנוי, *makom
     pnui*) for beings to occupy. Thus "[w]hen [*Ein-Sof*] determined to create its world
     and to issue forth the world of emanated entities, to bring to light the fullness of His
     energies […], names, and qualities, this being the reason for the creation of the world
     […], *Ein-Sof* then withdrew itself from its centermost point, at the center of its light,
     and this light retreated from the center to the side, and thus there remained a free
     space, an empty vacuum." As the Divine presence clustered at the sides, in the middle
     tehiru, a void, was produced. In the same process, *Ein-Sof* shed the elements of harsh
     judgment, *Din*, which remained in *tehiru*. In this way, they amassed into amorphous
     matter, *golem*, encircled by *Ein-Sof*. This preliminary phase of Creation involves, so
     to speak, a preparation of materials going into Creation proper. Interestingly, Luria's
     metaphors draw on the paraphernalia of an artist or a sculptor as after *tzimtzum Ein-
     Sof* sends a beam of its light towards the matter of *golem* to give it shape and mould
     it like a sculpture, making vessels (*kelim*) emerge from it that will serve to take in
     Godhead. Nevertheless, when the vessels were being filled with Divine light, they
     turned out incapable of holding perfection. Only the first three vessels were able to
     take in the God-emanated sefirot while the following ones fell into pieces. In this way,
     קליפות, *kelippot* – shells of shattered vessels composed basically of the dark matter of
     Judgment – came into being, still containing some sparks of light. Some of the sparks
     are souls lost after the fall of Adam. The primordial catastrophe of Creation directly
     necessitates salvation effected through partial acts of *tikkun*, repair, to which man
     is summoned. See Lawrence Fine, *Physician of the Soul, Healer of the Cosmos: Isaac
     Luria and His Kabbalistic Fellowship* (Stanford, CA: Stanford UP, 2003), pp. 126–44,
     quotation on p. 128.
     Luria's system is very elaborate. Additionally, the various accounts of it handed down
     by Luria's students differ widely. However, the fundamental structure of this Kabbalah
     is recognisable. It frames Creation as consisting of two movements: (1) first, *Ein-Sof*
     contracts as a result of *tzimtzum*, whereby a space is created to hold both beings and
     the matter from which they will be formed; and (2) then, *Ein-Sof* creates the world. At
     the latter stage, the catastrophe takes place.
42 BQ I, p. 160.
43 BQ II, p. 224.

When I call to God, I call to the Sense of the Void.[44]
God's absence is the infinite void that holds up the world.[45]

Clearly, Jabès does not simply assume that God does not exist; rather, building to a degree on Nietzsche, he presupposes *an event* as a result of which God does not exist in the present.[46] God's non-existence is not a simple refutation of the thesis that he exists; instead, it is a real, piercing and nearly palpable absence that calls for embracing the fiction of the disaster in which God died leaving emptiness behind. Therefore, God continues to be a fundamental structure organising the world, but its principle lies in absence now. "He is an image of lack."[47] If in Western metaphysics God could be the fullness of being, in Jabès he is the centre of absence:

... *God, the Absent, but beyond the power of absence, hence bound to be present where all presence has been revoked?*[48]

The disappearance of God does not affect only him; on the contrary, it stamps itself on reality as such because in place of presence it instils absence as a constitutive principle. And if absence has replaced presence, the new, absent God has likewise replaced the old God. But on closer inspection, we can see that the event did not change some primordial, "normal" reality into a new, absence-based one. As in Luria, *Creation itself entails absence*; the negative principle of reality has been in force since the very beginning.

Thereby, Jabès turns out to be an heir to a vast philosophical and theological tradition that differentiates between God from before Creation (in the Kabbalah usually referred to as *Ein-Sof*) and God after Creation.[49] The latter is

44 *Ibid.*, p. 157.
45 F, p. 20.
46 Cf. Handelman, "Torments," p. 56.
47 P, p. 34.
48 BQ II, p. 230.
49 For example, the *Zohar* speculates that in the opening of the Torah, *'Elohim* in "*bereszit bara 'Elohim*" serves as the direct object rather than the subject. As such, it reproduces, so to speak, the creation of God-*'Elohim* out of *Ein-Sof*. *'Elohim* in turn is God whose name combines two attributes: *Mi* and *Eleh*. *Mi*, i.e. the Hebrew "who," refers to the subject – to "the eternal subject...the great Who, Mi who stands at the end of every question and every answer" (Scholem, *Jewish Mysticism*, p. 220). *Eleh* is the "determinable world," a sphere of "this and that" – of all the attributes of the Divine being about which questions can be asked and answers obtained. Simplifying somewhat, *'Elohim*, by merging the realms of *Mi*, the subject, and *Eleh*, the object, belongs to the world in which there is knowledge, attributes are separable from the thing and the knower from the known. *'Elohim* overshadows unknowable and unobjectifiable *Ein-Sof*, barely pointed at as a glimmer on the horizon but entirely incompatible with thinking (see *Ibid.*, p. 221).

co-determined by Creation or, even, was created in it himself, supplanting the primordial, undifferentiated God from before Creation. The fiction of these two forms of Godhead is conveyed, for example, in the following passages:

> God let go of God in death and set himself up as an example.[50]
> God, the uncreated, that is, created before God, being where nothing exists. God, the creator and hence destroyer of God, because the All had to show proof of its innate Totality as it faced the void down to the final stripping where victim and hangman embrace and sink into baffling absence.[51]
> Time affirms, confirms what is; eternity denies.
> God is in time, not in eternity.
> Thus God has killed God.[52]

God-the-Creator replaces God-the-Uncreated. In the principle of reality, which is absence, *he can exist only as the absent one*; that is why the God present before Creation had to die. In Jabès' thoroughly paradoxical, apophatic thinking, *God still exists but, exactly, as non-existent* because Creation is now grounded in absence.

However, unlike Luria, Jabès identifies the act of Divine vanishing with God's use of the word, with Divine speech. In other words, Creation and Revelation, *tohu vabohu*, as well as Sinai, are one and the same event to him. God dies not only in the act of Creation but also in his book:

> *God is silent for having once spoken in God's language.*
> […] The death of God in the book has given birth to man.
> […] "If I spoke the language of God," […] "Men would not hear me. For He is the silence of all words."[53]
> The divine word is disquieting smoke. It has never been a blast of strange and terrifying sounds, but a harmonious coiling of a trace burning in the warm air coming down from Sinai. Trace of a trace reverberating in its infinite interdiction.[54]
> *"God was the first to break silence," he said. "It is this breakage we try to translate into human languages."*[55]
> *"We read the word in the sunburst of its limits, as we read the Law through Moses' angry gesture, through the breaking of the divine Tables," he said.*
> *In the exploded word, God collides with the hostility of the letters.*
> *Even outside the Name, God is a prisoner of the Name.*[56]

---

50 BQ II, p. 186.
51 *Ibid.*, p. 225
52 BQ II, p. 277.
53 BQ I, p. 224, 226, 255.
54 BQ II, p. 188.
55 *Ibid.*, p. 353.
56 *Ibid.*, p. 377.

This would imply that God is the only writer, and every book a privileged moment in the reading of the Book.[57]
The Book holds God's absence. O word sealed for oblivion. Men received it not, but loyal to the Letter, they multiplied the book [...].[58]
God spoke, and what He said became our symbols. [...] *His voice is inaudible, but it is the supporting silence which allows our sounds to be discrete* [...].[59]

This is where one of Jabès' most essential assumptions lies. Namely, as the passages above imply, the death of God is linked to him leaving a *message*. In other words, God is subject to the same process as any writer and, generally, any creature that produces an utterance within a symbolic system. Of course, the thesis could be construed as rehearsing a Romantic cliché: the author disappears from the text and, as he is no longer present in it, only his trace is left behind, bedimmed. But Jabès posits something far more poignant: he views each utterance as a failure caused by the very structure of reality, for articulation entails subordination to the order which is structurally other to the utterer. The utterance means dismantling the illusory sovereignty of a being that interacts with a network of structures. *Any attempt at speaking leads to a fundamental ontological displacement whose effects are marked by the catastrophe.*

The same displacement happens also in the act of creation. That is why Jabès can identify Creation with Revelation. They are, apparently, completely different acts: in Creation, God issued forth things while in Revelation He handed down the Law, thereby leaving his utterance behind. Nevertheless, in Jabès' view, both these events involve the C/creator entering the realm entirely beyond H/him, in which H/he fails. Creation – or the utterance – produced in this way is erected upon the absence of the C/creator. Therefore, it can be proposed that, in fact, the originary disaster is not a *cause* of the disintegration whose outcomes we witness. Rather, it seems the first manifestation of an inevitable conflict inscribed in the very structure of reality.

This is what lies at the core of the universality of the Jabèsian *tzimtzum*, the mechanism of which involves God as much as any writer.

57 *Ibid.*, p. 378.
58 *Ibid.*, p. 386.
59 *Ibid.*, p. 400. In this passage, Jabès seems to draw directly on the *Zohar*'s vision of Creation: "God spoke – this speech is force which at the beginning of creative thought was separated from the secret of *En-Sof.*" In Scholem, *Jewish Mysticim*, p. 216.

Tzimtzum as an Ontological Principle

Having discussed the consequences of the catastrophe and its underlying mechanism, we can engage in more abstract philosophising. I will attempt to show how the effects of the catastrophe – therein the change of presence into absence and of God-the-Uncreated into God-the-Creator – are all reducible to a fundamental ontological displacement which can be identified with the Jabèsian version of *tzimtzum*. Jabès' *tzimtzum* differs essentially from Luria's, and the two will be compared below. My analysis is informed by the idea that any act of creation and the writing process are identical.

The following three passages are crucial to my interpretation:

We are all equal before language.[60]

Before the Creation, God could expect everything of God, just as the writer can expect everything of his pen before the book, and the book everything of the book before it is written.[61]

God's heritage could only be handed on in the death He ushered in. [...] At this time before time, [...] one small point in space contained, like a bubble, all the wanderings of the worlds. When it burst, it freed the universe, but gave form to exile. God had disappeared, existing only in Creation. [...] Never again will we escape exile. The book is among its true stages.[62]

The first passage implies that by "language" Jabès does not mean human language. Rather, "language" designates first of all – and in keeping with some insights of Jewish tradition (picked up anew in the 20th century by Benjamin) – a *system whose rules one must observe to actualise anything*. Everybody, God Himself including, is equal before it. Therefore, God finds Himself in the same position as a writer starting to write. This position is encapsulated in the second passage: any creation is preceded by envisaging or hoping; a maker can "expect everything." Jabès seems to suggest that God and a writer both expect to produce a perfectly tractable work and to execute fully the conceived design. Before the act of creation, no element defiant of the author mars the vision.

The third passage discloses, however, that the vision is just an illusion engendered by the creator's specific position *before* the work, and fails in and with the act of creation. The "time before time" evoked by Jabès is nothing other but the illusory time possible only where the real time has not set in yet. The illusory time is a period of a unique pleroma, where "each point in space contains all the

---

60 LR I, p. 79.
61 BQ II, p. 224.
62 *Ibid.*, pp. 143–4.

wanderings of the worlds." As in Parmenides, it is sphere-like and impeccably symmetrical. Hence the space from before creation is perfectly homogeneous. Given this fact, the C/creator's misbelief must be induced by the illusory time in which he is steeped, and the perfection he envisages must reflect only this primordial, empty homogeneity.

This idea finds further confirmation in the third passage, which describes the catastrophe that happens at the moment of the real creation. Jabès foregrounds at least two of its aspects. First, a previously hidden dimension is revealed: "the universe is freed." The earlier sameness is destroyed, and a new, internally asymmetrical space comes into being. In this optics, the fullness of the initial vision seems to veil a space that has already been there and *is entirely incommensurable with the vision*. The act of creation turns out to be self-destructive as it puts an end to a vision that made it possible in the first place and, at the same time, reveals an otherness that defies the design. Second, the author (God, too) is himself destroyed, which indicates that also his existence was part of the initial vision. As a result, the space of the created things becomes a domain of exile. This means that the author, in a way, lingers on after the catastrophe, but he does so only in a mutilated form: his nature, as entwined with the fullness of the vision, remains fundamentally incompatible with the created space he is now destined to inhabit.

These conclusions will help us specify the mechanisms of the Jabèsian take on *tzimtzum*. Emphatically, unlike in Luria, Jabès' *tzimtzum* is not a single disturbance in the act of Creation but *a permanent effect of a fundamental incongruity between the imaginary and the real*.

The Imaginary and the Real

What is the difference between "the imaginary" and the "real"?[63] How come they are so fundamentally incommensurate that when they meet, a disaster happens?

---

63 Importantly, although "the imaginary" and "the real" may be redolent of the Lacanian imaginary-symbolic-real triad, here they have a decisively distinct meaning of their own. I propose to understand them without any Lacanian subtext. Separated from the real by *tzimtzum*, the imaginary penetrates deeper than RSI by shuffling off *l'imaginaire*, an element that is essentially alien to the triad and a residue of Lacan's early thought. In Jabès, the imaginary is closer to the symbolic. Thus, the realm that Lacan theorises only through *le réel* could be rendered by us in two categories: reality and *tzimtzum*. This, as I will show further in this book, makes it possible to grasp both the indescribable outside of the symbolic order, where it collapses, and the realm of multiple unmediated

Here, we come across a compelling element of Jabèsian thinking that sets him apart from Luria's cosmogonic speculations and brings him more in unison with the core of modern Western philosophy. To Jabès, the difference between the imaginary and the real does not mirror the incommensurability of the Divine power and the capacity of the "vessels" which are to hold it. Such a classic Lurianic explanation, albeit potentially relevant philosophically, does not accommodate the issues pondered in Kantian and post-Kantian philosophy. Jabès, on his part, locates the principle of *tzimtzum* in re-configuring *the relation between singularity and multiplicity*, which immediately confronts him with the same problems that bothered Kant.

To explore these insights, we can start from observing that in Jabès the domain of the imaginary makes up a singular symbolic system that has multiple equal elements for its objects. The imaginary enables the author to shape his work at will, assuming a dominant position vis-à-vis his subordinate objects. The imaginary itself does not seem to be subject to temporality at all: at any moment, the elements appear to be determined in the same way and can be combined and re-combined as the author wishes. The imaginary is thus analogous to the Kantian and Hegelian understanding (*Verstand*). First, it seems universal in the realm it organises; second, it predetermines certain objects, making them amenable to arranging in freely chosen relationships; and, third, its basic construction seems unchangeable over time. Consequently, *the imaginary is a mode of shaping relations between singularity and multiplicity in which the apparent unity of a system enables it to produce an effect of multiplicity within it. Nevertheless, this effect is possible only at the cost of a fundamental, internal limitation (selectiveness) of the system and its elements.*

The real functions in the opposite way. Its primary organising principle is multiplicity of fundamentally incommensurable elements. Each of them is singular in an entirely different way than elements of the imaginary: rather than embedded in a universal system (a "concrete universal," to use the Hegelian term), singularity is primordial and inexplicable. For this reason, in Jabès, the real is asymmetrical and does not allow either passing freely from one element to another or, even less so, arranging them in relations. As such, the real on this model cannot be accommodated in one dimension of time, for, as Kant showed, this would presuppose a homogenous "temporal series" shared by all the elements whereas the "elements" of the real resemble the Kantian things in

---

symbolic orders, in which a given form of the imaginary-real oppositions turns out to be one of many.

themselves, lacking a shared dimension in which to compare them. Hence, the Jabèsian real is *a mode of forming relations between singularity and multiplicity in which the primary multiplicity of "elements" entails their radical singularity. As such, the real is not subject to any limitation and seems to encompass everything that exists or can exist.*

Thus, the imaginary and the real seem to be uniquely interrelated and mutually dependent. The imaginary would not be possible without the real, which it conceals and, subsequently, reveals when failing. At the same time, the real could not be known even in a flawed way were it not for the symbolic system that fosters the imaginary.

Notably, Jabès employs a characteristic strategy. He does not explore the details of mechanisms behind the imaginary and the real, unlike his contemporary structuralists and poststructuralists (e.g. Lacan and Derrida), who puzzled over them, albeit under different names and in different configurations. Instead, he is preoccupied with the dislocation of the relation between singularity and multiplicity and with the effects thereof. Of course, this focus is easily explained by recalling that Jabès is more of a poet than a meticulous theoretician, but his strategy might be informed by a deeper philosophical insight. Namely, he analyses the most elementary structure of relations that seems to determine both knowledge and existence. Hence, he can think in the same way of Creation and Revelation, of bringing forth a being and writing a sentence and, finally, of God and a writer. There is, in this strategy, a striving to radically simplify, in which central concerns of modern Western philosophy are given a re-thinking and which, unexpectedly, revives traditional themes speculated on of old in Jewish thought, such as framing Creation as a linguistic act.[64] Paradoxically, the simplicity of this radicalism can make Jabès come across as questing for some species of "first philosophy" in confrontation with the wilderness of post-war thinking. That is why in this, and only this, sense, the conclusions his works suggest can be referred to as ontology even as this ontology overthrows all tenets of Aristotelian ontology.

Tzimtzum as the Principle of Discontinuity

Having outlined the differences between the imaginary and the real, we can resume our discussion of the mechanism behind the Jabèsian *tzimtzum*. As already mentioned, *tzimtzum* is engendered by the incommensurability of the imaginary and the real. But what is *tzimtzum* as such? We can posit that, to Jabès,

---

64 See Gross, *L'aventure*, pp. 19–20.

tzimtzum – manifest in any act of creation or writing – constitutes a moment of discontinuity in which the imaginary collapses and mutates into the real. Given the properties listed above, it entails a dislocation of the relation between singularity and multiplicity. In *tzimtzum*, the prior multiplicity of the elements of the imaginary is revealed as spawned by a single system, with this apparently universal system being at the same time exposed as one of many. If, earlier, multiplicity ensued from the basic singularity, after *tzimtzum* singularity of *entire systems* is disclosed to be an effect of their fundamental multiplicity. Clearly, Jabès' insights about *tzimtzum* are directly related to Derrida's notion of inscription, albeit they concern (conventionally speaking) the ontological plane.

Starting from these observations, we will attempt to discuss the essential features of the Jabèsian *tzimtzum* not as explicitly portrayed by the poet himself, but as translated into an ontological abstraction. First, to Jabès, *tzimtzum* is not a lone event that separated *Ein-Sof* from the creation once and for all; instead, it is a perpetually repeated *point of dislocation* of various relations between singularity and multiplicity. Jabès actually does not envision a universal history since history is either a perspectival construct (referred to above as the illusory time) or a persisting discontinuity of the real time. Hence, there cannot be *one*, single, definitive event. To construe it as an incessant repetition of *tzimtzum* or as a manifestation of one and the same *tzimtzum* is equally valid.

This has far-ranging implications. First, the function that philosophy tends to attribute to time is, in Jabès, invested in space, and in a specific, extended sense to boot. Since time is dependent on the transition from the imaginary to the real and both forms of time – the illusory and the real – exist either before or after a given act of *tzimtzum*, time as such can no longer feature as a universal series for all events. The role is, instead, performed by space conceived as a set of all *points of tzimtzum*.

Second, *tzimtzum* is a point of discontinuity. Indeterminate though the term is, we would be hard pressed to come up with a better moniker to describe the collapse between the imaginary and the real. Discontinuity as conceived by Jabès is a successor to both negative theology and the Kantian "things in themselves." As such, it cannot be accounted for or depicted other than from a distance, for it demarcates the boundary between two orders of being. And it is the outermost point in each of them. For this very reason, no account provided by these orders can accommodate discontinuity; namely, the imaginary does not explain how a created thing comes into being while the real does not render the moment of moulding by the meaning that was part of the imaginary. *Tzimtzum*, therefore, seems not only a transition point between the orders, but also a site where they are revealed as mutually determined. *Tzimtzum* as such, however, is *nothing*; as in Luria, it can be described only in terms of negation – as a curtailment or a withdrawal that wrecks one order and commences another one.

Third, in Jabès, *tzimtzum* stamps each of the two orders with a primal flaw, which makes them incomplete. As a result, neither of them is adequate in and by itself. Let us look into them one by one. The order of the imaginary is incomplete insofar as it calls for a real creation. Despite its correspondence to the pleroma, it lacks the realness which it tries to form in its semblance. It is therein that its "original sin" lies:

> [...] original sin was only an insane quest for divine harmony. To be a world in a hand and a word. To say what is written, to create what is read.[65]

Jabès ascribes to each of these orders a moment of utopia, located exactly where their imperfection resides and inciting the respective order to move towards self-transcendence and, thus, towards the *tzimtzum* point. The utopia of the imaginary is a utopia of harmonious creation in which the meaning and the matter of writing remain in perfect concord.[66] The real is incomplete insofar as it cannot find contentment in its material, mute existence but continues to strive for self-understanding, thereby breeding a new imaginary. Its utopia lies in self-understanding and self-accommodation. Through these moments of utopianism, *tzimtzum* imbues the world with an inner dynamics.

These observations indicate that *tzimtzum* takes place not only in the passage from the imaginary to the real (that is, creation or writing in Jabès' model) but also in the opposite conversion. For if both the imaginary and the real are incomplete orders interlaced in a certain discontinuity, *tzimtzum* seems symmetrical to them. But when is it that a transition from the real to the imaginary takes place? As Jabès suggests, it is when a new writing design surfaces.

If so, *tzimtzum* would be the node that binds the imaginary and the real, determining both these orders and experienced whenever one folds into the other, which happens as a result of their internal movement propelled by incompleteness.

To trace this movement, I will now analyse the cycle of *tzimtzum* as it unfolds in the act of writing.

---

65 BQ I, p. 401.

66 It comes in the form of a future harmonious creation and of the past lost perfection. It is in this sense that Jabès writes that "the age of transparency haunts [*hante*] human memory" (LSLS, p. 282).

An Example of the *Tzimtzum* Cycle: The Act of Writing

As already discussed, the structure of *tzimtzum* determines all creation – both Divine Creation and the work of a common writer.[67] Although *tzimtzum* as such is not directly graspable, if it constantly repeats itself, it can be experienced in a way. With this in mind, we can follow Jabès and try to pinpoint manifestations of *tzimtzum*. Undoubtedly, we come across them twice. First, *tzimtzum* must give rise to the imaginary by abandoning the domain of the real and bringing forth a design of creation. Afterwards, it will come to pass again as the design fails.

To start with, let us explore the first *tzimtzum*. It is expressed in the following passage:

> If anything exists, there is no creation at all [*Si quelque chose existe, il n'y a point création*].[68]

Jabès, a kabbalist of the French language, mingles two ideas in this sentence. First, he suggests that if anything *already* exists, creation is out of the question. For creation must enjoy a stretch of freedom, of emptiness unmarred by any prior existence. By the same token, a writer cannot venture to write knowing that something has been written before. How is it then possible that creation happens anyway? This is explained by the other insight, conveyed by the operator of negation "*ne... point*" ["not at all"]. The negation, namely, can be construed in keeping with the Jabèsian premise of the negative nature of existence proper. On this take, "*ne... point*" will mean *the negative existence of a point dividing the existing thing from creation*, and the whole sentence will read "if anything exists, there is a point of creation."

What does it mean? In the light of Jabès' other observations, it means that *since some things exist before new creation, creation is possible only if preceded by the rise of a dividing point of discontinuity*. All creation must eschew the past and

---

67 Like many Jewish thinkers before him – such as, for example, Jehuda Halevi – Jabès equates Creation with the foundation of writing, a matter formed by meaning in a way. Cf. Gross, *L'aventure*, pp. 53–4. In this way, he subscribes to thinking about creation as writing and about the real as made of Divine signs, a movement initiated by the *Sefer Yetzirah*. See Gershom Scholem, "Name of God and the Linguistic Theory of the Kabbalah," part 2, *Diogenes* 80, 1972, pp. 164–94, on pp. 181–6. The late kabbalists, such as Moses Cordovero, identified this process with a rupture in which the erstwhile complete Torah accrues materiality and becomes the imperfect textual corpus that we know. Gershom Scholem, "La signification de la Loi dans la mystique juive," in *Le Nom et les symboles de Dieu*, p. 133.

68 LH, p. 50.

engender its own, separate plane.[69] It is in the moment of this primal – and *specifically* determined – reduction of reality that the contraction of *tzimtzum* takes place, fostering the design of creation. A writing venture, likewise, is possible only if the past is erased:

> [...] All creating involves a splitting of time [*fraction du temps*], which, devoid of the past, is obliteration in itself.[70]

The "first" *tzimtzum* entails thus an erasure of the past and a breakdown of time: as the real folds into the imaginary, the real time mutates into the illusory time. The way to the "pleroma" of the creative imagination is opened, and the *freshly arisen* author is at liberty to manoeuvre the building blocks. Now, however, he inexorably faces a creative act bound to induce another manifestation of *tzimtzum*.

So much for the "first" *tzimtzum*. Its second manifestation can be gleaned from a longer passage in an interview with Marcel Cohen:

> Writing is risk-taking [...] There is a notable difference between expressing oneself orally and in writing. One does not speak up without having a more or less clear idea of what one wants to say. In the first case one can say only what has been done, achieved, finished. The spoken word is limited by time and space. It is a first degree *récit* [a story, a telling]: everything has happened and the end is known beforehand.
> In the second case [of writing], everything is in flux, in gestation, and we are riveted to this world of vocables being born. We are ignorant not only of what the book will be, but also of what it tries to express objectively – and even implicitly against us – insofar as the words have the initiative. *The risk consists in indefinitely opening the book to the book. This opening also is the chasm, the abyss in which the writer stands* [emphasis added].
> [...] What book is written? What book is read? Are we facing anew risk, perhaps the greatest of all, for if the future comes through words [*passe par les mots*] – and words are never innocent and prepare enactment [*passage à l'acte*], in the sense that the book forms our minds and sensibilities at the same time – what future is it?
> Any author [*createur*] would thus be, against himself, responsible for a future [*un futur*] which he has no way to command. Simultaneously, he fully grasps the importance of interpretation, commentary which can distort the text so much that it will be irreversibly adulterated even though no adulteration will have happened.[71]

---

69 Jabès shares this belief with Benjamin, to whom the bare, absurd continuity of history is just a pile of debris. Creative practice hinges upon an originary curtailment. Both Benjamin and Jabès describe this reduction using the notion of oblivion.

70 QQLS, p. 17.

71 DB, pp. 81–2.

In the excerpt above, "the spoken word" is contrasted with "writing" as the former lacks the originary *tzimtzum*: it refers to things that have already happened, relates the past and does not seek to create anything new. Therefore, a spoken utterance is easily formed since it does not rely on a design but on what has already come to pass. Writing, in turn, entails risk, including also existential risk, because of *tzimtzum*, which opens and closes it. In the latter (closing) *tzimtzum*, an incongruity is revealed of the imaginary and the written words expected to execute the design. No longer safeguarded by the illusion of the imaginary, the words return into the real. That is why *tzimtzum* cuts off the design from the execution, imposing on the author a peculiar responsibility for the future he cannot control. *The future belongs to words which exist in a different temporal order than the one available to the author.* Therefore, the catastrophe is intrinsic to the act of writing itself as the design must concern the domain which it does not encompass due to the very fact of having been executed.

In Jabès' account, *tzimtzum* turns out to be an inexorable discontinuity which makes creation possible (because the real alone cannot craft anything without the imaginary) and, at the same time, causes its disintegration (because the imaginary cannot be fully transposed into the real). The discontinuity must be transcended twice – before and after creation.[72] As a result of *tzimtzum*, created things bear indelible traces[73] that represent the specific rhythm of the toppling

---

72 Also in this respect, Jabès' *tzimtzum* parallels Luria's. In some versions of Lurianic thinking, the process of creation commences from God inscribing the Name into the emptiness of *tehiru*. The inscribing starts with the letter *jod* (י), often identified by the kabbalists with a point. See Marc-Alain Ouaknin, *Concerto pour quatre consonnes sans voyelles. Au-delà du principe d'identité* (Paris: Payot, 2003), p. 96. This inscription becomes a trace of the Divine presence that has removed itself from the world. God must first undergo a contraction to later perish in writing. In a further analogy between Jabès and Luria, *tzimtzum* is a prerequisite of the sheer possibility of writing – of the formation of the triad of a writer, a design and matter in which the inscription is made. Only then can the withdrawal of the writer from the work take place.

73 To express the discontinuity of *tzimtzum* that stamps the creation, Jabès frequently uses the metaphor of a wound. The first *Book of Questions* opens with musings on wounding: "*Mark the first page of the book with a red maker. For, in the beginning, the wound is invisible*" (BQ I, p. 13). Waldrop argues that it concerns both a writer and a Jew, in whose case wounding appears as circumcision, which makes him part of a community irrevocably marked by the event of Law-giving (*Lavish Absence*, p. 3). Nevertheless, also this discontinuity is only a re-enactment of the primary discontinuity resulting from Creation itself. For, as Nahon emphasises, "the primordial separation" is a kind of continually repeated "wound" or "burn": creation takes place incessantly and each moment witnesses a cut of a new beginning. Nahon, "Question," pp. 67–8.

of the imaginary and the real. The traces are easily observable in writing, which always makes "too little" sense to be fully interpretable and, simultaneously, "too much" sense to be treated as a common, material thing. So while the act of writing embodies the cycle of *tzimtzum*, its outcome – the text – offers a model of any created thing that is fragmented, harbours inner contradictions and defies any interpretive closure.[74]

Tzimtzum in Jabès and in Luria

Having outlined the theory of *tzimtzum* useful in interpreting Jabès' writings, we can examine how it compares with Luria's original framework. Which elements of Luria's concept are re-configured in Jabès and why? And, essentially, with Jabès, have we not strayed too far from the proper Safed mysticism to speak of *tzimtzum* legitimately in the first place?

To start with, I must admit that, in the foregoing, I identified Jabès' *tzimtzum* with two moments of creation which Luria viewed as entirely distinct, i.e. *tzimtzum* and *shevirat ha-kelim*. The Lurianic *tzimtzum* conveys the undifferentiated pleroma of *Ein-Sof* into a ruptured universe consisting of the central void – *tehiru* – filled with the dark matter of *golem* and enveloped in the withdrawn light of *Ein-Sof*. This Divine "inhalation" generates only two dimensions

---

74 Commenting on this Jabèsian idea, Derrida insists that writing generally provides a model of a specific kind of creation – ruptured and fragmented: "No 'logic,' no proliferation of conjunctive undergrowth can reach the end of its [writing's] essential discontinuity and non-contemporaneousness, the ingenuity of its *under-stood* [...] silences. The other originally collaborates with meaning. There is an essential *lapse* between significations which is not the simple and positive fraudulence of a word, nor even the nocturnal memory of all language. To allege that one reduces this lapse through narration, philosophical discourse, or the order of reasons and deduction, is to misconstrue language, to misconstrue that language is the *rupture* with totality itself. The fragment is neither a determined style nor a failure, but the form of that which is written. Unless God himself writes – and he would still have to be the God of the classical philosophers who never interrupted nor interrogated himself, as did the God of Jabès. (But the God of the classical philosophers, whose actual infinity did not tolerate the question, precisely had no vital need for writing). As opposed to Being and to the Leibnizian Book, the rationality of the Logos, for which our writing is responsible, obeys the principle of discontinuity. [...] *Assuming* that Nature refuses the leap, one can understand why Scripture will never be Nature. It proceeds by leaps alone." Jacques Derrida, "Edmond Jabès and the Question of the Book," in *Writing*, pp. 71–2.

in which Creation-writing will be possible, referred to by Luria as the Divine light and matter. Only after this division can Creation (giving shape to matter) be attempted, which results in a disaster – the shattering of material vessels intended to hold the Divine light. On this take, *shevirat ha-kelim* explicitly hinges on *tzimtzum*. In Jabès, the undifferentiated pleroma is already part of the imaginary bred by the primordial curtailment of the real. His *Ein-Sof*, a hopeful writer, was engendered by *tzimtzum*. Unlike Luria's God, who is the master of the universe at the beginning at least, Jabès' C/creator is already thrust into it, subject to its laws, and *tzimtzum* is not so much an activity of the C/creator himself as a movement that predates and gives rise to him. That is why the catastrophe that unfolds in the act of writing is the same primordial movement working in the opposite direction. The writer emerges from the real only to dissolve in it again, together with his design.

Two properties of this cycle – i.e. that it is continually repeated and uncontrolled by any power – suggest that, unlike Luria, Jabès views *tzimtzum* and *shevirat ha-kelim* as two facets of the same event. Of course, he implicitly distinguishes "*tzimtzum* as such" (the onset of a new book) from *shevirat ha-kelim* (the failure of the creative act), but he is preoccupied with one, central discontinuity manifest in both these events. For this reason, in my account of the Jabèsian version of *tzimtzum*, I used the term in its deeper meaning of any crack between the imaginary and the real.

Intriguingly, on this view, Jabès uses a nearly Kantian strategy to re-work the Lurianic myth. Instead of rendering the single event of cosmogony in a metaphysical description, he focuses on its conditions of possibility. In this essentially structural elucidation, the Lurianic *tzimtzum* and *shevirat ha-kelim* are one and the same mechanism of ontological displacement. Consequently, instead following Luria in the study of the origin of the fragmentation of reality by tracing the homogenous history back to its beginning, Jabès in fact analyses *one point* which is both prior and posterior as it eludes historical continuity. From which angle the point is examined – whether in terms of the contraction of the real into the imaginary or in terms of the perishment of the imaginary in the real – is irrelevant to the rupture that this point constitutes. Also, it can be experienced in any time. Hence, Jabès, as already mentioned, inscribes time in an abstract space.

Therefore, we may ask whether *tzimtzum* is actually a valid notion in the framework of Jabès' thought. The answer is positive because the movement of "shrinking" and, then, "breaking" of the creation is based on the idea of *reduction*, of delimiting an area by contraction, which is tantamount to *tzimtzum*. Moreover, the Jabèsian *tzimtzum* is not just the moment of Creation anymore, but a fundamental and common law underpinning reality as a whole, with beings not so much experiencing it, the way they did Luria's *Ein-Sof*, as rather arising because of it in the first place. With *tzimtzum* governing the Jabèsian universe, there is no space free of it: free space as such is, exactly, an effect of *tzimtzum*. Clearly, Jabès not only picked up Luria's old idea but also radicalised and expanded it.[75] This transition from 16th-century Safed to 20th-century Paris would not have been possible without the legacy of modern philosophy. In conclusion, I will address the role modern philosophy had in re-inventing *tzimtzum*.

Conclusion: The Jabèsian *Tzimtzum* as a Philosophical Idea of Modernity

Let us first recapitulate the insights of this Chapter. Starting from ascertaining the inevitable fictionality of thinking about the initial catastrophe, I surveyed the consequences of this catastrophe, all of which are classifiable as *incommensurability*. Incommensurable are the illusory and the real time, writing and reading, the possibility of a meaningful account and its validity over time, a perspectival truth and the liminal "truth of the void" and, finally, the meaning and duration of life itself. The disaster is also an event that has left behind the palpable absence of God and, generally, changed the principle of existence from presence to absence. In the next move, relying on the structural correspondence of C/creation and the act of writing, I sketched the dislocation of the relation between singularity and multiplicity, which embodies the nature of *tzimtzum*. *Tzimtzum* is the basic determinant of the Jabèsian universe as it brings forth, divides and determines the imaginary and the real as well as triggers their constant movement vis-à-vis each other. Finally, I spelled out the difference between *tzimtzum* as conceived by Jabès and Luria, showing that Jabès, though indisputably indebted to the Lurianic tradition, distils it radically to define *tzimtzum* as, essentially, an ontological relation. Thereby, he locates his work at the centre of modern philosophical concerns. At this point, we can ask what *tzimtzum* would eventually mean in the modern philosophical language.

---

75 There is a relevant parallel between the literal connotations of *tzimtzum* (holding the breath) and Jabès' metaphors. He often references inhaling and exhaling as a basic rhythm that determines writing. Inhalation is the beginning of the book, as it makes place for it, and exhalation is its execution. Besides, embodying the Freudian category of symptom, Jabès experienced this movement in his own body. Namely, he suffered from asthma, which subsided as he commenced a new text and suddenly worsened when it was submitted to publication.

First, it would mean the point of the primary reduction of the real to a limited symbolic order. Second, it would be where this order bordered with its own outside. As such, *tzimtzum* is a basic break within all meaning, in which a single element must be related to the entirety of the order it belongs to and, at the same time, this order is one of many like ones. In this sense, *tzimtzum* represents the paradox of perspectivism. Third, and most importantly, the Jabèsian *tzimtzum* is *absence as a construction principle behind all existence that is based on a distance between the real and the symbolic order within which this existence unfolds.* On this take, individual existence arises because, though determined and brought forth by the symbolic order, it contains its own *ne plus ultra* – a chasm in which it reveals itself as being one of many orders. For this reason, a thing is not exhausted either in its attributes or in the assumption that it exists outside of them. On the contrary, *it exists as this very rupture that is nothing else but tzimtzum.* This peculiar "atemporality," which forces existence out of its current, albeit historical, framework and makes it deafly inert vis-à-vis meaning – with the inertia seemingly stemming from time immemorial, though in fact only abolishing *the illusory time in which the imaginary comes into being, and yet not passing into the real time* – is a mode of existing in the Jabèsian universe. Consequently, *tzimtzum* can be construed as the central principle of the world that is given to us, a world that defies being definitively contained in any symbolic order, exposes the multiplicity and particularity of these orders and, at the same time, produces the effect of a deaf, deceptively primeval, meaningless thingness. Therefore, *tzimtzum* would be a peculiar, empty *haecceitas* of the modern world, a site of an inner superfluint of all being.

On this model, there is no simple existence as such, no Aristotelian "being at hand." Existence arises where the symbolic order contacts its outside. In other words, in each thing there is a chasm between a meaningful world and all the worlds in which this thing has had other meanings once. Hence the essentially modern effect of superfluity of things and their resistance to meaning, which is so peculiarly bound up with the experience of their materiality and primordiality that Jabès conjures up time and again. The effect, however, would be nothing else but a consequence of the modern perspectival universe. The new materialism surging in the age of *modernitas* would then be necessary for *the emplacement* of the excess ensuing from *tzimtzum*.

If we juxtapose this notion of *tzimtzum* and the concept of Jewish philosophy of modernity as outlined in Chapter One, *tzimtzum* would seem to embody the collapse of transcendence as an ontological principle, i.e. one of the basic tenets of this philosophy. "Restful" and discrete substances of autonomous existence are replaced by objects as defined by Kant, i.e. given shape by certain a-priori orders. In Jabès, these orders are identifiable with the imaginary. By necessity limited and incomplete, they find themselves in constant tension with the outside from which they mark themselves off. The tension is aptly theorised in the Jabèsian *tzimtzum*, which first gives rise to the curtailed imaginary only to unveil its selectiveness and return to the real. *Tzimtzum* punctuates also the incessant internal movement of the universe that has been stripped of transcendence, consequently becoming superfluous and "restless," to use the Hegelian diction. Finally, *tzimtzum* is the same unthinkable boundary between the continuous series and its singular beginning, which corresponds to the antinomies of pure reason in Kant.[76]

Second, Jabès' *tzimtzum* is the "originary" event in a paradoxical manner. Although a fiction in itself, it must be presupposed because of the fragmentation of reality. At the same time, because of its effects, it cannot be considered a single, one-time event; on the contrary, it incessantly manifests itself in subsequent re-enactments. As such, it demolishes the differentiation between an event and being that arises from it. *Tzimtzum*, though ostensibly an act of creation, does not create any being separate from itself because it must persist as the void to bind and, at the same time, divide the orders of the imaginary and the real.

Given these two properties, Jabès' *tzimtzum* can be said to work within the structure found in Jewish philosophy of modernity. On the one hand, it evokes the fiction of a primordial event which determined the entire reality and which thinking strives to fathom. On the other hand, however, it is still a functional construction principle of this reality. Reeling back to the event of the beginning, thinking only reproduces its continually effective condition. In other words, it examines in the fiction of the origin an empty residue that constitutes its current structure. It is no coincidence, therefore, that Jabès implicitly evokes the event of *tzimtzum*, which engrossed Scholem and Bloom, two other "Jewish philosophers of modernity." Perhaps *it is in the persistent resumption of the idea of tzimtzum that this thinking renders its own trace left in it by the shift of modernity.*

In conclusion, Jewish philosophy of modernity seems to be a crucial factor in the Jabèsian re-working of Lurianic inspirations. *Tzimtzum* is no longer the cosmological event of the beginning, but rather an abiding empty centre of the

---

76 "All figures tell the limit. The unlimited could not be a number. It is *before* the limit, *before* figures," writes Jabès, addressing directly the same problem as Kant did (F, p. 75).

world. It can be associated with the originary catastrophe, but such an association must be of mythical nature. Thus, Jabès portrays a world which, at the fundamental level, has been cut off from its beginning, wrested out of the continuum of history and formed by the ubiquitous force of negativity.

As it is still *tzimtzum*, it is Jewish philosophy, but the essence of the event consigns it to modernity.

4 Negative Ontology I: The *Vocable*

Having discussed Jabès' take on *tzimtzum*, we can now examine the philosophy that emerges from his poetry. In this Chapter, I will focus on an underlying grid of recurrent structures. I propose to call this grid negative ontology[1] as it is nothingness that has a central role in it.

To start with, I will discuss the *vocable* – Jabès' basic quasi-concept.[2] As we shall see, the *vocable* can be interpreted as a modern, negative equivalent of being in classic Aristotelian ontology. I will attempt to derive its model from the poet's scattered observations and remarks. Subsequently, I will use this category to outline Jabès' fundamental philosophical insights. Specifically, I will show why *tzimtzum* makes it impossible to describe reality directly and ushers in two modes of rendering it: representation and repetition, each of them defective in its own way. Afterwards, I will explain why Jabèsian ontology cannot be framed as a set of propositions but must become a sustained practice of writing. I will seek to show that Jabès radically re-invents the way in which philosophy can argue anything. I will also define the function of the text that comes into being in this way. These conclusions will help me outline the basic structure of Jabès' ontology,

---

1   I realise that the term "ontology" as used here can stir serious doubt, to say the least. Jabès' thought and classic Western ontology, starting from Aristotle and ending with early Heidegger's fundamental ontology, are considerably incommensurate. The recourse to this category invites already classic objections raised by Derrida, especially in his early texts. At the same time, it is difficult to come up with a less awkward term. Consider only the trouble one is in for talking of, say, "metaphysics." I agree with Matthew Del Nevo, who also addresses Jabès' ontology with the reservation that he does not mean fundamental ontology as conceived by Heidegger, but rather "ontology as a matter of writing." Matthew Del Nevo, "Edmond Jabès and Kabbalism after God," *Journal of the American Academy of Religion*, 65/2 (1997), pp. 403–42, on p. 421. Also Eric Gould believes that although Jabès indeed rejects transcendence, he retains ontology, which is based on writing from now on. Eric Gould, "Godtalk," in *The Sin of the Book*, p. 170.
    To justify the use of the term, I would simply define ontology as an idea of basic relations between forces which come out in the practice of thinking and *cannot have any further attributes*.

2   I will use here the term "quasi-concept," popularised by Derrida, to highlight that Jabèsian categories must not be thought of as stable, logocentric notions. Cf. Jacques Derrida, *Positions: Entretiens avec Henri Ronse, Julia Kristeva, Jean-Louis Houdebine, Guy Scarpetta* (Paris: Editions de Minuit, 1972), p. 124.

with *tzimtzum* and *vocable* as its components. To end with, I will look into how this ontology is related to modern philosophy and to Kabbalistic thinking.

The *Vocable*: The Concept and its Contexts

Jabès' ontology is tightly intertwined with the writerly imaginary. Hence its key concept – the *vocable* – is a term borrowed from the lexicon of linguistics. As the poet admits, when he started using the word, it had been long out of popular circulation and was employed only by linguists.[3]

In Jabès' mature thought, the *vocable* replaces *mot* – the word – which emphasises that the word cannot possibly exist as a unity of meaning and script. More than that, the *vocable* takes on such a fundamental function that it can be regarded as an equivalent of "being" in traditional ontology. Therefore, I shall start my account of Jabès' ontology by discussing this very notion. Exploring the poet's writings, we can distinguish four essential contexts in which the *vocable* appears.

First, the *vocable* is contrasted with *parole*, "living speech." This invites one to play with Romantic clichés of writing as preserving speech while annihilating it at the same time. It is announced in *Yaël* that "The book is always beyond the word [*parole*]. It is the place where the word [*parole*] dies,"[4] and knowing that the book consists of *vocables*, we can define the *vocable* as the death of speech.[5] What "death" is that? It is not just the loss of the author's "presence" or "intention." It is, emphatically, a consequence of *tzimtzum*: in *Aely* Jabès insists that "our words [*vocable*] testify above all to divine obliteration."[6] Speech, as expressed above in the passage from an interview with Marcel Cohen, is a utopian model of the equivalence of meaning and written form,[7] which is ruled out

---

3   See DEJ, p. 308.

4   BQ II, p. 23.

5   Warren F. Motte stresses that, in Jabès, writing is to speech what the desert is to the world we know – its death. Motte, *Questioning*, p. 8.

6   BQ II, p. 214. In the interview with Benjamin Taylor Jabès adds that the unpronounceability of the Tetragrammaton is an ultimate proof of the difference between speech, which persists in the present, and writing, which lasts beyond the moment of being written down (QJQW, p. 17).

7   Jabès would disown himself if he directly prioritised either of an opposition's elements. Without assessing either "speech" or "writing" (therein the *vocable*), he frames speech as a "live" spirit, a writerly intent which "dies" in writing, whereby he emulates old concepts dating back to German Romanticism. But, as we have already seen, he views speech as closed to the future and owing its freedom to the fact that it only re-tells past events. Writing, in turn, is to be the only proper reality or, more than that, the

in the *tzimtzum*-founded world. Therefore, in the first context, the *vocable* is a *vestige of the imagined "full speech"* – still a vehicle of meaning, yet a mutilated and absence-branded one.

Yet Jabès, with dialectical finesse, proceeds from this to a broader notion of the *vocable* and the second sense in which the term is used.

As a nomad his desert, I have tried to circumscribe the blank territory of the page. I have tried to make it my true place, as the Jew has for centuries tried to make his the desert of his book, desert where the voice [*parole*], profane or sacred, human or divine, encounters silence in order to become word [*vocable*], that is, silent utterance of God and final utterance of man.[8]

The strategic moment of this passage lies in that "the voice encounters silence in order to become *vocable*, that is, silent utterance." What does it mean? It means that Jabès introduces a middle term – silence – into the simple opposition of "voice/speech" and "*vocable*." The *vocable* is no longer a vestige of speech, but a unique synthesis of speech and silence. That is why Jabès refers to it as "silent utterance." This paradoxical coinage implies that the *vocable* not only gestures at speech, whose silencing it constitutes, but *is the utterance of silence itself*. If speech is an illusory making-present, what the *vocable* makes present is absence. As such, the *vocable* is a positive means of expressing the negative.

This is consistent with the writer's insights at the Cerisy colloquium:

I called this speech [*parole*] of the book, *this speech of silence*, a *vocable*. For fifty years, writers have not used the word *vocable* anymore. Only linguists have employed it. The way I used it, it was nearly a neologism. I created it almost anew. I did so to underline in how far the listening [*écoute*] of the book is not the listening of everyday... To hear the speech of silence [*silence*], we must perhaps make ourselves more silent [*silencieux*] than

---

very substance of creation. The love of letters alternates in the poet's writings with the hate of their lethal nature. This characteristic ambivalence has been captured by Derrida, who placed it in the context of 20th-century debates between two sets of representations – "Judaism" and the "Greek spirit." As Derrida argues, "[i]n the work of Emmanuel Lévinas can be found the same hesitation, the same anxious movement within the difference between the Socratic and the Hebraic, the poverty and the wealth of the letter, the pneumatic and the grammatical"; Derrida, *Writing*, p. 89. According to Derrida, Jabès is torn, in a degree, between the two traditions, just as Lévinas is. On the one hand, he intuitively draws on the resources of Western literature and philosophy to depict how the writer, unable to express himself, dissolves in the word, and on the other, as if wary of the peril of oversimplification, he resorts to Jewish tradition with its more or less strongly emphasised primacy of writing.

8   BR II, p. 45.

silence itself. There is nothing more silent than the word, and yet it speaks. All sounds are in the word [*mot*], and the written word envelops them in silence.[9]

In the second context, thus, the *vocable* is "speech" which *expresses and makes present nothingness*. Jabès effects a truly dialectical reversal here: the sign that refers back to its referent and cannot make it present is equally a means through which this very absence is expressed. The *vocable* turns out to be the symmetry centre of presence and absence: that which it cannot express is at the same time the other side of what it must express.

The third aspect of the *vocable* is associated with its etymology, which links this word to *vox* – voice.[10] Jabès himself adds that the *vocable* is a derivative of *vocare* – to call.[11] In this framework, the *vocable* is more than a trace of speech, which it was in the first context; it is a trace of a scream. What scream is meant here? The answer is: the primordial, inarticulate response to the disaster and mutilation of creation. Nathalie Debrauwere-Miller offers an illuminating account of this:

> Jabès' work resonates with a scream, a scream of the human being doomed to revolt, a scream of writing that through its rhythm merges with the collective scream of the Shoah survivors, a scream of God, whom his work tries to administer the extreme unction. […] Only the rebellion that persists in a scream belongs, paradoxically, to the order of speaking [*dire*]; [it is] a scream, however, that cannot be screamed out, it is a whisper that ultimately breaks silence to challenge the muteness of God and expose the lies invented by Theists. […] In its essence, Jabès' revolt is not against the absurdity of existence, and it does not express the desire to find man his proper place; the "scream" of remonstration is directed against God, whom, because of his withdrawal from the world, it blames for the absolute evil exemplified to the utmost in "Auschwitz."[12]

In Jabès, the scream is an outcry against absolute evil, which is immanent in the structure of the world after God' withdrawal. Because it is inarticulate, it can be pure expression, for instead of interacting with the world through meanings it *opposes the entire creation as such*.[13] Therefore, it is not only a protest in the

---

9   DEJ, p. 308.
10 According to Helena Shillony, the *vocable* "underscores the dimension of audibility. The word is first a sound, a voice that screams or whispers in the desert." Shillony, *Edmond Jabès*, p. 12.
11 BR II, p. 78.
12 Nathalie Debrauwere-Miller, "La 'Conscience d'un Cri' dans la poetique d'Edmond Jabès," *French Forum*, 30/2 (Spring 2005), pp. 97–119, on pp. 97–102.
13 See also Sydney Lévy, "The Question of Absence," in *The Sin of the Book*, pp. 147–59, on p. 149.

world completely wrecked by a catastrophe,[14] but also the very "spasm ripping the womb of creation."[15] As such, it is both a response to *tzimtzum* and its projection. Thus if in the third framework, the *vocable* is a trace of a scream, it also betrays scream to "collaborate" with words but anyway remains the scream's sole available marking.[16] As Motte points out, the idea of the *vocable* serves Jabès also to underscore the powerlessness of a writer when faced with a real scream as an expression of suffering.[17]

In this third context, the *vocable* acquires an existential dimension.[18] If the *vocable* is a placeholder of being in Jabès, it is not only a mutilated "being" but

---

14 Thomas J. J. Altizer states that in *The Book of Questions* a scream is that which apocalyptically unites nature, history and God; Thomas J. J. Altizer, "The Apocalyptic Identity of the Jew," *Journal of the American Academy of Religion*, 45/3 (September 1977), p. 361. Gabriel Bounoure, writes that "there is a truth of the scream. It is a truth experienced only within an individual existence and remaining a forever unanswered question. An answer could only come from another sphere of life in which the exception of scream would induce a manifestation of speech." Bounoure, *Edmond Jabès*, p. 58.

15 Debrauwere-Miller, "Conscience," p. 108.

16 That is why for Jabés writing "unfolds around a scream" (BQ II, p. 260), constantly addresses it and processes it. How does it happen? It happens in the process of inner self-purification and self-simplification, through which the act of writing is "becoming aware of a scream" (BQ I, p. 16).

17 Warren F. Motte, Jr., "Jabés's Words," *Symposium*, XLI/2 (Summer 1987), pp. 140–56, on p. 143.

18 There are close parallels between this notion of the *vocable* – and, in broader terms, the category of scream in Jabés – and Gerschom Scholem's take on lament in "Uber Klage und Klagelied." See Gerschom Scholem, "On Lament and Lamentation," trans. Lina Barouch and Paula Schwebel, *Jewish Study Quarterly*, 21 (2014), pp. 4–12. Scholem views lament as the opposite of revelation, which for him is a manifestation of linguisticality as such. Adam Lipszyc explains that "the defining feature [of lament] is its liminal character: it is language on the borderline between the said and the withheld, language on the verge of falling mute. Hence lament has no object and no content. If revelation is devoid of any specific content, being, as it is, an absolute fullness of linguistic positivity, lament is devoid of content as language on the threshold of obliteration, a perishing language." Adam Lipszyc, *Sprawiedliwość na końcu języka. Czytanie Waltera Benjamina [Justice on the Tip of the Tongue: Reading Walter Benjamin]* (Kraków: Universitas, 2012), p. 172. In Scholem, lament entails accusation, specifically an accusation of language as a whole and pitting the power of its immanence against it to achieve liberation (cf. *Ibid,*, p. 175). Like in Jabés, the scream embodied in the *vocable* is a complaint against ensnarement in language, a protest against collaboration with the closed symbolic system and advocacy for those disenfranchised in the past. The parallel was brought to my attention by Professor Agata Bielik-Robson.

also one that permanently evokes memories of past tragedies.[19] The very incompleteness of the *vocable* serves as a sign of the disaster and, at the same time, preserves the primordial act of protest against it.

The fourth context is provided by those of Jabès' texts which foreground the materiality of the *vocable*,[20] showing, in particular, how the act of writing down confers on the word [*mot*] a materiality which it did not have before. "All last words are pre-*vocables*,"[21] as Jabès concludes, stressing how important the shift from the word to the *vocable* is in which this materiality effect is produced. Motte theorises writing as

> a process through which normative denotation is put sharply into question, sidestepped or deliberately neglected. The word assumes materiality in the written text; the objectivity of the thing to which it normally refers becomes secondary to the acquired objectivity by the word itself.[22]

The transition from the word to the *vocable* is, of course, tantamount to *tzimtzum* discussed in the previous Chapter. If the word is a function of the symbolic order in which it is meaningful, the *vocable* with its materiality is involved not only in semantic but also in spatial relations as it has a shape, a colour and a position that situate it relative to other things. Compared with the word, which fully belongs to the imaginary, it carries a surplus beyond the dimension of meanings.

To sum up the four contexts before discussing the philosophical concept of the *vocable*: the *vocable* is: (1) a written record of speech that puts its freedom to an end; (2) a sign not only of speech written-down but also of silence which it has confronted; as such it is a *point* in which speech (absent presence) and silence (present absence) meet; (3) a sign of scream as a trace of the disaster and a protest against it; (4) a specific intersection of meaning and materiality.

---

19 In his commentary to *The Book of Questions*, Blanchot juxtaposes Jabés's silent scream in the *vocable* with Buber's vision of Hasidism, where prayer and exalted fervour are abandoned for a soundless scream which is "the Jew's reaction to his own great sorrow." Maurice Blanchot, "Edmond Jabès' *Book of Questions*," *European Judaism: A Journal for the New Europe*, 6/2 (Summer 1972), pp. 34–7, on p. 36.

20 As Motte observes that "[e]ven the dictionary [...] insist upon the material quality of the *vocable*, which is defined as a syntactic rather than a semantic artifact, a word considered as a grouping of orthographic or phonetic integers rather than as a unit of meaning." Motte, "Jabès' Words," p. 144.

21 P, p. 56.

22 Motte, "Jabès' Words," p. 146.

The *Vocable* as an Element of Negative Ontology

Now I will attempt to construct a model of the quasi-concept of the *vocable*. My argument will be fundamentally informed by the idea that the *vocable* negatively takes the place that being has occupied in the long tradition of Western ontology. In that sense, the model can be based on the comparison of the *vocable* and Aristotelian being.

Founded on the legacy of Aristotelian thought, which first set out to explore being as such, Western ontology privileges the concept of *ousia*. As already mentioned in Chapter One, *ousia* is a self-contained being whose qualities can be studied, whereby the study and *ousia* are not fundamentally separate, which makes the classic concept of truth possible. Of course, Aristotle himself assumes that there are various orders of studying (which he comprehensively differentiates while analysing under what aspects beings can be studied in particular ways), but they can freely be selected to refer to various aspects of being without affecting being as such. At the same time, the singularity of a given *ousia*, even though its cause is a weighty philosophical problem, is something that *is there – at hand*.

The *vocable* clearly repudiates this ontological paradigm as it is not a "being at hand." As writing, it is a *particular* combination of meaning (a remnant of the imaginary) and matter (the real). Its singularity does not stem from the originally given independence of *ousia* but from the intersection of *a* symbolic system with the realm in which it is inscribed. The "meaningful" component of the *vocable* is merely a function of the order that pre-determines things (wherein Jabès is revealed as a post-Kantian thinker) while its "material" component remains inscribed in reality as an outside of the order. That this concept is post-Kantian is revealed in that it does not know "being as such," studying which would be *secondary*. Hence, rather than in being itself, the principle of singularisation lies in the *place* where a given order of representation and reality are brought together, that is, the place of *tzimtzum*. As such, the *vocable* explodes the opposition of ontology and epistemology.

The second characteristic ensues from the first one: any *vocable* is a place where *the entire* isolated symbolic system confronts its outside, whereby each *vocable* is fraught with the utter tension of the transcendental boundary. As explained in the previous Chapter, it contains two moments of *tzimtzum*: a rupture between a given perspectival order and reality and the former's repeated breakdown in reality. Brown has observed that the *vocable* is an intersection of universality and absolute singularity.[23] In light of our discussion on the imaginary and the real,

---

23 Llewellyn Brown, "Le rythme et le chiffre: *Le Livre des questions* d'Edmond Jabès," *Litterature*, 103/3 (1996), pp. 52–62, on p. 53.

Brown's observation can be specified as follows: the *vocable* is a site where the inner multiplicity of one order and the multitude of singular orders break down; as such the *vocable* is *a radical particularity that results from the displacement of relations between singularity and multiplicity.* The *vocable* is a crack between the symbolic order and the fact that it is one of many orders; this is what makes the *vocable* utterly singular.

The third characteristic is that the *vocable* cannot be said "to be." What this means is that while being a point where two dimensions dovetail and break, the *vocable* is not subsumed in either of them and, thus, cannot be fully described as "existing," whether as an object or a material thing and, even less, as *ousia.* Just like Derrida's *différance,* it resists thinking and differentiates away the movement that would strive to apprehend it. Thereby, it produces an effect of estrangement as it always generates a gap between "itself and itself."

Consequently, the *vocable* is internally excessive, as compared with *ousia,* in not being a "restful" entity. It embodies both the invasion of the real into the imaginary (which is revealed in the materiality of writing) and a trace of the imaginary in the real (the *vocable,* namely, is this part of matter which sets itself apart through the meaning impressed onto it). As such, the *vocable* has its inner dynamics, and any attempt to capture it from either side produces a shift to the other, which entails a repetition of *tzimtzum.*

More than that, the *vocable* "contains" an emptiness, an ontological displace- ment which has already been identified as Jabèsian *tzimtzum.* The *vocable* came into being "as a result" of *tzimtzum* and still "lasts" in it (inverted commas seem necessary when using metaphysical notions). This emptiness is a *particular* way of separating and, at the same time, tying the two dimensions, a paradoxical centre of symmetry that cannot be experienced other than by the internal asym- metry of one of them.[24] Unlike *ousia,* it is based on the void.

I called the *vocable* a *place* to highlight that it does not belong to the real- imaginary constellation. We could ask whether this place is only a result of the

---

24 This is why it is impossible to define how many "internal elements" add up to a *vocable.* Theoretically, it seems that there are three such elements – a "meaningful" part, a "real" part and an emptiness between them. If it were indeed the case, the *vocable* would resemble the Hegelian negation that cuts two corresponding dimensions apart. But, in each of them, the *vocable* appears as both (1) consisting of two elements (as it belongs to one dimension and contains a "particle" of the other at the same time); and (2) consisting of one element in a peculiar way (as it is an element of this dimension and "something more" at the same time).

two orders collapsing or, rather, a site of connection prior to them. One feature of the *vocable* is that this question cannot be conclusively answered. It can be regarded both as a peculiar illusion of an excess place emerging in a confrontation of the two dimensions and as *a place which is part of still another space*. What space would that be? It would be an assemblage of all possible configurations of the imaginary and the real. Jabès calls it the whiteness of the Book on which *vocables* inscribe themselves. I will discuss this in detail in Chapter Seven.

If we assume this space, we should conclude that *vocables* interact with one another in specific ways. Because for Jabès the whiteness of the page and *vocables* together make up the Book, this would serve as a plane of these interactions. It would mean, however, that, besides separating particular configurations of the imaginary and the real, each *vocable* had an additional dimensions that determined its placement in the Book. Hence, the *vocable* could also be said to be a cut-off point of a *particular imaginary-real configuration from the infinite number of such configurations*. In this way, the concept of the *vocable* opens huge theorising vistas as it makes it possible to differentiate between (1) the real as an ensemble of several symbolic orders, yet not as the entire set but as one viewed from the perspective of the order whose singularity is revealed in writing; and (2) the Book as a set of configurations of symbolic orders and their *corresponding* dimensions of reality. The *vocable* is thus the point of rupture between (1) and (2). Consequently, the *vocable* is a concept that urges to go beyond any as-yet thought-of outside of a given order as already marked by its formation. Also, the *vocable* makes possible abstract theorisation of an order as one of many without defining this multiplicity, which would entail it being determined by this order.

Finally, the *vocable*, which always refers to its own impossibility and to the illusion of completion whose loss it seems to be, refers also constantly to the past catastrophes which have left palpable absence behind. The *vocable*, a mutilated "non-being," is an embodied scream.

Thus, the concept of the *vocable* enables Jabès to construct a specific "a-ontology" in which "existence" – insofar as it is still possible – is based on a fundamental sundering within creation. For the *vocable* is neither an entity nor a nonentity, nor a signifier,[25] nor pure matter. It has an inner dynamics of *tzimtzum*

---

25 According to Francois Laruelle, Jabès' *vocable* is, in a sense, a transformed sign as de Saussure defined it. While de Saussure understood the sign as a pure point of reference in relation to other signs, the *vocable* is a whole, a singularity, which unhinges oppositions. As such, rather than a point where relations with all other signs intersect, it is a particularity that resists reduction to a bundle of its relations. Laruelle grasps here a significant difference between the sign and the *vocable*, without however being able to

inscribed in it, and therefore it seems to form the very movement of the folding in of the order in which it is read, rather than its stable foundation.

Having described the concept of the *vocable*, we can now see how very different ontological thinking can be constructed based on it. We will watch the *vocable* in action.

To start with, I will attempt to show how the *vocable* enables Jabès to focus on the category of the "unsayable," that is, on the presupposed and ousted other side of the symbolic order. Afterwards, I will discuss the way in which the *vocable* undermines the idea of representation. Finally, I will proceed to demonstrate why Jabès' thinking is founded on the constant practice of writing.

The *Vocable* as a Trace of the *Indicible*

The *vocable* eludes the order which tries to think by means of it. As such, it holds more than this order could put in it. Hence, an essential difference emerges between the meaning intended to be invested in the *vocable* and the outcomes of writing, which, in Jabès, manifest themselves through reading. Namely, the retrospective reading implies that there is something more in the created *vocable* than in the order that gave rise to it. That "something more" is, in fact, an outside of this order impressed on the *vocable*. Jabès calls it *indicible*:

> As soon as it has been formulated, every sentence is confronted by something unsayable [*un indicible*] on which it founders.[26]

Notably, the act of formulating and giving a definitive closure to "a sentence" is, of course, *tzimtzum*, as a result of which this sentence transforms into a *vocable*. As such, it contains its own "unsayable" [*indicible*]. The *indicible* seems to be a dialectical category as, first, it is what cannot be uttered at a given moment and, second, its limits appear retroactively as that which "the sentence" has not said, even though signalling it negatively. The *indicible* seems both a reason for the failure of the sentence (that which it cannot effectively express) and its consequence as it comes forth only after the closure of the sentence, when it has

---

theorise it or to explain why, after all, the *vocable* conveys a certain meaning. I believe that only by linking the *vocable*, instead of to a single sign in a symbolic order, to an entire particular symbolic order which breaks in it can we grasp the essence of the singularity of the *vocable*, the discontinuity separating it from other *vocables* and the constitution by it of a liminal unit, not of meaning, but of an entire order in which this meaning is produced. See Laruelle, "Le point sur l'Un" in *Écrire le livre*, pp. 12–32, on p. 127.

26 DB, p. 44.

already morphed into a *vocable*. This is why the *indicible* can be recognised properly only succedently in reading:

> [...] When writing, you write to say something. Yet you never say it: something else gets said – something more powerful than what you wanted to say. You never believe that you wrote what you wanted to write. But, in reality, you wrote that, and it is in the book. [...] We could say that after the break with Egypt, after exile, the reader may say: there is something that happened in his life. But in writing, you do not understand at all what happened.[27]

The passage suggests that, for Jabès, the surplus of the "unsayable" beyond the meaning one wanted to convey in writing does not result directly from an event external to writing-down but is an inevitable consequence of the *tzimtzum*-based structure of writing itself. Hence, the *vocable* can be interpreted not only as a mutilated sign of what one wanted to write in it, but also as a sign of what, as a result of *tzimtzum*, will *have* to be impressed on it, that is of the *indicible*. Consequently, Jabès often evokes an additional voice that speaks through writing, as a rule associating it with the figure of death:

> All dialogue [...] involves three voices: the voice of one that speaks, the voice of one that answers and the voice of death, which makes them both speak [*qui les fait, tous deux, parler*].[28]
> *Night comes ajar for us, vacant reverse of a life.*[29]
> *So it seemed that, once death had blasted him with his own pen, the writer would finally be able to speak, on the far side of the night. But to whom? And for what purpose?*[30]
> *"Death is also a thought – like life, which is an infinite thought of death," Reb Kambi said. And he added: "Death is in every thought as a thought of thought."*[31]

What is this voice of death? Death opposes speaking just like reality opposes a given imaginary order. The voice of death is, thus, the effect of the *vocable* which reveals the demarcated order of free utterance as one of many and, consequently, as an internally impossible order. This observation helps us posit that the *indicible* is an *irremovable vestige of the originary severance of the imaginary from the real following the first tzimtzum, which made speaking possible in the*

---

27 EEJ, pp. 67–8.
28 LH, p. 76.
29 BQ I, p. 289.
30 BQ II, p. 415.
31 LR I, p. 34.

first place.[32] "'To forget the text that gave birth to the text. We began to write with this forgetting,"[33] insists Jabès. It turns out, however, that – as in the Freudian repressed – this severance, this "forgetting," continues to mark the speech it made possible, accompanies it like a shadow and imprints itself on the *vocable* as an *indicible*. The concept of the *vocable* enables us to think this primordial negation, which made all utterance possible.

> "One cannot write without first silencing the words that stir us. The white page is an imposed silence. It is against this background of silence that the text gets written."[34]
>
> "You always speak from a silence on which you will break.
>
> Behind and before us, there has always been *il n'y aura jamais eu… que*] but one and the same silence: the first one," Reb Yahid had written.[35]

The first *tzimtzum* – "an imposed silence" – which is a prerequisite of speech is, at the same time, the cause of its failure. Unlike words, however, *vocables* make it possible to grasp this interdependence as they always display their dialectically suppressed other side.[36] In this way, they reveal that *each utterance must be inexorably marked with prior silence, which it suppresses to come into being.* For there is no writing without oblivion and oblivion flickers back in writing.

Representation and Repetition

This breeds another consequence of thinking with *vocables*: they are closer to reality than words are as the former render effects of *tzimtzum*. Let us look into the following passage:

> They [words] only reflect [*reflètent*] the impossibility of appropriating [*de s'approprier*] things because there is no reality, because reality may be only this absence of reality the vocables underline in their powerlessness to take hold [*cerner*] of it – which, for a vocable, would be somehow to circumscribe [*circonscrire*] its own reality. But that too is impossible because it also is only the expression of an illusory reality, of an abyss.[37]

---

32 This clarifies Jabès' statement that the *indicible* is an "unimaginable thought back before what is before thought" (*l'avant avant pensée inimaginable*) that persists in thought as its "leaven" and "origin" at the same time (BM, p. 17).

33 BD, p. 51.

34 DB, p. 89.

35 BR II, p. 11.

36 In another formulation, Jabès said that *vocable* is "distance within non-distance, that is, the width of a gap that every letter stresses while bridging it. What is said is always in relation to what will never be expressed" (BM, p. 31).

37 DB, p. 92.

As the passage suggest, "words" misconceive reality and cannot take hold of things. Why not? Because they belong to the order of the imaginary and ignore *tzimtzum*, whose imprint things bear. The originary partition gives words a space of freedom at the price of obliviousness to their own nature, which is unveiled beyond their reach – in the failure of the utterance. The *indicible*, being the other side of their partition, never appears for words such that they could refer to it while *vocables*, as already discussed, are "words that have internalised debacle," pushed asunder in themselves by *tzimtzum*. As such, vocables *are by nature akin to reality which they seek to apprehend* since they contain an element of absence. This is what makes them better aligned with reality than words are.

According to Jabès, two ways of referring to reality seem to correspond to the words-vs.-*vocables* opposition. One of them is representation, which is clearly connoted by the activity ascribed to words, i.e. *refléter* – "reflecting" and "mirroring." Representation seeks to take hold of things and order them in its own way (even to "appropriate" them – *s'approprier*). Nevertheless, because representation itself continues to suppress *tzimtzum*, it cannot fully capture things, for things bear the mark of *tzimtzum*. For this reason, *in representation tzimtzum exists between the representing and the represented, determining their ontological incompatibility.*

Vocables take a different course, being more "adequate" vis-à-vis reality insofar as they are internally marred with *tzimtzum*. That is why *their own inner impossibility is of the same kind as the impossibility of reality.* Yet this very fact precludes *vocables* referring to reality as they cannot be effective signifiers. If we think through them, the object of our thinking is, by necessity, not reality as such but the very *vocable*, which draws attention by its own impossibility. Jabès clearly implies that attempting to grasp reality by means of the *vocable* leads only to "circumscrib[ing] [*circonscrire*] its own reality." The language in which the poet describes the *vocable*, instead of "reflecting" or "mirroring," connotes "encircling," "defining" and "writing" as such (the *scrire*/scribe suffix). Why? The answer is that the *vocable* does not seek to convey the entire reality but itself only, that is, the part of reality which it demarcates itself through writing. Clearly, in return for a better marking than is given to words, the *vocable* is doomed to radical singularity. For this reason, I would like to refer to this way of describing reality as *repetition*.

Clearly, *tzimtzum* cannot be adequately depicted either in representation or in repetition. It stands in the way of description in both cases, the difference lying only in the position in which *tzimtzum* is placed. Representation is coherent but, essentially, illusory as it fundamentally diverges from what it seeks to present because it places *tzimtzum* between itself and the represented. Repetition, even though conveying *tzimtzum*, does it at the price of being limited only to the fragment of reality encompassed by the *vocable*. To describe the entire reality is impossible, as Jabès assumes, yet *vocables* at least make it possible to gesture at this impossibility. We should notice also that the aporia between *vocables* and words seems to be closely related to the legacy of modern perspectivism. As a result of the fragmentation of reality, representing it as a whole is a perspectival illusion while indicating the fragmentation must be limited to marking the inner fragmentation of the indication itself.

Writing as a Philosophical Practice

As stated in the foregoing, the *vocable* allows a retrospective recognition of the *indicible* – the effect of the primordial severance that produced the symbolic order. It also makes it possible to "circum-scribe" at least this part of reality that it demarcates itself. As a result of the two, it is impossible to settle for one *vocable* only, and, furthermore, time is needed to retroactively recognise what it brings forth. Hence, Jabès' "ontology" is dynamic, which means that it must sustain itself in and by producing new *vocables*, unable to stop at one, complete and definitive representation of reality. That is why, over a conclusive philosophical proposition, Jabèsa privileges the continuity of writing that transmutes into a unique meditation.

His notion of writing is one of its kind. Writing, namely, is an alternating cycle of writing the *vocable* that "circum-scribes" subsequent regions of reality and reading it, which gives rise to a new *vocable*:

> The first sentence is free. [...] It could be anything. But already the second must follow from the first. And the third from the first two. You must read what you have written. If you read correctly what you have written, the text writes "itself."[38]

The first written *vocable* – whose vocation is to encircle, to "close in on," the real [*cerner le réel*][39] – will "circum-scribe" a fragment of reality irrespective of the representation that accompanied the writing. Since in Jabès' universe all acts of "creation," in particular of *vocables*, have the same structure, their content has no meaning at the start. The poet suggests that it is from this encircling that the *indicible* marked in it must be extracted. How does it happen? The category of reading, which has already been introduced, comes in handy. At this point,

---

38 Edmond Jabès in Waldrop, *Lavish Absence*, p. 60.
39 BD, p. 55.

we could usefully digress from our main argument and explore two aspects of reading in Jabès.

First of all, reading entails unveiling the layer of *indicible* sedimented in the written-down *vocables*. Correct reading reveals the other side of writing, in which "what had not been expressed were finally heard [*entendre*] and read outside the words."[40] We should note the characteristic relevance of the anteriority of the read *vocables*: only the lapse of time between the writing and the reading, redolent of Bloom's "belatedness," enables the reader to find the *indicible*. Only in reading can what, by necessity, eluded the writer be discerned. As "a potential writer" and "an unsuspected creator,"[41] the reader is consubstantial with the writer and, consequently, bears considerable responsibility. Jabès compares this[42] to the responsibility borne by one reading the Torah, who must complement the text containing only consonants and some *matres lectionis* with full-stops, *nikudot* and vowels, without which words cannot be formed. Reading thus compels "more than a profound comprehension of the text, a true intuition of the text."[43] This intuition seems to be related to the Nietzschean "suspicion," which, as a major philological instrument, helps decipher the unsaid.

In Jabès, reading has also another facet which resembles deconstruction rather than the hermeneutics of suspicion. Namely, if the *indicible* within a *vocable* is found, the *vocable* itself reveals its specific nature – a nature of the line between the directly said and the *indicible* bound up with it. Both these aspects are, in a sense, symmetrical to the inner gap of the *vocable*, and hence, either of them can be shown as a sign read in the language of the other.[44] The *vocable* turns then into a *place* where the opposition is located and where its elements are separated and

---

40 *Ibid.*, p. 38.
41 DB, p. 47; BR III, p. 65.
42 DB, pp. 81–2.
43 *Ibid.*, p. 81.
44 Which is what Jabès often does, relying on oppositions – such as death vs. life and voice vs. silence – dialectically and stating, for example, that "life is a voice of death." In this way, he underscores that each opposition of notions can be read from two directions. One of them is, as a rule, more natural to us, but it is only habit that makes us neglect the other one. Jabès shows that it can always be read from the other side. Ultimately, we cannot settle the order of the opposition's elements as they reflect each other. What else remains? The very place where the elements are divided. The *vocable* is this place. The *vocable* is a cut that determines the axis around which the opposition is built. While all oppositions are insoluble, there is one certainty in Jabès: the certainty that the *vocable* exists. We cannot resolve the oppositions, but we can show around which place they have crystallised.

articulated at the same time. In other words, the second level of reading would involve saying, while pointing at a given *vocable*: "at this place, the line between the direct utterance and the *indicible* ran so and so." This locatedness directly on the dividing line is an ultimate effect of the text which reading should reveal. Of course, it is not a limit as Hegel conceived it; rather, it is a place where an enunciation is disturbed by the *indicible* and where, also, the *indicible* is conditioned by the directly said.

Having examined these two aspects of reading, we can resume our analysis of Jabèsian writing. As already mentioned, it is founded on the alternating sequence of circumscribing the *vocable* and reading it, which gives rise to a new *vocable*. Consequently, reading in Jabès serves not so much to deconstruct the existing texts (which is the case in Derrida) as to *make writing turn to itself*, or more precisely: to make it analyse the consequences of the "circumscribing of reality," which it performed at the previous stage. As this is the quintessence of Jabès' writerly and philosophical practice, let us examine it in more detail.

The "writing turning to itself" is not simply a progression of writing-down and deconstructing. On the contrary, *each consecutive act of writing down is formed within the compass of deconstruction of the former so as to, by using its enduring effect, try and shape a new line between the said and the indicible.* "I write by the light of what is not revealed in what I express,"[45] states Jabès. However, because this "unrevealed" side will only show itself when the word is written, Jabès seems rather to be writing in the light of the *indicible* delimited by the previous *vocable*. Still, by reducing the distance between the previous *vocable* and reading, in which a new one will be written, Jabès *comes closer, asymptotically to apprehending the line between enunciation and the indicible in the particular vocable written down.* In this sense, he writes "in the light of what is not revealed in what I express," shortening the distance between the word and its unsayable. By this token, he nears the gap dividing the imaginary and the real, the plan of creation and its outcome, himself and the work being created. Briefly, in the strain of his writing, he approaches *tzimtzum* as closely as possible.[46]

Clearly, though applying practices akin to deconstruction, Jabès sets a different aim for his writing than Derrida does. Namely, he seeks to turn writing to itself in order to explore *tzimtzum*, whereof writing emerges[47] and, consequently,

45 BQ II, p. 126.

46 See Richard Stamelman, "Nomadic Writing," in *The Sin of the Book*, pp. 92–114, on p. 105.

47 That is why Jabès claims that each book fathoms incessantly its own origin, yet not all of them undergo "true reading" which reveals this fact (Cf. BD, p. 37).

to convey, through the mechanism of repetition, *tzimtzum* of reality itself. As a result, his texts are chains of *vocables* which, in their tension, embody particular moments of *tzimtzum*. The book that is produced in this way is like a *continuous border marked off by particular points of tzimtzum.* In this way, it reduces to a minimum the line between the reading (description) of *tzimtzum* and the immediate experience of it. Hence Jabès can identify his writing with a unique *creatio continua*: "Ah, write, write to keep alive the fire of creation,"[48] and creation itself with an ongoing catastrophe: "There is no reading of the book. We only read its being consumed in the ever-revived fire of creation."[49] That is why the text written in the proper tension of self-reading[50] becomes a *manifestation of tzimtzum unfolding in its continuity from the first, random marking of the vocable.*[51]

The Role of the Text as a Path of *Tzimtzum*

We can glimpse now the finale of the Jabèsian practice of writing. We have already seen what kind of text is produced in it. We could however probe deeper: What ends are served by the text that has unfurled from a random primordial trace and "renders" in and by itself the event of *tzimtzum*? What does such a text show? How is it relevant to philosophy?

I have already mentioned that *tzimtzum* is a place of differentiation and, in a degree, of dissemination as Derrida thought of it. In the written-down text, *tzimtzum* manifests itself through a *deflection* from the trajectory outlined by the imaginary and through a perspectival refraction. As such, *tzimtzum* is a structure that conditions the final shape of the text, makes it excessive and overdetermined, whereby it also affects meanings inferable from it. In Jabès' modern universe, the grid of *tzimtzum* points seems to demarcate a peculiar grid of negative forces, whose lines determine the course of all discourse.

---

48 BS, p. 99.
49 *Ibid.*, p. 110.
50 Hence Jabès believes that "a badly written text is a text badly read by its author" (DB, p.50); cf. BM, p. 11.
51 *Return to the Book* insists: "The work imposes its choices on us. Only much later the writer becomes aware of this" (BQ I, p. 398). In Jabèsian practice, the text clings as closely as possible to the original "cut" of the *vocable* which initiated it. This cut charts the line of texts across subsequent *tzimtzums* and in this sense "imposes its choices on us."

In this context, Jabèsian writing can be viewed as a reversal of dependence between this grid of forces and the planes of discourse it conditions. Namely, instead of regarding the *tzimtzum* grid as a map of undesirable inner disturbances, or even instead of showing its role in shaping the final text (within deconstructive practices), Jabès *seems to use all meaningful content only to focus on the grid of tzimtzum points*. His stories are skeletal, his sentences are elliptical, and the fabric of his text is tattered because the fundamental "object" of this text is the very path of successive *tzimtzums*, imprinted on the inner breakings of writing. Moreover, Jabès deliberately prunes the content of his text to prevent extending the intervals between *tzimtzum* events. In the last *Books* in particular, the content suffices only to highlight the discontinuity of transition. The world is reduced in them to the opposition of Nothing and All, divided and intertwined by the void of *tzimtzum*, imaged in the relocation of letters in the "NUL – L'UN" [NONE – ONE] formula.[52]

In this way – at the price of an unusually powerful movement of simplification – Jabès seems to expose the negative grid of forces working beneath the surface of modern discourses. Trimming its own content to a bare minimum, his text serves to show how a grid of *tzimtzum* points develops out of a first, haphazard "cut." At the same time, the concept of the *vocable* does justice to dialectics, acknowledging how the two "sides" (cor)respond to each other and recognise themselves in the other, but also marking *a particular empty place of tzimtzum* that separates and links the two sides. In this way, the *vocable* steps beyond dialectics, whose oppositions get inscribed in a broader whole.

We can now draw conclusions which will answer our opening question about the role of writing practice. Namely, Jabès' text, in self-simplification down to a line of *tzimtzum* events, *draws a line in a peculiar space of all possible tzimtzums and, thereby, as a whole, is a sign of this space*.

This is, at the same time, one of the nodal metaphors the poet relies on, repeatedly framing writing as arduous path-blazing in the desert, where no roads are to be found. As a path in the desert, the line of text is a *trace* which makes it possible to mark an ungraspable whole. Let us examine the following remarks Jabès makes:

> The book is woven into an elsewhere [*un ailleurs*] which leaves us out. It is the word already thought, but which rethinks itself while it is written down.[53]

52 BQ II, pp. 390–1.
53 BQ II, p. 316.

On one side, writing: what is done, what is written in the book. On the other, facing it, non-writing: what is undone and erased in the book. And as if erasure were writing in order to be erased.[54] Every book includes a zone of darkness [*d'obscurite*], a shadow-layer [*une epaisseur d'ombre*] which one cannot evaluate and which the reader discovers only gradually. It irritates him, but he does sense that this is there where the real book lies, the site around which the pages he is reading organize themselves. This unwritten book, both enigmatic and revealing [*revelateur*], always slips away. And yet, only the reader's intuitive grasp pf it enables him to approach the book's true dimension; this intuition enables him to judge if the writer has indeed come close to, or, on the contrary, has wandered from the book he had the ambition to write.[55]

Jabès assumes then that a well-written – that is, well "read" – text is formed in relation to the "real book around which pages organize themselves." If the book is "well read," "the other side" cannot possibly be the *indicible*. On the contrary, this "non-writing," this "unwritten book" and the like are *a space of all the tzimtzum points*, in which the entirety of a particular text imprints a trace. Ultimately, the goal of Jabès' writing is to mark this space. I will describe it in more detail in the following Chapters. At this moment, I would only like to elucidate the philosophical meaning of the text that marks this space.

To do this, I will briefly describe Jabès' writing practice. First, his text systematically discloses its own *indicible*, that is, the effect of the originary severance from reality. Second, it shows dialectically the mutual correspondence of the *indicible* and the direct enunciation, whereby it makes the *vocable* a place of their symmetry. In this way, the *vocable* is not (unlike in Hegel) just a boundary of two dialectically corresponding fragments, but it has its own emplacement that determines a particular way of binding the oppositions. This resembles Derrida's concept of "infrastructures." Third, as the content is reduced in relation to this constantly reiterated centre of emptiness, the text is revealed as a trail of particular *tzimtzums* impressed on the *vocables*. Fourth, the text as such becomes a sign of the space of all possible *tzimtzums*.

This practice suggests that Jabès, rather than only showing that every utterance is conditioned by its *indicible*, uncovers also the underlying grid of negative forces of *tzimtzum*, which organises the connection between utterances and the *indicible*. In the next instance, however, he shows that this very grid of forces has emerged from the space of possibilities and indicates it through its own

---

54 BR II, p. 79.
55 DB, p. 82.

incompletion. Therefore, his text ultimately becomes a sign of all the possible formations of the said and the *indicible* which have not been actualised in it. As such, Jabès' text serves to explore two "phenomena" at the same time. One of them is the emergence of *tzimtzum* from the space of possibilities and the subsequent rise of discourse around this "primal" regulation – this particular disjunction-and-linkage of the imaginary and the possible. The other is that coming close to apprehending an act of *tzimtzum* in its very unfolding, Jabès perceives it also as a *sign* of the space of possibilities of *tzimtzum*, which is indirectly marked in this way. Importantly, the two aspects of the text are inseparable: the "glimmering" of the act of *tzimtzum* in writing "illuminates," in Jabès' metaphor, the space in which it occurs. *Tzimtzum* gives rise to a particular configuration of discourse and, at the same time, signifies because the way in which it happened gestures at all possible ways in which it did not happen. Jabès seems to parse the category of happening (as Heidegger defined it): *happening as such divides "the happened" from the space in which happening occurs, being its sign.*

This is how far the *vocable* pushes philosophical thinking. The *vocable*, which I started discussing from an ostensibly simple "writing-down," turns out to be the fulcrum of comprehensive negative ontology. It is, first of all, an axis relative to which each singular symbolic order discloses its unsaid other side, produced in its very coming-into-being. More than that, the *vocable as a totality of the connection of the symbolic order and its outside* points to the inaccessible space of the Book. For this very reason, the *vocable* makes it possible to render a given order as one of many but also transcends the horizon of the negation it introduces, that is, the division between the order and *its* pluralistic outside. In this way, the *vocable* conveys the inscription of this division into a space whose content is basically unknown to us. If there is, indeed, any Jabèsian "ontology," its object is this space and happening that occurs in it.

In this way, starting from a veritably inconspicuous phenomenon of writing and through the self-focused practising of it, Jabès finds the underlying grid of forces responsible not only for how texts arise but also for how symbolic orders arise that make up a myriad of human worlds. *Tzimtzum* works even where the text is emptied out of any content: this is where the matrix of these dark dependencies that mark every whole with a wound is to be found.

Conclusion: Kabbalistic vs. Modern
Meaning of the Ontology of Writing

Concluding, I would like to integrate the implications of this Chapter with the book's organising idea, i.e. recognising Jabès' work as a site where modern structures of thinking border with Jewish tradition, in particular with Jewish mysticism.

Notably, this broad and heterogeneous tradition contains approaches in which script and writing are used as a blueprint for interpreting Creation. The anonymous *Sefer Yetzirah*, dated by Scholem to the 2nd or 3rd century of our era[56] and founding Jewish mysticism, describes God's Creation of the world by means of 10 sefirot (still conceived as numbers) and 22 letters of the Hebraic alphabet.[57] It frames beings as created out of combinations of letters.[58] The ideas of the *Sefer Yetzirah* were picked up by the Kabbalah, which started to evolve in the 13th century and interpreted the process of Creation as a language movement.[59] Isaac the Blind, a prominent Provençal kabbalist and commentator of the *Sefer Yetzirah*, frames his doctrine of emanation of *Ein-Sof* as a movement of Divine thought towards "the beginning of speech." The second sefirah – wisdom – is the source of language from which all other sefirot emerge, assembling in various configurations and producing letters of the alphabet.[60] As Scholem emphasises, linguistic mysticism is a mysticism of writing.[61] The kabbalists were clearly fascinated with writing as a site where meaningful content intersected with the palpably real. Given that already in the Torah Creation is associated with articulation of the creative force of Divine words, writing appears to be a model of all thing *tout court* poised at the border of content and "matter."

According to Scholem, the kabbalists understand writing as a place that harbours mysteries.[62] The model of all writing – the Torah – bears an imprint of God's creative word. The role of language is highlighted in the repeatedly mentioned and employed ambiguity of דבר, *davar*, which means both word and thing. Isaac the Blind interpreted it as foregrounding the immanent linguistic nature of Creation. Scholem emphasises that in the Kabbalah, which privileges linguistic mysticism, the world of language is the world of the spirit as such.[63]

The affinity of writing – as depositing the meaning in matter – and Creation lies at the core of the work of Abraham Abulafia, one of the greatest pre-Lurianic

---

56 Scholem, "Name of God and the Linguistic Theory of the Kabbalah," part 1, *Diogenes* 79, 1972, pp. 59–80, on, p. 72.
57 *Ibid.*, pp. 72–3.
58 Scholem *Kabbale*, p. 75.
59 Scholem, "Name of God" 2, p. 166.
60 *Ibid.*, p. 167.
61 *Ibid.*
62 *Ibid.*, p. 167.
63 *Ibid.*, p. 168.

kabbalists. He explains that in the act of creation, God brings language within the compass of things, leaving his signatures in them. The process unfolds as follows:

> The secret that lies at the basis of the "host" (of all things) is the letter, and every letter is a sign (symbol) and indication of the creation. Just as any writer holds the plume in his hand and with it takes up drops of ink and in his mind traces out the form which he wants to give to is substance, at which moment the hand is like the living sphere, and the inanimate plume, which serves as the hand's instrument, moves and links itself to the hand in order to spread the drops of ink across the parchment, which represents the body, which is used as the bearer of the substance and the form – in precisely the same way do things occur in the matter of the creation in its upper and lower spheres, as the intelligent person will understand, for it is not permitted to explain it more closely than this. Therefore are the letters set up as signs (symbols) and indications, so that through them the matter of reality, its forms and the forces and overseers which motivate it (that is: the intermediate parties), its minds and its souls can be given some form, and therefore is wisdom (in the sense of true knowledge) contained and gathered up in the letters and the Sefiroth and the names, and all these are composed the one from the other. The letters themselves have substance and form, especially in their written form of being, though far less so or rather in a spiritualized sense in their spoken or conceptual form. What, in the image above, was the ink, which translates this formal element into matter, is, in the organic creation and in the human realm, the seed, which already contains the substance and the forms which shall evolve from it.[64]

Adapting the Aristotelian categories of matter and form, Abulafia is resolved to erect writing into a model of all creation. Importantly, such association enabled many Jewish mystics to put forward theories which can be usefully applied to describing modern perspectivism. As Scholem reminds, one of the major kabbalists of the 13th century, Joseph Gikatilla, distinguished three worlds: the world of the spheres, the world of the angels and the earthly world.[65] Each of them is governed by different laws, but they are all united by the Torah, which remains the same across the worlds. The Torah is framed here as a universal text which is nevertheless *meaningless in itself* and acquires meanings only within particular worlds, different ones in each. Moreover, each of these worlds consists of millions of worlds, in which interpretations of the Torah differ as well. Each of the interpretations is complete and partial.[66] The assumption of the identity of writing and creation enables Gikatilla thus to think of reality as one world that

---

64 Qtd. in *Ibid*, pp. 185–6.
65 *Ibid*, p. 180.
66 Scholem, "Signification," p. 110.

is internally fragmented as a result of the fundamental divergence between the dimensions of writing (the Torah) and meaning (interpretation).

One more tenet relevant to our argument to be found in Kabbalist tradition is striving to obliterate the difference between ontology and epistemology. As Scholem notes,[67] the kabbalists often use two different languages to describe Creation, either rendering it as effusion of energy from *Ein-Sof* and emergence of the sefirot as Divine attributes or relying on the metaphors of letters and writing, in which Creation is a process unfolding between the Divine Name and letters. According to Scholem, this duality of language can be seen as an attempt to capture the difference between the order of creation as such (the notions of energy and sefirot) and the order of revelation, in which creation manifests itself (the notions of writing and letters associated with the Torah as revelation in script). Still, *the two orders are parallel*: creation and cognition are based on the same structure. Scholem explains:

> The process of creation, progressing from stage to stage and reflected in non-divine worlds, and in nature as such, is for this reason essentially identical with the process expressed in divine words and in documents of creation, which are believed to preserve these words.[68]

Consequently, the kabbalists who assume such parallelisms presuppose that it is possible to apprehend Creation through acts of creation in writing. This highlights the intellectual affinity between such strands in the Kabbalah and Jabès' thought and practice. His category of the *vocable*, which replaces being, refers directly to writing and, besides, makes it possible to theorise reality as immanently perspectival. Also, writing is for him a way of knowing reality as ontology and epistemology are secondary to a common matrix of creation, existence and knowledge.

However, Jabès gives these notions a strictly modern tinges. As already underscored, the difference between the *vocable* and being lies in the processing of post-Kantian philosophical insights. The *vocable* is a "limit" of *the entire given* symbolic order and its outside. Unlike in Abulafia, writing in Jabès does not embody the difference between matter and form but a transcendental difference as each moment of writing bears a radical apophatic tension.

Also, writing in Jabès is not a combination of matter and form, of materiality and meanings readable in it. In this, Jabès parts ways with the kabbalists of old. Here, writing is not a simple whole of two components, be

---

67 *Ibid.*, p. 105.
68 *Ibid.*

they only ideally differentiable. Instead, it is founded on a rupture between the two dimensions – on the still active *tzimtzum*; hence writing as such is an excessive entity subsumed neither in the imaginary nor in the real but, instead, in the constant transition between the two. At the same time, the transition is an outcome of perspectivism, which Jabès shares with modern philosophy. Essentially, writing as such does not exist for him as it is a *gap* between the two collapsing orders. The gap is theorised by Jabès as a *place*, which results in assuming a specific space of the white and the Book that comes into being in it.

Such an idea of "place" and "space" also goes beyond the traditional Kabbalistic speculations and is explicable only in the context of modern philosophy. For it is not a space in the proper sense of the term, but a space of certain possibilities thought of as places. The places of possibilities as such, rather than beings, are "basic" ontological decisions, that is, *particular acts of tzimtzum*. This type of space is a way of conceptualising perspectivism. That is why, if Jabès resorts to "spatial" or "materialistic" thinking at all, it is not to ponder the relationships of material beings to the area they occupy. On the contrary, like his contemporary theorists (Lacan, for one, and, to some extent, Derrida[69]), Jabès employs "materiality"-related categories to describe the dimension which *transcends the symbolic order and is this order's condition of possibility*. If the Book is based on "space," this "space" is just an attempt to apprehend the dimension available to us only partially from the side of symbolic order inscribed in it. It is the dimension that we sense to encompass all fundamental ontological resolutions though we cannot define it in any detail. Jabès' "materialism" is a philosophical casing of perspectivism, without having much to do either with the kabbalists' considerations on matter or with ancient materialism.

Joseph Guglielmi certainly seems right to claim that such "spatial" materialism ensues from in-depth re-thinking of atheism as non-existence of a central, meaningful principle of reality.[70] As a result, places of meanings become primary to meanings themselves, to *entire* orders of meanings, let us add.[71] The whole

---

69 Cf. Derrida, *Positions*, pp. 87–8.

70 Joseph Guglielmi, "Journal de lecture d'Edmond Jabès," in *Écrire le livre*, pp. 87–105, on p. 105.

71 Laruelle observes that, building on its Jewish legacy, Jabès' thought is a radical reversal of Platonism. As the One that integrates reality is overthrown, the space of writing comes into being. Things cease to be metaphors, becoming radically and inconceivably singular. See Laruelle, "Le point," pp. 123–5.

of the world can thus be theorised only as a space because only space allows thinking about co-existence of orders that defy any meaningful comparison.[72] Therefore, Jabès' "ontology" is a strictly modern phenomenon even though it draws on borrowings from the kabbalists.

---

72 For this reason, Joseph G. Kronick can contend that the existence of writing precludes the existence of God. See Joseph G. Kronick, "Edmond Jabès and the Poetry of the Jewish Unhappy Consciousness," *MLN*, 106/5 (December, 1991), pp. 967–96, on pp. 975–6. God had to withdraw not only vis-à-vis language but also vis-a-vis the space that appeared as a result. In his essay on *The Return to the Book*, Derrida aptly talks of Jabèsian "negative atheology." See Derrida, *Writing*, p. 375.

5 Negative Ontology II: God, Nothing and the Name

The previous Chapter outlined Jabèsian ontology yet passed over one of its central aspects, that is, the poet's radical mono(a)theism. This is where Jabès starkly differs from other philosophers who embrace the oceanic Nothing that engulfs all being. Briefly, there is in his thought a vestige which lingers on relentlessly and is identified by him with God. Given this fact, Jabès cannot be possibly associated with any *vanitas*-riveted metaphysics, where Nothingness is the first and last spawn which brings forth and annihilates creatures that barely keep clinging to being. He resists such classification because his crucial notion is the name which rips both the cohesion of being and the very possibility of insight into Nothing.

Within the simple opposition of Athens and Jerusalem, Jabèsian radical mono(a)theism would exemplify Jewish thought *par excellence*. However, this mono(a)theism is divested of presence and corresponds to the desert landscape, in which the sky and the earth – vaster than the echo of any human word – bear witness to the ruin of creation. For what is created more *today* than the impervious silence, the inner deafness of resting matter? The capacity to hear it is not a thing of Athens – it is a thing of *modernity*. And that a poet like Jabès – "a Jew and a writer" – knows how to listen to it seems seriously to undermine the Athens-vs.-Jerusalem binary.

Thus, in searching for connections among Greek, Jewish and modern thinking, one must look into Jabèsian ontology once again to try and identify relationships of Nothing, God and the name. Though surveying ontology form another angle, this attempt draws on preceding conclusions about *tzimtzum* and the *vocable*. In fact, it again *repeats* the attempt to provide an account of the Jabès' negative thinking. Perhaps the fracture of the two parts of ontology represents the fundamental impossibility of putting a closure on Jabès' philosophy. The fracture is something more than a mere failure here: it is a point of creation and, basically, the only thing to be looked for.

God – Nothing

Jabès' writings re-engage time and again in efforts to describe Nothing as a foundation of existence. For this reason, Derrida calls *The Book of Questions* "the interminable song of silence."[1] Some passages seem to suggest that Jabès sought to develop the concept of nothing, or the void, so as to erect it into an Absolute. This reverberates in several passages, for example:

The sky is absence.[2]
The Real, which is the sand, and the Nothing, which is the sky, are my two horizons.
[...] *"No matter how solidly you build your house,"* said Reb Alkem, *"it will always rest on sand."*[3]
All I care for: to live the absence of God.[4]
Every creature is allotted an acre of void to settle in.[5]
The void bears the weight of the universe, though light as air.
All truth is airy [*aérienne*].[6]
The word is a world of emptiness.[7]
"What strength could rival that of the void?" asked Reb Basri. "It is nothing and, all by itself, sustains All."
[...] "People of the Book," were you not the people fascinated for millenia with an extreme sense of Nothing sustained by the letter?
... an extreme sense of the void?[8]
"What holds you up?" Reb Asri asked Reb Debban.
"The void," replied the latter.
And added: "Does it not hold up the universe?"[9]

In the quotes, Nothing features as the foundation of the existing world, a kind of intrinsic, essentially negative principle that supports all being. In relation to it, the world becomes a whole, one that is internally homogeneous like the desert and sharply demarcated off the void. Nothing finds its particular incarnation in the word.

---

1   Derrida, *Writing*, p. 83.
2   LSLS, p. 287.
3   BQ I, pp. 199, 269.
4   BQ II, p. 90.
5   *Ibid.*, p. 102
6   *Ibid.*, p. 287; in *aérien* Jabès plays on the homophony of *a et rien*, "a and nothing." In this way, he suggests that the air is comparable to the void that supports a certain "a" or to an "a" that bears the weight of emptiness. Of course, he plays also on the function of the letter א, which opens the Hebraic alphabet and having no sound equivalent except a glottal stop, encodes the whisper of narrowing breath which, so similar to *tzimtzum*, only supports other sounds and allows pronouncing them.
7   *Ibid.*, p. 417.
8   LR I, pp. 51, 126 (the first line in *From the Book to the Book: An Edmond Jabès Reader*, trans. Rosmarie Waldrop [Hanover and London: Wesleyan University Press, 1991], p 158).
9   BR III, p. 81.

Therein Jabès seems to build on the legacy of Mallarmé and Blanchot, who view words, disjoined from the things they are supposed to refer to, as embodying an entirely autonomous quality. Due to the very nature of meaning, language, as based on emptiness produced by the dissociation of word from thing, calls into question the idea of presence. This, on Jabès' take, makes the emptiness-underpinned word parallel to any existence that emerges vis-à-vis the negative principle of – capitalised – Nothing.

With the key role invested in Nothing, Jabès can rehearse Kant's, Hegel's, Nietzsche's and Heidegger's earlier gesture of granting the essentially negative a positive function of the "foundation." In other words, the poet relies on the scaffolding of classic metaphysics, which positions being in relation to its variously conceived foundation, but takes Nothing as a new *hypokeimenon*. This means that absence, emptiness and lack do not refer to the withdrawal of something present that should be there, but are autonomous entities in their own right. Being marks itself off from them as it emerges from the originary non-being. Although we are on the side of being and our language is modelled on it, it is still possible to reverse the position of Nothing and make it a positive factor. This is what Jabès seems to have sought:

> [...] and yet, maybe I wrote this sentence only to give absence the status of presence. O perennial presence of an unbelieving absence [ô *pérenne présence d'une absence incrédule*].[10]

This "reversal of Nothing," which can be described as a substitution of *present absence* for *absent presence*,[11] produces a formal paradox. Namely, in the new model, the world can be founded on Nothing. Although this word – nothing – carries a meaning, it is supposed to designate something that eludes meaning. As such, it is a very special word: it functions as all other words in language do, but its content refers to something from beyond language. In Jabès' view, it harbours – just like the words "death" and "infinity" – a chasm faced with which we are swept off our feet.[12]

---

10 P, p. 50.
11 Discussing absence framed as presence, Strauss writes: "After Auschwitz, after the disappearance of God in whom Jews put trust or believed to do so – after the vanishing of illusory God into thin air – Jabès attempts to convert [*convertir*] this absence, this silence into a new identity located in the *vocable*, the *vocable* that *names* absence, which dwells in exile, in the desert." Strauss, "*Le Livre*," p. 298.
12 LH, p. 15.

Thinking Nothing as the foundation of reality results, symptomatically, in that *the entire reality is revealed as one whole* – "All" in Jabès' language. Whatever exists stands sharply against Nothing, and the bare fact of existence unites it with all other things existing. That is why, when confronted with its foundedness on Nothing, reality surrenders its inner heterogeneity and amalgamates into a specific oneness:

All is faced with Nothing which will engulf it.[13]
ALL was engulfed [*s'abîma*] in NOTHING.[14]
I give my all, and this *all* is but ashes of countless nothings [*d'innombrables riens*].[15]
The word will start from Nothing in order to dissolve in the All.[16]
Where there is nothing, All is intact: only fragments can be grasped.[17]
We are at the heart of creation, absent from the All, in the marrow and moire of Absence, with the Void for recourse, for a means to be and to survive. So that, in the creative act, we are and even surpass the Void facing the restoring All.[18]

The passages can be read as implying that Jabès replaces God with Nothing, granting it the same rank and position vis-à-vis Creation. Such reading would make sense insofar that God disappeared replaced by the void as a result of the primal disaster and, consequently, the void should be recognised as a new God. Let us for now put aside the question of how this Nothing of God should be comprehended – as an all-embracing and all-engulfing nihilistic emptiness to which everything returns or, perhaps, as a central point of negativity – and focus on Jabès' considerations in which God is identified with Nothing.[19]

---

13 PHD, p. 121.
14 BUS, p. 49.
15 BM, p. 90. In this passage Jabès uses an interesting property of the French language, in which the word for "nothing" (*rien*) is derived from the Latin *res* (thing). Hence, it is easier to speak of a multiplicity of "nothings." Also the etymological link between "nothing" and "thing" helps frame nothingness in positive terms as something both present and real. Shillony highlights Jabès' unique usage of the word *rien*: "Jabès, listening to the hidden memory of words, does not forget that *nothing* [*rien*] means also a 'thing.'" Shillony, *Edmond Jabès*, p. 31.
16 BQ II, p. 225.
17 *Ibid.*, p.439–40.
18 BQ I, p. 398.
19 Importantly, Jabès has a long line of Kabbalistic predecessors. It is, crucially, as Nothing that *Ein-Sof* in the created world tended to be perceived, which underscored his incommensurability with creation. For this reason, some kabbalists re-interpreted the notion of creatio ex nihilo to mean the world emerging from God as nothingness rather than God creating the world out of nothing. This re-casting enabled them to

In a conversation with Marcel Cohen, Jabès suggests that, for him, "God is the metaphor for emptiness."[20] The name of God[21] – Hebraic השם – performs the function of the word "Nothing" as both belonging within language and exploding its structures:

Man is All, God is Nothing. Here is the riddle.
The glide towards Nothing. Perennial slope.
[...] When I call to God, I call to the Sense of the Void.
[...] It is to be asked if God is not the one inadmissible question, the deep avowal of this inadmissibility through which the world is cut off from the world and man from his divine ancestry.[22]
A man of writing is a man of four letters which form the unpronounceable Name. God is absent through his Name.
Writing means taking on God's absence through each of the four.

---

reconcile God's separateness with the idea of emanation; see. Gershom Scholem, *Kabbale*, pp. 173–5.

20 DB, p. 57.

21 In Jewish mysticism, the name of God is not only the basis of theological speculation but first and foremost a liminal point in language as it is both one of its words and the only word that must not, or even cannot, be pronounced. This reveals a prohibition of representation within language and highlights that, even though having words to describe everything, language encounters in one of them an impassable limit to its efficacy. As Marc-Alain Ouaknin observes, "the name is a hole in language, a silence from which all other words get the power of meaning" (*Concerto*, p. 30). Jabès adds: "the name of God is the juxtaposition of all the words in the language. Each word is but a detached fragment of that name. 'Man' is only a word. All relations between man and God pass through the word [*vocable*]" (DB, p. 102).
In Jewish mysticism, the Name is a limit of language just because the essential mechanism of signification is inscribed in it. Besides, as the Name lacks vowels – which are not written and the tradition of pronouncing them has fallen into oblivion even before the demolition of the Second Temple – it cannot be uttered and, as such, assimilated. In that sense, God cannot be made an object of an utterance. Cf. Ouaknin, *Concerto*, p. 108. Though unpronounceable, the name can yet be commented on. Thus, God does not conceal the knowledge of himself fully. Nevertheless, he appears always *at a distance* from the word meant to grasp him, just like the commented-on name remains a material thing rather than a functioning part of language (cf. *Ibid.*, p. 109). Ouaknin insists that the name is not an instrument but, at most, an experience of the void that emerges based on its own laws (*Ibid.*). Clearly, Jabès' thinking is deeply embedded in the tradition of Jewish mysticism.

22 BQ II, pp. 129, 157, 158.

Thus any page of writing is fashioned under the sign of four letters which are the masters of its fate, with power to make it disappear through the expedient of the words containing them.

[…] God's language – language of absence, language of a language that has weathered fire and marble Frost – is unalterable, as if spelled by death.

[…] Thus, because it cannot be heard, the name of God wants to be unpronounceable and sterilize the letter at the height of its meaning.[23]

[God] is image in the absence of image, language in the absence of language, point in the absence of points.

[…] like God, emptiness has no name. The eye from the far side of silence turns to stone with the final period of the book.

No word is spoken after.

[…] God is the high calling to this presumptuous and harrowing departure towards a totality eager to absorb us in its own annihilation.[24]

"The questioning of God is the questioning of the void. Thus, the pure, objectless questioning of the questioning."

[…] "Isn't God's unpronounceable name," he said, "also the erased name of the unthought which all thought meets and founders against?"[25]

In all these passages, Jabès associates God with the void. God is framed as the great "Absent One," "present where all presence has been abolished."[26] This means not only that God disappeared and left absence behind, but also that *absence itself has become God.* If it is indeed the case, should Jabès not be charged with nihilism? Does he not believe that only Nothing exists properly, generating and engulfing beings that expire barely leaving a trace? Essentially, such Nothing, rather than a placeholder for the monotheistic God, would be a variety of the Greek *apeiron*; and there would not be a major difference between it and the world, with every being spawned by it vulnerable to absorption by the void. All this basically boils down to asking: Is Jabès a Jewish monotheist or, rather, a conservative nihilist?

Tzimtzum and the Exigency of Monotheism

Despite the deceptiveness of some formulations Jabès offers, the answer is rather straightforward as, even though God and Nothing are equivalent in a way, Nothing is by no means the primordial emptiness that consumes beings

---

23 *Ibid.*, pp. 250, 300, 301.
24 *Ibid.*, p. 353, 375, 439.
25 LR I, pp. 67, 68.
26 *Ibid.*, p. 40.

entirely and inexorably. On the contrary, it takes the position of the Jewish God, who is radically separated from the world, rather than of the pagan *apeiron*. In his enquiries into the role of Nothing, Jabès relies on his own interpretation of Judaism, in whose Jerusalem Temple the Holy of Holies, as Tacitus famously comments on the Romans' surprising discovery, was untenanted – contained nothing.[27] "Behind there is nothing,"[28] concludes the Jabès, suggesting that a privileged experience of Nothing is part and parcel of Judaism:

> Thus we became the people of Nothingness, of the limpid splendour Nothingness, through four letters that attained the silence of inaccessible crests.
>
> . . . people of Nothingness, of the intact void on which was built the world; stone on stone, beehive on beehive, sky on sky, nothing on nothing.
>
> *("What silence everywhere," said Reb Armel. "And this crushing presence of the void! God is there. I feel it.")*[29]

This suggests that Jabès does not perceive Nothing as an all-encompassing void that engulfs things newly emerging from it but, instead, views it as the foundation of existence, which remains a distant and inaccessible place – "silence of inaccessible crests" – an equivalent of God. Nothing cannot thus be worshipped through pagan wisdom, which sees all things as doomed to inexorable destruction. It is amassed as a mystery in an isolated place, a certain Holy of Holies, storing all the concentration of the void after the withdrawal of God. Therefore, *Nothing and the world are radically distinct even though one is the "foundation" of the other*. So, if Nothing takes the place of God, it is only within a negatively conceived monotheism. That is, Nothing is an outermost point which, though essentially impossible, is the only position from which the world can appear as a whole:

> Could the void [...] be just the introduction to a beyond which would give us back not only to ourselves, but to the world which we had only half imagined? To lose, to forget all in order to embrace the world of a glance...?[30]

Given the above, Nothing as conceived by Jabès cannot be regarded either as more primordial or as more substantial than the world. It is dialectically related to the world as a non-existent centre it produces. Therefore, the claim that Nothing is the "foundation" of things should be approached just like the unavoidable, yet false, myth of the beginning.

---

27 BR II, p. 30.
28 *Ibid.*
29 *Ibid.*, p. 32.
30 BQ II, p. 189.

Such positioning of Nothing is closely associated with a paradox that Jabès persistently revisits. Namely, Nothing – as identified with God – has a Name that inherits the peculiar status of the divine Name in Judaism: it is unpronounceable and inaccessible. In fact, it forms the central, empty point of language and is, at the same time, its condition of possibility and a place where it collapses. Had Jabès understood Nothing as an all-embracing emptiness pre-existing all being, he could have talked about it directly. Yet, as exemplified in the quotations above, Nothing can be addressed only via the paradoxical Name, whose very "use" in itself ushers into language the negative force of Nothing with all its workings. It turns out, thus, that Nothing cannot be talked about in an ordinary fashion, for as soon as we attempt it, it is bound to explode our utterance. In God that is Nothing, all meaningfulness generally breaks down: "Readability is a human invention, and […] God is an unreadable relation."[31]

In Jabès, Nothing is a peculiar point in *language* where it strives to gaze at itself ecstatically from outside.[32] God revealed Himself to Moses as the pinnacle of absence in His Name, writes Jabès,[33] and so does Nothing reveal itself in its name today. Definitely, Jabès by no means embraces pagan wisdom since he views God that is Nothing as a language phenomenon, encoded in one peculiar Name, which, additionally, is not inalterable over time but rather *preserves in itself a trace and memory of the catastrophe.* Furthermore, as Nothing is constantly entangled in mechanisms of language, it cannot be made present and revealed. Let us have a look at the following lines:

> You show yourself only to hide what you are, O void, O nothing. What is not wants to be free to be. And this freedom becomes the obstacle you run up against.
> […] The obstacle is inside.
> […] Giddy with the space, the wind ends by dropping pitifully.[34]

---

31 LR I, p. 96.
32 Of course, Jabès builds here on the vast resources of Jewish mysticism of the Name. In esoteric Judaism, the Name unveils a fundamental fissure that stamps language as the fabric of reality. In other words, the name indicates that not all the spheres of language can be known by man as there is an inner dimension of communication that eludes him. According to Scholem, the name has been central to Jewish esoteric thought ever since the 2nd century, described by an internally contradictory term of שם המפורש – *Shem ha-meforash* – which means the name both "made known," and "pronounced" as well as "separated" or "hidden." This duality represents a fundamental insight: the exposure of the essence of language must involve separation from it and falling silent; see Scholem, "Name of God", p. 66.
33 Cf. BQ II, p. 437.
34 *Ibid.*, pp. 287–8.

In a classic double bind, Jabès suggests here that the condition of possibility that gives voice to Nothing is at the same its condition of impossibility. Nothing manifests itself in striving "to be free to be," in an effort to become a stable, "existing" Nothing, and it is exactly this striving, this effort, that precludes its manifestation, since Nothing harbours the very obstacle in itself. What is this obstacle? The passages above suggest an answer. *Nothing has a Name, and this prevents it from being fully constituted.* The name is its inner obstacle that precludes its autonomous, self-contained existence and makes it only an impossible point in language.

For this reason, Jabèsian Nothing cannot be a pagan, nihilistic pleroma, to which beings that it has newly generated inevitably return. Nothing has a Name, and, consequently, it belongs to the created world and is subject to its laws, without transcending it in any way. This world's own flesh and blood, Nothing is also this world's mirage. Hence, any attempt to express it is doomed to failure, for, engaging with it, we plunge into notions and metaphors of "the unthought":

> We do not think death, the void, emptiness, Nothingness, but their innumerable metaphors: one way of getting around [*contourner*] the unthought [*l'impensé*].[35]
> [...] man ha[s] invented God only for the purpose of hoisting up his thought up to the point of the unthought [*l'impensé*].[36]
> Unable to stand *the unthought* [*l'impensé*, original emphasis] we take shelter in thought, as if it were a stranger to the former.[37]

"The unthought" seems to be a specific point *in which* dark knowledge about the construction of the world is supposed to be deposited.[38] Perhaps it is only because a Name – e.g. "the void," "Nothing," "death" or "God" – is crafted for this point that the point is assumable in the first place. For the name gives a notion a surfeit above its meaning and locates it on a different plane – one of writing. "The unthought" would then be an effect of giving Nothing a Name.

---

35 BUS, p. 71.
36 DB, p. 57.
37 BM, p. 92.
38 This point also locates God after Creation. As Edward Kaplan observes, developing his "atheistic theology," Jabès regards God as a metaphor for the void that serves to elevate thoughts up to the unthinkable. "The questioning of God," insists Kaplan, "is the questioning of the void. Thus, pure questioning, without object [*objet*]; questioning of the questioning. [...] How to understand God? God does not let Himself be enclosed. God's closure, is God: a non-closure or an after-closure." Edward Kaplan, "The Atheistic Theology of Edmond Jabès," *Studies in 20th Century Literature*, 12/1 (1987), pp. 43–63, on pp. 46–7, 50.

Furthermore, it is only due to the Name that an *act of assuming* can work at all, for to think something that, though world-funding, is inaccessible directly, an elementary difference is necessary, a deferral between a notion and its written form. The name gives God that is Nothing a weight which makes us relinquish penetrating the meanings of this specific notion and assume that *they are held by the place created by the Name*. In this way, the Name becomes the empty centre of language – a walled fortress which thinking approaches and recoils from, leaving trails of flawed, circuitous thoughts. A passive participle, *l'impensé* suggests that God and Nothing are always *already unthought*, that is, not so much inaccessible a priori, "not being thought" or "unthinkable" (*l'impensable*), as rather revealed in a failure of an already undertaken attempt to probe them.

They remain on the path already walked, as unapproached points against which thinking has crashed. That is why Jabès so often employs metaphors that associate Nothing with the empty centre and with the always dislocated – past or deferred – present:

"Where is the center?" "Under the cinders" [*Où est le centre? – Sous la cendre*].[39]
The last obstacle, the ultimate border is (who can be sure?) is the center.
[…] "The center is failure. The Creator is rejected from His creation. Splendor of the universe. Man destroys himself as he creates."[40]
The center is the moment. If God is the center He cannot exist except momentarily.[41]
Inside and *outside* are only the arbitrary part in the dividing of an infinity-time whose promised minute keeps calling the center in question.
Every minute is an apex of nothingness.[42]

Summing up this argument, we could say that even though in his pursuit to grasp Nothing Jabès enters many side paths which, incidentally, might imply absolutising Nothing, the position accorded to Nothing in his thought parallels the position of the Jewish God. Nothing is radically disjoined from the world even though it sustains this world. Ungraspable and incomprehensible, it is represented, in language, in a Name which is a liminal, unpronounceable point of this language.[43] Finally, it is always non-present, assumed and deferred. Ostensibly, it

---

39 BQ I, p. 360.
40 *Ibid.*, pp. 359–60.
41 BQ II, p. 159.
42 *Ibid.*, p. 363.
43 In his interesting comparison of Celan's and Jabès' philosophies, William Franke observes that, unlike Celan, who uses poetry to grasp that which lies beyond language, i.e. the originary event that language cannot reach, Jabès embraces the apophatic approach which always recognises absolute silence as an effect of language. William

occupies the centre, but the centre is a mere mirage, an empty place onto which the vision of the dark origin is projected.

This line of thought could be taken further. As a result of Creation, Nothing acquires a Name which, if written down, is nothing else but a *vocable*. Consequently, a split haunts Nothing/God. Therefore, *it shares in the lot of all things created in that it does not form a stable whole but a non-Whole*, to use Lacan's term. For this reason, in Jabès, neither Nothing nor God himself can be "substances," perfect beings, kinds of pleroma. As even Nothing is not a fullness of non-being, Jabès could not possibly endorse the pagan perception of being as "a vice" punished by reversion into the proper condition of non-being. Even Nothing is trapped in the dialectical loop of the *vocable* as a boundary point of a broader structure.

These insights help us understand the radicalism of Jabèsian monotheism, which after all identifies God with Nothing. God that is Nothing is both the apex of absence and the void, a place that makes the negative principle of being thinkable in its entire intensity. But, *at the same time*, God is not himself, remaining absent in his absence and, consequently, internally split. Undoubtedly, in this gesture Jabès overthrows the mode of thinking inherent to classic Western metaphysics. On the one hand, he retains the idea of God as the middlemost point of reality, but on the other, he supplants the fullness of being with the extreme concentration of Nothing. It turns out, however, that *changing the construction principle of God from positive to negative results in God's inner self-differentiation*. In other words, an attempt to conceive of God as "fullness" of Nothing turns him into a non-Whole and precludes stabilising him in one place. Hence, also,

---

Franke, "The Singular and the Other at the Limits of Language in the Apophatic Poetics of Edmond Jabès and Paul Celan," *New Literary History*, 36/4 (Autumn 2005), pp. 621–37, on pp. 628–35. In other words, also the ultimate experience of Nothing is, for Jabès, a liminal moment of expression rather than an extra-linguistic experience. Hence, Jabès' writing, even if apparently "striving to fall silent" in a tendency identified by Celan as part of contemporary poetry, constantly goes on. According to Franke, a distinct feature of apophatic poetics, which sees negativity as an effect of language, is an assumption that there is a special word, a special place in language, in which it contacts its own beyond and is, at the same time, funded by this place (*Ibid.*, p. 635). The Name of God is usually this word. And indeed, unlike Celan, Jabès very often refers to the idea of the Name with all the connotations it accrued in Jewish thought. Franke states, finally, that, in Jabès, all apophatics starts in the space of perpetuated language – in the Book – and leads back to it (*Ibid.*, s. 633). Wrestling with Nothing does not represent an attempt to go beyond language but involves, ultimately, accompanying its transformations.

he has a Name.[44] Perhaps, it is an ontological anti-proof: *God is so perfect a void and does not exist so utterly that, unable to exist as God, he differentiates himself from himself.*

The paradox of Jabès' theology is easily perceived by comparing it with Aristotle's thought. In the Stagirite's metaphysics, God is a thought thinking itself and, as such, the only being that does not depend on other ones.[45] This *noesis noeseos* is *one,* central point of short circuit in Aristotelian ontology and affects all other beings. If in Aristotle God contains himself in his fullness, in Jabès the opposite is the case. His God, an aggregation of absence, is self-referential based on an indelible difference. Though supposed to be a fullness of Nothing, he has an inner crack – grounded in the *vocable* – which always produces an impression that there is a deeper, even more primordial Nothing. By this token, there is a permanent tension between Nothing and Nothing, and between God and God.

Jabès states that God is "so deeply Himself in the incommensurable absence of Self" [*Soi-même dans l'absence incommensurable de Soi*].[46] In the world after *tzimtzum,* where all that is, is founded on God's absence, God is – that is, *is not* – most of all. Since he found himself on his own absence, he can never be stabilised. Moreover, according to Jabès, God is a "murmur [*rumeur*] of absence within absence."[47] What does it mean? There are no less than two absences here. One of them must be a common absence in the post-*tzimtzum* world, which is this world's structural principle. *Different from this common absence is another absence with one being a murmur against the backdrop of the other.* A particular absence murmurs in the common absence that separates itself off from it. *At the same time, this murmur sets God apart from God and makes him visible by marking him.* Here lies the utter difference between Jabèsian monotheism and the primal pagan Nothing, which, having no Name, is essentially invisible: it cannot be set against any backdrop as it is the ultimate backdrop in and by itself. God,

---

44 Importantly, the notion of God as a fullness of being recurring throughout medieval philosophy in fact precluded him having a Name. It is by no means a coincident that in Christianity, which fed on Greek thought, God himself is nameless. Having a Name, the Jewish God, in turn, is a dialectical product *par excellence.* This is also how the Hegelian apology of Christianity as a religion whose triune Godhead fosters developed dialectics can be opposed. The Jewish God is not only paradoxically One but also has an unpronounceable Name that differentiates him internally.

45 See Aristotle, *Metaphysics,* Book XII (Λ), 1072b, trans. William D. Ross (Oxford: Oxford University Press Reprints, 1924).

46 BD, p. 63.

47 *Ibid.,* p. 81. (quotation altered)

in turn, can be differentiated and *is audible*, for his Name makes him internally differential. This vision of God can be formed only when ultimate conclusions are inferred from the way language works based on the elementary difference between the *vocable* and what it refers to. The *vocable* shatters the stable being of God that is Nothing but, at the same time, makes referencing him possible.[48]

Back to our comparison between Aristotle's and Jabès' theologies, if the Stagirite's God is a restful whole that fully overlaps with its own name and an object of contemplation and *seeing*, Jabèsian God that is Nothing is *audible* in the act of ongoing self-differentiation of absence from absence, constantly parted by the Name.

This jettisons him from the immanence of this world and likens to the God of Jewish monotheism.

Language and Monotheism

This reasoning leads us to where Jabès' writings yield two compelling insights. First, God identified with Nothing is a hub of a continually renewing difference, an oscillation around an inner fissure. Second, this position of God that is Nothing is somehow associated with the fact that, albeit re-worked, it is still the God of Judaism who has a Name. Both these components seem to correspond to Jabès' vision of language, where language is a universal system with even the Creator subject to it. At this point, these links deserve a closer analysis.

Let us start from a remark from Jabès' last work: "A sign [*un signe*] invents the *vocable* – and suddenly the universe finds itself confronted [*se trouve confronté*] with itself."[49] In the light of what we said about the *vocable* in the previous

---

48 That the *vocable* enforces a specific concept of God – a differentiated and internally deferred one – is associated by Jabès with the Torah's prohibition on image (see QQLS, pp. 12–16). Because there is the *vocable*, i.e. writing, truth and being cannot be stabilised. Truth defies expression in words, which, as an image, would perpetuate it for ever. Writing must thus only gesture at that which cannot be expressed, fleetingly presenting it for reading (*Ibid.*, p. 14). Consequently, there is no sacred or profane writing as such: sacredness is a momentary tension of writing, which strives to express the voice of silence through itself (*Ibid.*, s. 15).

49 LH, p. 55. The French original emphasises that where there is a *vocable*, the universe is already confronted with itself. The "process" of this confrontation is not accessible to us, for it is a discontinuity. Either there is nothing and unexpressed, pure Nothing exists or there is a *vocable* and Nothing is already constrained but, consequently, also expressed. Writing entails experiencing how Nothing emerges from the dark and is briefly illuminated by a lightning of the *vocable*.

Chapter, the sentence can be interpreted as saying that when the *vocable* – which is no longer an ordinary sign – comes into being, *a rift appears within that which is*. In the void that is emptied out in this way, being is forced to face itself and, thus, differentiates within. While a sign could be viewed as a transparent label of being with a referential function and nothing more, the *vocable* belongs on a different plane, and its split separates it permanently from the thing "named." In this way, Jabèsian writing explodes being's quiet existence. Ever since the *vocable* appears, being is "confronted with itself," inscribed in the void of a dislocation between the imaginary and the real. However, if one sign can refer to one being and only to this being, the *vocable* places that which it refers to in a relation to all existence, which is marked with *tzimtzum* to boot. A thing bears an imprint of belonging to the whole system brought forth by Creation. That is why, as Jabès insists, the *vocable* makes the entire universe confront itself. This confrontation leaves behind a vestige of the irremovable rift, i.e. *tzimtzum*, which defies evacuating as long as the *vocable* exists.

Let us move on and focus on the poet's following statement:

By virtue of its letters Nothing becomes absence in its written materiality.[50]

By receiving a Name, and thus a *vocable*, Nothing, i.e. God, transubstantiates into absence. Just as any thing is "slain" in the *vocable*, Nothing as well loses its "presence." In other words, by coming into the world created after *tzimtzum*, even Nothing cannot be present. *For this reason God that is Nothing shares* with the created world *a common condition: his "being" is based on a gap – on his own absence*. Even though we describe the void itself as "God" or "Nothing," we cannot wrench it away from a dialectical relation with Creation. In this way, God that is Nothing is subject to the same laws to which any and all being is subject. Nothing is closer to things than the split God that is Nothing. He is the condition of rupture incarnate.

What is that difference between the *vocable* and the thing to which it refers that it carries the fissure on even into God? The answer suggested by Jabès' thought is far-reaching. First of all, we must notice that *this difference concerns equally language and ontology*. It means that the rift between the thing and the *vocable* divides the signified from the signifier and the "referent" from the "sign" (with, importantly, the *vocable* not being a sign) as well as being from Nothing. In the post-Creation world, Jabès can see no difference between having a *vocable* and being. To have a *vocable* means to be irreversibly severed from Nothing and,

---

50 BQ II, p. 248 (quotation altered).

thus, to exist. Yet, at the same time, wherever the *vocable* emerges, Nothing is "encased" by a thing split into two. A fissure that is produced in this way points at the thing. Thus, *the same split brings forth being and produces a fundamental form of language.* As the *vocable* comes into being, we see both language in statu nascendi and the stirrings of emergent ontology. As mentioned in the previous Chapter, in its peculiar way the *vocable* expresses both Nothing and the word that got dissolved in it. Intertwining Nothing and the word seems, for Jabès, to determine the ultimate line where being and language are indistinguishable.

In conclusion, as the *vocable* comes into being, something existing is brought forth and is bound to a unique name confined in materiality. The *vocable* still bears a fissure of *tzimtzum*, which makes the generated being always already internally ruptured. In this rupture, it is confronted with itself and self-differentiated as well as its relation with the entire universe is revealed. Being named and existing coalesce thus in the *vocable* as both are based on the same separation from Nothing. A minimum gap necessary for the *vocable* to refer to a thing jolts it out of its restful existence and breaks it into two, irreversibly stretching it between the imaginary and the real.

Consequently, all things in the Jabèsian universe exist in as far as they have names. Emphatically, it is not that a thing exists *due to* a name or that it has a name due to existing – being and having a name are two facets of the same event. This vision of reality could be said to comprise immanent elements of Jewish thinking: things are radically singular though they are related to the entire world, and the particularity of each of them ensues from its relation to the specific form of name that is the *vocable*. In a sense, each thing has its own unpronounceable name and each is based on self-differentiation. Thus, Jabès can easily make a final step and derive radical, apophatic monotheism from the very way in which reality functions.

Let us also take a final step and try to specify how God is to be thought in a world cleft by *vocables*.

It is a God formed in the semblance of the Judaic God, but an *already* non-existent one. He has a Name which is a paradigmatic *vocable* – material, unpronounceable and permanently disjoined from its "designee." The Jabèsian God comes out of utter purification; while things that have *vocables* are always deferred and non-present, God has never been there at all and, consequently, his Name, instead of upon some positive content whose mirage it defers, acts upon Nothing itself. Perhaps, there is no "content" whatsoever in this God as he becomes just a chart of relations between a thing and a *vocable*. In this sense, God seems an offshoot of the perception of reality as formed by language, one, let us add, that is radically modern. Once the *vocable* is thought, a thus-conceived

God is brought in. Owing to a cut that separates him from pre-modern thought, Jabès can describe the primal link that entwines language's generative role and monotheism. Indeed, impenetrable is the irony of history that offered us a solution to the enigma of the connection between One God and his creative language only when we can no longer decide whether the enigma had been there before or whether it surfaced, as we know it, together with modernity.

Conclusion: Relentless Theology and the Fate of Jerusalem

The deep structure of Jabèsian negative "ontology" harbours theology. In this context, there is an odd ring to Heidegger's critiques of ontotheology, which – prevailing in Western thought – was supposed to relegate Being to the background and replace it with being that draws its existence from the supreme and perfect being of God. For Heidegger, ontotheology belongs to an era that is just being rolled back by philosophy. Jabès' thought, however, is born not in the past but in the ongoing movement of simplification and purification. Monotheism features, as a relentless vestige, the last point of difference that precludes oceanic Nothing becoming reality. Unlike Heidegger, Jabès does not dismantle ontotheology but reverses the scaffolding of metaphysical thought still lingering in modernity to unveil its monotheistic vestige. Theology is a term that serves to describe the elementary phenomenon of the vestige which persists when thinking is emptied out of all content.

In this Chapter, I have reiterated the difference between the pagan concept of Nothing as *apeiron* that engulfs all beings and the monotheistic notion of impossible, split and deferred Nothing associable with Jewish monotheism. This difference, of course, is rooted in the Athens-vs.-Jerusalem opposition. The argument above showcases the utility of this opposition to thinking as its central rupture props thought and gives it grounding in the differentiating of material. Without the opposition, we likely could not go that far. Within an after all strictly modern inquiry, it helps form dialectically related, opposed camps: "pagan" and "Jewish," each attributed its particular features. Ultimately, the Athens-vs.-Jerusalem dualism is a definitive difference that remains after a text has been interpreted and thought through; juxtaposing two options at odds with each other, the dualism oscillates around *a pure split*. As the split persists, thus-constructed "Greek" thought and "Jewish" thought find themselves in an unequal relation, *with the latter comprising in itself the effect that is imprinted on it as on an element in an opposition.* For it is through Jabèsian "monotheism," founded on *tzimtzum* and the *vocable*, that the relentlessness of that final vestige, which survives as an ultimate difference, could be explained. What does it imply for the Athens-vs.-Jerusalem opposition?

I defined Jabès' theology as a re-interpreted Jewish mono(a)theism since it insists that when the Name appears, an irremovable split takes place and persists. But as soon as this theology was to be called, *to be given a name*, its being burst and a gap arose that links it to the other, mute companion, ignorant of its position – to "Greek thought." Perhaps, the opposition of the two metropolises does not a priori form Jewish philosophy but rather is brought forth by the very movement of naming it? Should this indeed be the case, *philosophical Athens would be only a self-differentiation of Jewish philosophy of modernity.* For, importantly, Jewish philosophy of modernity comes to account for the final vestige, which it associates with Judaic monotheism, and, at the same time, defines itself as recognising this vestige. Because of the latter, *in order to sustain itself, Jewish philosophy of modernity needs a name that, as a vocable, would also differentiate it from itself.* In other words, the movement of difference affects the very construction of Jewish philosophy of modernity, enforcing an inner rupture on it. If it is the case, "Athens" is just another form of "Jerusalem," which can reach its aim only through self-differentiation. The name of this conceptual Jerusalem – "Jewish philosophy" – is an emptiness that it cannot fathom. If "Jewish philosophy" is indeed interpreted as a *vocable*, it becomes clear why most effort within this current of thought is wasted on fruitless attempts to find a self-definition and sustain a constant difference from what it is not. "Jewish philosophy" is a material name that goes beyond what it "refers" to; at its centre lies a void that continually attracts the movement of thinking towards itself. But it is still impossible to descend into this void. The only possible step is self-differentiation in which "Jewish philosophy" becomes a boundary of two akin territories, one of which must represent permanence and limitation while the other directs the movement of difference, assuming the position of the self-differentiated, alienated and transgressive. Based on Jabèsian thinking, this is how the Athens-vs.-Jerusalem opposition, as well as the necessity constantly to traverse their boundary, can be explained. If it is indeed the case, the vestige that Jabès himself puts in the position of the Judaic God is not so much a re-interpretation of Jewish monotheism as rather *a final projection of Jewish philosophy of modernity on its own content.*

The relentlessness of modern theology is thus a cornerstone of a new philosophical Jerusalem and its own impenetrable enigma.

6 Messianism of Writing

In the previous Chapters, I provided a rather static account of Jabès' thought. I sought to grasp the fundamental structures and factors that govern his texts. Now, I will focus on their dynamics. This Chapter will show how the consequences of *tzimtzum* lead, inevitably, to messianism. As already indicated, *tzimtzum* is an excess place productive of a utopian moment. And this is where it essentially ties in with the movement of Jabès' messianism, a signature feature of his thinking.[1] Building on this link, I will attempt to establish in how far this messianism stems from Jewish tradition and to what degree it represents the groundwork of modern philosophy.

I will draw on the conclusions of the previous Chapters to give a theoretical introduction to my theme. First, I will discuss the essence of the utopian moment directly generated by *tzimtzum*, and then I will show how deeply this utopia-induced messianism is rooted in Jabèsian ontology. These theoretical insights will culminate in addressing the relation of messianism to time and truth. Against this backdrop, I will outline the dynamics of Jabès' messianic thought and its existential poignancy. My argument will proceed in a few stages. First, I will explore the utopia of the Unity of things, the ultimate goal of the messianic act, and then I will reveal its inner structure of impossibility. This will help me depict a deferral inscribed in Jabès' messianism. Finally and crucially, I will show that messianism is an effect of a gap between things and language, a gap resulting from *tzimtzum*.

---

1 "Disenchanted" messianism of Jabès' work has not failed to attract the commentators' attention even though none of them has addressed it comprehensively. For example, Josh Cohen observes: "Rather than seek its redemption, Jabès makes torment's irredeemability the organizing principle of his writing. And yet, […], this irredeemability is not to be seen in opposition to redemption. The messianic horizon which haunts all of his texts takes the paradoxical form of its non-achievement; the affinity of Judaism and writing lies in their shared thinking of redemption as that which is maintained in its promise rather than in its realization. It is for this reason that perhaps the most privileged term in Jabès' thought is the *question*, for the question is the form which maintains itself only in its irresolution, the originary form of incompletion." Josh Cohen, *Interrupting Auschwitz: Art, Religion, Philosophy* (London and New York: Continuum, 2005), p. 109. I believe that Jabès' messianism and its complex structure deserve a more thorough analysis.

In the last section, I will compare Jabèsian messianism with similar ideas developed in modern philosophy and formulate its implications for thinkers of a messianic proclivity, such as Benajmin and Agamben.

Hope for the Definitive Book

To analyse the messianic structure of Jabès' writing, we must first focus on the utopian moment inscribed in both the imaginary and the real. In an explicit play with Mallarmé, and in fact also with Hegel, Jabès frames this moment as the *hope for the definitive book*. What would this book stand for?

> God […] expected from man the book, which man expected from man. The one, in order to be finally God, the other in order to be finally man. The book of the order of the elements, the unity of the universe, of God and of man.[2]

It would thus be a book removing all incompleteness immanent to every being and putting the entire world in the definitive order. It would also round off the process of becoming God and man. As they are both authors, we can assume that, in and through this book, the author would definitively execute his design. Consequently, the book would itself evade the rupture between the imaginary and the real. More than that, it *would definitively put this rupture to an end*.

In this sense, if the book came into being, it would be a historic event and an end of history as we know it. As such, it could not be questioned by any other later book, and its text would abolish the very possibility of there being any other texts in the future. The book would mend the fragmented universe by eliminating its haunting *tzimtzum*. Re-uniting the real and the imaginary, it would give the erstwhile real an ultimate self-knowledge and the erstwhile imaginary a full enactment. Like Mallarmé's Book, it would transcend and bridge the gap between meaning and matter as, by being both meaningful and material, it would entwine the two inextricably. By this token, it would also remove the fundamental contradiction between the bare, persisting life and understanding of it:

> Isn't writing the attempt to abolish forever the distance between our life and what we write of it between us and the *vocable*? Between us and us, between word and word?[3]

As this passage suggests, cherished by writing, the hope for the definitive book would also promote comparison and agreement between "beings" which are now inevitably sovereign and isolated – between "us and the *vocable*" (which

---

2 BQ I, p. 172.
3 DB, p. 105.

would obliterate the chasm of *tzimtzum*), "between word and word" (which would evacuate a fundamental ontological incoherence from the text) and, even, "between us and us." The latter can be variously construed: as abrogation of the discontinuity of time, which incessantly explodes identity from within and differentiates "us" from later "us," or as a removal of differentiation intrinsic to every attempt "we" make to self-understand "us." Finally, as "we," like everything else that has a name, are burst by *tzimtzum*, the book would abolish it.

A vision of such a definitive book is located at the intersection of Jewish messianism, in particular its Lurianic version, and modern philosophy. Of course, messianism in general gives this vision the idea of restitution of that which was broken at the beginning. Still, Luria's possible influence lies in that making such a book is, to some extent at least, man's responsibility – his *tikkun*. The book is a human work which, once accomplished, transforms reality and paves a path to messianic renewal, which transcends man. Importantly, however, unlike in Luria, *tikkun* is here first and foremost an intellectual endeavour: the book is an act of definitive self-knowledge of the real by the real, mediated by man's work. As such, it is intimately associated with Hegelian absolute knowledge, as are Mallarmé's ideas about the Book. The Jabèsian book shares with Hegel's thought a modern assumption that the world is structured by knowledge, internally fragmented and incomplete as this knowledge is.[4] Like in Hegel, the act of knowing is an event which is more than just a discovery made by a certain person at a particular moment. The externally contingent place in which the book appears becomes a messianic event of universal compass.

In Jabès, the hope for the definitive book motivates every act of writing (as he conceives of it), gives rise to a new book and sets it in motion:

The first phrases of a work are always full of hope. Doubt creeps in and blossoms on the way. At the end there is double despair: that of the writer and that of the witness.[5]
Hope is bound to writing.[6]

---

4   The interdependence of "word" and "world" is explicitly expressed, for example, in: "A word joins other words in order to further first of all the sentence, then the page, and finally the book. In order to survive, it must take an active part in freeing the world of speech, must be a dynamic agent of its transformation and unity" (BQ I, p. 227). In Jabès, the Book gives things their correspondences, doubles and opposites (BQ I, p. 32) and, thereby, is the very basic structure of reality.

5   BQ I, p. 60.
6   BQ II, p. 155.

Hope is a utopian moment that reflexively illuminates the depth of fragmentation. It is accompanied by inexorable doubt, a final disappointment at the end of the work. However, characteristically of Jabès and connecting him to Jewish messianism, which hopes despite and, even more, *because of* historical disappointments, this hope cannot be relinquished.[7] *It corresponds to tzimtzum, which opens the beginning of a book, just as despair is involved in its collapse.* Hence, the act of writing is informed by its own specific moment of universal hope:

> I write because, while trying to get to the end of what I could say, I think, every time, that next time I will succeed.
>
> [...] An unformulated thought means hope to join word to word, means waiting for signs in search of their graven form [...].
>
> We do not know beforehand what regions we will cross because the end is between the tracks of adventure, between the lines, never between standing columns.[8]
>
> *To desire something passionately means suppressing the heat of any other desire, means fusing all your desires into one, possessing nothing in order to claim everything at once. The most deprived have the maddest desires. Emptiness desires to be filled.*
>
> [...] *Way off, there is a thought which will soon sweep away all others in order finally to take hold of silence and the dream of words sleeping in rows.*[9]

According to Jabès, writing is fuelled by this specific, maximalist desire – claiming everything at once. "Everything" means understanding which will repair reality. The abysmal failure of *tzimtzum* is paralleled by the hope for the definitive book; the state of fragmentation seems so agonising that writing cannot rest content with moderate claims. It is for this reason that hope is a utopian moment which, resulting from *tzimtzum*, precludes stopping either at a partial imaginary or at a partial real.

Messianism and Jabès' Ontology

Having seen how the hope for the definitive book imbues writing with dynamics, we can explore Jabès' messianism in more abstract terms and juxtapose it with the "ontological" structure outlined in the foregoing.

The mechanism of his messianism tallies with the specific position which the act of writing takes vis-à-vis the entire reality. As suggested above, each new "book" – or, more broadly, each symbolic order – is engendered by its

---

7   See EHW, p. 37. Hope is, as Gould concludes, the irremovable "sin of the book" – "the mad search for divine harmony" (Gould, "Introduction," pp. xvii, xxii).

8   BQ I, pp. 224–5.

9   BQ II, pp. 310, 316.

own primordial *tzimtzum* as a reduction of this reality. *Tzimtzum* demarcates the boundaries of this order and determines the compass of its own *indicible*. However, this order seems universal in the world that it creates while the *indicible* remains hidden.

Therefore, the messianic structure of each perspectival order can be said to be conditioned by a specific nexus of universalism and partialness embodied in the *vocable*. In this optics, messianism designates simply *a desire to enact universalism immanent to a given order ("book")*. In this sense, messianism would involve surmounting an ostensibly removable barrier that prevents an order from becoming the order as such. "The word which shatters the word in order to break free, for a moment holds the key to the book,"[10] writes Jabès, suggesting that it was the primal severance from the real in *tzimtzum* (and thus "shattering" of and "breaking free" from the burden of the past "word") that produced a feeling that the created order could achieve a messianic consummation.

Consequently, messianism is not a delusion and even less a removable delusion. It is *the other side of that "oblivion,"* to use Jabès' term, into which the symbolic order must slide to be constituted in the first place. Furthermore, in each case, a particular shape of this messianism is likely to be bound up with the limits determined for the order by its *tzimtzum*. In other words, *seeking messianic fulfilment, an order heads, in fact, towards its own, hidden limit*. Pushed forward by the hope for the definitive book, it paradoxically moves towards its own "origins" ("our sources precede us,"[11] insists Jabès). It is clear therefore why Lurianic *tzimtzum* and *shevirat ha-kelim* had to be coalesced into one moment of *tzimtzum* sensu largo: messianic hope leads an order back to its moment of primordial reduction. *Tzimtzum* remains a permanent condition of possibility, and the movement between the "originary" curtailment and the "ultimate" consummation entails moving to and from *tzimtzum*.

Similarly, the messianic drive in the act of writing comes from its condition of possibility and causes the originary *tzimtzum* to be rehearsed, as a failure this time. Demanding everything because of its claim to universality, the act exposes the limited grounds of such claims and, thereby, discloses that it is *only one of many*. This in turn, as explained in Chapter Three, means a transition from the imaginary to the real, that is, a failure of *tzimtzum*.

Therefore, the messianic act can be said to reveal a fundamental lack in an order, the same lack, actually, that emerged where the order was cut off from the

---

10 BQ II, p. 348.
11 DB, p. 85.

real. The concept of the *vocable* renders the pattern, showing the hope-fuelled movement as moving within the imaginary delimited by *tzimtzum*. Exercising its magnetic impact, *tzimtzum* forces the act of writing to make messianic claims. As if by the Hegelian "cunning of reason," the claims actually represent a given act's self-analytical impulse since in demands ultimately to comprehend the real, it ironically attains self-comprehension and discovers its own limitedness.

Before concluding this section, let us consider a pertinent question: Does anything remain of this circular movement, to which messianism belongs seemingly *despite* and actually *because of* its hopes? Do repeated messianic cycles generate anything new? A possible answer would be: what a messianic cycle leaves behind is the *vocable* as a *particular* nexus of the imaginary and the real. Only the rise and failure of an order can reveal it and make it known to us. And the *vocable*, as I will show in the next Chapter, is a key to analysing the space of the Book. If Jabès can write that

> [...] the book is a universe in motion which our eyes fix.[12]
> ... point [...] visible to the world for a fraction of a second because of my wish to explain.[13]

it is only because of the messianic structure that makes it possible. For it is in the messianic structure that the point of *tzimtzum* is *circumscribed*, which gives rise to a particular order, sustains this order's "wish to explain" and is a place where it dies. And *the point itself*, rendered by one entire book in its rise and failure, is "a universe in motion which our eyes fix." Studying this universe through snapshots of particular books is what Jabès commits himself to doing.[14]

Therefore, failure does not render the act of writing futile as it produces a *particular point* that preserves both the moment of its own creation and the moment of the radical messianic claim.

---

12 BQ II, p. 146.
13 *Ibid.*, p. 392.
14 *The Book of Dialogue* insists: "The mind does not think what it knows. It can only think what it does not know. It is ignorance of Knowing which its thinking enriches" (BD, p. 67). This nearly Hegelian thesis encapsulates the relationship between messianic acts and Knowledge that they produce. The acts ensue from ignorance, originary forgetfulness, and keep heading toward knowledge which is concealed from them. It takes an entire messianic cycle to reveal it, and in this way Knowledge, the forgetting of which gave rise to the act, is augmented.

Messianism, Time and Truth

With the preliminaries behind, we can scrutinise the distinct features of Jabèsian messianism in more detail. In this section, I will argue that it is essentially and compellingly related to time and truth, which connects it to the legacy of Kant and Hegel. As explored in Chapter Three, the "real" time differs from the "illusory time," and, naturally, the act of writing, which unfolds within a certain order instituted by *tzimtzum*, takes place in the latter. That is why time is measurable in this act, with there being both a past that contains the originary event and a future that holds messianic hope. Still, it is only possible at the cost of the originary limitation of the "real time," where the *point of this delimiting* becomes a "moment" *inaccessible to this temporal series*. As the act of writing revolves around its *tzimtzum* event, which is both past and future, the "temporal series," to use Kantian terminology, available in a given order, oscillates constantly around a point that eludes and entirely undermines it. Hence, similarly to Derrida, Jabès' act of writing is always belated-deferred and refers to that which is behind or ahead of it, for that which is "right before" and "present" refuses to be captured in it and is, emphatically, utterly "absent." At the same time, it is the point that seeks to accommodate writing.

Such insights seem to inform passages in which Jabès' reflection on the present comes strikingly close to both Hegel and Nietzsche:

Man carries time. We play against. Time is becoming, a second's blaze rekindled.
[…] Man is a merchant of ashes. Out of the world, I save the moment, my portion of eternity.[15]
The center is the moment. If God is the center He cannot exist except momentarily.
Therefore God passes in whatever, by virtue of renewing itself, does not pass.
Eternity is constant renewal. So that entering eternity means becoming conscious of all that begins all the time, means becoming yourself a beginning.[16]
"A search for harmony," she had said at the crossroads where we were drawn and quartered by our contradictions. […]
"at every instant of the book, which is a vibrant mirror of death."
[…] Ah, who but ourselves can perform this miracle on us at the hour of our death?
Creating your truth means exalting the instant. I salute eternity from one second to the next.[17]

---

15 BQ I, p. 135
16 BQ II, p. 159
17 *Ibid.*, p. 248, 280.

"When you write, you do not know whether you are obeying the moment or eternity."
[…] Moments have a spicy aftertaste of eternity.[18]

Following Nietzsche, Jabès sees eternity compressed in the present moment. The act of writing is fraught with constant tension as it turns towards this absent centre. The centre is, at the same time, a site of the concentrating happening/enowning that keeps deferring itself and makes itself visible only in dislocations as past or future, where it is but a trace in the "ashes" into which writing will turn after it passes.

All associations with Heidegger's late thought, unavoidable though they seem at this point, are ousted by a fundamental difference produced by the relation of Jabèsian messianism to time. In Jabès, namely, there is no language to persist through happening/enowning (as Heidegger's "Dwelling of Being" does) and allow approaching it. On the contrary, Jabès' messianism is stirred by the fact that *the centre of happening/enowning can be approached only in a one-off mobilisation of an order in which this order evanesces.* This is the already evoked attempt to achieve the definitive understanding, which is bound to end in failure.

In the passages quoted above, Jabès seems to describe this attempt, relying on the notion of "truth." In Chapter Three, I distinguished a "perspectival truth" from the inaccessible and fictional "real" truth; here, there is still another truth – one located exactly where the other two intersect. This third truth seems *the outermost point of a perspectival order where this order bumps against the boundary of its reality.* Still within this order, it conveys this order's *tzimtzum.* Since, as stated above, in a messianic effort to understand the real, an order comes to understand itself or, rather, its own limitedness, this third meaning of truth is a liminal moment of understanding the real in its own perishment.

Let us return to the relation of messianism and time. The central emptiness of the present can be "seen" in such liminal truth as, disclosing the *tzimtzum* of an order, it deciphers this order's inaccessible, withdrawing centre. At the same time, it propels *tzimtzum's* reverse movement, in which that central truth of an order turns out to be one of many truths. In other words, the moment of universality of an order lies in the instant of its fall, when its immanent perspectivism is exposed. The concomitant shift in the functioning of time is structured in the same way: *the moment of messianic fall is the point where the "illusory" and the "real" times intersect.* Indeed, it is a Jabèsian "moment of eternity" – an oxymoronic coupling of "eternity" and "moment." Eternity appears as the illusory time encounters its own boundary and condition of possibility. Since it cannot be accommodated within a temporal series it determines itself, it is "eternal" for the

18 *Ibid.,* p. 407.

entire series. And the "moment" is a moment of the real time in which the *entire* illusory time is inscribed.

The association of truth and time is specifically Jabèsian. Just as truth in Hegel,[19] when truth in the third of the senses defined above *is revealed, it immediately halts time*. In both cases, the time we perceive results from the persistent "alienation," and knowledge that abolishes alienation simply removes time. In Jabès, however, unlike in Hegel, there are multiple "times" and truths bound up with them. Each of them perishes in its "absolute knowledge," and the moment of messianic claim and its collapse produce an inextricable nexus of the "moment" and "eternity." In this sense, Jabès' thought is a kind of Hegelian disillusioned thought, a Hegelian morning after: *absolute knowledge is not one but forms an end of every symbolic order*.

Concluding, Jabèsian perspectivism is radical in its connection to messianism. Only the uncompromising demand of ultimate truth unveils "the moment of eternity" and, at the same time, inflicts failure on the order that made this demand. In finding truth, the act of writing makes good on its exclusive chance and, as Jabès expresses it, *saves the moment, its "portion of eternity."* As *Le Parcours* insists, "[it is] as if, at a particular moment, opening eventually gave passage to it alone, opening to itself."[20] This line can be understood to mean that the moment an order falls is actually its opening as it opens to itself, recognising its *tzimtzum*, and offers a passage. Where to? I will address this issue below.

---

19 Hegel writes: "*Time* is just the notion definitely existent, and presented to consciousness in the form of empty intuition. Hence spirit necessarily appears in time, and it appears in time so long as it does not *grasp* its pure notion, i.e. do long as it does not annul Time. It is the *pure* self in external form, apprehended in intuition, and not grasped and understood by the self, it is the notion apprehended only by intuition. When this notion grasps itself, it supersedes its time character, (conceptually) comprehends intuition, and is intuition comprehended and comprehending. Time, therefore, appears as spirit's destiny and necessity, where spirit is not yet complete within itself; it is the necessity compelling spirit to enrich the share self-consciousness has in consciousness, to put into motion *the immediacy of the inherent nature* (which is the form in which the substance is present in consciousness); or, conversely, to realize and make manifest what is inherent, regarded as inward or immanent, to manifest that which is at first within – i.e. to vindicate it for spirit's certainty of self." Hegel, *Phenomenology*, pp. 470–1.

20 P, p. 77.

The Risk of Messianism: "The Edge of the Book"

So far, I have outlined the theoretical structure that elucidates Jabèsian messianism: its connections with ontology, the nature of utopia that fuels it and its relation to time and truth. Now, I will explore the very act of writing in more detail, as a messianic event and a real, existential experience.

To begin with, let us explain why, as *an event*, the act of writing is radically dangerous. Let us have a look at two key messianic passages in Jabès:

"You write, but doesn't what you write hold only for a moment?"
"We don't own the coming moment at all [*ne...point*]."
"If so, how can we own the present moment?"
"The coming of the Messiah is for tomorrow [*La venue du Messie est pour demain*]. The change will be for tomorrow [*Pour demain sera le changement*]."
"Is the present whiter than the past? Our words cast shadow on the present, but what shadow would challenge the immaculate whiteness of tomorrow?"
"...will tear the night of my ink, of the *vocables* swollen with my black blood, the Messiah amidst them as a shipwreck on the ocean.
All my words bring change."
[...] "*How will the Messiah come in, o answer!, if the book were a closed world?*" wrote Reb Nachman
"*The Messiah is the condition of change, an incarnation of this condition,*" Reb Akkad said....[21]
Is writing simply to rise up against silence, a twitch of life within death, and finally to die of its passion? Die with its passion whose death catches us unawares with its loss of energy like a setting sun? O night, vast tomb of oblivion
[...] Around what is not expressed, what we could never formulate, we talk like the deaf and write blindly, outside time. But *life is there, on our heels, life come to meet us where we stoically tried to do without it* [emphasis added]. What does it want from us? And first of all, what hold does it have on the book? O weight of the prelude. All steps are under its signs. But life carries death in its womb, and we have eaten of this death.[22]

In the first passage, Jabès clearly links the messianic element to deferred time. What we write, he insists, holds only for a moment while the next one is not ours at all [*ne...point*]. This is another reference to the point as a moment of the discontinuity of *tzimtzum*. But, in fact, this point divides us also from the present as between the illusory and the real times there is an irremovable chasm, which prevents us from meaningfully describing and "appropriating" happening. *For this reason, that which will happen is the realm of messianism.*

---

21 LR I, pp. 121–2.
22 BQ II, p. 285.

The Messiah, as Jabès claims, will come *"pour demain,"* which can have two implications. One of them represents messianism's brighter facet, with tomorrow still structurally uncertain and possibly bringing a kind of "salvation." The other implication expresses messianism's extreme ontological threat as we are divided from the next moment by a discontinuity so radical that the depth of the impending change deprives us of understanding. The two implications merge in the word "condition" used at the end of the first passage: the Messiah is both a condition, i.e. a prerequisite of change (a hope for a new world in the closed, fallen book), and its condition, i.e. a state, an incarnation of uncertainty and risk. The messianic danger is further portrayed in the second passage, which implies that the ultimate mobilisation attempted by the act of writing *arises from its desperate inadequacy vis-à-vis the imminent, radically discontinuous time.* Writing is a "dash of life in death": its own death, for its attempt to understand is self-destructive. One of the rabbis quoted by Jabès is named Nachman, and for a reason, too: Nachman of Breslov believed that writing could grasp the mystical essence of reality only when it was put down and then burned.[23] In Jabès, this thought is even more radical as destruction looms not only for Kabbalistic writing but also for any endeavour to understand life completely. Life, which is "on our heels" and is "come to meet us," forms a surplus that, incomprehensible to us, continues to bring failure upon us.

So, if writing, as Jabès conceives of it, is based on the structure of messianism, it cannot be a quiet meditation on *tzimtzum*; rather, it means experiencing absolute, unbearable mutability:

> For me [the idea of the Messiah] represents the idea of a great writer, because, as we face a text, what are we keyed to if not change? And what are we exposed to but the unforeseeable change we owe to its brutality? Messiah is also a *vocable*.
>
> In our task [*à la tâche*], we are like believers buoyed up by immense hope and at the same time shaken by unutterable fear. It happens that a writer commits suicide at the edge of a book. But never will a nonwriter die *for* a word [*une parole*].[24]

Tellingly, in Jabès, while a writer is *like* the Messiah, the Messiah is a writer. What do the two have in common? Both survive subsequent failures. For Jabès, the two roles – of the writer and of the Messiah – involve the highest risk embodied in the vision of the "edge of the book" [*bord du livre*].

---

23 See Marc-Alain Ouaknin, *The Burnt Book: Reading the Talmud*, trans. Llewellyn Brown (Princeton: Princeton UP, Lieu Commun, 1995).
24 BR II, p. 47. (quotation altered)

What is this edge? Based on our argument so far, the answer can be: it is a boundary between the messianic representation of the following moment and its coming, that is, between *an attempt to achieve an ultimate understanding and pure duration, which puts it ultimately to an end.* Awaited with "unutterable fear," "the edge of the book" is a moment when the act of witing is over, and that which has come into being will be faced with abiding reality. This entails also verifying the messianic attempt and showing whether the Messiah was real or false. As such, it is not only a theoretical but also an existential experience of *tzimtzum.* Consequently, the writer is one that dares take this ultimate risk, which other people shun, as he demands truth and pays for his claim with a failure. The Jabèsian writer and the Aristotelian ideal of a calm contemplator of truth are thus worlds apart.

> "Do you believe," he said, "that one can reach the gilded pinnacles of the night and return to the starting point intact?"
> […] "There are no pinnacles of writing," he said. "Writing itself is a pinnacle."[25]

God as the Ultimate Reader: Messianism and Monotheism

Such is the existential risk implicated in Jabèsian messianism. Before describing the very experience of messianic endeavour and failure, I will focus on the relation between such messianism and monotheism as crucial to my further argument.

To start with, the messianic attempt is an act of definitive understanding that seeks to fathom the moment inaccessible to it. As such, it is also an attempt to halt time itself since the Messiah is expected to put closure to history. "The edge of the book" is a moment where all happening/enowning should cease. But what comes to pass when the attempt fails? Time goes on, defying expectations and explanations. It is the reason why the failure of the messianic act *reveals pure, incomprehensible duration after everything has been put on the line and lost.*

It turns out that an attempt to attain ultimate understanding, which seeks to prevent happening/enowning once and for all, is confronted with a dimension that radically transcends it. Thus, the messianic act can be posited to be pure duration what the Messiah is to God. In other words, *the Messiah's failure gives God space; more than that, it is this failure that reveals him.* Let us have a look at Jabès' phrasing:

---

25 PHD, pp. 115–116.

To write as if addressing God. But what to expect from nothingness where any word is disarmed?

[…] Here I have to stress how strongly the word is attracted to the nothing around it, for which it is the preferred prey. It is the same attraction God has for the universe of the ultimate utterance.

[…] Page by page, we answer the end of the world with our own end.

[…] God is the accepted challenge of the word. But the word does not lead to God. Only silence could.[26]

Writing is followed and heard up to the point where it stops being writing and becomes the deep sense of a passionate deletion.

[…] The word remains objective where subjectivity afflicts us. Truth is objective. / The law is objective. / Death is objective.

We must think of God as an objective Totality.

He said: "Am I the man God did not recognize? If so, I have done searching. For me God is nowhere."[27]

What you cannot read

He is reading.

[…] "God hears what no one hears and sees what no one can see" […].[28]

"The broken tables are an unrivalled model of the book" […].

"You will break the book," wrote Reb Shmuel, "not in anger, but in love; because in breaking it opens to divine speech."[29]

The vision of God that emerges from these passages is built around three fundamental relations. First, God is presupposed to transcend the messianic attempt. Second, he is a force that attracts "the last word" and generates the tension of "the end," i.e. "the edge of the book." Jabèsian messianism is thus inscribed in the divine and owes to it – to its beyond as it were – its dynamics. Third, *the divine is a plane of reference in relation to which the entire messianic act is a sign.* This is why the act becomes utterly unintelligible after failure as it is read where it cannot reach itself. Bare, meaningless duration is where understanding itself is subjected to an "objective" understanding incomprehensible to us.

Paradoxically, thus, the ultimate "reading" of the real takes place when reading itself is read in a space inaccessible to us. That is why Jabès can claim that "*only what disappears will have called for us.*"[30] This idea echoes both Nachman of Breslov's "burned book" and Lacan's great Other, who "sees" us, albeit in Jabès such seeing is necessarily discontinued and what remains is a liminal moment

---

26 BQ II, pp. 153, 161, 169.
27 *Ibid.*, pp. 216, 223.
28 *Ibid.*, pp.395, 403.
29 LR I, pp. 99–100.
30 BQ II, p. 154.

in which reading is "read." God is the ultimate reader as he reveals himself in pure duration after understanding fails. He is also a reader of the failure itself, its recipient and a place where it is written in a peculiar way. God guarantees thus a unique memory of failures, which but for him would vanish without a trace. Emphatically, even though the failure of writing entails a fall of understanding, it is at the same time an act that brings us closer to the position of God. It is only in the ultimate failure of comprehension that we stand closest to God although always at a distance which separates writing from the reader. All the accrued meaning must be destroyed *for God to manifest himself in the extreme concentration of meaninglessness.* As Jabès claims, the real writer, as well as the Messiah, wrecks his work – "breaks the tables." He has distilled the ultimate, definitive legibility, making present the entire meaning here and now, in one "table," only to be able to crush it and make room for God.

Concluding this argument, we can describe the relation between Jabès' unique versions of messianism and monotheism. Messianism of failure reinforces monotheism and precludes idolatry defined as identifying a certain representation with God. Any particular meaning one could choose to identify with reality is destroyed in the messianic failure and returned *vis-à-vis* the divine that transcends it. Messianism never removes the minimum difference between the Messiah and God.[31] Furthermore, radicalism of the hope to understand the real leads directly to revealing pure duration and, thus, a surplus that God is in relation to a finite meaning. Therefore, *"the edge of the book" is a place of God's revelation through a failed messianic attempt.*

Oneness and Equality of Things

With these insights, we can proceed to the central part of this Chapter, in which I will seek to provide a philosophical account of the experience of the messianic act of writing. Because, as already ascertained, in this act writing breaks in transition from the imaginary to the real – and crosses the boundary or *tzimtzum* – this experience helps re-think *tzimtzum* "directly" rather than in abstract terms. My final thesis of this Chapter is that in the moment of messianic failure *the very*

---

31 The kabbalists always maintained this difference as well. For example, Isaac the Blind believed that speculation could climb to the level of the sefirot, reaching pure "Thought," a source of human thought. That, however, is not the Divine as such, which is unreachable. Achievable is *devequt*: clinging to God, but not uniting with him. See Fine, *Physician*, p. 224.

gap between the imaginary and the real, between the meaning-producing order and things, is revealed.

To arrive at it, I will first argue that Jabès identifies the messianic act with unveiling a peculiar "One." To start with, let us observe that Jabès offers many descriptions of getting to the "edge of the book." In many of them, he suggests that the process is accompanied by a sense of nearing oneness in which everything that is enters a new community of things without forfeiting its own singularity:

> Before the One comes the dazzling void which we experience as the near advent of One. We came to the end of the night, and suddenly the world turned white. / We stopped at the threshold of the path, overwhelmed by all this whiteness. / Unable to speak or make any gesture, we sat on the last milestone. / We were evenly white.[32]
>
> [...] we wander within ourselves (up to the point where we are still ourselves, but different) to find the obscure spot which hides the sun and which, we know, is that privileged place where dark and light touch in order to be two and still only one in revealing the universe.[33]

What is this One? Jabès apparently implies that it is an ecstatic experience of the unity of the universe, discovered at the end of the messianic attempt to understand. *The One is a basic plane where differences themselves touch and divide.*

> "I no longer see words," he wrote; "I see only the place of their birth and death, which is blank."[34]

The line seems to indicate that it is an area where words, yet or already without meaning, only differentiate, that is, pass from "pure whiteness" to existence and the other way round. As such, it is not a plane of language but a plane of the *very condition of possibility* of language provided by there being differences at all. This is a plane where differences not so much exist as only emerge, still embedded in a specific oneness.

For this reason, if the messianic act reaches it through an utterance, it dissolves in this oneness. This means that the experience of the One entailed by the messianic act absorbs this act as well, obliterating the difference between the act and the event it brings on:

> You try to say all, own all. You think in the end you could disappear.[35]

---

32 BQ II, pp. 321, 353.
33 BQ I, p. 225.
34 BQ II, p. 439.
35 BQ I, p. 333.

Characteristic of the messianic act, an attempt "to say all" makes this "all" engulf and replace also the act itself. Paradoxically, the one, the advent of which Jabès presupposes, is the end, effect and erasure of the act. The messianic act thus revels a peculiar unity of the world to which it belongs itself as well. This unity is a site where differences as such emerge and vanish. It is a matrix in which differences come into being but still cluster together. It is both the place of the origin and the place of the end, the beginning of differences and the purpose of the messianic act. *Tzimtzum* again appears as both endpoints of the imaginary.

Having established what is specific to the space of unity, we can now ask where this unity comes from. In answering, we can be guided by an elliptical passage that Jabès placed in his last work's final section, closest to the "edge of the book," where the messianic tension is at its highest:

ALL THING(S) EQUAL [TOUTE CHOSE ÉGALE]. This is the [writer's] point: a thing.[36]

What does this statement imply? The second sentence states that the writer's point in all his searching is a "thing." What "thing"? This is what the first sentence, capitalised throughout, expresses, seeming as much an idea as a trace of a direct discovery made by Jabès at this particular moment of writing. The dual function of the word "tout" makes the French phrase "*toute chose égale*" ambiguous as it can mean both "each thing equal" and "all things equal." The idea inferable from this is that the "equality" Jabès talks about is comprised *both* of one equal thing and all equal things. Cross-referencing this passage with the portrayal of unity in the messianic act, we can conclude that it is an internally equal unity which is *at the same time* (1) one thing; and (2) a unity of all equal things. Finding it is the aim of writing.

Arguably, it could be a purely mystical unity, about which nothing more can be said, but our previous argument suggests its essential, structural similarity to certain insights of modern philosophy. I believe that this mystical unity can be explained by an issue that Kant and Hegel strove to settle: the basic division between "things in themselves" and knowledge. As we cannot discuss it in detail here, let us only note that Kantian "things in themselves" are both "one thing" and a multiplicity of things. Why? Multiplication of "things" is caused by knowledge to which a "thing" is external. The pluralism of the knowable world in which multiple objects (as Kant conceived of them) exist makes us think about multiplicity

---

36 LH, p. 89.

also in the case of "things in themselves." Yet, as external to knowledge, they are "one thing" because phenomenal categories are inapplicable to them.

Based on this reasoning, I will provide a philosophical interpretation of the Jabèsian "One" by drawing on one more idea to be found both in Kant and in Hegel, who investigated a fundamental plane on which "things in themselves" border directly with knowledge. This is the lowest possible level of differentiation, which gives grounding to all differences in knowledge and, at the same time, the level where this differentiation transitions directly into the unity of the "things in themselves." To avoid recapitulating the conclusions of Chapter One, I will only remind that this is Kant's concept of "temporal series": time as a basic form that brings together "things in themselves" and makes them into objects. Hegel, in turn, analyses the same problem relying on the category of "understanding" (*Verstand*), which distils from the chaos of primal undifferentiation a certain rudimentary structure underpinning knowledge and language.[37]

With these analogies in mind, we can posit that, in Jabès, the messianic attempt to write involves the experience of the One because it reaches the lowest level of differentiation between "the thing in itself" and the multiplicity of the symbolic order that corresponds to it.[38] Where the Kantian "thing in itself" is in constant tension with "things in themselves," the unity of "*toute chose égale*" is experienced in Jabès. This insight is resonant with the premise of Chapter Three, where *tzimtzum* is defined as a moment of discontinuity between the external multiplicity of the imaginary and the real unity of the particular. The moment of the messianic failure *is this very tension between the imaginary and the real, a moment of their ecstatic passing into each other*. In other words, it is an experience of *tzimtzum*.[39]

---

37 See Hegel, *Phenomenology*, pp. 31–3.

38 The following excerpt from *Return to the Book* aptly shows the symbolic order (metaphorically rendered as "a voice") causing disintegration of "the thing itself": "One pebble discovered another and said: 'I see myself.' And then: 'Who has split me off myself?' The surprised pebble answered back: 'You are a pebble, like me. Where do you come from?'" Disappointed, the pebble said: 'So you are not me? We do not have the same voice.' The pebble answered: 'As neither of us can move, here I am you; where you are you are I.' 'Will we one day be a single pebble?' […] And the pebble said: 'All over the earth we are the same stone.'" (BQ I, p. 347).

39 This concept explains also the "halting" of time in the messianic act. In it, the messianic act reaches the lowest level of differentiation, that is, a plane in relation to which time is perceived, following Kant's suggestions. It is, so to speak, "the eye of the storm," where extreme differentiation of the moments of passing time means, at the same time, stopping time. The structure of the messianic act of understanding suggests that it regards

Concluding, the structures recognised by Jabès in writing can be interpreted as references to various layers of mystical, therein Kabbalistic, thinking,[40] but they are explicable strictly within modern philosophical tenets.

Equality of Things: Possibility and Impossibility

Yet, can the equality and unity of things be really experienced? And what *experience* is it in the first place? The further part of the passage quoted above is illuminating in this respect:

What would the primordial/essential [*de primordial*] thing the writer has to say be other than the thing which is all he seeks to say, but by applying/fitting himself to it [*dans s'y appliquer*], no doubt, in order to leave it to/let it say itself [*pour la laisser… se dire*] indirectly.

As if that saying [*ce dire*] protected it against itself, doubling the access [*en redoublant les accès*] to it; for this thing, in the depths of silence, is the secret of the last word [*du dernier mot*].

Dust [*la poussière*] has its compelling reasons [*raisons fortes*] as well.[41]

We must disentangle this cryptic passage step by step. Jabès seems to assume that writing is motivated by saying something that is both essential and primordial – originary – as well as coming. Writing looks for a "thing" which is "all the writer seeks to say." Because this thing is involved in each moment of writing as its goal, it can be supposed to be also *the primordial condition of writing*, achievable if the writer, so to speak, "applies himself to it." It means, likely, that the writer not so much enunciates this thing as lets it enunciate itself in his act. In a sense, the writer *leaves it, lets it say itself.* In Jabès' usage, the verb *"laisser"* resonates with

---

itself as ultimate, "atemporal" understanding. This, however, results from the fact that, actually, it descends to its *own* lowest level of differentiation, which is a temporal series of *its own order*. The messianic act seems universal because in the order in which it unfolds, no beyond is actually seen anymore. For this reason, the messianic act seems definitive and ultimate *to itself*. Nevertheless, its failure makes it clear that from the very beginning the act was connected with a particular order which has just passed. The difference between the illusory time and the real time is a difference that separates a perspectival order from the unthinkable space in which all such orders are located.

40 For example, *Masoret ha-Berit*, a Kabbalistic work dating back to the 13th century, presents God after Creation as nothing that still has more being than any existence in the world. If all things returned to nothing, they would again become an undifferentiated One; see Scholem, *Kabbale*, pp. 174–5. By the same token, God is presupposed here as a dark centre in which things become one by losing their differences.

41 LH, p. 89.

the same insight as Heidegger's *sein lassen* because the aim of the utterance is to put an end to utterance as uttering-something – *and let this thing be*. Only when the writer withdraws, making room for it, can it articulate itself. Still, without deceiving himself in the least, Jabès means only a mediate utterance.

Impossibility and mediacy of the act are restated in the following sentence. Namely, the utterance "protects the thing against itself, doubling the access to it," because "this thing in the depths of silence is the secret of the last word." How should we construe it? First, we should notice that the last word – *this* last word with a definite article: "*le dernier mot*" – seems to be both an inevitable expectation in the messianic act of writing and something impossible because of the very structure of this act. This thing could ultimately be said only if the last word really existed. As another passage implies, only this word really matters to the book:

> The totality is not made up of all the vocables, but of one, the last one, which one can still foresee but which one can no longer pronounce and on which all the others have foundered. It is this ultimate word [*parole*] which gives the book its weight. From this word the book gets its charge [*charge*].[42]

"The last word" aggregates the words that precede it and gives weight to the book by articulating the "thing." But, in fact, it is still impossible as the hope of the last word is not this thing *yet* while the silence of duration *already* is not this thing. As such, this thing is never present, but rather opens before or closes behind us, in this sense protected by "the double access." This thing is "a secret of the last word," which inhabits the messianic act of writing for a fleeting moment only to show that it just *seems* the last word, and it seems so because, essentially, *it cannot be one*. For it is a middle point visible only in dislocation, perceivable only from a place before or behind it. It completes the whole without being seen in it:

> Enter the center: *between* seeing and seen.
> The hand writes between points. Along with the word, it is forever center.[43]

As the end of writing, "equality of all things" is thus something that appears as impossible and *because* it is impossible. Each time, the end appears where it is not, and Jabès insists: "there is no goal that, at the very moment it is reached, is not already surpassed." Writing is trapped in its own impossibility since everything it craves to express and is also founded by continues to be its constantly and obsessively searched goal, defined by its very unreachability. It is *embodied*

---

42 DB, p. 102.
43 BQ II, p. 359.

in the one, still missing word, a word both originarily forgotten and expected in the future:

> What if the book were only infinite memory of a word lacking?
> Thus absence speaks to absence.[44]
> All writing invites to an anterior reading of the world which the word urges and which we pursue to the limits of faded memory.[45]

With this word lacking, writing has the structure of constant deferral:

> The victorious eye trumpets its truth. The vanquished eye takes refuge in its defeat. The book escapes both. […] The end is always in the next word.[46]
> Between me and myself there are innumerable words whose ways and will I do not know. They move me away from the book which, sentence by sentence, has moved away from them.[47]
> At the finish there is nothing, but this boundary is not yet the fatal end [la fatale fin].[48]

The structure of this goal makes it thus essentially unattainable. It appears either as a future event – "finish" or "end" [fin], which provides the point that suffuses writing with all tension – or as something that is already transcended, when it turns out to have been nothing in fact. It is not the "fatale fin," claims Jabès and, in the spirit of Blanchot's musings on the impossibility of death, suggests that it is entirely incommensurable with the "real," mortal end.

Consequently, even the actual last word before death does not warrant fulfilment. The structure of messianism admittedly tempts us to consider it to be closer to that "which the writer had to say," indeed, perhaps even to be most authentic. But Jabès believes that while the "last word" may be the most vivid and extreme one, its structure does not differ from that which conditions every messianic act of writing, i.e. from the structure of internal impossibility. That the end is really near does not remove the fundamental disruption between the imaginary and the real and, consequently, cannot make the utterance immediate. Jabès conveys this insight, for example, in the following assertion, which exposes the double bind of the last word's "truthfulness":

> Our true face is the one we have in the hour of our death, and death contrives to reduce it to dust.[49]

---

44 BS, p. 27.
45 BQ II, p. 150.
46 *Ibid.*, p. 409.
47 *Ibid.*, p. 126.
48 LH, p. 27.
49 BQ II, p. 265.

To conclude this section, as a result of *tzimtzum*, writing has a specific structure in which the movement forward is fuelled by heading to one particular point, which is the point of consummation and impossibility at the same time. This point demarcates the "edge of the book," a moment of ultimate messianic tension in relation to which the entire act of writing is positioned. Because, on coming, it turns out to have already been transcended, it is the condition of possibility of writing, which completes and, also, splits writing through its inaccessibility. Therefore, the experience of *tzimtzum* is impossible, which, in the Jabèsian chiasm, means that *tzimtzum is an impossibility and it is experienced as such.*

The Essence of Messianic Utopia

Consequently, the equality and unity of things that transpire in the messianic fulfilment of writing have the structure of internal impossibility inscribed in them. But, in Jabès, this does not mean solely a limitation as it also has a positive facet to it. For although we cannot experience this unity, *we can generally enunciate it, albeit indirectly*, as it is internally fettered by conditions of utterability. And should such experience be given to us immediately, it would require falling entirely silent in mystical, incommunicable stillness. This, however, is not the case since there is no pure experience. Hence, paradoxically, writing can venture into the realm that this unapproachable silence would occupy even though it can articulate it only mediately. The *fact that all utterance bears the messianic structure of inner impossibility implies that there is no portion of the real that it could not describe.*

Building on this observation, we can explain a very important part of Jabès' writing, in which he seeks to convey *the relations between things as such*. One of such phrasings has already been quoted: "dust has its compelling reasons as well." Other statements of this kind locate reflection within things themselves, so to speak: in dust, sand, desert, heaven and the sea:

I come from the desert as one comes from beyond memory. I brought the salvation of sand. [...] *"The desert is homesick for the sea,"* observed Reb Safad. *"This explains why it fascinates us."*
[...] *Water obeys water and maintains the fish. Air obeys air and maintains the bird.*[50]
"I am, the tree calls to the tree, and the pebble to the simple pebble."[51]
Great is the freedom of light at the hour the sky grows dim.[52]
[...] it is certain that the pebble sees the star.[53]

---

50 BQ I, pp. 197, 270, 194.
51 *Ibid.*, p. 322.
52 BQ II, p. 173.
53 *Ibid.*, p. 218.

The universe is caught in the point like the sea in a drop of water.[54]
The sea rocks the earth and enfolds it. The wind breaks the wind.[55]
A pebble speaks only to pebbles, but with words of the universe.[56]
"I can't know myself otherwise than through you. But who am I?"
"Does fire know fire?"
"Does wood know wood?"
To the wood it devours, fire owes being fire, just like wood owes ceasing to be wood to the fire, which turns it into ash.[57]

In such sentences Jabès, a writer of the impossible, captures with surprising suggestiveness the sense of relatedness which we could feel were we "things as such." He does it relying on his trademark merger in which things can be attributed specifically human relations and human relationships can be suggested to, at a certain level, have a *thingness* to them. "Seeing," "homesickness," "freedom," "knowledge," indeed, the very "being-something" seem not only to pertain to things but also to be based on *elementary relationships among them*. Consequently, the lines above presuppose a liminal level of reality, where two realms meet: (1) things, which "exist" in undifferentiable continuity; and (2) language, which is inhabited only by the already differentiated objects. We got a glimpse of this liminal level when we described the Jabèsian One and concluded that it was the plane of differentiation as such, where differences emerged, vanished and remained in a specific unity. Now we can elaborate on this depiction to state that *this level is describable only because of the knotting of the world of "language" and the world of "things,"* or of the imaginary and the real, to put it in Jabèsian terms.

Consequently, the internal impossibility, which seems to be a bane of writing, in fact affords it an opportunity to evoke the liminal plane, where the basic structuring of the world comes to light. In this way, writing makes it possible to explore the connection between messianism and formation of reality. This relation is as follows:

The plane where relations "still" exist but "no longer" destroy the unity and equality of things is the essence of messianic utopia. Things simply "are" there, side by side, but no relation reduces one to another. At the same time, relations are like lightnings that illuminate this status of universal equality as they appear briefly enough to show the unity that obtains among things. "Briefly" is just our word, for, in fact, there is no time here and whatever happens has already

---

54 *Ibid.*, p. 393
55 LH, p. 48.
56 BS, p. 17.
57 P, p. 37.

happened. As in the imaginary, all relations constantly morph into each other, but they lack an immanent, perspectival limitation. *The totality of all possible relations is poised in an ecstatic equality and imbues things with unity.* Utter differentiation and complete unification dovetail in this utopian point.

This plane is both the condition of possibility of the perspectival world and the fulfilment that this world pursues, as viewed from its inside. To leave everything the way it is and, at the same time, to shift it slightly to prevent one thing dominating another – to such Benjaminian and Agambenian messianic insights Jabès could subscribe and, more than that, he could explain why salvation dwells in the gap between things and the language-shaped word

Messianism's Bi-directional Movement

It was Benjamin that posited a specific relationship of language and things. He suggested that messianic transformation involved human efforts targeting not so much other people as things.[58] Jabès seems to have shared this idea to a degree. As Didier Cahen aptly notices, at the core of Jabès' experience, marked by memories of the desert, lies a desire to "become one with things" [*faire corps avec les choses*],[59] where we join the realm of things through our corporeality. Moreover, by bringing salvation to things, man can be said to bring salvation to himself as a peculiar thing governed by language.

To explain these propositions, I will now attempt to show that messianic utopia entails both: (1) bringing the human being closer to the realm of things; and (2) giving salvation to things in this way. This is a bi-directional movement that *aims to bridge the gap between the two dimensions.*

I will start from the former. Across his texts, Jabès repeatedly presents things as if they were formed by a unique, internal quasi-order which is, generally, *an asymptote of all order.*

> If the tree had no intelligence, it would collapse. If the sea had no intelligence, it would devour itself.[60]
> The inside of the pebble is written [*est écrit*].
> From time immemorial [*de tout temps*] and for ever [*pour toujours*] legible.[61]

---

58   See Cahen, *Edmond Jabès*, p. 68.
59   Cahen, "Jalons," p. 264.
60   BQ I, p. 194.
61   LH, p. 13.

In the first passage, "intelligence" is the inner ordering of things, due to which they can continue. But unlike the perspectival order of the imaginary, this ordering does not issue from one system that gives life to particular objects. On the contrary, things survive "in themselves" and "by their intelligence." Of course, Jabès relies here on Kant's insights as his "things" are sovereign, not subordinated to the order of knowledge and endowed with an ability to last. Separated from knowledge by a transcendental boundary, their realm seems to be shaped by the "writing of reality itself" as expressed in the second passage. What may this writing be? Let us postulate that it is *the structure of reality before the perspectival reduction.*

Of course, "the inside of the pebble" evoked by Jabès is not the inside of the pebble as an object, but its thingness, which is structurally inaccessible to us. This is where this peculiar writing is located of which *this pebble as a thing is an entity.* Notably, Jabès makes two assumptions in Kant's spirit: (1) things are inaccessible to knowledge and "resist" the linguistic meaning embodied in their bare materiality; and (2) on this inaccessible plane, there is a writing, full of order which our finite orders cannot reach. The relation among things as entities of this writing would consist in co-existing in one reality, in an ultimate space which holds everything that has ever existed. At the same time, it is a realm of the real time, as Jabès suggests in an ambiguous last verse of the second passage: the inside of the pebble preserves "all time" – that is, unreduced time – and, as such, remains essentially beyond time as we know it.

Thus for Jabès, the realm of things would be a writing that we cannot comprehend – the complete writing in which the particular does not become a unit of an a-priori order but co-exists with other particularities. The movement of messianism would head towards this fullness.

Yet Jabès posits also an opposite movement – one progressing from things to language. Why? Because the fullness of things needs articulation to sustain its elementary differentiation:

Does the sound of the see prove the existence of sound or of the sea?
And the silence of the sky?
Dependent on *saying* [*du dire*],
on the cry.[62]

It takes the simplest possible enunciation, such as the cry, for things to be brought forth from the unity of the real. In other words, things need language to illuminate the connection between their unity and differentiation. Messianism cannot

---

62 BM, p. 86.

thus entail siding entirely with their "fullness." For it is not fullness in as far as it would not be visible as fullness on being accomplished and, consequently, would in fact contain less that the world before the messianic repair.[63] This suggests a paradox that triggers messianism's bi-directional movement. Embracing entirely either side – things or language – is a reduction. *If salvation were to salvage the fullness of the world, it would have to remain poised on the liminal line of the nexus-division of the two realms.*

This helps us proceed to the conclusion of this Chapter, define what Jabès' messianism consists in and formulate its implications for modern philosophy.

There Is No Salvation Beyond Writing

Jabèsian messianism is an inevitable consequence of *tzimtzum*. It is a movement which seeks to overcome *tzimtzum* and, in the same gesture, only returns to it, discovering its own condition of possibility. Because of *tzimtzum*, in each tangled realm – of the real and the imaginary, or of "language" and "things" – a surplus appears and induces messianism's bi-directional movement. *At its core, thus, messianic utopia means entering the central gap between the imaginary and the real,* a gap that is *tzimtzum.*

From the perspective of this gap, things appear as an *already* uttered and, thus, broken fullness while language as a system stamped with a central lack, elimination of which seems to lie in the fullness of things. As such, this gap is a place whence the world reveals itself in its extreme rupture between the two realms. *For it is also a place which negatively fills this rupture.* For this reason, by reaching this point, one experiences the world in the extremity of its internal disruption between "things" and "language," and one takes at the same time the position of the void that binds this disruption. This relation is explicit in the act of writing, which in its messianic attempt both becomes nothing, veritably vanishing in *tzimtzum,* and seems to sustain the entire structure of reality.

Jabèsian messianism stems directly from conjoining "things" and "language." Whatever content a particular order of the act of writing invests in its messianic attempt, the possibility and effect of this attempt are based on the structure of movement it undergoes. Notably, the *content* is here entirely secondary to the

---

63 In this sense, Motte is right to claim that Jabès' writing as such is fuelled by a permanent split between words and things, which wrestle with each other but never achieve harmony. See Motte, "Jabès' Words," pp. 146–7. "Harmony" would indeed be a deprivation rather than a repair of the world.

pattern of *forces* that compel the emergence and failure of this content. Jabès' messianism can thus be said to be structural and circular. Consequently, it is impossible to abide in the gap sought by writing. The place appears in permanent dislocation – either nearing or bygone – and manifests itself briefly only in one, outermost moment of the "edge of the book." Therefore, in the Jabèsian act of writing, its end is its sole goal, both expected and post-poned – an object of fear and hope. Characteristically, it takes the entire cycle of the "book," from the originary *tzimtzum* to the final catastrophe, to hit this cen-tral, still-sought point. In each act of writing, it is given once only.

Admittedly, Jabès' messianism is based on the structure of circular movement, but *reaching the empty centre of each cycle is a radically singular event*. It is a par-adoxical point where particularity and universalism fold into each other because even though it seems to recur in subsequent acts, these repetitions are incom-mensurable. So the point of *tzimtzum* is an inseverable linkage between the quasi-universal structure and the fulfilment of one, unrepeatable act of writing. Since the two realms intersect, the moment of messianic failure is the only event that eludes any description by virtue of its radical singularity. At the same time, because of this intersecting, Jabès' thought is admittedly circular, but each cycle is a necessary deferral on the way to knowing the *once-given, particular* point, which irreversibly perishes and makes room for another one.[64]

Consequently, Jabès is compelled to "practise" rather than describe *tzimtzum*. All his mature works are devoted to experiencing this specific structure that binds the cycle to the space in which the cycle's central point of *tzimtzum* is inscribed as something absolutely singular. The singularity of the cycle is embodied first and foremost in the book. Purification and simplification of language help Jabès, however, encapsulate this structure even in a single sentence, with his aphorisms forming a "microbook," a circle that fuses the beginning and the end of its order, singular as a whole.

Still, a question offers itself whether Jabès' messianism is only fulfilled in writing or perhaps entails a "real" change in the world.

---

64 Gabriel Bounoure aptly grasps the radical novelty ushered in by every new messianic attempt: "As the last word falls silent, nothing more can be known. And even that which is now known is darker than what was known before. Still, a transformation has taken place which will help us kindle other flames of questioning in an entirely new form. […] The questioning thought pushes relentlessly towards the extreme, the contradic-tory and the negative, towards impossible truths. The ever more extreme extreme to which it heads tirelessly and without end: this is the unity of the Book." See Bounoure, *Edmond Jabès*, pp. 94, 98.

The answer is far from obvious because *tzimtzum and messianism it produces seem to Jabès to structure the entire world given to us*. He views Jewish history as patent evidence that messianic hope and its failure are responsible for real and traumatic events. Consequently, in the Hegelian and Marxian spirit, it could be assumed that by recognising the structure of *tzimtzum* and messianism we will be able at least to influence our own history. Yet Jabès' work seems to suggest that, paradoxically, knowledge of the messianic structure, best available in writing, does not offer any *applicable* knowledge. It offers only an experience of messianism and an unstoppable desire to repeat it. Writing is a privileged site for messianism, but it is also a trap. It may be, like the point of *tzimtzum*, an empty place where intuiting the messianic structure entails self-loss.

I would posit that, in Jabès' universe, messianism is ubiquitous but, once recognised in writing, *it is henceforth possible only in writing*. For the movement of recognition itself has a messianic structure and, through subsequent cycles, impels the writer to the position of the void. Nothing more: salvation brought to oneself and things only means reaching the central void of *tzimtzum* through writing, and, as such, rather than an ideal accomplished in writing and realisable in the "world," it is an experience intrinsic to writing.

Salvation in writing is exemplified in the following passage from *Le Livre de l'Hospitalité*:

> Not a farewell [*adieu*] to things, but – o night! – salvation for things, shimmering back farewells [*miroitantes d'adieux*].[65]

Salvation of things does not mean saying farewell to them, but rather dispatching them to God (*à Dieu*), who could support them. Salvation is a coming "night" in which we co-exist and co-reflect ("*miroitantes*" reverberates with "*miroir*" – a mirror) with things in a state of equality. The *word* ("*adieu*") is replaced by *a shimmer – reflection*. Things thus shimmer back. In the last verse, "*adieu*" is no longer a farewell but a reflection of non-God, of God's absence (*a-dieux*), in which things dissolve.

Salvation is, thus, an effect of writing; it is a moment when, as the word fades away, language leaves the thing alone, letting it be.[66] *And we, watching the dusk fall,*

---

65 LH, p. 19.
66 As Stephane Mosès rightly observes, such passages in Jabès are similar to Benjamin's "constellations" as words mutate in them from vehicles of meaning to a material arrangement of signs, a thing. See Stephane Mosès, "Edmond Jabès," p. 47. The messianic effect results from the fact that a text morphs into a thing while language abandons itself, so to speak, and strays from its own formulation, looking at it as at a thing moving away.

feel that we have reached the line between language and thing and, with it, achieved the state of messianic equality.

Conclusion: Jabès' Messianism and Modern Philosophy

Throughout this Chapter, the structure of Jabès' messianism has often been shown to be deeply embedded in modern philosophy. First, it is an effect of perspectivism and, by inducing ever new attempts at definitive understanding, it enhances perspectivism even more. Jabès' writing resembles Benjamin's Angel of History, who tries to collect past ruins, but his drive only adds to them. Second, messianic failure is essentially akin to an entire bundle of issues explored by Kant and Hegel, such as the status of "things in themselves" and transcendental boundary, the relation of a continuous series to singularity and the link between time and knowledge. Third, an attempt at definitive understanding integral to Jabèsian messianism is similar to Hegelian absolute knowledge and, in its failure, also to the fate of Hegelianism, i.e. the confrontation with time it cannot survive. Fourth, the specific combination of circularity and unique course of happening/ enowning links Jabès' messianism to Nietzsche's concept of eternal return. Finally, the possibility-impossibility structure inherent to Jabèsian messianism is the same one that Derridean deconstruction tackles later.

Clearly, in its messianic investment, Jabès' thought discovers the same structures that an essential portion of Western philosophy has explored since Kant. At the same time, explicit references to Jewish tradition help the Jabès describe these structures in a language adequate to them. The intertwining of messianism and *tzimtzum* explains the hope that writing finds in movement[67]while the historical burden of Jewish messianism explains why this hope persists through subsequent failures. Finally, uncompromising monotheism results in maintaining a radical difference between the Messiah and God. To put it philosophically, this difference designates the incommensurability of the messianic attempt and the realm its failure reveals – a realm which not only transcends it, but also in which it has been inscribed since the beginning.

---

67 Of course, messianism is not necessarily connected to *tzimtzum*. In the Talmud, Yochanan ben Zakkai says that the created world has preserved an immanent tendency to catastrophe, a will of fall, expressed in an unquenchable desire to gain infinite knowledge, which results in another fall. See Raphael Draï, *La pensée juive et l'interrogation divine. Exégèse et épistémologie* (Paris: PUF, 1996), p. 106. Still, *tzimtzum* explains how the messianic attempt is engendered by the primal limitation.

Do these links between Jewish tradition and modern philosophy offer implications for the latter? After all, the structures of secular messianism have lingered in modern philosophy at least since Kant, motivating the internal movement of Hegel's philosophy, making an imprint on Marx's and Nietzsche's thought, essentially affecting, under their own name, 20th-century thinking in, for example, Benjamin, Bloch and Rosenzweig, and being compellingly revived in our times in Derrida's mature thought, Badiou's concept of an event, Žižek's philosophy and Agamben's reflection. That such different philosophers can be listed meaningfully in one sentence is made possible by the power of the messianic structure. What is it that Jabès' messianism can tell us about messianism of modern philosophy?

First, it suggests that messianic hope should be viewed in its proper context, that is, not as a real chance of salvation but as an effect and expansion of the catastrophe. In this perspective, the very idea of going beyond the modern pattern of messianism-as-failure is, in itself, an execution of this pattern. Always appearing a viable and only chance, the endeavour fully to overcome the fragmentation in place is a mechanism that serves this very fragmentation. In other words, the problem is not that there is no way out. On the contrary, there is a way out, and this is exactly a pitfall because the way leads to another failure and expansion of ruins. Claiming everything, we extend the modern desert. For this reason, Jabès can insist that "all we do by writing is [...] to throw ink on the fire."[68]

Jabès seems to reverse the proportions as his messianism, rather than a quasi-Gnostic expectation of intervention entirely heterogeneous with respect to the modern world, is an intrinsic component of this world. Perhaps this insight can help us think a completely different kind of messianism, one Kafka seems to have suggested.[69] It would be a messianism exhausted in a fleeting thought that

---

68 BQ II, p. 394.
69 In his Zürau notes, Kafka wrote: "A first sign of the beginning of understanding is a wish to die. This life appears unbearable, another unattainable. One is no longer ashamed of wanting to die; one asks to be moved from the old cell, which one hates, to a new one, which one will only in time come to hate. In this there is also a residue of belief that during the move the master will chance to come along the corridor, look at the prisoner and say: 'This man is not to be locked up again. He is to come with me.'" Franz Kafka, *The Blue Octavo Notebooks*, trans. Ernst Keiser and Eithne Wilkins, ed. Max Brod (Cambridge, MA: Exact Change, 1991), p. 88. This unexpected liberation can be interpreted as a messianism whose idea is unalloyed with unredeemed reality and, as such, refers to the complete end of the heretofore order, including messianism of failure it contains.

cannot be developed without being entangled in the inevitability of failure. Such messianism would be an idea of a sudden and unanticipated liberation. It can be understood as putting all logic of the modern universe to an end. Still, Jabès does not opt for such messianism and, rather, implies that all attempts to think about transcending this universe are doomed to be sucked back into its movement. Another implication for modern philosophy would be a protest against pessimism potentially bred by "messianism of failure." Jabès seems to call for a sober balance of profit and loss that messianism produces. Besides the obvious loss of repeated failure, there is also a profit of successive, unrepeatable acts of understanding. Admittedly, "after its spectacular victory in the very wreck of its unity, the world will be destroyed by the world as man is every night by man,"[70] yet each new act of understanding leaves something fundamentally new behind. To Jabès, every word is the first one, claims Stephane Mosès.[71] More than that: *the radical novelty of each subsequent act is possible only because of the utter perishment of the previous one.* At the price of total failure, we are thus given a possibility of obtaining a fleeting and entirely new glimpse of the world:

All is the origin. Nothing is invented. All and nothing are repeated. O miracle of repetition – a regular escape to All, a passionate return to the origin [...].
We could never tell the old language from the new.
Repetition is our subversive way; for it moves by an inborn need to destroy and be destroyed [...].
Repetition is a chance for continual change.
[...] "You are never twice either the same or the other," he said.[72]

Messianism thus paves the way to continual change.[73] Furthermore, it is only through messianism that we can explore that "All" and "Nothing" in their mutual

---

70 BQ II, p. 112
71 Mosès, "Edmond Jabès," p. 45.
72 LR I, p. 88.
73 This passage implies that messianism not only introduces constant change but also precludes stable identities as the breaking between hope and failure is imprinted on everything that exists. For this reason "being" itself fears its own fulfilment and, internally halved, both wants to and cannot arrive. Therefore Jabès writes: "'The night hesitates before the forbidden night. This moment's hesitation clinches the vertigo above the abyss, salutary halt at the fatal edge of time. 'Even death is afraid of death.'" (BQ II, p. 158).
"Hope: the following page. Do not close the book."
"I have turned all the pages of the book without finding hope."
"Perhaps hope is the book." (BQ I, p. 243).
"'The word would have to revive before we could approach its life [...]'" (BQ II, p. 150).

relations. And, finally, it is through messianism that we are given an experience of pure duration after failure, which means the experience of God in Jabès.

Jabès seems to urge to recognise messianism in all its complexity, that is, in the inextricable and arduous nexus of hope and hopelessness.[74] For modern philosophy, this would mean an injunction to become aware of its intrinsic messianic component, to realise that the depth and novelty of its acts of recognition come at the price of radical transience and to think on despite being conscious that thinking leaves a vastness of ruins. This implies a third conclusion – the necessity of repetition. Because of Jabès' messianism, *no statement is capable of stopping the movement of understanding*; even understanding the structure of this movement cannot accomplish the feat. Hence the coercion of repetition, which in Jabès is often also a celebration of reiteration:

"You repeat yourself. You say the same all the time. You have grown old," said Reb Saman to Reb Jaffe.

"Indeed, I say the same all the time; but is the moment a following moment? The other that comes from me says every time what I said long ago; this is my way to survive, through these few words, my truth," he answered.[75]

Repetition is not a nihilism of disappointed old age but, each time, a new truth that suits the moment when it emerges. Because there is no continuity in time, *formulating subsequent truths is a way to survive, that is to out-last, subsequent moments of one's own dissolution.*

What does it entail for modern philosophy? It means that successive radical acts of understanding, such as Hegel's absolute knowledge, are not *errors* to be avoided in search of a simple, "local" and time-immune reflection. On the contrary, Jabèsian messianism seems to suggest that the scale of the philosophical attempt and the sheer magnitude of its catastrophe lie at the core of philosophising in the modern world. Of course, not all philosophy in modernity is compelled to practise it, but universality of this messianism makes its *movement* reproduce, with more or less precision, the cycle opened by *tzimtzum*. This implies that philosophy resolved to seek a radical act of understanding produces at least one effect: it illumines messianism that conditions it. Through its own failure,

---

"*The word will start from Nothing in order to dissolve in the All*" (*Ibid.*, p. 225).
"*Developing a thought means first of all the death of this thought for the benefit of another, which chance or its own strict requirements raised to strike it down in turn*" (*Ibid.*, p. 242).

74 The connection is conveyed, for example, in: "Faith buries faith for the promised resurrection" (BQ I, p. 301).

75 PHD, p. 122.

it represents the discontinuity of time and affirms itself as an unrepeatable act of understanding suited to one moment only rather than as *philosophia perennis*. Jabès' thought indicates what sense philosophising makes if determined in advance by a perspectival messianic structure. It does makes sense but not because it finds universal, time-defying truths (though this remains philosophy's inalienable utopia). What sense does it make then? Following Jabèsian thinking, we could say that it makes sense in two respects.

First, philosophy's role is to *put an end to the claim of radical understanding*, which is part and parcel of each perspectival order of knowledge. In other words, philosophy is to reveal and appraise the messianic element of this order. What for? To unveil its originary limitation and, thus, to show how the primordial gap of *tzimtzum* opens and closes an entire world form. This intent would not only be deconstructive towards orders which make claims to timeless truth but, first of all, serve to render happening as such since happening, as Jabès conceives of it, means the rise and decline not so much of beings as of *entire orders*.

Second, philosophy could use this practice to examine the very structure of the modern world, which we have described following Jabès. In other words, particular orders of knowledge would serve it as *elements* which, in their movement of emergence and failure, render a grid of forces that eludes any substantive account. Evidently, a similar expectation has been more or less explicitly articulated in modern philosophy since its dawn. As early as in Kant, philosophy explored conditions of possibility of *concrete species of metaphysics*; and in Hegel, the object of philosophy was the movement of *particular forms of knowledge*, therein various forms of philosophy. In other words, the former and, in intent, complete philosophical frameworks were turned into entities whose movement only served to infer conclusions. Compared with Kant and Hegel, Jabès looks nevertheless as an advocate of a general simplification, reducing the content of particular elements to a bare minimum and scrutinising the very principles of their movement. They are reduced to pure differences that help grasp the movement from *tzimtzum* to failure. Entities arising in this movement would serve to support reflection on the space of all instances of *tzimtzum* (Jabès' Book), which could become a new philosophical concept.

This leads to a third, and final, implication concerning the relation between Jabès' messianism and modern philosophy. Namely, philosophy that follows the path of this messianism is a *practice of writing* – an activity that transcends the existing ideas of literature and philosophy. Neither theoretical nor practical, the activity constantly fathoms the rise and messianic fall.

What lies at stake in this practice should not be neglected, and Jabès' mature work is, in fact, devoted to chiselling it. Constituting the *shared* "zero level" of literature and philosophy, the practice relies on simplification to reveal the structure *it produces in the very movement of its simplification*. That the shared, reduced plane combining literature and philosophy is at all possible is both a reason for and an outcome of writing. This paradoxical loop shows that Jabès' idea that "sources precede us" concerns the foundations of his thinking. The practice of writing is a sovereign movement in the sense that it produces its own conditions of possibility. Ultimately, it resists the question whether it indeed reveals some structural patterns of the modern age or just presupposes them itself. This indeterminacy is perhaps its most modern facet. Finally, the only thing that could be said about modern philosophy turned practice of writing would be: *it is*.

7 The Concept of the Book

We have discussed Jabèsian messianism. Now let us address the Book, one of his central and, at the same time, most interesting quasi-concepts. In the previous Chapters, I outlined the Book as the space of all possible points of *tzimtzum* and, thus, of all possible constellations of the imaginary and the real. We know also that the singularity of the Book contrasts with the multiplicity of books, just like the singleness of God contrasts with the multitude of messianic acts.[1] In this Chapter, I will elaborate on these preliminary insights and propose a philosophical concept of the Book.[2]

To start with, I will show that this concept contains two basic components which, drawing on Jabès' quasi-Kabbalistic metaphors, I will refer to as *the whiteness of the Book* and *the script of the Book*. With this initial distinction in place, I will discuss each of the components in some detail. Whiteness is related to three categories: (1) continuity and legibility; (2) survival; and (3) succession. The script of the Book, as we will see, is a specifically conceived history. Having described the components of the Book, I will depict the significance of this concept. In particular, I will attempt to show that, because of the Book, philosophical

---

1 The capitalised "Book" appears in Jabès relatively late and is more frequently used in *The Book of Resemblances* cycle. Still, in *The Book of Questions*, similar connotations are evoked by *le livre* (the book) as opposed to *un livre* (a book).
In the following, I discuss the idea of the "Book" as defined and interpreted in the light of Jabès' reflection on both *le Livre* and *le livre*. Importantly, not all instances of the former in Jabès' texts designate "the Book" as understood here. As with other quasi-concepts, each passage must be separately interpreted in terms of the meanings it attributes to the even non-capitalised "book."

2 Notably, as Motte observes, Jabès' idea of the Book is indebted both to the sacred and secular traditions, gradually developing the concept inspired equally by the Talmud and Aristotle, the Kabbalah and Mallarmé. He pits these traditions in a heated dialogue, in which each questions the other ones. Motte, "Hospitable Poetry," p. 40. Capitalising the "Book," the poet seems to allude to the Bible as the only proper book and, concomitantly, to a writer's ultimate book – his *opus magnum*. Cf. Matthew Del Nevo, "Edmond Jabès and the Question of the Book," *Literature & Theology*, 10/4 (December 1996), pp. 301–36, on p. 307. The Bible is indisputably central in this context, as Del Nevo rightly claims (*Ibid.*). Still, Jabès' ontology should also be factored in as the Book is the Bible in the aftermath of his version of *tzimtzum* and, as such, is founded on God's non-existence. While the Bible was permeated with Divine presence, the Book is there because of God's withdrawal.

knowledge – a definitive, lone act – is replaced by ceaseless writing. This conclusion will come from a comparison of the Jabèsian Book with Hegel's Absolute and Mallarmé's "Book." To conclude, I will ponder the relevance of the thus-conceived Book to Jewish philosophy of modernity.

Introduction: The Layers of the Book

Let us first establish how the concept of the Book is structured. To do so, we need to revisit our previous insights concerning "the end of the book."

Reading Jabès' texts suggests, crucially, that the end of the book is bound up with a traumatic experience. Jabès himself talked about the fits of asthma which would repeatedly bother him whenever he was finishing a book – as if the rhythm of the book itself emulated breathing in and out.[3] In writing, this torment is envisaged in the recurring visions of the "abyss" and "darkness." The following passage perfectly exemplifies this imagery:

> The hour to abandon his book had come.
>
> He took it in his hands not to reread it, but with a long, gentle caress fingered page after page, line after line in order to soothe and close forever the thousand questioning eyes fixed on him, words [vocables] of which, at the end of the abyss, only a stare was left.
>
> Immediately, all the stars in the sky went out. He felt paralyzed facing utter night, the absolute negative of the unknowable.
>
> It is not nothingness that roots us to the spot, but the sight of the Void [la vision du Rien].[4]

What is it that happens at the end of the book? So pliable before, the words suddenly become *vocables*: something substantial and thing-like – lumps of matter that reflect meaning. They do not explain the world anymore but, through their bare materiality, side with the inexplicable. Additionally, they begin to *stare* at the writer. The book he wrote is becoming not only radically alien to him but also capable of gazing. As the night of absolute negativity falls, Nothing crops up. The unimaginable horror of the unknowable is paralleled by a momentary, *frozen gaze* of the paralysed writer, reflected in the gaze of Nothing itself. This Lacanian conjunction of the gaze and the Real reveals something about the Book; namely, *confronting it is a trauma of being seen by something far more powerful than we are*. The gaze of Nothing itself is an aspect of the Book.

---

3   IEJ, pp. 15–16. This declaration should undoubtedly be read in the context of Lurianic *tzimtzum*, with its connotations of "exhaling."
4   BS, pp. 86–7.

But this does not describe the Book fully. Further, *The Book of Shares* says:

For the first time he felt weightless. Unburdened to an extreme degree. Disintegrated. O ashes of contentious immortality within God's radiant immortality in ashes. Dust. Dust. God turns away from Himself.
Could He accept His defeat calmly? Lasting history of dust. History of man and the universe.
Have we not paid dearly for our shared dream of eternity?
And did God know that immortality was only the other side of death?[5]

At the end of the book, the writer is obliterated together with the order that produced him. He turns into "dust." But his "own" experience is accompanied by a *vision* of past annihilations: of a vast, layered expanse of "dust," of the ruins of the past, with God-the-Creator lying amidst them. The end of the book is the instant when the writer is included in this space. What can it be other than the sequence of "having been read" by the "ultimate reader" – by absent God, for whom the failing messianic act is just one of many?

So, essentially, "the end of the book" is not a uniform moment. It is split into: (1) a solitary confrontation with Nothing; and (2) the vision of joining, as "dust," the rubble of all past failures. This rubble is thus another aspect of the Book, besides its traumatising gaze. The two elements seem to be mutually entangled. For, importantly, the writer cannot contemplate this space of ruins directly. If not, how can he glimpse a vision of it? The answer is that, confronting Nothing as "the ultimate reader," the writer is spotted and destroyed by it. *Without the condition of his radical loneliness in the face of Nothing being lifted,* the writer can however think future confrontations with it. It is from the very position of "dust" to which he has been reduced that he surmises about the space of "dust" accumulated in the former failures of understanding. His thinking about the past wreckage is only possible through the mediation of Nothing. For Nothing, as the place of ultimate scrutiny, is not accessible to the writer, yet *the gaze it reciprocates* enables him to conclude about the space that such gaze alone can see.

Consequently, the gaze of Nothing is the ultimate guarantee of (utterly paradoxical) continuity between particular symbolic orders, i.e. books in Jabès' lexicon.[6] The place whence this gaze looks is inaccessible from any point within the

---

5   *Ibid.*
6   Jabès called the period between one book and another "*the book of torment*" (BS, p. 3). See also Waldrop, *Lavish absence*, p. 97. This "Book of Torment" was in fact a *link* between subsequent books and a plane of unbearable discontinuity, whose gaze could be averted only by a new writing design.

Jabèsian universe; indeed, as Jabès suggests, the place holds the eye of God, i.e. the most non-existent one. The burden of Nothing gazing at various orders is one of perennial themes in the Jabès' writings, particularly in *Elya*.[7] Jabès envisages a plane where all orders are situated side by side. This is the negative of Hegel's Absolute as no point of reconciliation is envisaged where one could say "The Absolute speaks through me." On the contrary, referring to Nothing, one can only say "I am looked at by it." Unlike the Hegelian philosopher, the writer cannot gaze at unity himself and can only see its reflexion in Nothing's gaze fixed on himself. As such, Jabès' thought seems to expose a fundamental distortion in Hegel's philosophy: real unity that it attributes to absolute knowledge is possible, but *only in the place of Nothing*. Absolute knowledge does not recognise unity by itself but only *triggers the gaze that Nothing turns to it*. In this gaze, knowledge sees a reflexion of the actual co-existence of all orders. Consequently, the Jabèsian writer is not faced with the problem that secretly gnawed the Hegelian philosopher, i.e. How can the validity of absolute knowledge be maintained after the book has been written? For the writer, a flash of "absolute knowledge" comes the moment *after* the book is written, in the perishment of the book.

While Hegel espouses the "Greek" notion of seeing as the co-presence and the consequent equality of the seeing and the seen, Jabès deems such seeing to be inaccessible. With seeing always coming out in displacement as an act in which the writer is passive, "seeing" in Jabès is only imaginary while *having been read*, i.e. an act that has always already taken place, is a real category.

In the light of this argument, the Book in Jabès seems to consist of two tightly interconnected and interdependent "layers." One of them is the very *plane* of ultimate continuity between discontinuous orders, that is, the plane of "Nothing," absent God and "the ultimate reader." Employing Jabès' metaphors, let us call it *the whiteness of the Book*. Superimposed "on" this layer, so to speak, there is

---

7   To provide just a handful of passages from *Elya*:

> "An eye catches and leads me astray. Though seen I cannot see myself.
> [...] "Do not think walls can keep you apart," he said. "They are pierced by an eye which belongs to no one." Eye of a world without God or of God without the world?
> [...] Eye is absence opening its lid.
> [...] God's eye is everywhere. / The void is a voyer.
> (*"An eye for an eye, / the look insists." "How come God refused to take this risk?"*)
> [...] From the other side of death, the desert stares at us with our own eyes.
> [...] *For the word, the invisible is the silence where God defines himself.*
> *To learn to see where there is no more world."* BQ II, pp. 213, 217, 231, 266, 278.

another one: a layer of particular orders – "books" – that co-exist due to this whiteness. Let us call it the *script of the Book*.

Notably, the traumatic experience of the whiteness of the Book, which appears at the end of the writing act makes it possible to think the script of the Book, i.e. the past of all failures. Therefore, the Book is never given directly but only in its liminal moment between the whiteness and the script, which point is, at the same time, *the liminal moment of a single book – its end*. It is only because of this interrelatedness that we can think of the Book

Whiteness: Continuity and Legibility

I will now discuss the concept of the Book in more detail and focus first on its former aspect. For Jabès, whiteness is where the definitively finished book is connected to the next book – a site of their shared inscription:

> From book to book, the blank space is place and bond.[8]

Since whiteness is a *place*, it can, but does not have to, hold objects (script). It can also be empty, and then it is an irreducible surplus – pure duration, which transcends script. In both cases, whiteness is that which *carries on* and connects over existence and over meaning. For if script is definitively divided by discontinuity, *this very discontinuity* can be said *to bring script together*. To script, whiteness is discontinuity, yet on its own, whiteness is an ultimate plane that stretches across both script and where there is no script. Whiteness is always a substratum though, *for writing*, its pure form is a token of discontinuity. "Continuity can only be assumed in the break…,"[9] insists Jabès. Moreover, with this reversal of the regular relation between continuity and discontinuity, *whiteness is presence while script is absence*, for Jabès. Combined, the two make up the Book:

> "In the book," he said, "writing means absence, and the empty page, presence. Thus God, who is absence, is present in the book."[10]

Whiteness is present just like the absence of God is present. Writing, however, is absent. Why is it so? Exploring Jabèsian thought, we are led to realise that for this "script" to be script at all, it must presuppose a specific plane. Script (1) constantly refers to it; (2) repudiates it; and (3) includes it as a place from

---

8   BQ II, p. 369.
9   *Ibid.*, p. 186.
10 *Ibid.*, p. 213.

which it can be read – all at the same time. Jabès believes that script can be both defined and singularised in relation to whiteness only if it persists in referring to the ultimate place from which this definition and singularisation can be seen; otherwise, such a script would be altogether impossible. *Whiteness* must be presupposed to be *the very condition of possibility of there being anything particular.* Paradoxically enough, it turns out that an inaccessible plane of continuity is necessary for discontinuity to be "seen" in Jabèsian language and, consequently, to be distinguishable. To articulate this thought in a self-echoing paradox, *continuity in discontinuity is a precondition of legibility.*

> And yet, separate in order to be recognised – for do we not need the blank space [between *vocables*], the fraction of silence between words [*paroles*] to read or hear them? – the words [*vocables*] have no tie to one another except this absence.[11]

Consequently, any particularity is possible only when it is assumed to be readable from the plane where it is inscribed together with other similar particularities. In other words, any particularity must presuppose being a passive element in the relation of being read, something that "is seen" but itself does not "see." This assumption determines its inner construction.

We can now explain why "whiteness is presence while script is absence." It is not about conferring a permanent ontological status on whiteness or script but about grasping their dynamic relationships. Script, namely, as consisting of units, must assume a constantly present plane which transcends it and from which the finitude of this script can be seen. In other words, script presupposes whiteness as a dimension that continues where script itself has already finished. As such, script bears an imprint of a relation in which *it is already absent and this absence is corroborated by the sustained presence of whiteness.*

Clearly, Jabès does not ascribe any stable ontological presence to whiteness, Nothing, God and the like. They are all *places* which the finite must assume to be able to recognise itself as the finite. This produces a highly interesting consequence as thus-conceived whiteness is an internal assumption of perspectivism. To think the fragmentation of the world into many incommensurable perspectives, it seems necessary to contrive a place of their continuity. Of course, this place is not accessible directly, for it transcends each perspective within which it could be grasped; but *the structure of its presupposed and deferred presence* is imprinted on all perspectives. As such, they refer to one plane which, admittedly, cannot be said to be shared by them (as in each perspective this plane is a trace

---

11 BM, p. 84.

only) but which recurs as the place of reference. This breeds Jabèsian repetition, which means, each time, that something so radically singular comes forth that its singularity indicates the imagined repeatability.

Let us conclude our argument so far. In Jabès' universe, all "being" has a dual condition. First, it belongs to a particular symbolic order, which forms it and subsumes it into the continuity of its temporal series. Second, this very order is finite and, in its finitude, presupposes its own inscription in the plane of whiteness. This plane cannot be said to "exist" since it only recurs as a trace in particular orders. Yet, each of these traces is a result of this plane being assumed as, by definition, an inaccessible plane of continuity from which a given order is looked at. In this way – through double external mediation – orders merge by assuming themselves to inhabit one place. This place is the whiteness of the Book.[12]

Whiteness: The Awe of Excess and Sur-vival

Whiteness is thus that which structurally transcends finitude and comes across as its excess. The end of a book is a privileged place of whiteness. But, in fact, whiteness ensues wherever *something senseless that is the condition of possibility of sense comes forth after sense has collapsed.* Therefore, whiteness is wherever something finite comes to an end against the backdrop of a plane endlessly persevering in its excessiveness.[13] It is not for no reason, as Jasper observes, that

---

12 In the "Letter to Jacques Derrida on the Question of the Book," Jabès cites the vision of medieval kabbalist Isaac the Blind and writes that the book is written in black fire on white fire. The metaphor was polysemous to the Kabbalah scholars, such as Gershom Scholem and Moshe Idel; nevertheless, it undoubtedly rendered the relation between the written and the oral Torah. According to Idel, the true written Torah is white fire, which forms the substance on which writing is performed while, paradoxically, black fire is the secondary oral Thora. In Scholem, in turn, white fire symbolises the oral Torah from which the written Torah emerges (cf. a discussion of this problem in Del Nevo, "Edmond Jabès and Kabbalism after God," pp. 408–9). Whichever version of the Torah is given precedence in Isaac's original metaphor, what it means in Jabès seems clear in the light of my foregoing argument. Whiteness is the basic raw material of reality as its continuity and present absence whereas that which exists is a particular negation of whiteness just as the black ink vis-à-vis a blank page. Still, to come into being and be read, black needs white. By the same token, existence comes into being against the "background" of continuing reality by setting itself against the present absence. Therefore, his absence – whiteness – founds everything that exists.

13 In another passage Jabès relies on another metaphor: "Sound diminishes sound. 'Between the lines of the book,' you said, 'there are levels of absence.' The bottom of the page is everlasting absence" (BQ II, p. 403). In this vision, "the bottom of the page"

a blank space conjures up a vision of the desert in Jabès.[14] The desert, for one, cannot be destroyed because destruction only expands it; and, additionally, by simply continuing, the desert exposes the finitude of things that enter it.

Jabès suggests that two fundamental modes of experiencing this interrelatedness of duration and excessiveness are life and writing. I will now focus on the two, starting with life. The following passage continues the description of the book quoted above:

> "When God wanted to destroy the earth, a great fire burst from the ground sweeping Him into the conflagration.
> – But God is not dead.
> When God wanted to blot out the sea, a giant wave broke from the others and carried Him off in its fury.
> – But God is not dead.
> When man opened the book and shattered it – o, grief! – a ravaged landscape lay before his eyes. And he drowned in his tears.
> – But man still exists. Here is the miracle," he said.[15]

Though drawn into a whirlpool of destruction, God and man live on instead of dying. What does this "life" mean? Blanchot would say that it means surviving beyond the disaster – the impossibility of death. Evidently, life in this sense surfaces, according to Jabès, only where it is inexplicable and where its pure duration crosses its demarcated limits:

> "Life is at the end […] Life is at the end, I am sure of it … And at the end there is nothing."[16]
> Life is in survival.[17]

Characteristically, "the end" – the outermost point that determines the symbolic order – is bound up with the appearance of "nothing," which is at the same time a form of "life." Like in the presence-absence dialectics of whiteness and script, life is both an absent thing (in its utter senselessness and indeterminacy) and the only present thing (in its persistent continuation where finitude has passed). As

---

is everlasting silence, which however is not absence but, rather, the lowest level of the sound – a silence from which all sound itself from to come into existence. Like whiteness, "everlasting silence" is present absence, an element that makes both writing and sound possible, a fullness from which singularity sets itself apart.

14 Jasper, *Sacred Desert*, p. 85.
15 BS, p. 87.
16 BQ I, p. 126.
17 *Ibid.*, p. 183.

such, life is knowable only in the moments of the end, binding them and determining their legibility. Failure, particularly the failure of the book – that is, of
understanding – reactively illumines life. For this reason it is "survival" – *survivre* – both "living-though" and "living-on."[18]
Consequently, Jabès views life as a traumatic experience. Its incomprehensible
continuity despite subsequent debacles inspires awe – admiration and dread
alike. This is also what makes living more difficult than not living:

You have to be mad to accept death, and wise to resign yourself to living.[19]

"To resign yourself to living" is not a fortuitous turn of phrase as life is not a
simple choice but rather the more difficult of two options. It is not natural and
primordially given; rather, it is a predicament that takes resigning to. To Jabès,
life is more of a burden than death is, for life forces one to face up to duration,
which is not clothed in sense:

Anguish at the flight of hours, not because I fear death, but because it is impossible to
live, impossible to follow.[20]

Still, the sage chooses life, his choice is consonant with the spirit of Jewish messianism, described above, in which the failure of an attempt is, indeed, despair,
nonsense and the end of everything, yet also something that is sur-vived trau-
matically while watching bare duration annihilate meaning. "The Jew expects
each day to live,"[21] states Jabès, suggesting that life is never *here* but always *afterwards* and, as such, must be waited for.
To recapitulate, the structure of life vis-à-vis that it which makes it possible
mirrors the structure of whiteness vis-à-vis script. Transcending finitude, life is

---

18 Of course, Jabès' idea of life as sur-viving resembles, in many respects, Blanchot's pre-
    occupation with the concept of "survival." For example, Blanchot states in *Le pas au-
    delà* (opulent punning of the passage is hardly translatable): "Survivre : non pas vivre
    ou, ne vivant pas, se maintenir, sans vie, dans un etat de pur supplement, mouvement
    de suppleance a la vie, mais plutot arreter le mourir, arret qui ne l'arrete pas, le faisant
    au contraire *durer.*" Maurice Blanchot, *Le pas au-delà* (Paris: Gallimard, 1973), p. 184.
    Cf. "Survive: not to live, or, not living, to maintain oneself, without life, in a state of
    pure supplement, movement of substitution for life, but rather to arrest dying, arrest
    that does not arrest, making it, on the contrary, *last.*" Maurice Blanchot, *The Step Not
    Beyond*, trans. Lycette Nelson (Albany: State University of New York Press, 1992),
    p. 135.
19 BQ I, p. 89.
20 BQ II, p. 276.
21 BQ I, p. 143.

an inaccessible dimension of continuity.[22] This is the reason why Jabès' universe cannot simply live: with *living always elsewhere*, only "being lived" is actually possible. We think of "our" life, but this life is, at the same time, utterly strange to us and utterly our own. Just as a blank space amidst script, life appears only as a trace and, thus, as a place of being marked with something in-finite. Hence, to survive means to experience the whiteness of the Book.

The other experience that reveals the structure of whiteness is writing. As Jabès' concept of writing was outlined in Chapter Four, in the following we shall just highlight its aspect of continuity. Writing means persisting in putting down. Writing is not about executing a design to "create works" but about *experiencing continuity above the design*. Jabès envisages the writer as continuing to be after the successive debacles, i.e. the books he has written so far. "His" writing is structurally tied to "his" life. This is a paradoxical and unbearable continuity that shows the catastrophe of books in its sheer horror. For there is a space where they co-exist and wreck each other, which can be seen only in writing.

It is for this reason that writing discloses whiteness as an excess and duration. Persisting in writing, the author can recognise the dimension that binds particular books above their separate worlds. Therefore, rather than on the work at hand, the Jabèsian writer focuses on what follows the work's end and what, through the void of *tzimtzum*, leads to another work. Indeed, he uses subsequent books to explore this paradoxically continuing void. The void ingests the lost book and carves a place for another out of its own excess. Each blank in the Book seems to offer new land, writes Jabès.[23]

Writing is paradoxical insofar that it traverses the place where script is no more:

> The route of writing goes through the night. Will other eyes see for us where we can no longer see?[24]

Thus, the continuity of writing mirrors that which is impossible and ungraspable, excessive and enduring, in one word – whiteness. As such, writing is a counterpart of life ("I know that without writing I will die,"[25] claims Jabès). Besides, writing registers for us – or, rather, for the meaning we need in order to understand – that which we cannot see. Writing is "our eyes," which let us appreciate the truly incomprehensible – the continuity of duration ("What is mysterious in

---

22 Cf. JW, p. 27.
23 BQ I, p. 72.
24 BQ II, p. 218.
25 LR I, p. 45.

the book is its light [...] not its obscurity,"[26] insists Jabès). As Derrida writes in "Ellipsis," "within this movement of succession, writing keeps its vigil, between God and God, between the Book and the Book."[27]

Hence writing consists first in [...] spying continually on a voice whose barren efforts perforate time from the inside.[28]

Notably, the gesture Jabès presupposes is dual as only the decision to persevere in the continuity of writing (structurally analogous to the decision to persevere in life) makes it possible to unveil whiteness and, simultaneously, turns writing itself (and life) into whiteness.

With the last word [vocable] of the night, an empty space stretches towards us while we try to cross behind the narrator ...[29]

To keep going beyond the end, beyond the last *vocable*: this is the point *where our own perseverance becomes co-extensive with the dimension it exposes, one that is ostensibly independent of it* – whiteness. "We try to cross an empty space" because it stretches towards us. But doesn't it stretch just because we made a step to cross it?

Whiteness: Existence as Incompletion and Succession

We know now how whiteness marks a symbolic order, transcends it and is a place in which it is inscribed. Let us now review what we know about symbolic orders themselves.

Given that they are formed in tension with whiteness as described above, each of such orders – "books" – (1) is incomplete and (2) succeeds another order. Both these consequences mingle in one of Jabès' key sentences: "The book survives the book."[30] I will now elucidate this statement, addressing both the aspects.

Let us start from incompletion. "The book survives the book" means that every book carries in itself the possibility of its being surpassed – that it will be survived by another book. However, at stake is not simply this book's completion and exigency to retreat in order to make room for a future book. We must bear in mind that, in Jabès, sur-viving is a traumatic event. In "being survived," the

---

26 BQ II, p. 425.
27 Derrida, *Writing*, pp. 371–2.
28 BQ II, p. 291.
29 BQ I, p. 181.
30 *Ibid.*, p 191.

book will have to suffer an outright defeat and confront whiteness. In turn, the excess of whiteness will give rise to a new book. Hence, *each book bears a trace of a catastrophic event which only lurks ahead for it.* Furthermore, the book not only assumes its disaster to be witnessed by whiteness but also presupposes *a new book to come into being in this whiteness and bear direct testimony to the prior failure.* Consequently, each book carries the inevitability of its own repetition as it presumes it will perish and be supplanted by a new book.

This idea is a cornerstone of Jabès' perspectivism. It explains the fundamental variance between the imagined future duration of a given order and its actual lot. The order, namely, imagines that it will simply go on existing and, at the same time, that it will inevitably be repeated. What we retrospectively perceive as a lack of continuity in time is, in fact, the symbolic order's "internal" structure, formed in tension with whiteness. Such perspectivism has poignant consequences in Jabès. First, *each whole is incomplete and already disenfranchised.*

> *The book is destroyed by the book. We shall never have owned anything.*[31]

Second, once the temporal factor – development, duration, and the like – has come into play, the emerging order is constantly invaded by a recurring break, shift, "wound" in Jabès' lexicon.

> The *Book of Questions* is from beginning to end interrupted in its unfolding. Each interruption is a cut. Gaping white wounds.[32]

The first passage implies that an unfolding whole is marked with "wounds" in the way suggesting that whiteness itself uses the texture of this whole to overwrite itself. Thus, for Jabès, internal shifts within each whole – a text in particular – are *traces with which the Book makes its imprint on a book.* Furthermore, the Book overwrites itself with them:

> "'This absence which claims the book in order to rewrite it, is this God and, therefore, the hope for a divine word which devours us?' he asked."[33]

This is how Jabès' writings should be read. As mentioned in Chapter Two, *The Book of Questions* as a cycle of, ultimately, seven parts was written gradually. Its final structure, as we know it now, was not preconceived. The subsequent books came into being in succession, as "survivals of the book by the book." Instead of a prior design, Jabès was only "conscious of a movement," as he asserts himself,[34]

---

31 BQ II, p. 337.
32 *Ibid.*, p. 261.
33 *Ibid.*, p. 275.
34 DB, p. 53.

which tossed in successive books. Already *The Book of Yukel* (to become part two of the future series) made Gabriel Bounoure observe that it "takes over *The Book of Questions* and replaces it to see whether this lifeless life can be infused with survival."[35] The heptalogy was thought of only later as a retrospective attempt to piece together a whole which is nonetheless affected by the structure of survival. At the beginning of *The Book of Resemblances*, Jabès proclaims it to be a book in its own right, albeit possible only in the aftermath of *The Book of Questions*.[36] Both the writerly designs and all efforts to put the past in order are disrupted by whiteness in Jabès. Therefore, the structure of incompletion and impossibility haunts every whole, in particular a book.[37] Whiteness is not only excess revealed *in the aftermath of* a book but also a book's "inner" wound. For this reason, a book's incompletion can be read as a trace of the Book itself.

"The book survives the book" implies also that the book at hand follows on the former one, with "succession" based on the structure of survival and, thus, necessarily imprinted by whiteness. In other words, every *already* existing book is a book that has survived and, as such, has the vast and inscrutable past of failed books *behind* it. Whiteness not only follows but also precedes it, concealing the boundless ruins.

"*You dream of writing a book. The book is already written.*"
[…] The past is never foreclosed.
We are soldered to God in the hour and man.
[…] "A madman who wants to destroy the Word by words, and the Book by books."
[…] "*Death is the past that persists.*"
[…] The present is alone, grubbed. Being on the margin means having reached the place of the present. The place of before-and-after-place.[38]
"*God follows God, and Book follows Book.*"[39]
Everything is before Everything. The word is the day after the word, and the book the day after the book.[40]
"I will write [*aurai écrit*] only one book," he said. "'The first one [*Le premier*]."
But it was already written."[41]
"In every created thing, there is a space left empty by the thing created before."[42]

---

35 Bounoure, *Edmond Jabès*, p. 37.
36 LR I, p. 9.
37 Cf. Motte, *Questioning*, p. 122.
38 BQ I, pp. 207, 246, 254, 283, 301.
39 *Ibid.*, p. 329.
40 BQ II, p. 121.
41 LH, p. 57.
42 F, p. 102.

In terms of the continuity of writing, each book is inscribed in the impenetrable past of that which has already come into being. The past persists in the blank space and "is never foreclosed." Whiteness thus forms a *place* where all past books can be thought.[43] Taking shape, a new book must curb this excess. This, of course, is an act of *tzimtzum*, which produces "a place of before-and-after-place." The concept of whiteness complements Jabès' vision of *tzimtzum* insofar that it shows the dimension of continuity, in which *a perspectival order exists only in following other, already bygone orders.* This insight helps us decipher the following passage, central to Jabès' ontology:

> Je suis celui qui suit. [*I am the one that follows*], says the page to the page, the word to the word, the point to the point.[44]

In this sentence, which reverberates with the biblical אהיה אשר אהיה – "I shall be who I shall be" (*Shemot* 3, 14) – Jabès acknowledges that every existing order (rather than being, the subject or God![45]) is specifically related to another order, and this relation is expressed in "I am the one that follows" [*je suis celui qui suit*]. It exists in existing-after as, generally, to exist means to succeed something. In utter contradiction of the traditionally construed Cartesian *cogito, ergo sum*, the sentence grounds existence not in "being as such" but in relatedness to things past, which relation ousts and conceals the past.

What is more, the homophonic arrangement of *suis* and *suit* seems to underscore that being "oneself" means being "something else."[46] Being coherent is

---

43 Incidentally, Didier Cahen insists that the "Book" refers in a sense to the Bible. Each writer writes after the Bible, in the wake of the book that was or was supposed to be the right and only one. Thus, by writing, one questions, in a way, the sanctity and singularity of the Book as the Bible and alters its meaning since, even though not adding anything to it, one deprives it of the last and proper word and expands the context in which it is interpreted. Nevertheless, Cahen claims that it is the Bible's fate to perish in writing. The Bible can be correctly interpreted only where it loses its exceptional status. Didier Cahen, "Les réponses du livre," in *Écrire le livre*, p. 60. In this sense the Bible is a model of the first fallen book which finds itself followed.

44 BQ II, p. 418 (quotation altered).

45 This sentence conveys the relationship of page to page and word to word, which are units of the text rather than of "being as such," which does not appear in Jabès.

46 Jabès expresses the same idea, which resonates with Rimbaud's famous "I am another" ("*moi est un autre*"), punning on *L'étranger. L'étrange-je?*: "The foreigner? The foreign I?" (F, p. 43). Similarly to Lacanian extimacy, that which is most our own is strange to us to the utmost: we are somebody else exactly where we are ourselves. See also Cahen, *Edmond Jabès*, p. 24.

impossible as a difference creeps in between "I am" (*suis*) and "I am" (*suis*), with *suis* morphing into *suit*, which is discernible in writing only. In carrying on being, one *already* follows and is already something else. Jabès' phrasing encapsulates also the parallel co-existence of two orders, represented here by speech and writing. In the former, identity ostensibly persists, but in the latter a disruption within identity is conspicuous.

This duality is inevitable in Jabès' ontology, and it is this duality that underpins the differentiation of a book from the Book, an act of writing from the continuity of writing, and meaning from life. Emphatically, however, Jabès does not rely on any presupposed dualism. The two aspects do not exist *side by side*. Where there is a book, the whiteness of the Book is unseen, hidden by the reduction of *tzimtzum*. And where whiteness unveils and discloses the ruins of the past, a book is obliterated. So a book and whiteness are intertwined and one makes the other visible. That is why whiteness is not the ultimate instance of presence, but rather a place where the entire past is present *as* absent.

Concluding, the concept of whiteness helps show that every book is based on the structure of sur-vival. It dissociates itself from the past in its own act of *tzimtzum*, which gives it an illusion of being the ultimate one. "Could the obsession of the book be only the obsession of a word able to survive all books?"[47] asks Jabès. "You must believe in the book in order to write it."[48] Yet, based on this messianic hope, the very existence of a book is sur-vival and, as such, a testament to *failures that precede it*. In other words: the rise of new books, therein Jabèsian messianism, results from this unbearable, excess continuity, which needs acts of delimiting to mark itself off.

Having outlined the concept of whiteness and its implications for the formation of the finite orders of books, we can now focus on the other aspect of the Book, that is, on script.

The Script of the Book

As mentioned in the foregoing, the script of the Book is the totality of past orders (books) inscribed in the plane of the whiteness.

Essentially, script in this sense is never given directly, but it surfaces as an object of contemplation from the vantage point of whiteness. Whiteness

47 DB, pp. 102–103.
48 LR I, p. 29 (in Edmond Jabès, "From *The Book of Resemblances*," trans. Rosmarie Waldrop, *Studies in 20th Century Literature*, 12/1, *Special Issue on Edmond Jabès*, 1987, pp. 13–25, on p. 15).

itself appears only at the moment of the book's perishment, as a place that sur-vives and will read it. What is script then? It ensues from the assumption behind the messianic fall of a book. This book, namely, yields itself to its ulti-mate reader and *allows presupposing other past books similar to it.* In other words: for this book, whiteness is not only the place of being read but also the place that *has read (and will read) past (and future) books.* If whiteness is the ultimate plane of continuity, there must be the corresponding totality of past singular orders which can be seen from it. This totality is referred to as script here.

Having settled this, let us have a closer look at what script involves. First, entire singular orders (books) are units of script. Consequently, each of them is a discrete organisation of the world based on another *tzimtzum.* What is more, as explained in Chapter Three, a unit of writing in this sense is *a given organisation of ("illusory") time and, as such, an entire given history.* Hence, Jabès repeatedly suggests that the Book is "history of all histories" and "eternity of all eternities":

> Time [*le temps*] begins with the book.[49]
> This time – like a book. All these books will have allowed us to do our time.[50]
> The book is the vague consciousness of going beyond yourself, the need for which will show only later.
> To wait, in the shade of time, for the time to come, the time which, tomorrow, will be ours [...].[51]
> [...] I dreamed of [...] a book [...] which would only surrender by fragments, each of them the beginning of another book.[52]
> A highway is also a humble crossroad, and most often we do not know where it leads.[53]
> *The time of the infinite is the time of borders crossed.*[54]
> "Every century leaves us a white page in bequest. Eternity is just a myriad of pages that fled writing."[55]
> "If eternity is the time of God, time of a continuous time where our time miscarries – a past more distant than the past, a future beyond the future – how could we, who can act only in time, reach God?[56]

---

49 BQ II, p. 23.
50 *Ibid.*, p. 163.
51 *Ibid.*, p. 197.
52 *Ibid.*, p. 247.
53 *Ibid.*, p. 281.
54 *Ibid.*, p. 346.
55 LR I, p. 19.
56 BR III, p. 64.

Jabès emphatically foregrounds the paradoxical nature of the Book, which is a world of elements that make up mutually exclusive wholes.[57] Each of these wholes has its own time while the Book is an assemblage of all these times, a time *within* which they are all contained, that is, "the time of borders crossed."[58] *For what is just a unit in the Book is, actually, the entire eternity of time in a given order.*[59] Consequently, there is no single history as each history is finite and perspectival by belonging to a particular symbolic order. The Book accommodates them all.

"To wait, in the shade of time, for the time to come" can thus be interpreted to imply that in the duration of the ultimate time of the Book ("the shade of time"), *its* moment comes which is in and by itself the entire time of a book. Passing from book to book in writing, we pass from one illusory time to another and from one eternity to another, though we still move within a certain ultimate time which aggregates all perspectival times as its moments. In this insight, Jabès is close both to Hegel (with his Absolute as "a time of times") and to Nietzsche (with his concept of eternal return). Still, he also draws on an important trend within the Kabbalah which revolved around the medieval *Sefer ha-Tmunah* (*The Book of the Figure*) and distinguished two types of the Torah: an absolute one and

---

57 The Book is, in a sense, "a set of sets." Hank Lazer observes that: "The perspective and the written expression that a woman or a man achieves, as she or he learns and makes manifest her or his precise particularity, become part of a larger Book. Such a poetics is akin to set theory – the individual contribution being an element of the all-encompassing set – and to Heidegger's thinking through of being, the individual existence being an instance of Being." Hank Lazer, "Is There a Distinctive Jewish Poetics? Several? Many? Is There Any Question?" *Shofar: An Interdisciplinary Journal of Jewish Studies*, 27/3 (Spring 2009), p. 79.

58 It is this "time of borders crossed" that stands for real eternity in Jabès. For the eternity of the book is not independent of and alien to the moment; rather it is the moment's "infinite extension" (QQLS, p. 15). In this sense, the search for such eternity entails sacralisation. Rather than in the eternal continuance of the sacred moment, sacralisation, the poet adds, consists in the constant tension of the profane, which tilts to its infinite extension (*Ibid.*).

59 In *Intimations The Desert*, Jabès suggests other names for these varieties of time. The time of the Book is named "eternity," and particular times – just "times." Their relationship is still the same, however: "Time measures only time, but measures itself against eternity./ The eternity of time is perhaps only time's eternal return to a time [*du temps au temps*] that repeals it, the repeal becoming an eternity of time [*un temps*] without common measure: frightening infinite. / All writing […] becoming the writing of its time" (BR II, p. 15). The Book's counterpart is thus eternity filled with books and their times. One time overthrows another and, thereby, highlights "a dreadful eternity."

one revealed in a given period (*Shmita*) of the universe. Each of one-thousand-year-long Shmitas had its own version of the Torah, based on the reduction of the original absolute Torah and determined by the attributes of its patron sefirah. In this vision, history was the passage from one Shmita Torah to another, with all of them being in a way accommodated by the absolute Torah.[60] In Jabès, the book is, similarly, the "absolute Torah" of individual books.

In this optics, *script is a totality of possible tzimtzum junctures*, irrespective of how they have actually panned out. "Eternity is a myriad of pages that fled writing," Jabès asserts and seems to suggest that units of the script of the Book comprise not only the discerned and implemented (e.g. in writing) orders but also their embryonic germs even if they managed to "flee writing." For Jabès, this makes the writer not so much an author of enunciations as a witness to the rise of entire worlds in which enunciations find their own place. Some of these worlds get to be developed, others only indicated, and still others may pass unrecorded in an utterance. In this sense, "a single letter may contain the entire book, the universe."[61]

This implies that Jabès develops the concept of the script of the Bok to think the past in a specific – and specifically modern – way. The past is not simply a past of "real events," but a past of orders that have come to pass. How developed they are matters less than the very fact that they came into being. Because of this, the script of the Book contains more than what is popularly conceived as the past, for it preserves also the orders traces of which have but barely remained. *The Book is thus an ultimate witness.* "Events" are registered in this past of the Book secondarily, only as elements of the orders themselves.

This insight leads us to conclude that, though in its basic meaning the script of the Book is the totality of the realised possibilities of *tzimtzum*, it also holds all the "real events" and objects belonging to the orders generated in particular *tzimtzums*. In this sense, the script of the Book hoards everything that has ever existed and become a thing of the past. The idea is intimated time and again:

> [...] Thus the chain is never broken. Death verifies the unity.[62]
> The book is a solitude of sand where every word leaves an imprint of its voice. You read in silence what once was said by all.[63]

---

60 Cf. Scholem, "Signification," pp. 139–46.
61 BM, p. 47.
62 BQ II, p. 189.
63 *Ibid.*, p 231.

[…] there are major works […] which are majestically turned towards ours; critical eyes fixed on all that is – or is to be – written. One day our books will die at their feet; […] it is our work that opens their eyes.[64]

Nothing is lost. Even trivial words and gestures are collected and preserved by death.[65]

"Think also about all the erased words which the words of your books have replaced," he said. "There are some traces of them left in your notes. Thus you will learn that absence bears witness to all infringed absences because it is written into their gradual dispossession."[66]

[…] every page of writing is in some way the journal diary of a dead man.[67]

A lack,

a gap of centuries

torments me.

[…] Stones, dust, cold slope of emptiness, hell where the murmur seeps down that once shook the Temple.[68]

The script of the Book contains all past "words and gestures" as well as former "works." "What once was said by all" – by which Jabès likely means commonly endorsed truths – today is but a trace which is read in silence. Thus, the script of the Book holds past verities which failed in their claim to ultimate understanding. Notably, if, in Jabès, the messianic attempt is an utter supersession of former attempts – a striving to institute a book as a universal one – the failure unifies all messianic acts. Lethal to them, the gaze of whiteness forms, at the same time, a plane of continuity against which they appear as units of the same script of the Book.

Moreover, they appear as equal units, for the words "erased" and "replaced" are subsumed in the script of the Book just like "important" and "present" words are. Why is it so? This can be easily explained if we remember the fundamental construction principle underlying the script of the Book. Script is, namely, the totality of possibilities of *tzimtzum*. From the perspective of *tzimtzum*, "erasing a word" does not entail replacing it without leaving a trace. For the erasure to invalidate fully that which has come into being, there would have to be one valid order abiding in time. Then the power of this order's *tzimtzum* reduction would nullify the past, including the erased things.[69] Yet in the script of the Book, the

---

64 *Ibid.*, p. 239.
65 *Ibid.*, p. 248.
66 *Ibid.*, p. 342.
67 *Ibid.*, s. 431.
68 *Ibid.*, p. 432.
69 *The Book of Resemblances* says: "'You think you can cross out a word by drawing a line through it. Do you not know that the line is transparent? / The pen doesn't cross out a word but the eye that is reading it,' wrote Reb Taleb" (BR III, p. 12). Jabès clearly

limitation of *tzimtzum* does not work anymore, and the past is manifest in its continuity. For this reason, in script, erasure is not a definitive effacement but only a point of transition from one order to another, with the two orders being equal. Hence, the script of the Book contains the crossed-out word *side by side* with its deletion and the new word.

Clearly, the concept of the script of the Book helps Jabès think much further than the popular notion of the past could enable him to do as the latter is, in fact, always only *a* sense-making history. The script of the Book, instead of making sense, forms a plane where all senses are contained despite their discord ("repulsion" as Hegel would have put it). Moreover, the script of the Book, which basically consists of entire orders rather than of meanings taking shape in them, reveals *the originary grid of tzimtzum reduction.* This, in turn, demonstrates how the mutual negation of particular meanings is powered by the difference of their source orders. In other words, this helps Jabès reduce the contradiction of various meanings at the *content* level to the more primordial forces of limitation and supersession which engender the orders themselves.

To conclude our argument about the script of the Book, let us consider materiality as another aspect exemplified in quotations above. Jabès persistently reiterates the idea that past meanings retain *traces of matter* in the script of the Book: "'The word leaves on imprint of its voice in the sand,'" "stones preserve the murmur that once shook the Temple," and • *(El)* tells us:

> *The unsayable settles us in those desert regions which are the home of dead languages. Here, every grain of sand stifled by the mute word offers the dreary spectacle of a root of eternity ground to dust before it could sprout. In the old days, the ocean would have cradled it. Does the void torment the universe, and the universe in turn vex the void? Roots buried in sand keep longing for their trees.*[70]

---

suggests that the past can be invalidated only by *the current reading* ("the eye that is reading"). It is reading that spots an erasure and takes notice of it, treating the crossed-out word as never existing. But such an erasure would be impossible without the new reading based on its own *tzimtzum*. In the Book, "the line [crossing out a word] is transparent" in being a sign *next to,* but *not instead of,* another sign.

70 BQ II, p. 415. Incidentally, the root metaphor in this passage has its ample antecedents in Jewish mysticism. For one, in Luria, reality consists of several hierarchised worlds, with each upper world being the lower world's soul, interiority or, as Luria put it, "root." The root is the principle of life and the anchoring of the lower world in the upper one. See Emmanuel Lévinas, *Beyond the Verse: Talmudic Readings and Lectures*, trans. Gary D. Mole (Bloomington and Indianapolis: Indiana UP, 1994), pp. 157–9. On this model, Elohim is a shared place of all worlds and functions in the same way as the Jabèsian Book in this passage.

This passage relies on the metaphor of the desert, where, after its tragic demise, each order (here "language") is literally *embodied* in a grain of sand. Each grain preserves a separate "eternity" and the hope of the world that arose from it. The desert as conceived in these terms is equivalent to the Book, with expanses of wilderness corresponding to the blank space of the Book and the grains of sand to the script. Where does this materiality-suffused imagery come from? It seems that, for Jabès, only a matter-filled space works as a metaphor that enables us to think the totality of all symbolic orders. The Jabèsian space has no demarcated places and, consequently, all orders are equal in it. At the same time, the orders can be imagined to co-exist, which is impossible within any one of them, where the limiting forces of its *tzimtzum* are at work. Such an intuitive notion of matter as "external" grounds the idea of an external dimension where the orders dwell together.

Let us round up our argument on the script of the Book. As explained, it amasses all the previous *tzimtzum* junctures together with the orders they spawned and the meanings engendered within these orders. Clearly, however, it is possible to think the script of the Book only if mediated by the idea of whiteness. It is so because only from the place taken up by whiteness and inaccessible to us can the script of the Book be gazed at. That is why we can think it only through participating in the fall of the messianic attempt of an order which finds itself confronted by whiteness.

Consequently, the script of the Book is a specifically defined "history" in Jabès. Unlike in the standard notion of common history, there is no comprehensible continuity between the units of this "history." This, however, does not mean that there is no history as such and that these units are completely unmediated monads. There is still "history" in Jabès, paradoxical though it may be. The plane which gives continuity to its units forms an inaccessible, presupposed place of scrutiny while confronting it amounts to experiencing utter discontinuity. Indeed, there is no communication between the units of such "history," but each of them, in its own fall, presupposes similar past falls. *So although the continuity of "history" is utterly inaccessible, it leaves a trace in each of its units, and this trace is located exactly where an order perishes.*

The script of the Book thus produces "history" not as a coherent, meaningful narrative of events but as an impossible continuity, inferable from the traces surfacing in debacles of orders. Paradoxically enough, Jabès' ultimate perspectivism requires presupposing an ultimate and uncrossable plane where all perspectives meet. This is the reason why the desert is the poet's favourite metaphor. For, in the desert, the utterly dispersed grains of sand make up the ultimate oneness of the desert as such.

Writing and the Book

At the beginning of this Chapter, I showed that the end of a book reveals a new dimension: the Book. Then, I described two "components" of the Book: whiteness and script. Let us revisit now the key moment of the book's fall and explore it, drawing on these insights.

Recall that the whiteness of the Book is the totality of possible *tzimtzum* versions, and its script is a set of its *effected* versions. Consequently, each act of writing is dual, depending on which layer of the Book it is juxtaposed with. First, writing is the rise of whiteness, which amounts to forming an order based on a given *tzimtzum*. Following and subsuming the former order, whiteness offers a new place where the originary limitation can produce an entirely new domain. Second, the act of writing ends, nevertheless, in the fall of the book and its inclusion within the script of the Book. Thus *the act of writing is peculiarly suspended between the emergence of whiteness and the incorporation in script*. Between these two extremes – the beginning and the end of a book – writing is forever dislodged vis-à-vis whiteness and script in not being whiteness *anymore* and not having turned into script *yet*.

What is the act of writing in this framework? In the chasm specific to the Jabèsian universe, it can be understood in two ways. First, the act of writing, i.e. one book, can be viewed as an inner movement within the field shielded by the illusion of the originary *tzimtzum*. What is the aim of this movement? Its aim is to bring the book to a close through returning it to *tzimtzum*, that is, through the messianic fall. In this way, *one book is the passage from the beginning to the dissolution which, as a whole, is a unit of the Book*. In other words, on this model, the act of writing means putting down one record in the Book.

In this optics, Jabès seems to assume that the book is a sphere of illusion which, inevitably, turns out to be just a unit of the Book. But this image is incomplete without the other way of viewing the act of writing. For *writing a book down is the only way in which the Book can overtly pass from whiteness to script, that is, happen as such*. In other words: the Book depends on a book as much as a book on the Book.

Consequently, one act of writing takes place, as it were, on two planes simultaneously. First, it produces a book – an order based on a given *tzimtzum*. Second, it is also the Book's movement from whiteness to script. This double engagement embodies Jabès' specific concept of writing as a circular movement of rise and dissolution and a unique, individual unfolding of *tzimtzum*, at the same time. This insight helps us draw a crucial conclusion.

Namely, for Jabès, writing is movement which, in the successive cycles of books, charts an unrepeatable trajectory in the Book's space. Out of all the possible configurations of *tzimtzum*, it enacts some and, thereby, marks the script of the Book against its whiteness. In this way, the book being written down becomes a transition point of the Book's whiteness into script.

Let us revisit now the *vocable* as discussed in Chapter Four. As explained there, the *vocable* is not only a place where the imaginary and the real are separated and joined in a particular way but also an entity inscribed in the whiteness of the Book. The argument of this Chapter helps us eventually explain why the *vocable* is also the breaking point between a *particular* configuration of the imaginary and the real (visible in the perishment of the book) and the space of *all* such configurations. The fall of the book, namely, unveils the whiteness and, through it, the script of the Book. Both dimensions, though accessible by assumption, are not accessible directly. The *vocable* is thus also the liminal point between the fall of one, particular book and the presupposition of the Book it makes possible. In other words, *the vocable constitutes a point dividing the book as a discrete whole from the book as an entity within a larger plane.* Consequently, Jabès conceives of writing not only as of philosophical practice, which I claimed in Chapter Three, for *writing is participation in the formation of the Book itself, that is, in happening/enowning.*[71]

This observation leads us to the last part of this Chapter, in which I will address two issues. First, I will consider the relation between writing and the Book in Jabès, relying on the comparison with Hegel and Mallarmé. Afterwards, I will examine the effects of passing from philosophical thinking to writing which draws conclusions from the nature of the Book.

Writing as Marking the Book: Jabès vs. Hegel and Mallarmé

As already stated, writing unveils and marks the Book in a way. But what is it that writing actually does? What does this "marking" involve? In this section, I will focus on the quasi-epistemological relationship of writing and the Book. To do this, I will contrast the Jabèsian Book with two apparently similar ideas: Hegel's Absolute and Mallarmé's Book.

Jabès envisions writing as a unique path in the Book. What does it mean? First of all, the journey of writing does not have a predetermined destination, for it unfolds in a space that refuses to have a destination imposed on it. The Jabèsian writer gropes in the dark, unable to anticipate what shape his book's

---

71 This makes Richard Stamelman observe that Heidegger's being-in-the-world becomes "being-in-the-book" in Jabès. Stamelman, "Nomadic Writing," p. 95.

new *tzimtzum* will take and, thus, which point of whiteness will be used in writing-down. This is why Jabès' metaphors envisage writing as conscious navigation through a space bristled with units of script like the sea with reefs:[72]

> *When adventure has reached its farthest point where the sea listens only to the sea, writing suddenly appears as a broken coastline which no map records.*[73]

Writing brings forth reduced worlds which lend themselves to meaningful, albeit limited, depiction. Yet, they are submerged in the abysmal "sea," without signposts and directions, where adventure reaches "its farthest point." This space is what Jabès dedicates himself to exploring. *For him, writing – instead of in creating works – consists in sustaining the movement of their rise and dissolution, which is movement through the Book.* Consequently, the Jabèsian writer is perennially incommensurable with the Book. It means, first of all, that the Book is a dimension he cannot fully grasp and convey since he is inscribed in it himself. This is seemingly reminiscent of the relationship of the Hegelian philosopher and the Absolute. Yet, this is, in fact, where an essential difference between Jabès' Book and Hegel's Absolute lies.

Hegel presupposed a position in which the Absolute, self-recognising in the philosophical act, speaks through the philosopher. Furthermore, the Absolute's self-recognition is possible because it uses the individual philosopher, abolishing at the same time the difference between itself and him in absolute knowledge. Yet for Jabès, such position is a sheer impossibility because of the specific separation of a book from the Book. All meaningful utterance can take place only in a book, but, there, it is already distorted by its *tzimtzum* limitation. The Book, in turn, is never accessible directly but always as a place of a book's inscription, visible prior to or after it. Unlike the Hegelian philosopher, the Jabèsian writer cannot have the Book self-recognise in him. And it is not for the lack of trying as messianism of the act of writing is nothing other than such an effort. Departing from Hegel, Jabès focuses on what *follows* this effort, instead of on the victory it proclaims. And what follows it is movement from the book that has failed to another book, that is, a displacement in the space of the Book. For this reason, *the Book appears as an ungraspable dimension in which the writer's movement takes place.*

Consequently, unlike Hegel's Absolute, Jabès' Book is recognised only through an incomprehensible shift one experiences. Furthermore, the Book is an assumption inferable from this shift rather than a dimension immediately

---

72 Cf. BQ II, p. 227–30.
73 *Ibid.*, p. 279.

given. A similar insight is to be found in Benjamin's Angel of History. Unlike the Hegelian philosopher, the Angel cannot give history a place for self-recognition, capable only of knowing its traces, ruins and relentless, destructive drive forward.

Having established this, we can now return to our initial question of how writing is related to the Book in Jabès. Evidently, not by knowledge as Hegel thought of it. Writing itself is watched from the position of the Book – *it is known by the Book and not the other way round*. Whatever writing knows about itself, this knowledge comes because the Book has been ascribed the position of ultimate scrutiny. So while knowledge pursues its object, *Jabès' writing presupposes itself as an object to reveal the plane from which it will be looked at as such*.

For this reason, I propose to define the relationship of writing and the Book as "marking." I believe that marking can be deemed an "equivalent" of knowing in the perspectival world. How do marking and knowledge differ? Knowing assumes that it cannot only strive towards its object but also exhaust it. Marking, in turn, represents the situation in which the knowing entity is not just finite but also stamped by the assumption that there is a dimension that knows it. What is marking then? Rather than movement towards an object, marking is *autonomous movement* which takes a step back from itself to think a dimension from which it could be seen. Marking brings in not so much knowledge – of writing or of the Book – as this specific distance, which channels the perception of their mutual incommensurability.

Hence, while Hegel's knowledge abolishes the difference between the knower and the Absolute, Jabès' marking highlights this difference because marking, as its very name suggests, is based on the referential role of a mark – a sign. *Writing means self-institution as a sign which can be read only in the Book*. As such, this sign is never "really" read and keeps forever referring only. This reference separates and differentiates the knower from the Book. Writing cannot read itself but, by assuming itself to be a sign, it makes the dimension of the Book visible and, *as a whole, refers to it*. But the Book is not a stable "reading" entity, either, but just an assumption. Consequently, the referential function of the sign is its sole function in Jabès' universe. *This sign does not serve to indicate something present but is the position a symbolic order takes in relation to the Book – the Book, which it presupposes itself by taking this position*.

To conclude the comparison of Hegel's knowledge and Jabès' marking, let us address another difference between them. Knowledge, namely, can be a lone act productive of a permanent outcome: absolute knowledge. This is impossible in Jabès. Writing as marking the Book must be a constantly sustained activity. It is necessary because, unlike the Absolute, the Book is never made present, with marking merely referring to it and the reference never being accepted. Hence, the Book cannot be shown and described once and for all; what can be done is continue marking, which makes its traces visible.

This distinct vision sets Jabès apart not only from Hegel but also from Mallarmé. Apparently, both poets share the idea of the Book capable of rendering all the relationships of the universe. Both also apparently deem such Book the regulatory idea of the writer's pursuits. It is in the view on making such a Book a reality where they differ. While Mallarmé seemed, at least for a time, to believe that one, definitive writerly act could bring the Book amidst ordinary texts,[74] Jabès knows that the Book cannot be made present and accommodated within one work. Even though, as he admitted himself, his ideas verged on Mallarmé's,[75] Jabèsian thinking surpasses Mallarméan thinking in being acutely aware that the condition of possibility of accomplishing the Book is, at the same time, its very condition of impossibility. Mallarmé wanted to write the ideal and ultimate Book thoughtfully and deliberately[76] while Jabès knows that rendering the real Book in a book would entail *extending* that which has already been written. Otherwise, such a book could not possibly be read.[77] Therefore, a writer's definitive book must be ruined.[78] In his conversation with Benjamin Taylor, Jabès says:

> If the sum total of things could be contained in a book, he [Mallarmé] reasoned, such a work would me more than human; it would be the work of eternity, the Book – literally – to end all books.
> But as I see it, the complete book of human knowledge would not be eternal but instead the most ephemeral of books. Because knowledge won't stand still more than a moment for the project of certainty. Reach after it and it evades you. What's true one moment turns up false the next. It seems this is the nature of thought. In any case, this is the presumption on which my books are based, and it's in loyalty to such a logic that they function. Each of my characters would speak in order that there may be an end to speaking, in order to fix the truth once and for all where it stands. But no one of them

74 In a letter to Verlaine, Mallarmé formulated one of the most celebrated articulation of this ephemeral concept. Expressing his belief that ultimately there is just one Book sought, be it even unawares, by anybody that writes, he states that such a Book would be *l'explication orphique de la Terre* (the Orphic explication of the earth). Stephane Mallarmé, *Œuvres complètes* (Paris: Gallimard, 1945), pp. 662–663.

75 DB, p. 83.

76 *Ibid.*

77 See IEJ, p. 22.

78 DB, p. 83. Comp. also Handelman, "Torments," p. 62.

can succeed, nor can they succeed in their accumulation. What together they amount to is the refusal of each one's purported truths.[79] I built my books on the lacks of the book. Every time, the book's lacks create a new book. In a book, gaps/flaws/failings are indispensable. […] Because of the lacks of the book, no book has ever stopped makings itself as a book [*se faire livre*].[80]

Learning a lesson from Mallarmé's failure, Jabès recognises that the space of the Book appears only in relentless continuation, extension and sur-vival:

I have always dreamed of a book that would reproduce [*reproduirait*] the process of life. First, it extends us [*il nous prolonge*], then it replaces us, […] That's why I thought that my books should make and unmake themselves [*se faire et se défaire*] indefinitely for the benefit of the next book.[81]

Whereas Mallarmé assumed a writer's life to be only a prelude to writing the Book,[82] Jabès believes that "life always comes after the book."[83] In other words, life in all its surfeit, failures and rebirths, in its persistently prolonged going-on, corresponds to the Book.[84] If one work were to show the nature of the Book, none of Mallarmé's project would do, but the Bible alone as it is an internally incoherent layering of books fostered through surviving each other and strung into a never pre-planned sequence.[85]

Bearing this in mind, we can now contrast Jabèsian marking and the notion attributable to Mallarmé, that is, having-written. Having-written is a single, definitive actualisation of the Book. Marking, in turn, means persisting in writing which refers to the Book but makes no claims to incorporating it within any existing work.

Having compared the two poets' respective projects, we can see the central axis of their dispute. In fact, Jabès accuses Mallarmé of omitting the moment of reading in his idea of the accomplished Book. If this moment is presupposed, it is necessary to think the dimension transcending the written-down. This dimension is what Jabès considers the "real" Book. In other words, his critique of Mallarmé concerns the latter's latent desire to stop time by the act

---

79 QJQW, p. 17.
80 DEJ, pp. 312, 314.
81 *Ibid.*, p. 83.
82 "The pure work implies the elocutionary disappearance of the poet, who surrenders the initiative to words," claims Mallarmé. Mallarmé, *Oeuvres complètes*, p. 366.
83 BQ II, p. 126.
84 See also Serge Meitinger, "Mallarmé et Jabès devante le livre: Analyse d'une différence culturelle," in *Écrire le livre*, pp. 133–143.
85 DB, p. 83.

of writing which would not be *read* anymore. Still, Mallarmé's formal experiments (e.g. in *A Roll of the Dice…*) suggest that he definitely sought to go beyond the realm where reading is bound up with succession. Instead of being read, his Book would simply reflect the universe beyond the human capacity to ascertain that reflection. Essentially, it would still be inaccessible to people. Paradoxically enough, failure would be part and parcel of accomplishing the book, for it could not be reconciled with the human world and its ineluctable reading founded on succession. Could such an "actualised" Book be anything more than just a trace in this world? Would it not appear as lost in the very moment of being achieved?

This is what Jabès seems to conclude from Mallarmé's venture, and his gesture seems less a polemics and more a thinking-forth of its consequences. Mallarmé's Book omits the dimension in which it could be read and, because this is the dimension of human life, the Book would be brought to pass only after the ultimate end of life. While life still continues, the Book must be inaccessible.[86] This conclusion can be gleaned from Jabès' following words:

> A writer tries to imitate the mythical book he will never write. This is what all writing consists in. We will never create this book for once we do, there will be nothing anymore … it would be death. Talking about Hebraic tradition, this book is also the book of books of people who will try to read it, reading themselves in their [books].[87]

The Book is entangled in the dialectics of life and death as well as of onceness and sur-viving. To Jabès, both Hegel's Absolute and Mallarmé's project would be a structural impossibility spanned between two possibilities. Either they would be carried into effect, but then they could not be followed by anything and, consequently, read, which would amount to the end of the human world; or they would be read, but that would imply being succeeded and becoming inaccessible the very moment they revealed themselves. A response to this aporia is found in Jabès' quasi-concept of the Book which is always displaced as an inevitable assumption and an inaccessible place at the same time. Writing does not aim to know the Book, less even to write it down. Writing only marks the Book.

---

86   Warren F. Motte believes that Jabès' working-through of Mallarmé's Book is affected by Blanchot – in particular by his notion of *livre à venir*: a book to come, a book that is only becoming without being a complete whole. Motte, *Questioning*, p. 102.
87   DEJ, p. 308.

Writing Instead of Knowledge

It is clear now what the Book is and that writing's relation to it consists in marking. It has also been explained why, on this model, marking of the Book is the perspectival world's equivalent of knowledge. Concluding this Chapter, I will ponder a change Jabès deems necessary, i.e. supplanting knowledge with writing. What is writing-based thinking like?

First of all, writing entails the end of a strong, knowing subject. Each subject turns out to be indebted to the Book as both his existence and the domain to which he wants to give shape are places in the Book. The Jabèsian writer realises the sheer size of his indebtedness and does not make any authorship claims to "his own works." On the contrary, he views them as *moments* of marking the Book. Each book is a lightning which irradiates the Book's boundless expanses. What is a writer than? A tool used by the Book to light up its own "existence." Jabès often plays with insights that correspond structurally to Hegel's philosophy but are invested with different meanings. The book can never personify and recognise itself in a writer, who cannot be the Book's prophet, either. Rather, his "works" shed oblique light on its space. Instead of places of encounter between the Book and the writer, they are a point that divides and illuminates them reactively.

Writing means then that the knowing subject is replaced by a new figure: a writer who yields his entire existence to the Book. To mark the Book, he must treat *his successive versions* as parts of books, which light up the Book. Writing equals the continuity of life for him.[88]

---

88 As already mentioned, writing is sur-viving. "To believe you still have something to say even when you no longer have anything to express. Words keeps us alive," writes Jabès (BUS, p. 68). A writer's life comes then to depend on the life-sustaining marking of the book. One of Jabès' protagonists – Yukel, a ghetto-survivor – is described by Bounoure as follows: "faced with numerous impossibilities of his life, of any life, Yukel chooses survival (*survivre*) and writing (*écrire*) – one would be tempted to say "sur-writing," for the prefix (*sur*) marks transcending that poor and dismal 'speck of ghetto' he has carried in himself." Bounoure, *Edmond Jabès*, p. 52. Bounoure focuses on this special aspect of "living-after" which was surviving the Shoah. Writing his own book (*The Book of Yukel*) would mean that the protagonist chose to sur-vive – and sur-write – the Shoah. The book that follows *The Book of Questions* conveys, thus, the mechanism not only of "the book being survived by the book" but also of the survival of a man who has been through a disaster but has not surrendered to it and lives on. Writing is here intertwined inseparably with life and survival, which is wittily expressed in Bounoure's apt coinage *surécrire*.

I am a man of writing. The text is my silence and my scream. My thinking advances with the help of words [*vocable*], moved by a rhythm which is that of the written. Where it runs out of breath I crumble.[89]

"The difficulty of writing," he said, "is only the difficulty of breathing in rhythm with the book." […] Listen to time breathing. Eternity's breath is imperceptible.[90]

I give to read not what I have read but what has read me unawares.[91]

Jabèsian writing is a practice that abolishes the difference between the knower and the known and transforms the subject so that his entire life boils down to marking the Book. It is no coincidence that Jabès envisages the writer's condition as exile: in his life, an exile may traverse innumerable places, but he always moves within a *space* that contains these places. The wandering writer is closely correlated with the Book, which Jabès clearly suggests in the following excerpt from *A Foreigner Carrying in the Crook of His Arm a Tiny Book*:

I left a land not mine
for another, not mine either.
I took refuge in a word of ink with the Book for space,
word from nowhere, obscure word of the desert.
I did not cover myself at night.
I did not shelter from the sun.
I walked naked.
Where I came from no longer had meaning.
Where I was going worried no one.
Wind, I tell you, wind.
A bit of sand in the wind.[92]

Second, writing is an exploration of the way in which particularity rifts and marks the space of continuity. To this purpose, writing produces traces which instantaneously show the difference between them and the field they have been inscribed in – a difference that elucidates their relationship:

A sound – uttered by whom? – and then nothing.
A word – written by whom? – and then a blank.
Listen to the nothing. Read the blank.[93]

If knowledge is first of all about the *content* of this sound or this word, what matters in writing is their *position* vis-à-vis whiteness. Jabès is interested in the

---

89 BR, p. 45.
90 BQ II, pp. 323, 327.
91 P, p. 36.
92 F, p. 79.
93 P, p. 73. (In Mark C. Taylor, "Foreword," BM, p. xi).

basic grid of relations between a book and the space in which it is inscribed –
the space of the Book. Writing is a continual exploration of this relationship.
Marking the Book, writing does not produce either propositions or a permanent
body of knowledge. Writing is not even about determining the relation between
particularity and the space of continuity; if such determinations are produced,
it is only as a side-effect of writing practice. Writing means confronting a book
with the Book, a point with space, through making their relationships *visible*.
Hence, Jabès' texts revisit time and again the same topoi: boundary, edge, beginning and end, threshold and its beyond,[94] end and sur-viving the end.

What is written flows from a summary of life which the letters restore to its accepted
boundaries. But farther off, out of reach, where life clings to its ruin and is nothing but a
memory of man's predestined passage, there the universe finally lets us read it from the
other side of memory. We alone, now, can do so.

[…] The end is the impassable obstacle. What ruse could we use to be done with it – to
be done with what is done? Considering the end as means, is this not also giving the end
the means to continue on into an after-the-end between two provisional ends in wait for
future prolongations?

[…] To keep within the sensible track, within a balance of life and death – of life in death
and death in life – at the heart of the fateful question to God, namely, Where is the end?[95]

…the distance covered between book and book […] when the blank crossing is achieved
within the blank. No shadow to count, no milestone, not the least little pebble near
or far. Infinite light! …except for a point in the distance which is no landmark, but a
mystery.[96]

"The book of life," I said, "opens in death."

[…] Hence no approach to God and the book could be conceived except in terms of this
endorsed point, that is, in terms of a book which we have discovered in the charge of
hope this point contains.

[…] Where recourse to the imaginary is exhausted, the book comes forward.[97]

And third, writing is also an experience of happening/enowning which is movement within the Book. How does writing approximate it? In this, Jabès, like
Heidegger, must engage with apophatic language. Writing is an experience of
happening/enowning for *it performs a movement which it perceives, at the same*

---

94 See Mary Ann Caws, "Signe et encadrement: Edmond Jabès ou *Le Livre en Question
    (I)." Les Cahiers Obsidiane*, no. 5 – *Edmond Jabès* (Paris: Capitales/Obsidiane,
    1982), p. 77.

95 BQ II, pp. 265, 310–11.

96 *Ibid.*, p. 392.

97 *Ibid.*, p. 419–20.

time, as the movement of the Book itself. This is a specific double bind of activity and passivity, of showing the Book and being read. Writing both opens the Book

> A word is tiny in its scope of revelation, immense in the scantiness of the sign. The book is always open.[98]

– and is overwhelmed by the Book –

> God taught us that writing is eternal, at the eyes' farthest reach. The book sees for all its words.[99]

This relationship, which makes it possible to make happening/enowning visible, is powerfully rendered, for example, in the following passage:

> *And Reb Fehad told this story:*
> *"I mingled with a crowd of people an asked:*
> *Where is the Book?*
> *A man in the crowd replied: I had it in my hands.*
> *I went up to him and asked:*
> *Show me the Book.*
> *The man laughed and said: I threw it into the river so the water could read it. Then I said: Earth furnished the pages. Water and fire the writing. Alas, the man was gone."*[100]

To sum up, writing is an experience of happening/enowning, for in one and the same gesture of having written a book it reveals the Book and is absorbed by it. The act of writing is a change, a coming-into-being of something new, something that is happening/enowning but also has *already* happened/enowned as a fragment of the vast space of the past. Finally, the act of writing is a change of perspective – a turn from seeing the Book as external and separated by *tzimtzum* to recognising oneself in it. But this change of perspective is an irremovable gap in and through which the Book makes itself visible and expands its compass.

This leads us to the conclusion of this Chapter, in which we must reflect on how the concept of the Book ties in with modernity and Jewish tradition.

Conclusion: The Book and Jewish Philosophy of Modernity

The idea of a book that encompasses the entire reality is an old Kabbalistic motif. Without doubt, it could not have arisen had it not been for the position the Torah took in Judaism after the destruction of the Second Temple. As Moshe Idel argues

---

98   *Ibid.*, p. 164.
99   *Ibid.*, p. 225.
100 BQ I, p. 313.

in his comprehensive *Absorbing Perfections: Kabbalah and Interpretation*, in the aftermath of the Temple's destruction, Judaism had to re-invent itself, relinquishing the holy place as the central point of reference.[101] With its role taken over by the Torah, the ensuing transformations re-cast the fundamental theological tenets: God ceased to intervene in reality directly and hid himself behind the text while his living voice was replaced by the holy book.[102] Furthermore, the Torah was accorded such prominence that God was represented not even as its author but as its reader.[103] Idel claims that in post-Biblical Judaism, the Torah was envisaged as pre-existing Creation and, moreover, embodying the paradigm of Creation. It contained all perfect knowledge, and to study it was a religious injunction even for God himself.[104] The Torah was also supposed to serve as the immovable basis for the world both ontologically and sociologically (i.e. for society).[105] This was fertile soil for the Kabbalistic beliefs that the Torah contained everything and was a "world-absorbing text."[106]

Jabès' book obviously draws on these representations. What is more, its inner dualism (of whiteness and script) consciously employs Isaac the Blind's idea of the "white" and "black" fires as components of the Torah, with the former as the mystical source of unity and the latter as the world inscribed in it. Whatever this whiteness could have meant precisely in the old Kabbalah, it was a homogeneous plane that conferred continuity on reality. For example, medieval kabbalist David ibn Abi Zimra insisted that whiteness in the book encompassed sings, just like God encompassed all worlds.[107] Jabès' whiteness has an analogous function as it incorporates books, that is, symbolic orders.

Yet, also here, mechanisms of modern thinking are to be found behind the Kabbalistic trappings. One of such mechanisms is the idea of a dimension which is radically external to knowledge. An encounter with this dimension is a trauma of experiencing something that transcends and determines the symbolic order. In Jabès, this dimension is the whiteness of the Book. However, whiteness is underpinned by the same structure as Kant's "thing in itself" and Lacan's "real,"

---

101 Moshe Idel, *Absorbing Perfections: Kabbalah and Interpretation* (New Haven, CT, and London: Yale UP, 2002), pp. 1–3.
102 *Ibid.*, p. 3.
103 *Ibid.*, p. 4.
104 *Ibid.*, p. 29.
105 *Ibid.*, p. 34.
106 See *Ibid.*, p. 37 ff.
107 *Ibid.*, p. 58.

that is, by the borderline between the continuous domain of knowledge and the radically particular.

Another modern mechanism involves the idea of a set of all limited symbolic orders. In Jabès, it is embodied in the script of the Book, corresponding to Hegel's Absolute though without a possibility of the Book's direct manifestation in the orders inscribed in it. Admittedly, like in the kabbalists, Jabès' Book comprises the entire reality, yet *reality itself is comprehended in different terms, that is, through the lens of perspectivism.* For the Book contains not beings but "books," i.e. entire symbolic orders.

This implies a third modern facet of Jabès' concept: *the co-dependence of the Book and books.* For the kabbalists, this "world-absorbing text," to borrow Idel's wording, was the ultimate plane of presence. Everything belonged to the Torah, which was the unique ontological foundation of reality. The kabbalist was to rise to its level, where the entire world was anchored. Yet in Jabès, even though the Book is a place where books are inscribed, it depends on books as well. It is through their rise and demise that it can expand; it is only by them that it can be marked. *The Book and books are thus inseparably linked.*[108]

This difference between the kabbalists and Jabès accurately reflects the difference between pre-modern and modern thought. The kabbalists' Book is a transcendent being, the basis and a warrant of the world. In Jabès, the Book is one of the moments of dynamic reality, a moment that must be assumed as a result of perspectivism even though it is revealed only in a dislocation. As I have attempted to show in this Chapter, the Book *is an indispensable presumption of Jabès' thought and gives it coherence.* "Abolishing [the idea of] the place means creating a non-place in proportion to place, [creating] a blank place within the blankness of a yet blanker infinite," states Jabès.[109] He suggests in this way that, unlike in the kabbalists, the Book is not just an existing, transcendent entity but *an outcome of "abolishing the idea of the place."* It is as if thinking something radically particular had to entail the rise of a backdrop that makes it so.

Juxtaposing the concept of the Book in the kabbalists and in Jabès, we can see that it mutated, apparently as a result of a shift in the very notion of being which took place at the threshold of modernity. For Jabès, there is no being as such. Existence stems from "having been read," that is, from being part of a symbolic order. And reading presupposes the ultimate dimension of continuity *against the backdrop of which* a particularity comes to the fore in its distance from the other

---

108 Motte, *Questioning,* p. 104.
109 QDLB, p. 229.

ones. Jabès' perspectivism makes the whiteness of the Book – the world's unde-feated void[110] – necessary. What is more, because of this very perspectivism, a particular order is seen not only against the background of the continuity of the Book's whiteness but also as *part* of the Book's script. As such, this order is both separate from and inscribed in the Book while the alternation of these aspects is, in fact, the movement of a book's rise and ruin.

In this way, the Jabèsian Book weaves a thread of distinctly modern thought into the texture of the Kabbala's archetypal concept.

---

110 Cf. *Ibid.*, p. 243.

8 Judaism and Writing

Jabès views Judaism and writing, which is (as discussed in the previous Chapter) the marking of the Book, as specifically interrelated. Their interrelation can be briefly described as a structural similarity. This perhaps best exemplifies the essence of Jewish philosophy of modernity. For Jabès, Judaism and writing are fully autonomous: neither of them precedes the other nor is a source or a model for the other. However, when structurally compared, they turn out to have developed in an analogous manner. The conclusion that writing, as conceived of by Jabès, is deeply rooted in the laws of the modern universe indicates that its affinity with Judaism stems from the fact that this very Judaism is, in itself, just a modern re-invention. As such, the analogy of writing and Judaism is due to their respective, inherently modern structures.

In this Chapter, I will examine this relationship. To begin with, I will show how the condition of the Jew parallels the condition of the writer. Subsequently, I will discuss a few aspects representing the identical structure of Judaism and writing. I will show that both – Judaism and writing – are based on the structure of the Book, originate from an event which Jabès calls "wounding" and, finally, are intrinsically historical. This reasoning will help me explain why Jabès regards Judaism as "religion after religion," which persists after the death of God. Afterwards, I will focus on where Judaism and writing are closest to each other, that is, on life understood as continual interpretation. To conclude, I will seek to locate the interconnection of Judaism and writing posited by Jabès in the context of Jewish philosophy of modernity.

Introduction: A Jew and a Writer

Undoubtedly, Judaism was not among the traditions that had the earliest formative impact on Jabès'. Jewish tradition is hardly ever evoked in his early texts, the least so in his Cairo poetry.[1] *Chansons pour le repas de l'ogre*, the only volume in which such references can indeed be found, is devoted to *dernier enfant juif*, i.e. to the poet's mother-in-law Édith Cohen, and in no way prioritises Jewish tradition. As mentioned in Chapter Two, Jabès considered some of his post-war works to be an indirect response to the Shoah, but they were meant first of all

---

1   See Jaron, *Edmond Jabès*, pp. 37–40.

to assuage the soul[2] rather than to ponder what had happened. This may be the reason why these texts barely evoke any recognisably Jewish experience.

This changed only in the wake of Jabès' exile from Egypt, which was provoked by a surge of anti-Semitic sentiments and policies.[3] Starting with that moment, when his Jewish origin affected his life so deeply, Jabès came to dwell obsessively on a handful of recurring questions: What is Judaism generally, and in particular today? How is Judaism possible after the death of God? What about Judaism after the Shoah? How do Jewish faith, customs and topoi interlace with and determine Jewish lives? What makes it possible for those who feel attached to Jewish tradition to form a community?

This is not an autonomous set of questions. Unlike Emil Fackenheim and his likes, Jabès does not just try to re-think Judaism after the Shoah.[4] In Jabès, Judaism and the lot of the Jews are bound up with apparently more general questions – queries about the status of God as such, about the mode of human existence in the world and about the relationship of writing, memory and the Book. It does not mean, however, that "universal" and "Jewish" questions simply alternate. Rather, *a structurally identical questioning is carried out on two different planes of reference.* One of them is writing, where the "subject" is an exiled writer who produces his writings and is constantly inscribed in the space of the Book he traverses. The other is Judaism, where the "subject" is a nomadic Jew who wanders across reality with no place to call his own.

Many Jabès scholars have recognised this double investment of questioning. Stéphane Mosès, for one, writes:

> Jabès' books always have a dual point of reference: writing and Judaism.
> […] The Jewish experience and the poetic experience keep referring to each other, in their different ways certainly, but in the same proximity, in the same approximation and distancing, which definitively precludes privileging either of these experiences as a simple allegory of the other.[5]

Yet, although writing and Judaism are interconnected in Jabès' texts, they never lose their own respective autonomy.[6] This is what Derrida notices when he calls

---

2   As Jabès wrote in this first poetry volume, "for there may be / a song of childhood / which in the bloodiest hour / stands alone against horror and death" (LSLS, p. 29).

3   See QJQW, p. 16.

4   See Emil L. Fackenheim, *To Mend the World: Foundations of Post-Holocaust Jewish Thought* (Bloomington and Indianapolis: Indiana UP, 1994).

5   Mosès, "Edmond Jabès," pp. 45, 47.

6   Despite this autonomy, which can be fully seen only when the entire structure of Jabèsian reality is considered, the poet has not escaped criticism from some commentators who

have accused him of trivialising the Shoah and reducing the Jewish exceptionality. This put Jabès within a broad movement of the post-war humanities that framed Jewish tradition as a victim of Western logocentrism and a stimulus to discard the logocentric structures. Maxim Silverman, who associates the poet with Blanchot and Lyotard, suggests that, like in the latter, where the Jew is turned into an allegory of what has nothing in common with Jewishness as such and serves to oppose Western rationality, Jewishness in Jabès is identified with the process of writing. In this way, Silverman insists, Jewish experience is generalised into a universal truth, which threatens to dilute the Jewish specificity. "Writing is 'Hebraized,'" writes Silverman, "while, on the other hand, the departicularized 'Jew' is thoroughly secularized. In a sense, this amounts to the ultimate form of assimilation of the Jew to a 'higher' cause. This is ironic – to say the least – given the professed desire of such theory to refuse to trap 'the other' within the oppressive logic of sameness and difference, and to return otherness to the 'other.' This universalizing of the Jew in this way moves perilously close [...] to eradicating the Jew all over again." Maxim Silverman, *Facing Postmodernity: Contemporary French Thought on Culture and Society* (London & New York: Routledge, 1999), pp. 18–28.

This criticism, though useful given the frequent, unexamined instrumentalisation of Jewishness and the Shoah in the post-war humanities, seems oblivious to what Jabès is always acutely aware of. Namely, in modernity, this more or less mythical "Jewishness as such" evoked by Silverman is in itself a play of differences – alternating particularisation and universalisation. Modern anti-Semitism and the Shoah prove powerfully that Jewishness is not just a simple, autarchic way of being, but a condition subject to constant interpretation – interpretation which verges on utter violence – by external agencies. It is also a condition which, as a result of the Jews' historical experience and of new trends in the humanities, continues to re-interpret itself. To demand respect for the exceptionality of "the other" by prohibiting interpretation of the other's tradition and by safeguarding it against any change means to remain within the logic of instrumentalisation *à rebours* (the mechanism aptly grasped by Jean Baudrillard).

To Jabès, the Jew indeed seems a universalised allegory of particularity. In this, Jabès is close to the post-war humanities, as referred to by Silverman, but a distinct feature of Jabès' take on of Jewishness is that even such universalisation is just one of many attempts at self-definition in the history of broadly conceived Jewish tradition. It does not in the least diminish the "Jewish exceptionality," which Silverman fears. Quite the contrary, it emphasises all the more that the Jewish exceptionality cannot be possibly fully rendered in any explanations. We would be hard pressed, indeed, to find a more unqualified philosophical justification of this exceptionality than is given in Jabès' notion of the trace which ultimately defies all interpretations and persists where they all pass. The impossibility of erasing the trace, of forgetting, causes, as Jabès sees it, the pain of the Jewish fate. It would be difficult to accuse Jabès of instrumentalising Jewishness, all the more so as, in his thought, Jewishness is interwoven not just with suffering, but with excess of suffering and its unbearable continuance.

Nevertheless, there is a pattern which Silverman's argumentation actually captures. Namely, modern Judaism is already re-interpreted and, in this sense, instrumentalised. Whatever it might have been before, the Jewish difference has come to rely on the

Jabès' "exchange between the Jew and writing [...] a pure and founding exchange without prerogatives."[7] Besides, as Josh Cohen suggests, "in insisting that it is writing itself rather than a given thematic or descriptive content that confers 'Jewishness' on a tale, Jabès undoes a key literary-critical distinction between form and content."[8] Writing dovetails with Judaism not because of its content but because of its *structure*.

This relationship has never been an a-priori assumption for Jabès. It is in the practice of questioning as such that writing and Judaism display their structural likeness. Jabès distinctly emphasises this in his retrospective self-interpretation, insisting that, as the consecutive parts of *The Book of Questions* were written, he grew more and more consciously aware that his texts were coming, unintentionally at the beginning, to resemble the way of questioning characteristic of the Talmud,[9] that is, questioning as a constant meditation rather than as a search for answers. "If there is anything Jewish in my work," wrote Jabès, "it is endless questioning, commenting, putting in doubt, uncertainty, accepting things which though seemingly true may not be true."[10]

This is an explicit expression of the double link between writing and Judaism. According to Jabès, writing is Jewish because it does not provide definitive answers, because it does not know truths that endure in time but constantly wanders across them. Still, in Jabès' account, the same Judaism is simultaneously very peculiar and unorthodox, to say the least. It is a construct with an affinity to the modern universe, which is presupposed in advance in it. Having ascertained this, we can raise an objection: Did Jabès not claim himself that he had discovered analogies between his writings and the questioning mode of the Talmud, which is at any rate a classical rather than a modern corpus of Jewish texts? Consequently, is it not about their affinity to the core of Jewish thinking in the diaspora era instead of to modern thought? The answer must be negative: the

---

modern mechanism of the remnant and the trace. This is the key factor in universalising Judaism and in stripping it of specificity, which no longer resides in Judaism's own "content" but consists in how it functions in the modern universe. Undoubtedly, modern Judaism is a tradition which has been re-constructed upon the originary loss, the status it shares with other religions and pre-modern knowledge. Thus, Silverman criticises, in fact, not so much Jabès himself as the structural mechanism that makes his thinking possible.

7   Derrida, *Writing*, p. 78. See also Raczymow, "Qui est?" pp. 166–7.
8   Cohen, *Interrupting*, p. 107.
9   EEJ, pp. 69–71.
10 *Ibid.*, p. 71.

Talmud is not viewed here from within Jewish tradition, through the commentaries of Rashi, the Tosafot and later exegetes. Jabès does not care either about the *content* of the Mishnah and the Gemara or about halachic argumentation. *The Jewish law is dead to him.* What he finds compelling is only the *logic* of the text made up of strings of inconclusive commentary. His view of the Talmud is external and modern; he finds in it what he himself wants to find. Consequently, there is no way of establishing whether Jabès' texts are "really" Jewish in their fashion of questioning. For "real" Judaism, however it might be defined, no longer exists in the modern universe, and the Judaism which is the framework of comparison for the poet has been "made out," that is, re-invented, in this very mode of questioning.

Therefore, the relationship of writing and Judaism as Jabès posits it goes beyond a simple similarity and is based on Jewish philosophy of modernity. Writing and Judaism are concurrent since each can be read in the context of the other. At the same time, there is an ineradicable difference between them. This is why Jabès is neither a Jewish writer nor a Jewish philosopher but "a Jew and a writer."[11] Through his *porte-parole* Yukel, Jabès can claim in *Return to the Book*:

> "First I thought I was a writer. Then I realized I was a Jew. Then I no longer distinguished between the writer in me from the Jew because one and the other are only torments of an ancient word."[12]

The intertwining of the writerly condition and the Jewish condition is paralleled by the interwovenness of writing and Judaism:

> I talked to you about the difficulty of being Jewish, which is the same as the difficulty of writing. For Judaism and writing are but the same waiting, the same hope, the same wearing out.[13]

Jabès' book is one text of "waiting, hope and wearing out" which writes itself twice on each of the two planes. Therefore, writing and Judaism can be said to be two particular fields of the modern universe underpinned by the recurring structure. *As the difference between them is irremovable, both writing vis-à-vis Judaism and Judaism vis-à-vis writing are a repetition in Jabèsian sense.* The "and" in "a Jew and a writer" conveys the parallel and, at the same time, the impossibility of identifying the two conditions with each other, being the locus of the ultimate constitutional difference in the modern world.

---

11   DB, p. 58.
12   BQ I, p. 361.
13   BQ I, p. 122.

These initial insights lead us to the next section, in which I will scrutinise Jabès' texts for the fundamental traits he ascribes to Judaism and writing. Without reducing one to the other, I will show their structural analogy in more detail.

Writing and Judaism: The Structure of the Book

One common trait of writing and Judaism, in Jabès, is their groundedness in the mechanism of the Book. As a result, they share a specific structure. They are not based on any enduring content, and they cannot be reduced to any definite formulation. Instead, they are *movements which pass through their particular finite forms* without being identifiable with them. In Jabèsian language, writing and Judaism are not definitive books durable in time but rather the sustained creation of book after book.[14]

Because I discussed writing in this respect in the previous Chapter, I will now focus on Judaism. First of all, Judaism as such has, basically, no permanent and invariably present traits, according to Jabès; instead, Judaism is movement in history which passes through particular forms that are taken to be Judaism at a given moment. More than that, Judaism is a line drawn in the Book as a result of combining mutually contradictory perspectival forms. *Jabès does not negate the internal contradictions within Jewish tradition, but, emphatically, he deems them to be the basic property of Judaism.* For, throughout history, Judaism can repeatedly take new forms which utterly diverge from the previous ones.

Consequently, *Judaism is continuity in discontinuity.* This feature has already been identified in writing: writing also consists in continuing across individual, mutually negating books. Judaism and writing transcend thus their consecutive finite forms. They seem to be, in a way, anchored in the Book, whose existence enables them to survive through the particular forms they take.

Another key consequence is that writing and Judaism are specific spaces of *memory*, in which their previous forms are discernible. In other words, writing and Judaism are not identifiable with their current forms; furthermore, their specific way of functioning *makes visible the forms they once took.* Writing and Judaism seem thus to be "the Book in miniature": as the Book is the ultimate space of continuity and inscription for all past, writing and Judaism make visible *a certain* ensemble of gone-by orders. This trait is well expressed in the metaphor of a line in the Book. If the Book is a continuity of all points, a line connects some

---

14 This is the reason why, as Jabès insists, the Jews while not having their own land for a long time, have always had their book, which has continued to expand with new parts and commentaries (QJQW, p. 16).

of them. This is exactly the role of Judaism and writing: they institute continuity among some of the past orders. As such, *in their entirety they mark the Book because they unfold in the Book.*

Now, let us look into specific consequences that grounding in the structure of the Book brings to Judaism. Jabès emphasises first of all the incommensurability of the "essence" of Judaism and its particular forms:

> […] we have wept so much over the centuries that to each of our tears there corresponds the brief twinkling of a star.
>
> […] We have molded our sun in pain, with our own fingers.
>
> […] Brothers of different covenants and a different abundance, you have built statues for your descendants, granted cathedrals to your cities, surrounded the desert with mosques.
>
> Your treasures have remained with your families.
>
> We mourn for the destroyed Temple.
>
> […] *"God is leaning against the dismantled wall of the Temple. From now on, no dwelling will be ours."*[15]
>
> The initial sin is a sin of memory. We will never get to the end of time.[16]
>
> In what has been said, in what has returned to silence, there is our solitude.
>
> For the Jew, having a place means finishing a book.
>
> The unfinished book was our survival.[17]
>
> You must always add five thousand years to the age claimed by a Jew.[18]

Judaism is always *not-here*; it is always something more than its current form. It is based on an additional dimension that transcends the here-and-now. Hence, the "essence" of Judaism seems to be negative vis-à-vis any given content. The Jewish God "is leaning against the dismantled Temple," and, as such, is supported by *sustained nothing*. Hence, he becomes an external point of scrutiny for whatever positively exists. Judaism constantly accompanies that which is Jewish, just as the Book accompanies the book, and adds to its present, finite form a vast expanse of the past.

The "essence" of Jabès' Judaism consist in that as soon as something comes to be recognised as Jewish, it is instantaneously blasted out of its closure and revealed as finite and inscribed in the space of ages-long, inexplicable continuity. To the Jew, Judaism is what the Book is to the book – it is the space of its inscription, rendering it in a way incomplete and unequal to itself. The Jews are "autochthons of the Book," says Derrida.[19] For Jabès, to be Jewish means to be illumined in one's

---

15 BQ I, pp. 187, 193, 233.
16 BQ II, p. 116.
17 BQ II, p. 309.
18 BR III, p. 21.
19 Derrida, *Writing*, p. 80.

own incompleteness by the legacy of Judaism. This legacy in itself is based on constant self-transcendence: "Judaism is always outside Judaism. It is a religion of leaving the word behind in its own absence and austere novelty […]."[20] Thus, Israel's wandering across history has no defined meaning of its own and is more like exile, with meanings only occasionally surfacing in it.[21]

Another consequence of grounding Judaism in the structure of the Book is that Judaism endures despite failures of its subsequent forms. Hence also the continuity of Jewish messianism. One of the many disasters visited on the Jewish people in the past could alone be a tragedy capable of putting an end to the nation, but Judaism has not only survived but also helped perceive the subsequent disasters from the outside. Judaism survives outside meaning and is reborn again in a new iteration.[22]

This concept brings to mind the biblical notion of שאר ישראל, she'ar Yisrael – "the remnant of Israel" – which is often dwelled on in the prophetic books (especially in Isaiah[23]). "The remnant" survives the disaster, salvaged from the total destruction visited upon the Jewish nation in its previous form. Yet, rather than re-producing this form in its original shape, it becomes the source of an entirely new form. The remnant of Israel embodies survival and pure duration throughout the discontinuity of the disaster. "The wound of all origin! To the death we survived we keep bearing witness,"[24] as asserted by one of Jabès' invented rabbis. Of course, survival crucially involves suffering. While regular pain has its limits since its excess would cause death, the pain of Judaism is *the memory of subsequent sufferings beyond any limits*:

> "Suffering," a sage said, "is the largest book for it contains all books."[25]

This verse depicts suffering as structurally similar to Judaism and writing, that is, as based on the mechanism of the Book. It is a surplus in relation to particular instances of suffering ("books") – it is the memory of them.[26]

---

20 BQ II, p. 291.
21 "To be Jewish means to have left home early and arrived nowhere" (BQ II, p. 439).
22 Cf. Berel Lang, "Evil, Suffering, and the Holocaust," in *Cambridge Companion*, pp. 277–300, on p. 282.
23 See, for example, Isaiah 10: 22.
24 BR III, p. 60 (quotation altered).
25 LH, p. 11.
26 That is why, Jabès says that "so white was the cry we had reason to think that pain simply meant feeling stages of whiteness" (BM, p. 95). One gap in the text – a blank

Concluding, Judaism and writing are founded on the structure of the Book. While Jabès' concept of writing ensues from the idea of the Book and keeps referring back to it – and its relation to the Book is obvious – Judaism fits this description only when re-interpreted. Admittedly, Jabès uses the concept of the Book to explain the excess continuity of Jewish tradition in time, but this happens at the price of a specific re-invention of Judaism. He casts the Jews as "the people of the Book" in an entirely new sense, which is aptly grasped by William Franke:

> Jabès' poetics of the inexpressible pivot not so much, or not so directly, on an extra-linguistic singularity or otherness as on the Book. Like the Neoplatonic One, also an All-Nothing, the Book is infinite and can be manifest only in fragments and finitude, never as a whole and intact. In finite terms the Book is nothing, that is, nothing finite can express it, and every word taken as a word of the Book cannot but be empty. The emptiness of the word, as abstracted and separated from the reality of things and as belonging to the Book, opens into the omnipresent infinity of Nothing, and the Jews, by dwelling in this exile of the word, are veritably the people of the Book (*gens du livre*). This infinity and emptiness of the word, as well as its totalization – the Book – is totally unsayable. But it is open in its emptiness, an open question and an open desert for wandering, a space of errancy. And only in this openness is there any room for human expression.[27]

This specific re-interpretation of Judaism makes Judaism highly useful in thinking about the Book but, at the same time, severs it definitively from the space in which the Book was not a universal world of exile yet.[28]

The Wound as the Beginning of Judaism and Writing

Another link between writing and Judaism is conveyed by Jabès in the metaphor of the *wound*. This suggestive expression is underpinned by a powerful philosophical structure. As already mentioned, the relationship of writing and Judaism to their various forms replicates the relationship of the Book to the book. Hence, each of their finite forms is marked by indelible excess. In Jabès, the wound designates this very excess, which shatters finitude and forestalls its

---

space – is a scream while the chain of the *already experienced* stages of whiteness is suffering. Whiteness – pure duration and bare life – is thus associated with suffering, in itself an effect of communing with the unthinkable.

27 Franke, "Singular," pp. 630–1.

28 Beth Hawkins explains that "as the space in which the Book is inscribed continually erases itself, grounding is removed, and exile becomes the established condition of both the text and the language employed in the text. The Book becomes the metaphor for wandering and exile. Specifically, the desert becomes the poetic space" (*Reluctant Theologians*, p. 174).

becoming equal with itself. As such, the wound quasi-conceptually renders the fact that the "essence" of writing and Judaism transcends their concrete positive content.

The first part of *The Book of Questions* opens with one of Jabès' most-quoted lines:

> *Mark the first page of the book with a red marker. For, in the beginning, the wound is invisible.*[29]

Jabès assumes that each book starts from a wound. The concepts and insights developed in the foregoing shed light on this notion. The wound seems to be a new way of describing *tzimtzum* – the originary contraction, which simultaneously (1) makes the book possible; and (2) leaves in it a trace of what underwent contraction. It is this trace that is the wound. Importantly, it is invisible first and is revealed only as the book develops.

The mechanism behind the wound is clarified in Jabès' remarks about *The Book of Questions*. Namely, Jabès stated that *The Book of Questions* meant, for him, making the primal trace which could be neither forgotten nor erased nor fully elucidated in writing that followed it. Jabès opened an "inexhaustible book" which he could not close anymore and, consequently, had to find himself *in* it.[30] It seems, thus, that the wound brings a boundless, negative remnant into the book, which has a number of consequences. First, this remnant rives the finitude of the book apart by indicating a dimension that the book itself cannot capture. Second, this remnant leaves in the book a trace that cannot be comprehended either from within the book itself or in later writing. This leads to the third, and most important, consequence: *this remnant is the axis of the displacement which makes the book as a whole into the book as an entity within another dimension*. Jabès starts writing, but, instead of an autonomous work implementing his design, "an inexhaustible book" appears, in which what was the "work" suddenly becomes a moment.[31] The wound turns out to be an unexpected opening of a new dimension which engulfs the book and the writer, forced to find himself in this peculiar space.

As such, the wound is an event that compels one to write in the Jabèsian sense, that is, to make oneself at home in the Book and perceive oneself as well as one's books from a distance:

---

29 BQ I, p. 13.
30 DB, p. 113.
31 "The book is a moment of the wound, or eternity" (BQ I, p. 196).

Writing forces us to adopt a distance in relation to ourselves. It is in this distance that our books are made.[32]

Making a book is by no means a narcissistic enterprise. On the contrary, it requires yielding to the pressure of the written – which can not only give us a faithful image of itself, but also of sustain all through our reading the salutary dialogue the book initiates in taking shape. For its pages are so arranged that, once the first is turned, none of the following can avoid the planned facing page [face-a-face].[33]

Therefore, the wound can be viewed as both (1) the originary event that initiates writing; and (2) an enduring remnant that shatters the narcissism of the strong writer-work relationship. The wound reveals that no book can ultimately abide in the limitation of its own *tzimtzum* because it will inevitably be confronted with other books. As such, the wound shows that the book does not establish any "truly" new beginning but finds itself *within* the Book:

"The book does not begin," he replied.
"All beginnings are already in the book."[34]

Jabès attributes structurally identical consequences of the wound to Judaism. Predictably, "the wound" in Jewish tradition corresponds to circumcision, and in this respect Jabès does not differ from Celan and Derrida.[35] In this perspective, circumcision is a trace imprinted on an individual that marks the continuing, excess memory of Judaism, which transcends this individual.

The effects of the wound as analysed for writing are fully consonant with the Jabèsian interpretation of Judaism. Like the wound at the beginning of the book,

---

32 DB, p. 104.
33 BD, p. 80.
34 *Ibid.*, p. 3.
35 Waldrop, similarly, concludes that this passage concerns both the writer's wound and the Jew's circumcision wound. Cf. Waldrop, *Lavish Absence*, p. 3. See also, Édith Dacan, "Le corps et l'écriture dans le *Livre des Questions.*" *Les Cahiers Obsidiane*, no. 5 – *Edmond Jabès* (Paris: Capitales/Obsidiane, 1982), pp. 18–19.

Circumcision is the motif common to Jabès and Derrida (see e.g. "Shibboleth: For Paul Celan" in *Sovereignties in Question: The Poetics of Paul Celan*, eds. Thomas Dutoit and Outi Pasanen [New York: Fordham UP, 2005], pp. 1–64). In Derrida, like in Jabès, thinking about circumcision as making a mark on the body is bound up with reflection on the trace and writing. Circumcision is a model of the event that traumatises through its incomprehensible singularity; cf.. Joseph G. Kronick, "Philosophy as Autobiography: The Confessions of Jacques Derrida," *MLN*, 115/5 (December 2000), pp. 997–1018, on pp. 1005–1006. In this regard, Jabès and Derrida follow a nearly identical path.

circumcision strips the Jew of a stable and complete identity and makes him refer constantly to the dimension of which he is himself a part. For this reason, the Jew watches himself from a distance. Furthermore, the wound of circumcision becomes an incomprehensible, inexhaustible and irremovable trace. Finally, it points to the inexplicable originary event that set Israel apart from other peoples.

Finally, an important thing is that in his re-interpretation of circumcision Jabès plays on an entrenched motif of Jewish tradition. The Hebraic word מילה (*milah*), which designates circumcision, is also an equivalent of the term "word." In some Jewish doctrines, circumcision means anchoring the word in reality and establishing a bond between the word and matter.[36] In Jabès, similarly, circumcision introduces the Jew into the realm of the Book, i.e. the ultimate instance of "reality." As such, circumcision is more than just a sign. As stated earlier, in writing, the wound is *the axis of the displacement* between the book and the Book. Circumcision works in a similar manner. Ostensibly just a sign of membership in the Jewish nation, circumcision essentially makes a man on whom this sign has been inscribed a part in relation to Judaism based on the structure of the Book.

To recapitulate, the wound is a notion issued by the very structure of the Book. Based on it, writing and Judaism override their particular forms, leaving a non-removable trace in them. It is the "wound in the beginning of the book" or circumcision. In both cases, it is a sign which reveals a new dimension of historicity that transcends finitude.[37] Historicity is what I will now focus on in more detail.

Historicity: Judaism as a Religion after Religion

Writing and Judaism are, according to Jabès, specifically associated with history. Certainly, the relation is not about them sharing the same narrative of the past, but rather about bringing *historicity* into each narrative that develops within them. With their "essence" located in the negative remnant, writing and Judaism

---

36 Ouaknin, *Concerto*, pp. 69–71.

37 The Jabèsian interdependence of historicity and the letter (and, consequently, circumcision) was also noted by Derrida: " […] in question is a certain Judaism as the birth and passion of writing. The passion *of* writing, the love and endurance of the letter itself whose subject is not decidably the Jew or the Letter itself. Perhaps the common root of a people and of writing. In any event, the incommensurable destiny which grafts the history of a 'race born of the book' (…) onto the radical origin of meaning as literality, that is, onto historicity itself. For there could be no history without the gravity and labor of literality. The painful folding of itself which permits history to reflect itself as it ciphers itself. This reflection is its beginning. The only thing that begins by reflecting itself is history." Derrida, *Writing*, pp. 7–8.

explicitly indicate that each of their concrete forms is inevitably historical. This has a very interesting consequence. Namely, these successive forms refuse to be integrated by any continuous narrative. Individual books – and, consequently, individual forms of Jewishness – must therefore be perceived as discrete, mutually negating entities linked only by *their common relation to the remnant* of writing or Judaism that transcends them. As writing was discussed in these terms in the previous Chapter, I will focus in the following on how historicity works in Jabès' Judaism.

According to Jabès, "he [the Jew] carries the weight of his history."[38] This means, first of all, that the Jew cannot forget about the past. Second, he heaps the "weight of history" onto every present moment, which amounts to inscribing this moment in the plane of impossible continuity. In this sense, Judaism works *against* oblivion associated with the limitation of each *tzimtzum* and destroys it by re-connecting to the Book. Third, the legacy of Judaism compels constant reflection on history, which defies erasure. That is why, Judaism, as Jabès puts it, is "but questions asked of History."[39]

This statement seems to echo Franz Rosenzweig, who insisted that only the Jewish nation, which is outside history rather than within it, can judge history.[40] Jabès, however, draws a more complex picture than Rosenzweig's. In Jabès' interpretation, Judaism cannot be conclusively defined as remaining outside History and separated from it by the immutability of the Law and ritual. On the contrary, Jabès' Judaism is a tradition that combines utterly different and changeable forms, which are without a doubt fully entangled in their historical conjunctures. Outside History, there is only the *negative remnant* of Judaism, which, by transcending Judaism's particular forms, makes History visible. Therefore, Judaism is both at the centre of History and outside it.

This distinct situatedness is highly relevant in Jabès' account. In his view, Judaism can restore historicity to contemporary culture, which tends to dwell in oblivion:

> What would remain for the Jew if he didn't at least have the hope that his history, his suffering, his anxiety will, after the fact, constitute a ferment, an exemplary experience everybody has to take into account? [...] it exists in order to wake up a consciousness that risks falling... What is at stake is our Western culture. All questioning that avoided Auschwitz, for example, would miss the essential.[41]

---

38 DB, p. 61.
39 DB, p. 29.
40 See Franz Rosenzweig, *The Star of Redemption*, trans. Barbara E. Galli (Madison: University of Wisconsin Press, 2005), p. 355.
41 DB, p. 61.

More than that, it is Judaism, with its boundedness to historicity, that makes genuine questioning possible.[42] To Judaism, everything that now exists appears in the context of the unforgettable past and is but a moment in the Book that is writing itself down.[43]

There is one more important consequence. Jabès' Judaism can continue religious questioning where religion as such is no more. Judaism is a *religion after religion*, a surviving witness of its own decline. Judaism after God still permits

to interrogate Judaism without ceasing to be Jewish.

The salvation of the Jewish people lies in the rupture, in the solidarity at the heart of the rupture [...] The rupture is primarily due to God who wanted to be absent, who fell silent. To rediscover the divine word means to pass through this rupture.[44]

Thus, Jabès regards Judaism as unique in that it can continue after the end of Theism, which seems to be intrinsic to the Jewish religion. Judaism persists even though there is no longer God, around whom it organised itself and the notion of whom it purified down to radical monotheism. Judaism is thus a religion after religion because its negative essence makes it a witness of that which has already passed. In this way, Judaism can recognise *within itself* a rupture left behind by the fall of classic Theism; it can find "divine word." In this optics, it is perhaps only Judaism that genuinely understands real atheism, for Judaism itself *is based on its own non-existence, which it has survived and to which it testifies*.

In this view of Judaism, Jabès is similar to Kant and Hegel, two Protestant philosophers of emergent modernity evoked in Chapter One. Their similarity lies in that all three of them consider religion to have been abolished in its erstwhile form by modernity. In the new space ushered in by the modern turn, religion can only be re-constructed in a form that is subject to the laws of modernity.

---

42 *The Ineffaceable the Unperceived* insists: "By calling himself and his faith into question [*mettant en question*], the Jew has taken the pathetic risk of placing all interrogation on the axis of the crucial question of man and God, of making his own the question of the universe and then bringing it back to the book. The book is his answer" (BR III, p. 69).

43 As *The Ineffaceable the Unperceived* states, the Jew refused to disappear and stubbornly embraced his past:

"Trying to kill the Jew means also tackling his time.

Being born a Jew means entering this time, and dying, leaving it for good. The duration of this time means crossing the desert, indeterminate duration of our endurance" (BR III, p. 61).

44 DB, pp. 58–9.

As such, this religion no longer derives from reality-transcending revelation but, contrariwise, is discernible *in the mode of existence of everything that is real*, including via direct, individual experience. This form of religiosity breeds a specific atheism: ostensibly, God still exists, but he is just a mechanism of the modern world.

Similarly, according to Jabès, "Judaism after God" continues to ask questions about God, but God is now the centre of the void intrinsic to the modern universe. In this sense, the epistemologically privileged status of Judaism should not come as a surprise: Judaism epitomises the modern space so accurately because it is itself based on the structure of this space. *The Ineffaceable the Unperceived* tells the following story:

> Reb Issah, the most controversial and, curiously, most feared of the commentators of the Book, taught that Judaism was based on itself alone [...].
>
> Thus, truth, like God, would be an arch-vertigo, an irresistible appeal of the void; [...] God [...] declared: "Whosoever dies in Me shall not die. For I am the life of all death, which unites Me with them."
>
> Outraged by Reb Issah's statements which had been eagerly reported, the three most famous rabbis of the region took occasion to summon him and make him explain himself.
>
> "Where did your read that God said: 'Whosoever dies in Me shall not die. For I am the life of all death, which unites Me with them'? In which holy scripture? asked the first.
>
> Proudly, Reb Issah replied:
>
> "In myself, for I am the source of my sources and the word of my words [*paroles*]."
>
> The second rabbi pounced on him, screaming:
>
> "'These are words of your mouth and not God's."
>
> "How would God make Himself heard if not through our mouths? How would we come to read Him if not in our books?" replied Reb Issah without flinching.
>
> "You reason like an ungodly man. But who could ever prove that these words are really God's?" asked him the third.
>
> "I will tell you," replied Reb Issah. I will tell you: *the words themselves*, because they fly higher than our own words, which die like flies in the attempt to hold them back.[45]

This dialogue marshals the key features of Jabès' Judaism "after God": God is the centre of the void, the site of the ultimate community in death. He needs neither Zion as a special place of revelation nor consecrated channels, such as the book, to transmit tradition. He reveals himself in the words of an individual human being.[46] It is so because God is a *function of thinking as such*, a

---

45   BR III, pp. 81–2 (quotation altered).

46   In Jewish thought, language is not reductively conceived of as just communicative and horizontal (i.e., limited to human relationships). Rather, it is seen as intrinsically harbouring a transcendent dimension as it refers to Divine Revelation; cf. Gross, *L'aventure*,

point of questioning inevitably presupposed by this questioning. Because of that "Judaism is based only on itself" rather than on a transcendent source. In conclusion, Jabès' Judaism is crucially entangled in a double bind. On the one hand, its relation to historicity enables it to persist after "the death of God" and gives it continuity, in which the effects of this event are visible. This is also how Jabès views Judaism, seeing in it a chance to restore "History" to the present. Yet, on the other hand, this re-construction of Judaism itself results from the modern rupture. It is possible to locate its "essence" in the negative remnant only because there is a structure in which this remnant emerges and works.

The Jew and the Writer: A Silent Community

Because writing and Judaism share the same common structure, their "subjects" – the writer and the Jew – take analogous positions. Their particular forms pass in time; nevertheless, the two "are," in a way, an enduring remnant. In other words, the Jew and the writer are forever torn between their historical forms and surviving based on the Book. To describe this position, I will first analyse the status of the writer:

> *You are the one who writes and the one who is written.*
> [...] I hate what is said in places I have left behind.
> [...] The word is bound to the word, never to man…
> [...] It is not I who answer. It is the sentences.
> *Words rush in and knock everything over. They want, each, to get their chance to convince. The true human dialogue, that of hands and eyes, is a silent dialogue. There is no such thing (spoken or written) as a dialogue between persons. [...] We are the instrument that takes itself seriously.*[47]
> At the origin of all, the word questions the universe for man's benefit. It precedes man in time. Man fashions himself in the word.[48]
> *"But isn't it always words that express us?"*
> *No doubt, at the moment my pen draws them, when my voice sets them free… But immediately after, I realize that I have not written, not spoken.*
> *"But in that case, what you read, what other people hear, what is that?"*
> *"A mixture of sounds of words bitterly remote in their alien truth."*
> *Man is mute I tell you. The only mute creature is man.*[49]

---

pp. 48–49. Here, Jabès connects this aspect to a modern form of this revelation, which instead of from God comes from reality itself.

47 BQ I, pp. 11, 19, 26, 65.
48 *Ibid.*, p. 226.
49 BQ II, p. 373.

In Jabès, the status of the writer is patently affected by a necessary dualism. Namely, on the one hand, the writer is what "the words express"; he is produced as an entity by the text itself. It is, naturally, his "own" voice that other people hear. But, on the other hand, the writer is what has perished in these words. Words are, for him, a strange universe with its own laws, which he has entered but has failed to take hold of. In neither of these forms is the writer more present or truer. He has been produced by words as an entity in the text while, as that which has been lost in them, he is merely a trace, a negative remnant. Thus Jabès' writer can be said to be a gap between a particular form that words confer on him and a remnant which is left over from this form. Hence the writer embodies the condition of man, "the only mute creature" – the only creature that has a symbolic language, which is exactly what makes him unable to express himself in it.[50]

---

50 To Jabès, the human being is a thing distinctively possessed of a linguistic being. The human being consists, so to speak, of two parts: a real one and a linguistic one. In Jabès, the former is the body while the latter is theorised usually in terms of the soul (cf. BQ II, p. 276,). On a number of occasions, especially in the *Book of Resemblances* series, Jabès reflects on the body as a substantive component of the human being. Alien to meaning, the body is silent and, inexplicably, manifests affinity with the community of all things. It exists before it comes to be capable of speaking; it exists as an absence only to be illumined by language where language does not reach (cf. BQ II, p. 107). The body is a separated part of the universe, communicating with the rest of the universe via the skin (cf. BQ II, p. 362). The body knows and apprehends the world in a primary way, outside meaning (cf. BR II, p. 81). As the body is matter, traces are imprinted in it (cf. BQ I, p. 139). *We are, essentially, like words written down because "we" means inscribing language in matter that is, in this case, the body.* In other words, subjectification is of the same nature as writing-down.
  The body makes meaning and thought possible (BR II, p. 37) though it does not speak itself. It is the foundation of our being across time as a mute and incomprehensible companion. "The body is the road," and "all roads start from the body and lead back to it" (*Ibid.*, p. 63). "Without body we would be a breath in the wind, a silence within silence. Without body there would be no book. As if absence of books were but suppression of the body. / But could we, without body, even tell presence from absence, waking from sleep, dawn from dusk?" (*Ibid.*, p. 81,). *As such, the human being is similar to the vocable in being stretched between "body" and "mind," in being a gap between oneself and oneself.*
  There is tension between "the body" and "the mind" as they have different ontological statuses and yet mutually condition each other. The body does not march to the beat of thought (cf. LR I, p. 34); it ages in another rhythm than one we can understand. "[W]e are older than our life" (BR II, p. 69), writes Jabès to suggest that the symbolic

Therefore, the writer belongs to the community made up of whatever is structurally positioned as a remnant. In this, Jabès' reasoning approximates Blanchot's *communauté inavouable* (unavowable community).[51] In perishing himself, the writer – "a shadow that carries man"[52] – *gives voice to that which similarly perishes in its particular, limited form.* At the same time, this voice is a subversive voice[53] of protest against the contraction. The scream, an aspect of the *vocable*, resurfaces here again. The perishing writer screams in his own name and on behalf of all creation, bearing witness to unfolding *tzimtzum*. Jabès' portrayal of the writer's condition is thoroughly entangled in the structure of the universe assumed by the poet, a structure I have defined as modern. The writer's position results directly from perspectivism, from the Book's existence forced by perspectivism and from the remnant produced in the Book. The universality of this position, as well as its affinity with the thought of Blanchot, Nancy and Agamben, does not

---

order always precedes the bodily order and never overlaps with it. Death is strange to us just because it concerns the body (cf. BR II, p. 63).

"The body is on the scale of the body, but what is the measure of the mind? I would not hesitate to say: that of the body. / "Then the limits of the body are arbitrary in life as in death," said Reb Ledin. / The strength of the body can never equal that of the mind. But the slightest ailment of the body – shortness of breath, a speck of dust in the cogs – can overcome it. / The body wields all the powers of the mind except one: the power to annihilate mind along with itself, at its end. / The body dies its own death; the mind, a death inflicted by the body. / Innocence of the murderer. / Death is first of all a matter of the body. / To think death, he said, is but to think the body" (BR III, p. 74; quotation altered).

Therefore, the body in Jabès can be said to be a site of *inscription* of the human being into reality. As the written word depends on the matter in which it has been preserved, the human being depends on his body but is unable to fathom the order to which it belongs. For this reason, he finds death, as "the body's matter," so utterly alien. *The mind waits for the death that the body will inflict on it.* The body is entirely innocent since it does not belong to the order of meaning, in which death can be defined as murder. In other words, *within our own bodies, we encounter the limit of language: a beyond that is "our own" and yet belongs to the entire universe.*

In this reasoning, Jabès is, of course, very close to the concept of "extimacy" developed by Lacan.

51 Maurice Blanchot, *The Unavowable Community*, trans. Pierre Joris (Barrytown, NY: Station Hill Press, 1998). See also Jean-Luc Nancy, *The Inoperative Community*, trans. Peter Connor, et al., ed. Peter Connor (University of Minnesota Press, 1991).

52 LR I, p. 21.

53 See Shillony, *Edmond Jabès*, p. 42.

seem coincidental. Rather, it is an effect of the same, basically simple structure whose reiterations inform a multitude of philosophical frameworks.

This insight is substantiated by Jabès' depiction of the condition of the Jew, which includes identical motifs: exclusion, remnant, solitude and silent community. The following passage is a perfect entry point for analysing this issue:

> [S]olitude has become the profound destiny of the Jew. [...] If the Jew is the other, it is because, trying at all cost to be himself, he is *also* each time a being from nowhere. [...] I would even say that this *also* – this *plus* which is in fact a *minus* because it is a void that needs to be filled up continuously – is his only difference. This lack is a source of his questioning.
> [...] To want to be [...] *the other*, isn't that, a priori, an unreasonable provocation? [...] However, if the Jew persists in wanting to be recognized in his difference – that is to say as the *other* – he does so first because he sees it as a fundamental progress [...] as a victory over the self's total intolerance. This [...] is [...] one of the "missions" of Judaism. How could an atheist not subscribe to it?[54]

The first passage clearly identifies the "essence" of Jewishness with the remnant that transcends all positive being (hence, the Jew is "from nowhere"). Vis-à-vis being, this remnant is at the same time something more and something less. The difference produced in this way is the source of questioning which cannot be entirely contained in any answer. The distinct character of Jewishness lies in the surplus in relation to meaning, as a result of which the Jew cannot fully dissolve in any given meaning and in his definition.[55]

---

54 DB, pp. 59, 60, 62–3.

55 That is why, like the writer, the Jew screams "to escape himself from the cruellest punishment: smothering in the word" (BQ II, p. 284) – that is, he marks his perishing in the script with a scream – and, consequently, "the Jewish soul is the fragile casket of a scream" (BQ I, p. 165), which scream finds itself in writing only as a description of persecution and incomprehension. The script entraps and is, in itself, persecution and incomprehension. The scream, which wants to break loose, perishes in the word that lies in waiting for it. The power of naming is destiny and death – the stoning of the scream (*Ibid.*, p. 167). In Jabès, Judaism is closely bound up with the scream, which is an ultimate sign of resistance against incorporation within a violence-based whole. The poet identifies the writer's protest against the arising script with the Jewish rebellion against the violence of "persecution and incomprehension" as based on the same mechanism. In both cases, it is about incorporation into a general meaning, about replacing the true voice of resistance with its meaningful surrogate (stoning of the scream). Along the Lévinasian and Lyotardian lines, Jabès regards meaning as violence, as coerced incorporation in the order governed by its own principles and not respecting the autonomy of things. "The act of writing may be nothing but an act of controlled violence, the time it takes to move to a new stage of violence" (BQ II, p. 348).

The second passage develops this concept. Jabès defines the Jewish condition not only as determined by the position of the remnant but also as *reflectively accepting this fact*. In his view, the Jew wants "to be recognised in his difference." It is not about a simple recognition of Judaism's otherness but, rather, about recognising *the universal condition of difference* embodied in Judaism. At this point, Jabès ascribes to Judaism another universal mission which involves combating the homogeneous, self-same, stable identity by disseminating differences. The particularity of the Jewish difference is supposed to be the source of the universal subversion, which would challenge and demolish firm and permanent meanings.[56] Attractive though this vision is, it is impossible to fail to notice that Judaism's universal mission again appears due to the common structure it shares with the modern universe. Judaism is not only a reflective acceptance of the position of the vestige imposed by modernity but also a modernity-propelled re-invented construct of earlier Judaism.

Because of the condition of the Jew, the Jewish community – like the community the writer joins – assembles the lonely and the singular, those who belong by not belonging:

> […] it is precisely in this break – in that non-belonging in search of its belonging – that I am without a doubt most Jewish.
> […] Salvation [*salut*] lies in this bet, kept until now, and which has denied any rest to the Jew. Jewish solidarity is a solitude that knows itself [*qui se sait*]. It is made up of all the individual solitudes.[57]

According to Jabès, the Jewish community is not founded on being the same or having the same definition, or on agreement in any shared meaning. On the contrary, this community is a *community of repetition*; that is, every member of this community repeats – through their own condition of solitude – the position of exclusion. Emphatically, this repetition is predicated on reflective processing of Jewish solitude, solitude "*qui se sait.*" On Jabès' model, it is less Jewish to cherish faithfully the tradition of Judaism and more Jewish to reject, re-formulate and

---

Writing is an act of "controlled" violence presumably because violence is authorised by the very perpetration of it; its effect – inscription in meaning – obliterates the traces of what has happened. This violence is, thus, self-legitimised. The victim becomes just an excluded "shadow," doomed to the "stoned" scream. Jabès' Judaism rebels against this violence: "the Jewish word opposes the hostile exclusion of the voice" (LR I, p. 116).

56 "Chosen by their God, they became a people set apart, bearing a universal message that later required that they give up – make restitution of? – a land they had nevertheless been granted" (BR III, p. 62).

57 DB, pp. 64, 59.

re-invent it. As he explains in the conversation with Marcel Cohen, Judaism "has always favored such excesses";[58] even the followers of Sabbatai Zevi considered themselves true to Judaism in the extremity of their heresy.[59] This shows Jabès' conceptual affinity with Scholem as both focus on the antinomic tendencies in Judaism and are fascinated with the continuity of Jewish tradition in its multiple and so contradictory forms.[60]

The only constant underpinning of Judaism's ongoing rebellion is, in Jabès, *the formal difference* rendered in the metaphor of circumcision – the primal wound. The wound is an infinitesimal material trace preserved by all mutually exclusive movements within Judaism.[61] But as Judaism corresponds to the modern world, so the Jewish community seems, to Jabès, to be part of the universal, repetition-based, *community of things.*

> *Excluded. Naked. Naked like the destroyed Temple, the witness wall.*[62]

The persisting of the Jew as the excluded one is on a par with the persisting of a thing, such as the destroyed Temple: while *the ruined wall looks with the ultimate gaze of a witness, the Jew gazes at the meaningful world in the same way.* Like the writer, the Jew lives the life of a "shadow," bearing witness to that which is excluded. He is the mouthpiece of material memory, which is as indelible as a substantive trace is:

> Reb Eloze said: "The synagogue is full of holes for the sky to get in. Thus it has a life of shadow and light until the end of time."
> And Reb Labri: "You cannot destroy a synagogue. You might as well try to bring down the sky."[63]

As the sky, which spans above everything that comes to pass and, in its continued duration, is a mute witness of History, cannot be "brought down," so Judaism cannot be destroyed, for it is essentially survival through destruction, the persisting of the remnant. Therefore, in Jabès, belonging to the Jewish community (and thus, paradoxically, non-belonging) involves being an ultimate witness and bearing witness mutely through sheer survival.

---

58 *Ibid.*, p. 65.
59 *Ibid.*.
60 See Idel, *Old Worlds*, p. 27 ff.
61 Cf. BQ I, p. 61.
62 BQ II, p. 298.
63 BQ I, p. 369.

The Fusion of Judaism and Writing: Life as Interpretation

It is clear now how and why Judaism and writing have analogous structures in Jabès. Before concluding this Chapter, let us focus on one more recurrent motif – one of life as ongoing interpretation, as "living in the word." In this specific aspect, Judaism and writing coalesce so thoroughly that, were it not for their different names, it would be difficult to tell the Jew from the writer.

The pivotal passages include the following:

The Jewish world begins with us, with our first steps in the world.

The Jewish world is based on written law, on a logic of word one cannot deny.

Every Jew lives within a personified word which allows him to enter into all written words.

Every Jew lives in a key-word, a word of pain, a password, which the rabbis comment on.

The Jew's fatherland is a sacred text amidst the commentaries it has given rise to.

Hence, every Jew is in the Law.

Hence, every Jew makes the Law.

Hence the Law is Jewish.[64]

[...] being Jewish means exiling yourself in the word and, at the same time, weeping for your exile.[65]

Judaism is always outside Judaism. It is a religion of leaving the word behind [...].

[...] *Dead of wanting to live against life, alive by virtue of being lost in death's labyrinth, he comes into his own survival, as if the beyond were his place. So his words remain prophetic and announce the return of those who left the time of man.*

[...] *Even more than by his speech, the Jew is a Jew by the silence or the vast murmur which encloses his eyes as a sea surrounds an island and makes it inaccessible.*

[...] The desert wrote the Jew, and the Jew reads himself in the desert.

[...] *Jewish solitude lies in the impossible outcome of the book [...].*[66]

I repeat. The sign is Jewish.

The word [*vocable*] is Jewish.

The book is Jewish.

The book is made of Jews.

Because the Jew has for centuries wanted to be a sign, a word [*vocable*], a book. His writing is wandering, suspicion, waiting, confluence, wound, exodus, and exile, exile, exile.[67]

You see, it is perhaps just there, where we are silent while talking, where nobody can read us while we write, that what I have called Judaism resides. The words of the Jews are buried in sand, forever silent, but every syllable, as if mesmerized by this living death, reports their immortal agony.

---

64 *Ibid.*, pp. 100–101.
65 BQ II, p. 165.
66 *Ibid.*, pp. 291, 299, 300, 302, 319.
67 *Ibid.*, 290.

[...] perhaps the only affirmation of the Jew is, paradoxically, that there is no such person as the Jew. There is only the exile of a word, which he came to take on himself, not to try and save it, or himself, but to guide it from dawn to dusk of the longest day, from the point catching fire to its grandiose conflagration.

[...] "Twenty centuries of wandering can only come to rest in a word both so dense and so light that it is carried off into space and swallowed by the wave."

"I have lived only within this word," he added.[68]

Whether talmudist or cabbalist, the Jew's relation to the book is as fervent as that of the writer to his text. Both have the same thirst to learn, to know, to decipher their fate carved into every letter from which God has withdrawn.[69]

Being a Jew and/or a writer entails continual interpreting: "Our lot is to interpret an unreadable world."[70] This thought, which lies at the core of modern Western thinking shaped by the legacy of the Reformation and Protestant hermeneutics, acquires a deeper meaning in Jabès. For it is not only about the Jew or the writer interpreting the incomprehensible world and himself in it. Namely, superimposed on this hermeneutical model is the structure of perspectivism and of the Book. As already shown, the Book is the ultimate reader, a locus of interpretation of all particularity. In relation to the Book, the Jew/writer is that which is interpreted. *For this reason, the state of permanent interpretation involves him striving to interpret the way in which he is himself interpreted by the Book.*

Consequently, if the life of the Jew/writer is a never-ending interpretation, it is so first of all because the "interpreter" himself is thrown into the world subject to interpretation, and he gets a glimpse of the place where he is read himself only fleetingly and in displacement. Hence, the Jew is not only the author of the book but also the book, the sign: "The desert wrote the Jew, and the Jew reads himself in the desert." The Jew enquires who he is, but he could discern it only from the position inaccessible to him. As this aporia is irremovable and structural, neither the Jew nor the writer exists as a stable, interpreting subject. Their being as such prevents itself from materialising. *For they embody one and the same gap between the perspectival world and the Book.* That is why they actually do not exist but are *a place* which divides and links two sides of the perspectival universe: the limited worlds (books, words, the Law) and the Book. Their spectral being illuminates this fundamental ontological crack.

Let us focus now on the quotations above. In the vision they sketch, the Book is the Jews' world, and each of them has his own personal word, "a word of pain,

---

68 *Ibid.*, p. 374, 429, 439.
69 BM, p. 173.
70 BQ II, p. 84.

a password." In these formulations, Jabès alludes to an old Kabbalistic motif, particularly pronounced in the Safed Kabbalah. According to Luria (in the *Sefer Ha-Kavanot*), the Torah was revealed in as many aspects and meanings as there were Jews who received it on the Zion (i.e. six hundred thousand, as tradition would have it). Each of these aspects gave rise to the root[71] (שורש, *shoresh*) of the souls of Israel, obligated to read and know the Torah in accordance with explanations specific to the root from which they arose.[72] Moses Cordovero (*Derisha b'Inyanei Malakhim*) believed, however, that each and every soul had its part of the Torah and its own, exclusive individual understanding of it.[73]

As is always the case in Jabès, the historical motif of Jewish tradition is reinterpreted in the light of his own modern thought. The aspect of the Torah becomes the Jew's own word – a word of pain, a key-word and a password, at the same time. Given the reasoning recounted above, *the Jew's own word can be understood as his position in the Book, which he cannot know despite his ongoing enquiries.* If only he could read this word, he would find a key to his existence. But because he has no existence, the word becomes a hidden determinant of his lot. What was a personal revelation to the Safed kabbalists becomes the Jew's own enigma in Jabès. The enigma arises as a result of perspectivism's structural principles. Moreover, the Jew/writer embodies the condition of modern man *tout court* as he lives his life in the world "from which God has withdrawn." The Jew/writer is a paradigmatic interpreter of the world which, in the wake of God's death, turned into a riddle and, first of all, made man's existence a riddle.[74]

---

71 Notably, the "root" is also the name of the conjugated stems of Hebraic verbs, which delineate the semantic field of derivative forms. Therefore, the idea of the "root" comes to connote functions of language, in particular the Hebraic language, in which individual words are based on elementary combinations of letters. Because of this, many kabbalists (starting from the yet "pre-Kabbalistic" *Sefer Yetzirah*) interpreted letters not as simple script-tools but as the basic fabric of reality because permutations of letters were believed to reveal the foundations of meaningful words.

72 Scholem, "Signification," pp. 126–127.

73 *Ibid.*, p. 127.

74 A similar gesture is to be found in Kafka: in the parable "Before the Law," "a man from the country" can be construed as a Jew who, cut off form tradition, interprets his own riddle of common Revelation. At the same time, he is a universal example of modern man. "The New Advocate," another of Kafka's parables, features Bucephalos. Without the master, the horse becomes free yet loses the peculiar blindness, which before enabled him to rush with Alexander to new lands and defy the fate. What does the modern Bucephalos do? He reads legal books. Instead of spontaneous action, he is overcome by a paralysing hermeneutic drive: the desire to understand what one is and what event founds the new form of existence. This desire seems to hold a hope of

Drawing on these insights, we can now answer the question why, in Jabès, the condition of the Jew and the condition of the writer are so similar in terms of the relationship between life and interpretation. Both modes of being – being a Jew and being a writer – *entail functioning as a sign in the Book, which sign self-reflectively interprets its own place.*

Does writing mean undertaking an ultimate reading, first in our mind, then through our own vocabulary [*vocables*], of a book whose necessity is our reason to be?[75]

The fact that there is the Book seems to doom modern man to be a writer entrapped between writing down his own books and being read by the Book. To Jabès, Judaism, in which interpreting the Torah has merged with life as such over centuries, can offer a wealth of its own experience to this modern condition.[76] Re-interpreted in this way, Judaism is still universal knowledge about "the exile of the word," and the difference that constitutes Judaism is based not on any particular content but on the very mechanism of "exile," typifying reality as such.[77] The position of the Jew, as Erbertz observes, means here "*conditio humana* in its extreme form."[78] In *The Ineffaceable the Unperceived*, Jabès builds on the etymology of the word Hebrew[79] to conclude that the Jew is a *passeur*,

---

regaining the lost naturalness even though this hope only exacerbates the paralysis. Thus, both to Kafka and to Jabès, modernity entails incessant, demotivating interpretation. "God's withdrawal" leaves a trace that calls for constant inquiry. The question about the source of the modern universe dovetails with the question about what one actually is. Both riddles are, indeed, traps resulting from situatedness in the structure of modern perspectivism and of the Book this perspectivism produces.

75   BR II, p. 11.

76   Matthew Del Nevo insists: "Jabès, as a writer and a Jew, is unlike the nomad who stands for the ability to transform silence and absence (as what is most environing) into a life-force. While for the (symbolic) nomad this transformative capacity may be second-nature, for the writer and the Jew, it is what remains to be discovered and is also, after the disaster, of the most pressing historical significance: to transform God's silence and absence into a life-force" ("Edmond Jabès and the Question of the Book," p. 303). Consequently, the writer and the Jew can be said to stand at the forefront of modernity's wrestling with the situation it has found itself in.

77   "To belong to what by nature rejects all belonging – the universal: this is the true Jewish vocation […]" (BR III, p. 31; translation altered).

78   Erbertz, *Poetik des Buches*, p. 43.

79   It is the traditional, albeit controversial, etymology of עברית, *iwrit* (Hebrew), allegedly deriving from the verb לעבור, *la'avor* (to pass, to cross over, to get past). This

one who crosses, wanders across the desert and guides others, at the same time.[80]

The notion of life as interpretation, which is central to the modern structure, is what ultimately binds Judaism and writing in Jabès. Judaism and writing undergo utter simplification in being reduced to the position of the remnant. The difference between them becomes just a trace, nothing more.

Conclusion: Jabès' Judaism and Jewish Philosophy of Modernity

One of the key motifs in Jabès' texts, the interconnectedness of writing and Judaism, of the writer's condition and the Jew's condition, reflects what I have called Jewish philosophy of modernity. Jabès consistently develops the parallel of writing and Judaism. The two are linked by the common dependence on the structure of the Book, the "essence" based on the negative remnant, the mechanism of survival, the shared transcendence of their respective successive forms, introduction of historicity into them and, finally, constitution of "subjects" – the writer and the Jew, whose life is ongoing interpretation governed by the Book. Such an analogy of writing and Judaism is clearly predicated on the structure of the modern universe and undermines the simple idea of the Jewish legacy as exceptional. If the exiled writer has the same status as the nomadic Jew, what could possibly determine the other's alterity in Jabès? Nevertheless, Jabès consistently maintains that Judaism is unique. Moreover, he regards Judaism as a tradition which provides experience relevant to modernity in that it helps accommodate to exile, survival and continual interpretation.

At this point, we can ask a question that exposes the aporia of Jewish philosophy of modernity: Where does this privileged knowledge of Judaism come from? Does it indeed come from its rich tradition? Or is it perhaps a result of the retrospective re-ordering of this tradition, underpinned by the modernity-specific structure? Should the latter be the case, Jabès' thought would be a peculiar tautology: *Judaism offers modernity a valuable experience only because it is in itself modern.* This would mean that Judaism is *a point* where modern self-reflection reached itself, revealing its disconnectedness from the past and foundedness on itself alone.

---

interpretation is explicitly associated with the vision of the Israelis' exodus from Egypt as a formative experience of the Jewish identity.

80 BR III, p. 12.

The way Jabès approaches pre-modern Jewish tradition seems to confirm this conclusion, for he finds in it what he actually seeks to find: exile, solitude, uncertainty, permanent questioning and persistent survival. Deconstructive reading, however, shows that the discovery of affinities between Judaism and modernity does not come as a surprise: *the modern structure was hidden in them even before its rediscovery.* In other words, Jabès' reasoning – which proceeds in the following stages: (1) Judaism is… (exile, solitude, constant interpretation, and so forth); (2) *ergo*, it offers modernity a useful experience – obscures that fact that this Judaism is already strictly modern. Perhaps, *obfuscating this premise proves the magnitude of the loss on which modernity itself is based.* The content of old Jewish tradition is still available in modernity, but it depends on the primary severance, which organises it into the structure of the Book, the remnant and survival. With this content defused in this way, it is impossible to establish whether it is "truly" Jewish. Consequently, Judaism with its ages-long tradition of memory, historicity and ritual finds itself thrown into the eye of the modern storm, *where any simple continuity with the past is demolished, and the past itself will always already be a construct.*

This is the lens to be applied to reading Jabès' insights about Judaism. To conclude, let us have a look at some of these insights, bearing in mind that the parallel of writing and Judaism proves that they concern, actually, modernity itself:

> Judaism is the only religion in which one breaks even. When a Jew reads a text, he always starts from the oldest commentaries and, later, interprets and questions them, as a result breaking even. He is always the same in his faith, but whenever he reads a text, he breaks even. […] Hence also […] this opening, this modernity of Judaism, which only few people see still.[81]
> Truth is always at the end of the questioning, on the other shore, behind the last horizon. To go towards truth, that is the essential preoccupation of the Jew. But what truth could resist such a questioning? Unless that fragmentary truth, always at a further remove, reveals itself [*se livre*] stroke by stroke [*touches successives*] in the very movement of questioning. Where God abdicates, truth glimmers.[82]
> *The Jew keeps his eyes on the horizon.*[83]
> "Never say you have arrived because, everywhere, you are a traveler in transit."
>   Reb Lami.[84]

---

81 EEJ, p. 72.
82 DB, p. 59.
83 BQ II, p. 298.
84 BR II, p. 62.

9 The Shoah and Anti-Semitism

In the previous Chapters, I discussed Jabès as a(n) (a)theologian, philosopher and writer. Now I will focus on a less pronounced, yet equally important, concern of his, involving history, politics, social life and ethics. Undoubtedly, Jabès' position on these issues originates in his reflection on the Shoah and, as a rule, turns back to it. In Jabès, the Shoah is an event in which history intersects with ontology as real experiences transform language and cap the process of God's withdrawal, exposing the entanglements of memory and forgetting. This is the reason why Jabès made (at least declaratively) the Shoah the cornerstone of his thought. But besides this ontological investment, the Shoah formatively affects also Jabès' social and ethical ideas scattered across his writings.

The discourse of Jabès' writings – his *Books* in particular – is governed by the laws of its own, and, unsurprisingly, events which they feature are filtered through a quasi-Lurianic ontology and poetic experience. Nevertheless, Jabès sometimes addresses also events of apparently journalistic resonance. They tend to be associated with certain forms and manifestations of anti-Semitism after the Shoah. Such developments powerfully affected Jabès' explorations of Judaism (as discussed in the foregoing) and, moreover, provoked him to offer spontaneous, topical commentaries. For example, when a Jewish cemetery in Carpentras, Provence – one of France's oldest hubs of Judaism – was defiled in May 1990, Jabès wrote an indignant letter to the press. A passage of the letter was later included in *The Book of Hospitality*, Jabès' last work, in which he strove to reach ultimate silence. The contrast of these discourses suggests that if there is any social reflection to be found in Jabès, it never strays from the central, underlying movement of writing.

I will analyse socio-ethical motifs in Jabès in two stages. In this Chapter, I will examine the role of the Shoah and Jabès' comments on anti-Semitism and on the complicity of discourse in the rise of violence. In the next Chapter, I will discuss the idea of hospitality, in which ethics is, again, inseparable from ontology.

The Shoah as a Disaster

In a text devoted to Blanchot, Jabès writes:

> The crematorium ovens were not their [Nazis'] only crime, but surely the most abject, in full daylight, in the abyssal absence [*absence abyssale*] of the Name.[1]

---

1   BM, p. 95.

The first conspicuous thing is that Jabès does not ascribe the enormity of the Shoah to the sheer magnitude of the crime; to compare it with other atrocities in history not infrequently means to insult the memory of all victims. Rather, the Shoah is highlighted – and prevented from being forgotten – by "daylight," the moment when the crime was perpetrated. In this context, reading "full daylight" as a metaphor for the existing law does not seem far-fetched. If so, Jabès is certainly right to say that the Shoah was not a crime *against the law*, perpetrated surreptitiously, in the dark of the night. It took place "in full daylight," that is, where the law should be present at its fullest. If so, why did the law not prohibit murder? Did the law fail to work? The key to this tantalising confusion is to be found at the end of the passage, which associates the "daylight" with the "abyssal absence of the Name." The law did exist and, indeed, set apart day from night, to be consistent with the metaphor, and organised human doings "in full daylight." Yet, stripped of its ontological embedment in the Name, it lost its ethical power or, rather, *showed that it had no such power at all*. The Shoah was a flagrant crime, arranged by the law and with the full sanction of the law.

Of course, Jabès does not engage in discussions which revived the distinction between positive law and (variously defined) natural law in post-war philosophy of law (e.g. in Radbruch). Emptied of any subtleties, such discourse brings the Shoah down to the level of radical philosophical analysis. In Jabès, law in this sense seems to be identified with the language-based organisation of the world. *The difference between the fact and law becomes in this way less important than the distinction between law and the silent, blank space of the Book, from which law dissociates itself, along with its world.* To a degree, like in Lévinas, the compass of ethical reflection shifts from within language to a relation that arises outside language and cannot be rendered in injunctions. Jabès' far-reaching premise seems to be that all forms of language bear more or less violence; more than that: that they are *meaningful organisations of violence*.

At this point, it is useful to evoke a sentence which Hannah Arendt brought into public knowledge: "Eichmann feels guilty before God, not before the law,"[2] as Eichmann's lawyer stated during the high-profile trial in Jerusalem. "In full daylight, in the abyssal absence of the Name," writes Jabès. If we put these statements together, we will see that Eichmann feels guilty before God, who is not there, but has nothing to reproach himself for in the light of the law, in full daylight. It implies that God, who – as already mentioned – is a human invention in

---

2   Hannah Arendt, *Eichmann in Jerusalem. A Report on the Banality of Evil* (Penguin Books, 2006), p. 19.

Jabès' view,[3] *serves to justify the law within the law itself, which waives all respon-*
sibility by making guilt the matter of God's judgment. In this way, calling upon
God as (in Eichmann's own words) a *Höherer Sinnesträger,* a higher bearer of
meaning, reduces all responsibility to compliance with the law, which in itself
has no legitimation and lingers in "the abyssal absence of the Name," with God
being its own hypostasis.

As a certain configuration of meaning, the law is founded on the void, which
it endeavours to veil with its notion of God as a being and a source of meaning
in one (which should be distinguished from Jabès' idea of God as the position
of a remnant). "They said that they served God and put God into their service,"
states *The Book of Hospitality.*[4] Consequently, ignorance of God's death – of "the
abyssal absence of the Name" – *helps make God part of the meaningful law and, in
this way, absolutise this law.* This is, I believe, the core of Jabès' ethical conclusions
from rethinking the Shoah: the persistence of meaning, "daylight," as dissociated
from the absence of the Name, makes for a structural mechanism of ultimate
violence, against which there is no protection. The Shoah shows that all forms
of the law work in the same way: that which law considers desirable is treated
as an order *per se.* Zygmunt Bauman argued that a change of the law-instituted
order of injunctions very easily produces a sense of its own naturalness. Very few
people are able to find an external grounding, and even if they do, it is not a result
of any ethical reflection but rather of a spontaneous, Lévinasian response to the
suffering of the Other.[5] Jabès reasons in a similar fashion:

> Auschwitz has radically transformed our vision of things. Not because such a degree of
> cruelty was unthinkable before. The unthinkable was the near total indifference of both
> the German and the allied populations which made Auschwitz possible. This indiffer-
> ence continues to defy any previous notion of the human. After Auschwitz, the feeling
> of solitude that lies at the core of each human being has become considerably amplified.
> Today, any sense of trust is doubled by an all-consuming distrust. We know that it is not
> reasonable to expect anything at all from others. And yet we hope – though something
> gnaws at the core of this hope, reminding us that the thread has been cut.
> […] It is therefore the very culture that supports us that we have to question. We must
> try to grasp *how* it was able to engender the greatest evil, and not only *what* made it
> incapable of warding off this evil; for is it possible to separate man from his culture?[6]

---

3   Cf. P, p. 106.
4   LH, p. 42.
5   Zygmunt Bauman, *Modernity and the Holocaust* (Ithaca: Cornell UP, Polity, 1989).
6   DB, pp. 61–2.

Jabès adds also that it is a gross mistake to regard the Nazis as "brutes from another planet." The common, widespread support they had from the German population implies that their actions must have seemed completely natural and obvious, which is exactly where the problem lies.[7] Therefore Jabès' conclusions denounce culture, the law and, more generally, all linguistic forms of the world. Whether they are criminal or not is entirely a matter of chance. God's withdrawal – "the abyssal absence of the Name" – divests them all of legitimation, which does not stop them from exercising their authority. On this model, the Shoah is an extreme case that exposes the nature of language most glaringly. As I will show further in this Chapter, in Jabès, it originates in the persisting mechanisms of label-tagging name-giving – in "the power of words over people." Is there any room left for ethical reflection given that if ethical thinking takes place within language, it is subject to the law while outside language it faces God's absence? Jabès strives to locate his thought nowhere else than in this paradoxical sphere of absence. This is also what Lévinas did in searching for ethics beyond morality and law, yet still underpinned by active God's commandment.[8] In Jabès, God is only a name of this structurally demarcated place of absence, the beyond of all meaning, where the poet seeks to resist language.

Taking this position, Jabès at the same time faces the dilemma which, in the wake of the Shoah, haunted to a greater or lesser degree other authors as well, in particular Paul Celan. Namely, the language which was to depict the Shoah was the same language that had so easily served to perpetrate it. There was no ontological difference between those two applications of that language. So the problem did not lie in the linguistic-vs.-inexpressible opposition, where language stumbled upon a barrier to articulating indescribable crimes. On the

---

7   *Ibid.*, p. 62.

8   Although Lévinas was one of the key forces in the rapprochement of philosophy and Jewish tradition in the 20th century, he never renounced loyalty to the strictly religious element in Judaism. This is the reason why Jabès had his reservations about Lévinas. In his conversations with Marcel Cohen, Jabès remarks that despite all possible similarities between him and Lévinas – and despite the speculative potential of Lévinas' thought – Lévinas abandons speculation when it comes, for example, to the Talmudic lectures, and subordinates himself to the already recognised thought for fear of profanation (EEJ, p. 74). Jabès seems to take issue less with abandoning speculation as such (after all the Talmud itself is based on the *Maloket* method) but with endorsing its religious delimitation, Theism in particular, be it even in its various weakened forms. Jabès' own speculation gathers momentum where radical atheism steps in.

contrary, the problem concerned two linguistic organisations of worlds which, though mutually untranslatable, were each meaningfully logical. Consequently, a question arose how one could be distinguished from the other, if, "in the abyssal absence of the Name" there was no point of reference provided by an external, law-giving God. Jabès and, even more so, Celan (to whom the language of the murderers was, at the same time, his "mother tongue" and the language of his poetry[9]) strove to re-think the suspicion against their own language because it did not differ ontologically from the language deployed as the murder weapon.[10] Celan and Jabès come to the same conclusions insofar, at least, that they reverse the common opposition of unimaginable crime and comprehensible, ethically informed language (a distinction upheld, for example, by Habermas, who sought ideal claims in language[11]). Instead of wrestling with language to express what has happened, both poets explore how much language itself has been undermined. Because the enormity was perpetrated with the full sanction of the law, which contrived to give it an axiological grounding, Jabès and Celan do not attempt to put this law in opposition to *any other* law, instead seeking to set the inexpressible *against* language. Rather than in speaking of the ineffable atrocity of the crime, the poet's responsibility lies in finding a sign for silence that could indicate it. The point is that the crime not only was directly communicable but also had its own, perfectly articulate language.

Thus, both Celan and Jabès grapple with the fact that language has in a way become estranged from them just because it is still theirs.[12] Language does not

---

9   Cf. Susan Gubar, "The Long and the Short of Holocaust Verse," *New Literary History*, 35/3 (Summer 2004), pp. 443–68, on p. 456.

10   Susan Gubar explains that "if language was therefore itself an instrument and casualty of the disaster, then literary artists confronted a confounding perplexity about their own medium, as Adorno knew they would. The enormity of the event, coupled with this suspicion about political or aesthetic productions, often propelled poets in two diametrically opposed directions: on the one hand, toward ellipses, fragmentation, in short poems that exhibit their inadequacy by shutting down with a sort of premature closure; on the other, toward verbosity in long poems that register futility by reiterating an exhausted failure to achieve closure." Gubar, "Long," p. 443.

11   Cf. Jürgen Habermas, *Theory of Communicative Action*, trans. Thomas MacCarthy (Boston, Mass: Beacon Press, 1981).

12   Jean Améry described the alienation of language amidst the horror of the Shoah in this way: "We, however, had not lost our country, but had to realize that it had never been ours. [...] The meaning of every German word changed for us, and finally, whether we resisted or not, our mother tongue became just as inimical as the one they spoke around us." Jean Améry, *At the Mind's Limits: Contemplations by a Survivor on Auschwitz and*

side with them as a tool for naming and condemning the crime but speaks against them. Such naming and condemning turns into a fight of word against word, in which no decisive criterion is available as we are faced with "the abyssal absence of the Name." Outside this conflict, there is nothing, and it is this paradoxical nothing that the poets must cross in search of truth: with language alienated as it is, this is the only place for them to go. In terms of negative theology, they rely on silence for scrutinising the conflict of languages from outside. Consequently, their texts focus not on the meanings conveyable in language but on the means of enhancing their distance from language.

Conceived in this way, Jabès' work testifies to the Shoah though in a different way than Primo Levi's, Jean Améry's and Elie Wiesel's did. In his conversation with Philipp de Saint-Cheron, Jabès insisted:

> You cannot speak of Auschwitz. People imagine that I tried to speak of Auschwitz. But I never tried to speak of Auschwitz because I did not go through Auschwitz. I cannot speak of it, yet Auschwitz is something we all went through, if it can be put in this way. This terrifying, unspeakable thing has made its way into words. Words, for me, have changed completely.
> [...] It is not my role to bear witness. Elie Wiesel can bear witness because he was in the camps; I did not know the camps, but it does not take away from me the right – not to talk about the camps, perhaps – but to say what we became in the wake of the camps.[13]

Though Jabès considers himself a Shoah survivor, he has no intention to bear witness the way camp survivors do. His testimony, if it is a testimony in the first place, is different since he describes how reality has transformed after Auschwitz, how language has transformed and how we have ourselves transformed. This choice tends to stir controversy. Berel Lang, for one, criticises Jabès for aestheticising the Shoah, for choosing not to speak of it directly and explicitly, and, as a result, diluting the uniqueness of the Shoah in reflections on a general, indefinite disaster. In this way, the Shoah is made, first, just one among the many events of the tragic Jewish history and, second, a proof of an all-encompassing disintegration.[14] On such reading, Jabès is indeed culpable for what Alain Finkielraut denounced as "narcotization" of the Shoah experience, i.e. its universalisation

---

Its Realities, trans. Sidney Rosenfeld and Stella P. Rosenfeld (Bloomington: Indiana UP, 1980), pp. 50, 53.

13   EEJ, pp. 68–69.

14   In Hawkins, *Reluctant Theologians*, p. 160.

and dissemination to the point of collective amnesia, with the Shoah's true historical relevance lost in the ubiquity of its evocations.[15] However, Lang apparently fails to notice the motivation Jabès cites in the interview quoted above. Jabès holds himself unauthorised to provide a direct narration of the Shoah, unlike its direct witnesses. His responsibility lies elsewhere – in the questioning which can prove consequential to the very possibility of bearing witness. In her polemics with Lang, Hawkins contends that, in Jabès, the Shoah results in the very impossibility of writing a continuous history.[16] In this way, Jabès joins a very broad post-war movement of "epistemological" reflection on the Shoah, which attempted to re-think such issues as bearing witness, historical truth and objective criteria of settling disputes. Still, Jabès follows his own radical path in this, problematising the entire linguistic structure of reality. According to Peter Boyle, Auschwitz shatters Jabès' poetry because "it [Auschwitz] is what it is, it is what happened" and, as such, it is entirely divorced from the words which attempt to covey it.[17]

The accusation of blurring the uniqueness of the Shoah, or even the very historicity of its events, for the sake of generalised ontological reflection misses out on a fundamental fact. Admittedly, Jabès thinks about the catastrophe as such, about Creation, which is at the same time a collapse, where particular events, therein the Shoah, seem to be only repeated re-enactments of the same general pattern. However, Jabès emphatically states that his *entire* writing is determined by Auschwitz:

I write from two limits.
Outside there is [*il y a*] the void.
Within, the horror of Auschwitz.
Real-limit. Limit-reflection.
Do not read anything but incapacity to ground balance.
Do not read anything but the harrowing and awkward
resolve to survive.
In one scream, life and death
– the despotic sisters –
fade away, intertwined.
Impenetrable is eternity.[18]

15 Cf. Bruno Chaouat, "Forty Years of Suffering," *L'esprit créateur*, 45/3 (Fall 2005), pp. 49–62, on p. 50.
16 Hawkins, *Reluctant Rheologians*, p. 160.
17 Peter Boyle, *Museum of Space* (St Lucia: University of Queensland Press, 2004), p. 25.
18 P, p. 95.

Even if the *Books* had been written without reflecting on the Shoah, they would anyway be inseparable from the reading framework imposed by Jabès. If, in his texts, references to the Shoah seem to be overridden by the disaster as such, it is the effect of *the utterly radical questioning that the Shoah spurred Jabès to pursue.* Justice, as formerly thought of, would respond to the horror of Auschwitz by trying to write a legible general history in which problems of bearing witness were excluded, the possibility of producing an objective record in language retained and ethical responsibility clearly defined. In Jabès, the experience that stamped itself on language makes such a history impossible, and if it were possible, it would rely on the same mechanisms as ultimate violence. Hence, the other limit evoked in the passage from *Le Parcours* is the void. One does not return from Auschwitz to the old world; the counterpoint to what has happened is found in the void.

Given the above, the Shoah in Jabès is an event which, in a sense, is not "an event," that is, a fact accommodable within the former framework of knowledge. On the contrary, it becomes a cornerstone of a new reality. The opposite of Auschwitz is not an intelligible, meaningful human world; the opposite of Auschwitz is the void. In this way, Auschwitz is cut off from the past by a radical discontinuity that can be rendered only in a set of concepts and metaphors which re-imagine the idea of the originary disaster in Jabès. If the Shoah loses its uniqueness, it is only because *there is no access anymore to reality not founded upon the Shoah.* The Shoah has become the formative event of our universe, as ubiquitous as God's withdrawal and permeating all things. As Guy Walter notices,[19] there is no before and after Auschwitz in Jabès since the entire history changes and starts anew with it. Similarly to Philippe Lacoue-Labarthe and Dan Diner, Jabès views the Shoah as a historical turning point, a radical shift in the relationship between the possible and the impossible, an event whose meaning unfolds only in history that follows it.[20] Interestingly, Carl Schaffer[21] summons in this context a well-known Kabbalistic idea of parallel events in higher and lower worlds, exemplified, for example, in the simultaneous exile of Israel and

---

19 Guy Walter, "La spiritualité du silence après la Choah dans *Le livre des questions*," in *Écrire le livre*, p. 75.

20 Cf. Alan Milchman and Alan Rosenberg, *Eksperymenty w myśleniu o Holocauście. Auschwitz, nowoczesność i filozofia*, trans. L. Krowicki and J. Szacki (Warszawa: Scholar, 2003), pp. 11–16.

21 See Carl Schaffer, "Chaos and Void: Presencing Absence in Edmond Jabès' *The Book Of Questions* and Juan Rulfo's *Pedro Paramo*," *History of European Ideas*, 20/4–6 (1995), pp. 859–864, on p. 862.

Shekinah. Interpreted in the Kabbalistic spirit, the Shoah must be a cosmic event that affects the whole of reality.

Hence, the position of the Shoah in Jabès' thought is, indeed, liminal: the Shoah has been attributed such a fundamental role that, as a historical event, it loses its uniqueness. The dispute over the uniqueness of the Shoah abounds in paradoxes of thinking about discontinuity which were spelt out already by Hegel. By enclosing the Shoah in the category in unintelligibility and unspeakability, we strip it of meaning in the meaningful world while by making it an absolute starting point of the entire post-Shoah reality, we strip it of uniqueness we wish to attribute to it. This is perhaps where the exceptional role of the Shoah in thinking lies: in a mesh of epistemological traps in which it ensnares us and in the inescapable clash of opinions which transfigures the dread of what has happened into the furious criticism of other views.

I believe that Jabès wished not so much to take a position in such polemics as to have his works demonstrate their simultaneous necessity and pointlessness. In Jabès, words never express what should be conveyed in them, and their incompleteness dooms us to perspectivism and the disputes it generates. The above passage from *Le Parcours* suggests that there can be no balance between Auschwitz and the void. No thesis could possibly explain the Shoah or settle the polemics around it. The only thing that remains is writing – an equivalent of "resolve to survive" – which meanders its way between the void and Auschwitz, fully aware that each particular form of writing is only a broken piece and not a full-fledged position.

Bearing Witness to the Shoah

The study of post-Shoah writing, therein Jabès' writing, can be inventively aided by the ideas Giorgio Agamben has been developing for a number of years now. In the third part of his *Homo Sacer* trilogy, titled *Remnants of Auschwitz: The Archive and the Witness*, Agamben focuses the figure of the *Muselmann*, a camp prisoner who, having lost speech and the ability to respond to stimuli, is terrifyingly reduced to his purely biological being.[22] As Agamben states, the *Muselmann* reveals the essence of humanity located in speech, which has invaded the biological being and makes man human in the regular sense of the term. The *Muselmann* is a liminal case of anthropology and ethics, a human as

---

22 Giorgio Agamben, *Remnants of Auschwitz: The Witness and the Archive (Homo Sacer III)*, trans. Daniel Heller-Roazen (New York: Zone Books, 1991), pp. 41–87.

such and no-longer-a-human – a fragile body emptied out of dignity, the will to live and the ability to say "I," which would constitute him as human in speech. Agamben writes:

The living being who has made himself absolutely present to himself in the act of enunciation, in saying "I," pushes his own lived experiences back into a limitless past and can no longer coincide with them. The event of language in the pure presence of discourse irreparably divides the self-presence of sensations and experiences in the very moment in which it refers them to a unitary center. Whoever enjoys the particular presence achieved in the intimate consciousness of the enunciating voice forever loses the pristine adhesion to the Open that Rilke discerned in the gaze of the animal; he must now turn his eyes inward toward the non-place of language. This is why subjectification, the production of consciousness in the event of discourse, is often a trauma of which human beings are not easily cured; this is why the fragile text of consciousness incessantly crumbles and erases itself, bringing to light the disjunction on which it is erected: the constitutive desubjectification in every subjectification.[23]

Agamben's idea ties in with Jabès' thoughts on the status of the writer, language and body (though, of course, while Jabès focuses on writing, Agamben is closer to Lacan, it seems, in attending to speech[24]). To Jabès, the write's role and harsh lot is to give voice to that which is excluded by language, which lingers just before the threshold of enunciation. This verges on Agamben's vision of the witness who has not experienced himself the events to which he bears witness, for had he experienced them, he would not be capable of bearing witness. Instead, he speaks on behalf of the one who cannot speak, *and the object of his testimony is the sphere that eludes testimony, the sphere that cannot be borne witness to*:

At first it appears that it is the human, the survivor, who bears witness to the inhuman, the *Muselmann*. But if the survivor bears witness *for* the *Muselmann* – in the technical sense of "on behalf of" or "by proxy" […] – then, according to the legal principle by which the acts of the delegated are imputed to the delegant, it is in some way the *Muselmann* who bears witness. But this means that the one who truly bears witness in the human is the inhuman; it means that the human is nothing other than the agent of the inhuman, the one that lends the inhuman a voice. Or, rather, that there is no one who claims the title of "witness" by right. To speak, to bear witness, is thus to enter into

---

23 *Ibid.*, pp. 122–3.
24 Jabès probably would not subscribe to Agamben's simple juxtaposition of speech and "the pure presence." Jabès views speech as something always already arranged, recounting the past and, as such, non-present. Even putting aside Derrida's critiques of binding speech to the present (which Jabès could fully endorse), for Jabès the present as such is never there but always displaced. Paradoxically, in his view, it is writing that exposes us most to the impact of time.

a vertiginous movement in which something sinks to the bottom, wholly desubjectified and silent, and something subjectified speaks without truly having anything to say of its own [...]. Testimony takes place where the speechless one makes the speaking one speak and where the one who speaks bears the impossibility of speaking in his own speech, such that the silent and the speaking, the inhuman and the human enter into a zone of indistinction in which it is impossible to establish the position of the subject, to identify the "imagined substance" of the "I" and, along with it, the true witness. This can also be expressed by saying that *the subject of testimony is the one who bears witness to desubjectification*. But this expression holds only if it is not forgotten that "to bear witness to a desubjectification" can only mean there is no subject of testimony [...]. Here it is possible to gage the insufficiency of the two opposed theses that divide accounts of Auschwitz: the view of humanist discourse, which states that "all human beings are human" and that of anti-humanist discourse, which holds that "only some human beings are human." What testimony says is something completely different, which can be formulated in the following theses: "human beings are human insofar as they are not human" or, more precisely, "human beings are human insofar as they bear witness to the inhuman."[25]

Jabès is not, strictly speaking, a witness to the Shoah, but he bears witness to what the Shoah revealed – to the discontinuous boundary between speaking and speechlessness, between pointlessness of speech and inexpressible validity of silence. It is not only that Jabès "bears the impossibility of speaking in his own speech," as Agamben's witness does; in fact, we would be hard pressed to find a writer who has dedicated himself more than Jabès to studying this ultimate limit, *the point* dividing silence from language, itself devoid of content and, thereby, registering the unsayable.[26] Agamben's concept shows why the Shoah can be

---

25   Agamben, *Remnants*, pp. 120–121.

26   Guy Walter offers a similar insight: "[In Jabès] silence hovers amidst words, within words, in-between the gaps of *vocables*, in-between the parting of the lips. [...] In this way, Auschwitz is always at the threshold, at the threshold between beginning and end, between the impossible opening of the book and it impossible closure. For, in every moment, the *threshold* opens in the book. The book, at every moment, is between the edges of the threshold, at every moment crosses these edges and steps inside the threshold. [...] In this way, Auschwitz is at the threshold of another history, the book of which records the wandering and forbids repetition. From then on, history continues at its threshold and cannot enter itself other than through this threshold. [...]. This is how the silence of the scream is perpetuated and gains from infinity the time which it intercepts and leads in-between parts of all [...]." Walter, "Spiritualité," pp. 81–82.
     Interpreting this rather enigmatic passage, I would highlight the two types of threshold it juxtaposes: the threshold that Auschwitz opens for history and the threshold that surfaces in the book time and again. Though rarely portraying details of the Shoah, Jabès' writing is cut out for thinking about the Shoah because it constantly

identified with the originary catastrophe, with the "wound of the word," as Jabès puts it, without being divested of its uniqueness while having its essential consequences exposed. Indeed, Jabès' texts rarely address the realities of the Shoah. As the poet himself states, particulars are redundant because "[w]hen you say: they were deported – that is enough for a Jew to understand the *whole* story."[27] The object on which his writing – like Claude Lanzmann's film *Shoah* – focuses, is absence as such,[28] present in the scattered bricks of the crematoriums in the divine fashion. Because absence needs a footing to show itself, Jabès employs a palette of devices discussed in previous Chapters.

His devices undoubtedly differ from Celan's: Jabès never deforms words, never degrades the syntax and never belts out chanted sounds, which, in Celan, reminded Primo Levi of "last inarticulate babble" or "the gasps of a dying man."[29] Franke elucidates this difference:

> Celan's language is witness to an event; it is in a state of shock. Jabès seems rather to be witnessing a predicament; the disaster that he expresses is there in language always already. Jabès' theoretical reflections and the glassy, cool composure, as well as the quietly fiery passion, of his sibylline aphorisms bespeak the disaster of the word as such. Every finite, human word is an annihilation of the infinite, divine Book. This annihilation is

struggles with crossing its own threshold. Similarly, Auschwitz produces for history a certain limit which cannot be crossed by understanding. Even if attempts are made to inscribe the Shoah into meaningful history, it bursts this history apart time after time. In this sense, the threshold – embodied in the point in Jabès – is the limit of incomprehensibility with which the writer constantly wrestles, re-enacting in this way the position of meaning vis-à-vis the Shoah. In Jabès, the impossibility of the book is the same thing as the impossibility of one, continuous history. Hence, Jabès combines reflection on Creation with thinking on the Shoah, as in the following passages of *Return to the Book*:

> "The last obstacle, the ultimate border is (who can be sure?) the center?
> [...] The center is threshold.
> [...] "Where is the center?"
> "Under the cinders."
> [...] The center is mourning.
> [...] Aside from challenging God, the center formed by the many extermination camps left the Jews – chosen people of the center – grappling with the interrogations of the race. Even those who could no longer think" (BQ I, pp. 359–60, 364).

27 Cf. Daniel B. Listoe, "Seeing Nothing: Allegory and the Holocaust's Absent Dead," *SubStance*, 35/2 (110) (2006), pp. 51–70, on p. 63.
28 *Ibid.*, s. 54.
29 In Agamben, *Remnants*, p. 37.

necessary to the existence of humanity, of the finite, which is otherwise totally annihilated by the infinite.[30]

Thus if Jabès persists in writing the point where speechlessness turns into language, the body into mind, and infinity into finitude, he resorts to different means than Celan. Falling-silent does not trickle down into the very tissue of his words; rather, it appears always as *a before* or *an after* of more coherent entities.

Reminiscent of Agamben's survivor, who simply survives in the bare worthlessness of survival (where all values are emptied of meaning),[31] Jabès evokes the "resolve to survive," on which his writing is based. "In one scream, life and death – the despotic sisters – fade away, intertwined," he writes in *Le Parcours*, intriguingly confirming Agamben's idea that sur-vival, enduring, is a state beyond life and death.[32] An equivalent of this state is found in the pure marking, in the point which – in itself ungraspable as a remnant that it is – divides life and death. *Meanings matter to Jabès, ultimately, only insofar as they can be obliterated in being used to mark the point.* In this way, Jabès re-thinks how culture, meaning and language contribute to violence. His answer seems simple in its paucity: meaning is erected on the basis which it cannot grasp and which it subdues. The poet's journey leads to exposing this basis in the nakedness of the point, which embodies the nakedness of continuing life. This is the only way the poet can bear witness to what is annihilated through the very testimony. At the same time, this is also the only way to unhinge the totality of meaning from its enclosure, destabilise it and reveal it *against* "the abyssal absence of the Name."

Thus, in Jabès' writing, a voice is indirectly lent to that which cannot have its own voice.[33] The entire reality is revealed to be a set of things on which language

---

30 Franke, "Singular," p. 632.

31 Agamben, *Remnants*, pp. 92–4.

32 In this way, as Kronick argues, in Auschwitz – and in the thought that tries to think it – death is no longer an element of "the economy," which it is in Hegel. Death in the Shoah evades the logic of gift and sacrifice in being something totally exterior to meaning, its exteriority forever refusing to be incorporated into dialectics. Kronick, "Edmond Jabès," p. 980.

33 One of the Talmud's classic ethical treatises *Pirke Avot* includes the following maxim: "One who cites an utterance in the name of its original speaker brings redemption to the world"; cf. Adam Zachary Newton, "Versions of Ethics: Or, The SARL of Criticism: Sonority, Arrogation, Letting-Be," *American Literary History*, 13/3 (Fall 2001), pp. 603–37, on p. 603. Jabès obeys this commandment in his special way. Because in the Shoah those who could be quoted did not have a voice, the Jabèsian writer cannot quote their words. Instead, he tries to employ pure marking to invoke that which has fallen silent. The conventional fortunes of the protagonists of *The Book*

works and which, for this very reason, cannot speak themselves. The Shoah unveils the limit to meaning, which turns criminal, and to man turned into a thing enduring in time. His truth is, in Jabès, the truth of Creation, a mute voice of being raised from nothingness. Bearing witness as a Shoah survivor, Jabès bears thus witness to truth which persists as a liminal point of meaning, thought and, also, all value.

However, we could ask whether the desires and hopes associated with finding truth are not dissipated in this truth. This is a truth that does not give anything while taking everything away and delivers us back to speechlessness of Creation, in which everything is equal and mute at the same time. The only alternative is the blindness of meaning, unaware of the nothing in which it is grounded. As Adorno insisted, it was the cold, bourgeois subjectivity that first made Auschwitz possible and now makes life after Auschwitz possible.[34] Therefore, Jabès tries to find a way between meaning and silence of Nothing, searching in this manner for *a place which was human once.* But because this is the place where pointless survival is at its most intense, as is the power of destruction pushing the writer – as Jabès himself states – into death, it *only shows how much more was wrecked in the Shoah.*

"Truth is not for sale. We are our own truth: this is the solitude of God and man. It is our common freedom"[35] Excluded and violated by language, pure duration is a site where God, man and things meet. As the quotation implies, this place is the centre of solitude but also affords freedom. Comparing Jabès and

---

of Questions, the voices of rabbis coming out of nothing only to disappear immediately and, finally, the cited utterances of the anonymous *il*, all do what *Pirke Avot* commands in the world in which a space of complete silence has emerged. Those who have passed away can be remembered only in the speech that verges on silence.

In this way, Jabès responds to the urgency of re-conceptualising testimony, quotation and remembrance in the wake of Auschwitz. The Talmudic maxim assumes that both the quoted one and the quoting one can be named; time does not encroach on identity and only consigns the original enunciation to oblivion. In Jabès, however, time destroys all identity and obliterates names. Therefore, quoting must head towards total anonymity. Paradoxically, the salvation evoked in *Pirke Avot*i is made possible only through an anonymous quotation from an anonymous source. Words, so to speak, quote themselves beyond their author and beyond the quoting one. This is the essence of the pure repetition of the point and its testimony.

34 In Brett Ashley Kaplan, "Pleasure, Memory, and Time Suspension in Holocaust Literature: Celan and Delbo," *Comparative Literature Studies*, 38/4 (2001), pp. 310–29, on pp. 313–4.

35 BQ I, p. 319.

Agamben, we can conclude that Jabès' witness would have a certain power of resistance, which Jabès describes as subversion. Registering the silence of duration is not a surrender to the power of meaning but a struggle with it:

> "My vision of God is horrible: blind, deaf, one-armed without legs."
> "Lord, I resemble You in my impotence to save You."
> [...] "My God, You gave the helpless the strength to act in order to rule the world through Your weakness."
> [...] "In silence, we always eavesdrop on death."
> [...] I believed we rebel so that the minute of chalk (which records the minute) should survive. I have now learned that revolt is the privilege of death.
> [...] You fight in those instants when the revery of life gives way to the dream of death.[36]

The first of the passages sketches the idea of "God after Auschwitz" – mute and mutilated, resembling the *Muselmann*. This God shares in the lot of victims in order to save them. Here, Jabès' thinking intersects with Hans Jonas' theology. According to Jonas, Judaism's difficulty with re-thinking the concept of God after the Shoah is greater than Christianity's. The reason is that, unlike Christianity, Judaism does not focus on salvation in the afterlife but sees this world as the "locus of divine creation, justice, and redemption."[37] With the Jewish God conceptualised as the Lord of History, theodicy after the Shoah is far more difficult.

Yet Jonas ventures to embrace theodicy despite all odds. He starts from marshalling the common argument that the Shoah proves that if God permitted it to happen, he either is not good or did not have power enough to intervene.[38] Then Jonas revisits the idea of *tzimtzum* and argues that creation from nothing inevitably implies a self-limitation of Divine power. God handed his autonomy over to the world, has "given himself whole to the becoming world"[39] and suffers with His creation. Expectedly, Jonas' conclusion assigns responsibility for the world as it is to man; because God has completed his action and cannot do anything more now, man is faced with an immense space of ethical obligations.

Jabès' thought differs symptomatically from Jonas' reasoning. While Jabès starts from the same point, i.e. from the idea of *tzimtzum*, he does not restrict it only to the relation of God and Creation. As abundantly pointed out, Jabès' *tzimtzum* frames the relationship of every author to every work, of the speaker to speech and of things to the linguistically formed world. Consequently, unlike

---

36 BQ I, pp. 241, 272, 273, 275.
37 Hans Jonas, "The Concept of God after Auschwitz: A Jewish Voice," *The Journal of Religion*, 67/1 (January 1987), pp. 1–13, on p. 3.
38 *Ibid.*, pp. 7–9.
39 *Ibid.*, p. 12.

Jonas, Jabès cannot claim that Divine *tzimtzum* has left a space for the human being to act freely in the autonomous Creation. Human activity is human ruin. That is why the human being does not replace God but *repeats God's position*. Indeed, Jabès does not intend to retain the previous ethics after Auschwitz, which Jonas is eager to do. The only ethical position in Jabès is the place of rebellion in the enslavement of all Creation, a protest encapsulated in a simple scream which, devoid of content, mimics the point. An ethical act is to recognise in what way the condition of things – therein of God and the Shoah victims – is repeated in the writerly gesture. An ethical act is to repeat a revolt against the injustice of meaning.[40] The salvation offered by the blind and mangled God means only stepping into the same position and suffering together, which does not save anything except the remonstrance itself.

This brings us to another major difference between Jonas and Jabès. Namely, for Jonas, God as the almighty lord of Creation undoubtedly does not exist *anymore*, but the sphere of ethical responsibility is still there, ceded to man. In this way, Jonas rehearses, to put it in very broad lines, philosophy's fundamental gesture ever since Descartes, that is, putting man in the place previously occupied by God. The Shoah does not alter this mechanism; more than that, it even inclines Jonas to rely on this mechanism. Jonas assumes thereby that *signs of God's action or inaction are directly correlated with his existence or non-existence*. God did not intervene in Auschwitz, *ergo*, he does not exist (at least not in his previous form). This perfectly illustrates the ontotheological structure of philosophy, to use Heidegger's terminology: God is a being which is the centre of ethical law-giving and of law enactment. God is *ex officio* obligated to act ethically, and if he does not do so, he does not exist. At its core, Jonas' reasoning retains the God of ontotheology and only negatively assesses the existence of this God. Moreover, it presupposes that *God and the place of his potential action are located in the same space; hence, God's non-existence can be inferred from his inaction*. Whether God exists or not, reality is subject to the same laws, and God's existence or non-existence has exactly the same impact on each of its places. This shows that Jonas does not offer any deep re-examination of the idea of *tzimtzum* on which he builds because God's withdrawal is only a cloak hiding reflection on reality still conceived as one whole.

Jabès thinks differently: *in Auschwitz reality is revealed in its truth to which God's existence or non-existence is irrelevant*. This idea is far more devastating

---

40 This rebellion reverberates with Améry's claim that dignity can be regained only if fear is re-forged into anger. Améry, *Mind's Limits*, p. 100.

than atheism of ontotheology. *God can even exist but this does not change any-thing.* Auschwitz is a place which, like in Kafka's parables, is too remote for God's power to reach it. If God did not intervene, it might be not because he does not exist but because reality is so fragmented that *at some places God's existence is entirely inconsequential.* It does not entail any expectations of intervention while God's ethical injunctions to man become simply negligible. The Shoah just shows the limit of meaning, and if God expresses himself through meaning and acts meaningfully, the very medium he purportedly uses lets him down. In other words, in Jabès, God is weak not because he has no power to enact an ethical duty, but because the ethical behest itself is erased and becomes undecidable. For this reason, the role of ethics can be assumed only by a powerless, inarticulate scream of protest, which dies out in the opaque world.[41]

Drawing on Gadamer, Cezary Wodziński observes that, in Celan's works, the poem is to speak for the Other so as to let the Other speak on his own behalf.[42] Jabès' writer speaks for all things, including God. Actually, all the things excluded by language speak in the same voice on their own behalf and, at the same time, on behalf of them all. In the passage quoted above, God can save Sarah because he is deaf, mute and mutilated: his powerlessness speaks for her powerlessness. Such speech is an ontological relationship, a relationship of the infinite to the singular. The writer, who has his real voice, is only a special instance of such relationship. In this way, things that have stopped at the threshold of being and all express this fact in and through their position come to form a unique *communio infirmorum.* The writer, in turn, whose position is slightly more privi-leged because of the possibility to write things down, can use that which causes exclusion – i.e. language – to speak for things. His situation is, thus, liminal: he is still within language but seeks to come as close as possible to the world of equal and mute things.

Thus, Jabès makes himself part of post-war French thought – epitomised by Lyotard, Blanchot and Derrida – which responded to the Shoah by mobilising

---

41 In a sense, Jabès has more in common with Buber, who thought that though after Auschwitz "one might still believe in a God who permitted the Shoah to happen," one could no longer hear God's words or sustain "an I-Thou relationship with Him." The new God does not resemble the old one anymore, and his change is historical, which means that Auschwitz did not show what God *has always been like* but revealed *what he has become like.* Tamra Wright, "Self, Other, Text, God: Th Dialogical Thought of Martin Buber," in *Cambridge Companion*, pp. 102–21, on pp. 115–6.

42 Cezary Wodziński, *Kairos. Konferencja w Todtnaubergu. Celan – Heidegger* (Gdańsk: slowo/obraz terytoria, 2010), p. 56.

the motifs of passivity, enduring and indistinction, indebted to Heideggerian *Gelassenheit* (and, by extension, to its source in Meister Eckhart's *Gelazenheit*).[43] The Shoah reveals God's silence so radically that it turns silence itself into a scream, as David Patterson insists.[44] According to Patterson,[45] Jabès views the Shoah as an irreparable rupture which founds a new history. In his silence, God speaks henceforth against his will, for the memory of the Shoah creates a new context in which silence, inaudible as it is, becomes obtrusive. In continuing writing, in "resolve to survive," the Jabèsian writer-and-Jew's apparent duty is to *continue marking in order to prevent the silence of God's speechlessness from ever sliding into oblivion.*

Given the above, the idea Gadamer formulated in his meditations on Celan's poetry is applicable also to Jabès: the poem is a cosmic event.[46] The poetic word does not rely on rhetoric, and it does not use metaphors.[47] Nor is it an allegory because it does not stand for anything else: it is just "itself,"[48] as Gadamer claims. In Jabès, the materiality of the word is embodied in the point that divides silence from muteness; in this way, the anchoring which makes silence visible is always sustained. Consequently, Jabès' work boasts ontological relevance as, in its moment, it embodies the forever repeating drama of universal *tzimtzum*. This final point, beyond metaphor and colloquial language, is *the ultimate way of expressing Auschwitz and a testimony to the impossibility of speaking about the Shoah.*

No doubt, it would be precious to know whether this channel of commemorating the Shoah is not, by any chance, just another of the many modern delusions and whether the simplification at which it aims is not, by any chance, one of the enemy's weapons at the same time.

---

43 Chaouat, "Forty Years," p. 55.
44 David Patterson, "Through the Eyes of Those Who Were There," *Holocaust and Genocide Studies*, 18/2 (Fall 2004), pp. 274–90, on p. 277.
45 *Ibid.*
46 Hans-Georg Gadamer, *Gadamer on Celan: "Who Am I and Who Are You" and Other Essays*, trans. and eds. Richard Heinemann and Bruce Krajewski (Albany: State University of New York Press, 1997), p. 121
47 *Ibid.*, p. 130.
48 *Ibid.*

Anti-Semitism as the Rule of the Name

Jabès' reflection on the Shoah is closely intertwined with his scrutiny of anti-Semitism. Like Celan, Jabès keeps an eye on displays of the hatred of Jews after the Shoahm a hatred which persists, albeit in less manifest forms. Jabès was haunted by a fundamental question: Why was it the Jews that fell victim to such a terrifyingly tenacious discourse – an entire system of beliefs, prejudice, associations and labels?

> Because I was exiled due my Jewish origin, the Carpentras event and its likes always make me ask anew: What does it mean to be a Jew? What does it mean that the Jew will never escape another's hatred?
> [...] It is as the moment came when the Jew is no longer perceived as anything else but a Jew. You may repeat in vain: "I am this and that, I have done this and that, I am a university professor, I am a writer, I am an engineer"; in response you will hear: "No, you are a Jew!" You are perceived only as a Jew and attacked – in the name of what? No idea. This is anti-Semitic discourse.[49]

What is most perplexing to Jabès in anti-Semitic discourse is its absolute reduction of complexity. Differences that add up to a person's individual way of being in the social space are discarded for one simple criterion – being a Jew. All *content* of human features is obscured by this act of naming. The word used in it subsumes all other labels, which Jabès himself experienced in post-war Egypt, when a campaign against "Zionists" mutated into an open witch-hunt against Jews.[50] Moreover, as Jabès suggests, the most mysterious thing about anti-Semitism is the fact that the content of the "Jew" label (which this discourse associates with various properties after all) is less important than *the very act of designation*. There is no telling in the name of what the Jew is attacked, Jabès observes: essentially, he is attacked in the name of the very name "Jew." While a human being is reduced to this word, inexplicable aggression is unleashed. Anti-Semitic discourse, as Jabès sees it, is the cause of violence, and as long as it continues – and not much changes in this matter – violence can return. Commenting on the calamity in Carpentras, the poet writes in *The Book of Hospitality*:

> After the defacement of the Jewish cemetery in Carpentras, silence followed; what else could happen? But this disgraceful, repulsive act is always only a logical and predictable consequence of the discourse, of a series of discourses sustained skilfully and cunningly, handed over, bolstered, sometimes condemned by some, but most of the time tolerated

49 EEJ pp. 66–7.
50 Auster, "Interview," p. 11.

by the majority in the name of the freedom of speech, which a democratic country grants to its citizens.
Anti-Semitic discourse – the oldest of them all –.[51]

To Jabès, anti-Semitism is a blueprint of all racist speech. As such, it represents a peculiar rule of the word – or word cluster – over human life. It is a way of doing things with words which Austin failed to include in his typology of speech acts. What are ostensibly not all too dangerous acts of elocution disseminate and consolidate latently only to erupt at an unexpected moment and provoke very tangible action. Jabès obsessively dwells on the silence that follows anti-Semitic acts and their more or less nominal condemnation. A newspaper lives one day, he concludes,[52] and then memory is wiped out. All the while, anti-Semitic discourse goes on underground, in its peculiar memory, in its doggedness to reiterate the same associations and resume the same patterns of action. And, briefly after coming to France, Jabès sees the following words on the wall:

MORT AUX JUIFS
[…] scrawled in white chalk, in caps.
In which street? In several streets on several walls.
[…] at each halt, at each corner…[53]

Jabès repeatedly reminds that anti-Semitic acts of violence are usually preceded by *writing*: writing which is public but anonymous and unsigned. A more vivid example of the written word that heralds and brings death is difficult to find. Communication in speech is broken, details of the individual's life are obliterated, and only a bare act of naming remains in total silence, which all the more emphasises that writing has taken place. From there, there is only a path to violence, which also takes place in silence, and even if it happens in speech, this speech is empty and purely instrumental, serving the perpetration of the crime. At this moment, Jabès, who devoted much of his work to exploring the writer-language relationship, cannot possibly fail to link this reduction-to-one-name to his other insights.

To discuss this link, we should first describe briefly Jabès' idea of the name:

In the first volume of *The Book of Questions* I say: "The world exists because the book exists." This is so because in order for something to exist it has to be named. Naming precedes us. It is therefore first of all this naming which I wanted to recover; a naming

---

51 LH, p. 34.
52 *Ibid.*, p. 33.
53 BQ I, p. 52.

which is only the becoming conscious of what is or will be; which has therefore preceded the thing and which will subjugate the universe.[54]

Naming means entering language and, consequently, also the language-shaped world; it means finding in language the word that is most one's "own," the place that is most one's "own," where, however, the contradiction between the named and its language form culminates. Like entering Kant's causal series, naming makes a thing part of the language order, renders it visible and gives its existence in the meaningful world. In this sense, naming determines the form and the fate of the thing turned object. Besides, as Jabès insightfully notices, the name is a place where a thing can "become conscious of what is or will be." This thought can suggest that in the act of naming, a thing, a human being *in particular*, is empowered to recognise the position it has been granted in language, which will also weigh on its future.

The role of naming is analogous here to Schelling's idea of "primordial choice," which predetermines human freedom without, however, being in contradiction with it.[55] Jabès seeks to grasp this primordial act in which a fundamental onto-logical decision about the form of a thing in language is made. At this point, we should recall our conclusions about human life being inscribed in the symbolic order, which is represented in Jabès' "premature birth." The poet uses another reference for a similar effect: his name is already in the Bible. The town of Jabèsh in Gilead ("Jabès" in the French translation) features, for example in the Shoftim (the Book of Judges). Referring to this, Jabès says that "the Jew does not quote the book; he is quoted by the book," which means that the name precedes and determines his existence.[56]

"It is thus simultaneously true," writes Derrida about the Jabèsian idea of naming – "that things come into existence and lose existence by being named."[57] Standing for a thing, the name replaces and, at the same time, excludes it. Rene Major observes:

> Giving itself, the name at the same time holds itself back. The name belongs equally to the one that gives it and to the one that bears it. To the one it entrusts with watching and to the one it watches; but the name itself guards itself against the one that gives it and

---

54 DB, p. 84.

55 See Friedrich Wilhelm Joseph Schelling, *Philosophical Inquiries into the Nature of Human Freedom*, trans. James Gutmann (La Salle, IL: Open Court, 1992 [1936]).

56 See Stephane Barsacq, "Dans la double dépendance du nom," *Europe*, 954 (Octobre 2008), pp. 277–9.

57 Derrida, *Writing*, p. 86.

the one that receives it. [...] The name evades the one that gives it and the one that bears it. It preserves the presence of the one and the other in their absence. Beyond death. Beyond erasure.[58]

God's Name is a paradigmatic example of the name. Because he exists in the Creation only as absence, his Name is absence at the extreme of its intensity. Franke argues:

> The Jewish God's uncompromising transcendence renders him absent from the world and especially from the *word* in which he is revealed but at the same time concealed. The word remains as a trace of God's withdrawal from the world. The withdrawing of God is the precondition for the existence of anything else. Otherwise God is all in all, and existence is saturated by his being alone. The word makes a beginning, interrupts eternity, and in so doing marks an absence of God by opening up a gap in His eternal presence.[59]

Having established this, we can return to anti-Semitism. Its manifestation *reveals the bare act of naming, which is the precondition of language.* Hence the reduction of complexity in which a human being is stripped down to a bare name. The anti-Semite believes that, it this way, he captures this human being's hidden essence, makes him fully present and reveals the "truth." But he finds nothing except a bare, meaningless name which is directly bound to what this name excludes. The void of naming is revealed in the alleged source of presence, and the one created and, at the same time, excluded by one's name, appears in the absence. That is why Jabès views anti-Semitism as re-enacting the primal gesture of violence that is naming.

What is more, anti-Semitism is a matrix of similar racist discourses because it turns against the Jews as representing the universal message of God's withdrawal and exclusion in the word.

> "If [the word] JEW could suddenly be spelled JEWE or JOU, perhaps the persecution would stop" [...] "We would be doubly persecuted" [...]: "in our alliance with the word and in its madness. God expunged the Name so it should never expunge us." [...] "In the permanence of this word lies our permanence, guarded by its letters graven into the infinite absence of the four divine letters."[60]

In Chapter Seven, I discussed the idea of the primal, non-absorbable trace that constitutes the Jewish community. At this point, we can elaborate on Jabès' vision. The trace is not exhausted in the use of a particular word. Because the trace

58 René Major, "Jabès et l'écriture du nom propre," in *Écrire le livre*, p. 15.
59 William Franke, "Edmond Jabès, or the Endless Self-Emptying of Language in the Name of God," *Literature & Theology*, 22/1 (March 208), pp. 102–17, on p. 104.
60 BR II, p. 46.

is founded on an erasure, it functions just inversely to the word that exists at a given moment. While this word can be simply forgotten or driven away and consequently disappear, memory works differently in the space generated by the trace. *Forgetfulness adds another layer to the trace.* As Judaism is memory based on the trace, memory in anti-Semitic discourse resists any simple erasure. On the contrary, each change of the name feeds this discourse and fuels its obsessions. Like a distorting mirror of Jewish memory, anti-Semitism erupts only to descend into the silence of ostensible oblivion, but in fact it accumulates the reserves of its representations and practices beyond meaning. Those return unexpectedly where no meaningful memory seems to have survived. So, if the word JEW were changed into JEWE, the persecutions borne out of anti-Semitic discourse could escalate. "We would be doubly persecuted: in our alliance with the word and in its madness," concludes Jabès. This can be taken to mean that if the name changed, anti-Semitic discourse would not only hold off the forgetting that the change of name was to effect but also construe *this change itself* as another reason for "tracking down the truth." Jews would thus be persecuted as Jews ("in our alliance with the name") and as those who changed their name in an attempt to push into oblivion the cruel past that has grown into it ("in its madness"). If the name is replenished, the obsession of anti-Semitism is projected on its subsequent versions.[61]

Therefore, if, as mentioned earlier, naming means making absent, erasing and replacing with a word, we can specify that *each act of erasure bolsters the working of the name.* As Judaism (and writing) bears an immense space of material memory, which includes everything lost in meaning, so the name accumulates absence nourished by each subsequent erasure. In this way, the Jews directly experience the mechanism of naming and, in doing so, join God, who creates a place in his Name where absence is concentrated. The letters of the Name, which is an "infinite absence," as the passage above puts it, guard the "permanence of the word": as long as God is wiped out in the name, serving, so to speak, as a paradigm of the name's operations in reality, the Jews are sustained by their word.

Their experiences, however, enable the Jews to apprehend the violence of naming. Just like the writer-and-witness evoked earlier in this Chapter, the Jabèsian Jew persists and bears testimony despite his name. In other words, where a particular meaning seeks to definitively imprison all things subordinated to it, the Jew recalcitrates:

---

61 This is how, "anti-Israeli discourse incrementally grafted itself on anti-Semitic discourse" (LH, p. 36).

"'The number '4,'" he said, "is the number of our ruin. Do not think I am mad. The number '4' equals 2 times 2. It is in the name of such obsolete logic that we are persecuted. For we hold that 2 times 2 equals also 5 or 7, or 9. You only need to consult the commentaries of our sages to verify. Not everything is simple in simplicity. We are hated because we do not enter into simple calculations of mathematics."[62]

The Jew goes toward the Jew who waits for him, pushed by what he thinks is inescapable fate – which is nothing but people's fury to destroy him.

[...] Thought respects words in their integrity, whereas society repudiates the Jews. Society often has as much contempt for thought as for the Jews.

[...] At the beginning, the Nazis sent only useless Jews to the gas chambers. Then even this notion of uselessness vanished: all Jews were to be exterminated.

Perhaps there will come a day when words will destroy words [vocables] for good. There will be a day when poetry will die.

It will be the age of robots and the jailed word.

The misery of the Jews will be universal.[63]

In Jabès, the Jew symbolises an opening – a *possibility* – of truth other than the commonly endorsed one: a freedom of thinking, as well as of poetry, which breaks the closedness of "the jailed word" subordinated to pure utility.

Conclusion: Anti-Semitism and the Modern Depletion

In order to conclude this Chapter, let us address one more issue. Jabès' thought and writing practice, in which the profusion of thought undergoes an utter reduction down to a repeated point, peculiarly parallel the possibility of reducing a human being to the pure name by evacuating all content from it. This affinity helps Jabès understand the phenomenon of anti-Semitism. We could nevertheless argue that instead of trying to understand anti-Semitism by discerning the practice of naming in the process of progressive reduction, it might be better to forgo such thinking and writing at all. By continuing it, we might ask, do we not concede somewhat to the depletion which can turn into the discourse we combat? How does the search for the ultimate, equal, contentless community of things differ from the anti-Semitic reduction? Both mechanisms are, after all, based on the same structure – one I will not hesitate to call modern: the structure of the remnant. Does Jabès' protest not rely, perhaps, on the same power grid that inflames anti-Semitism?

To answer these questions, we must notice that there is no option of choosing any other structure in Jabès' work. *Tzimtzum* and exile are the primary

---

62 BQ I, p. 92.
63 *Ibid.*, pp. 228–9.

conditions of the modern reality. After the Shoah, it is impossible to think otherwise. The only thing reflection can salvage, if at all, is *drawing a dividing line between discourses that seek simplification.* While the reduction process as such cannot be eliminated, it is possible to create within it a discourse that will reclaim the possibility to bear witness and to oppose the violence of language. Below, I will formulate three properties of such discourse which show that there still is an ethical choice in a deserted reality (though "choice" is hardly an apt word, for it is all about protest as instinctive as a scream of a tortured human being).

First, if Jabès strives to arrive at the point, at the last threshold of differentiation, he never stops at it as a conclusion. In continuing to write books, he *circles the point, resisting it and discovering ever new possibilities it organises.* What anti-Semitism and its likes do is performing a reduction and stopping there, taking it for the truth, oblivious to the fact that, when consistently re-thought, the point must overthrow this truth. It is the same blinded truth of "full daylight" that was discussed at the beginning of this Chapter.

For Jabès, the point is not the truth but a place which breaks all truth loose from its enclosure. The point as the basis of differentiation does not divide beings into categories because it *makes possible and, at the same, destabilises this very division.* Besides, the point is immanently linked to rebellion: in Jabès, the singularity and contentlessness of the point are paired with the scream as the most elementary and, simultaneously, all-encompassing sign of protest. Therefore, if anti-Semitism regards the bare act of naming as revelation of the truth, Jabès responds by framing it as the pinnacle of violence: revelation of the truth not about the one that gets named but about the functioning of language as such. Admittedly, anti-Semitism reduces the entire abundance of language to the bare name, but it does not judge this fact. Jabès' response is to reject *the entire language* which has in this way disclosed its essence. That is why Jabès is so resolved to look for a vision of existence liberated from language, a vision of things in their total equality.

Second, the point in Jabès is a *community of all things* while anti-Semitism reduces only a certain group of people to their name. What, across all books, turns out to be a gradual stifling, a levelling, a striving to reach the whiteness of the Book concerns all being. In doing this, Jabès balances on the verge of the highest and most hazardous odds: *his messianism differs from utter nihilism only in the slightest content-difference, which he prevents from fading.* Jabès' writing takes responsibility for all being. The whiteness of the Book is a locus of the complete and ultimate equality, in which things become at the same time utterly alone. Separation is an extreme condition of equality. For this reason, the community of these things means the termination of all violence as none of the things can influence any other one. Yet, as Jabès observes himself, the same kind of community seemed to arise as a result of the most horrible violence modernity has produced. *The difference is only a slight one and resides nowhere else than in the content, but it is perhaps only in this difference – rather than in the decisive mechanism of the remnant – that the boundary lies between ruin and salvation in modernity. And this boundary is what ethical thinking must uphold.*

Third, the Jabèsian point reverberates with all the lost contents and properties and, as such, it gives justice to things while anti-Semitic discourse seeks to reduce only a particular group of people to the name and maintain its own content at their cost.

> [...] To exclude another means to exclude yourself in a way. The rejection of difference leads to negating your fellow human being. Don't people forget that to say "I" is already to utter difference?
>
> [...] racism is only a renewed expression of negation of the human being, of man as such in his abundance and in his infinite poverty.[64]

Anti-Semitic discourse does not try to apprehend that reduction to the pure distinction is also a source of *its own* destabilisation. On the contrary, it seeks to reduce the other to the name in order to remove the other subsequently. Violence triggered by anti-Semitism is, to paraphrase Hegel, the fury of meaning that refuses to acknowledge its own nothingness. Reducing the other to the pure distinction, anti-Semitism desires in fact to erase its own constitutive difference and establish itself as the universally valid meaning. Racism negates the human being "in his infinite abundance and in his infinite poverty," as Jabès writes, emphasising the inseparable coupling of "abundance" and "poverty," which can be given justice only by the community of equal things that are, as already suggested, one thing and a multitude of things at the same time.

To conclude, reflection on the Shoah compels Jabès to recognise that after Auschwitz no other thinking is possible except thinking which has the desolation of reality as its fundamental precondition. Inconsistence in grasping this fact leads to perpetuating the violence of fragmented language and to the rule of blind nothing. To put it briefly: after God's death, maintaining God as a residuum, "an ethical ideal" or "the higher meaning-maker" is far more dangerous than consistent, conscious atheism. Jabès' ethical response is, thus, radicalism that seeks to *unveil nothing everywhere and in every form. But in this effort, radicalism endeavours to save the most elementary ethical difference – a difference in the aim of simplification.* Jabès' thought may bear the same patterns

---

as the thought of his opponent, Heidegger; but, unlike Heidegger, Jabès knows the consequences of simplification and pursues it with an ethical hope. In his radicalism, Jabès is very close to Nietzsche, who views "desertification" as irreversible and effort to resist it as breeding nihilism. In the reality they both depict, a real threat is posed not by the lack of meaning but by the persisting meaning unaware of its unfoundedness. This affinity with Nietzsche suggests to what Jabès owes his radicalism. Even though this radicalism seems to be autonomously derived from Jewish thought, modernity demands to be acknowledged also here.

10 Jabès' Ethics: Repetition, Resemblance and Hospitality

Three notions in the title of this Chapter chart Jabès' ethics, which is, as a matter of fact, closely related to his negative ontology. Nowhere else is Jabès' connection to his contemporary philosophy more conspicuous, with Lévinas' thought reverberating in Jabès' ideas particularly vividly. In this Chapter, I want to address Jabès' ethics – controversial though the term may sound in this context – and to identify its links to modern philosophy.

The three eponymous notions are key concepts which recur throughout Jabès' body of writing, with the latter two featuring in the titles of his books. Basically, they make up an underlying ontological grid on which the Jabès' entire thinking is founded as they map the relations which beings establish (repetition and resemble) or can enter (hospitality) with each other. In the sequence proposed in the title, the notions progress from the groundwork of ontology up to an ethical culmination. Below, I will discuss them in this order to conclude by exploring the possibility of ethics in simplification-seeking modernity.

Repetition

Repetition is the only notion I address here which does not appear in any title of Jabès' books. Sometimes it is admittedly difficult to draw the line between repetition as used by Jabès in its colloquial sense and repetition as charged with idiosyncratic connotations, which gives us a sense of Jabès' distinct take on repetition. Repetition is a consequence of perspectival reality, in which there is no simple connectedness among various perspectives – books, worlds, and so forth. Each perspective has its own meaningful world, without communicating with any other one. Therefore, they are neither different nor similar, for they are separated by discontinuity.

Nonetheless, Jabès does not presuppose an absolute impossibility of two things, two moments or two perspectives convening. This is where the notion of repetition comes into play, supplanting the colloquial concepts of similarity, sameness or identity. Repetition, as defined by Jabès, means that *there arises a being (a thing, a moment, a book) which is shaped by the same structure that has determined another being.* Because this very structure produces conditions of utterability, the structure itself cannot be depicted. Consequently, the instance of repetition cannot be proven because the repeated cannot be possibly brought side by side with the repeating. *Repetition is thus a mutual relationship of different particularities which defy comparison.*

Therefore, the act of repetition is unique and non-comparable with any other one even though it repeats this act. That repetition is taking place cannot be substantiated by anything external to this event. In this regard, the ascertainment of repetition corresponds to Hegel's infinite judgment or Nietzsche's thesis of perspectivism: *within a particularity*, this ascertainment tries to refer to what is outside it and, as such, is by definition impossible. Finally, each act of repetition embodies the repeated structure fully, and, in this respect, it is equal to any other one (even though it obviously cannot be uttered). For this reason, all imaginary depictions of the primordial disaster are mutually equivalent in Jabès, for each of them renders the same structure of unutterability, whatever specific content it may bear. Repetition transcends the same-other opposition ("you are never twice either the same or the other,"[1] writes Jabès in a spontaneous gesture of a-Heraclitism), for this opposition applies to things comparable rather than to things discontinuous.

A suggestive metaphor for repetition often employed by Jabès is the image of concentric circles:

> A circle
> and in the circle another
> circle
> and in the new circle still another
> circle
> and so on
> till the last: a forceful [*assujettissant*] point
> then an invisible point
> unbelievably present,
> majestically absent.[2]

The space in which these circles find themselves is that comprehension-eluding, ultimate space of all places, that is, the Book. To understand the image, we must grasp that the circles never intersect and, as such, never come in touch directly. Each of them is surrounded on both sides by its own blank space, which separates it from other circles. Therefore, each is alone against whiteness. At the same time, they are involved in a relationship, *be it only a*

---

1 LR I, p. 88.
2 BQ II, p. 11.

relationship as perceived from the point of view of that whiteness, which is the only space where no meaningful utterance can be formulated. Relationships among the circles are made possible by what is impossible for them but holds their conditions of possibility. At the same time, each of the circles fully embodies the condition of the circle: its emplacement in the space of the Book, circularity and being surrounded by whiteness, which is its radical beyond.

It is not without reason that Jabès' metaphor relies on circles rather than any other geometrical figure. Having no beginning and no endpoint, the circle is self-enclosed, a property that philosophy has used regularly for multiple purposes. In other words, *within itself*, the circle does not encounter any visible end. Such an end is demarcated only by the whole of the circle against the space which is impossible from the circle's point of view. It is in this space that the circle is finite and duplicates the position of other circles.

The image of circles epitomises Jabès' perspectivism: the relationship of circles is the relationship of perspectives, each of which, though self-enclosed and complete in itself, is finite and particular vis-à-vis the space in which it is located. The perspectives can obviously be identified with Jabès' "books." Circles can have radiuses of various lengths and, consequently, various perimeters; perspectives, likewise, can have more or less content, *but this does not determine their existence as such.* Content establishes the scope of a perspective but does not provide the principle of singularisation, which lies in the radical singularity of everything contained within the space of the Book.

This can be discerned in the central point of all circles. In Jabès' image, they all share the same centre, which lies beyond them all. The reduction of content, i.e. the depletion of perspectives, corresponds in this image to the gradual shortening of the circles' radiuses as they approach the central point. The point is absent, as Jabès says in the passage quoted above, which can be taken to mean that all content disappears in the central point, and the circle (perspective) becomes indistinguishable from the point (the principle of singularisation). This is the reason why *the circle can exist only where it keeps at a distance from its own centre, without overlapping with it.* Hence, the point is at the same time the circle's condition of possibility (and is, in this sense, "unbelievably present") as well as the boundary crossing which the circle ceases to be (and is, thus, "majestically absent"). Since we know that, according to Jabès, "when God wanted to reveal Himself He appeared as a point," we must realise that God is, to him, an absent centre around which all perspectives revolve – a centre which makes them possible and, at the same time, must be inaccessible to them (a "forceful," or as Jabès originally puts it, *"assujettissant"* point, which plays on the double meaning of the French word: "making subject to itself" and "turning into a subject"[3]). Just as the circle must "move away" from its centre to be distinguishable from the point, *God cannot appear within any perspective,*[4] *but must form its invisible centre of gravity outside it.* At the same time, the progressive reduction of perspectives, the depletion of content in writing, helps near the central point, without ever making it possible to reach that point. Therefore, the circle in Jabès, just like the Möbius strip and the Borromean rings in Lacan,[5] serves as the only viable, i.e. material (geometrical), representation of the position of perspectives.

As this image suggests, repetition takes place between the circles (perspectives). I believe that time must be seen as a factor in the arising of circles as it is not for no reason that Jabès talks of "new" circles. They differ in terms of their positions in the Book and, also, in terms of the singularising moments of their formation. Most fascinating is the position of the midmost point, which, contentless and always central, though each time different, *keeps repeating itself.* In Jabès' vision, the point is thus not the centre of stability and self-identity. On the contrary, it is the utmost concentration of distinction, which can be repeated at the same place only because it has no content and is differentiation itself. In Jabès' ontology, a thing can persist in the same place only when it is not stable at all but is just the principle of distinction – the point of indistinguishability

---

3   The double meaning of *assujettissant* has made the term popularly useful. It has been widely employed, particularly by Foucault, where its customary English translation is either subjectifying or subjectivating.

4   At this point, Jabès' thought coincides with the insights in Wittgenstein's *Tractatus*, which is deliberately evoked in *El*. According to Wittgenstein, God does not reveal himself in the world and cannot be an object of meaningful propositions but is a condition of possibility of the world that lies outside him (cf. theses 6.432, 6.41, 6.45). It must be borne in mind, however, that as Jabès develops pluralistic perspectivism, the transcendental boundary, which in Wittgenstein divides one world from its outside, is in Jabès the boundary of each perspective. This pluralism makes possible repetition as conceived by Jabès, and this repetition is the relationship of various Wittgensteinian "worlds" with each other. Obviously, Wittgenstein's philosophy form the *Investigations* period also expresses such pluralism though it abandons the *Tractatus* ontology. It can be posited that in some of his insights (e.g. in his reflection on the point), Jabès offers a pluralistic equivalent of the *Tractatus* philosophy: a kind of *Investigations*, which explores the forever repeating (rather than one) transcendental boundary, instead of examining colloquial language.

5   Cf. Jacques Lacan, *The Seminar, Book X: Anxiety* (1962–63), trans. Cormac Galligher; *The Seminar, Book XXIII: Joyce and the Sinthome* (1975–76), trans. Cormac Galligher, http://www.lacaininireland.com/web/published-works/seminars/.

between the present and the absent.[6] This corroborates the insights of Jabès' negative theology as discussed in Chapter Five.

Because perspectives repeat each other, every act of creation is a repetition of God's primary act:

> Repetition is man's power to perpetuate himself in God's supreme speculations. To repeat the divine act in its First Cause. Thus man is God's equal in his power to choose an unpredictable word which he alone can launch. I obey slavishly. I am master of the metamorphoses. Adventure is a property of words.[7]

The specificity of repetition makes the human act of creation free (in that it has its own unique place) and "slavishly obedient" to the First Cause, at the same time. Counterintuitively, the two properties, rather than being contradictory, are each other's perfect equivalents in Jabès' ontology. Repetition is both the performance of *the same* act, as it fully embodies the same structure, as well as its *subsequent* iteration from the point of view of the Book.

In Jabès' texts, repetition serves also as a prerequisite of creative practice. For if all creation is doomed to follow the same process of fall, it should also be doomed to cease when confronted with the past. However, exactly due to repetition, every act of creation has its own radically particular place, where it cannot be related to what has already happened. While two adjacent beings can be similar in a common way, in Jabèsian repetition the repeated and the repeating must be divided by destruction. In this way, Moses' Second Tables repeat the first – Divine – ones and are possible only when the former have already been shattered.[8] Each human book has the power to repeat God's book because God's book has failed. Thus, Jabès can insist that "repetition is our subversive way, for it moves by an inborn need to destroy and be destroyed."[9] Repetition is thus the principle of coming into being and perishing. Unlike in the principle of identity, that which comes into being through repetition has its structure inscribed in the material memory of the worlds which have already perished, making repetition possible, and appears within the horizon of its own perishment. As such, repetition can be considered a negative equivalent of the identity principle in Jabès' nothing-based perspectivism.

---

6   In crossing the principle of identity, Jabès follows the Kabbalistic tradition in an attempt, as Marc-Alain Ouaknin insists, to think and practice a "beyond" of the identity principle. Ouaknin, *Concerto*, p. 28.

7   BQ, p. 328.

8   Cf. PHD, p. 117.

9   *Ibid.*, p. 88.

It is also due to repetition that Creation perpetually goes on rather than remaining locked it its once-shaped being. As Jabès writes: "The Origin is All.
Nothing is not invented. All and nothing are repeated. O miracle of repetition –
a regular escape to All, a passionate return to the origin."[10] Repetition makes it
possible to experience originariness here and now only because the origin has
already been destroyed. Repetition re-opens the process leading to creation and
"is a chance for continual change."[11] Clearly, Jabès shares some of Benjamin's
ideas, who similarly described the process of recalling and salvaging the past,
including the notion of the origin which is ahead of rather than behind us. By
repeating, we do not imitate but *take the same place* that the repeated has occupied and, as such, we reclaim also all the possibilities it has had.

A fitting conclusion to the discussion of Jabèsian repetition is found in
Derrida's remarks on repetition in "Ellipsis." Derrida states that repetition
removes the centre and identity of the origin.[12] Repetition (return to the book,
in Derrida's essay) is elliptical in the double sense of the word as a geometrical
figure and a literary device:

> Something invisible is missing in the grammar of this repetition. As this lack is invisible
> and undeterminable, as it completely redoubles and consecrates the book, once more
> passing through each point along its circuit, nothing has budged. And yet all meaning
> is altered by this lack. Repeated, the same line is no longer exactly the same, the ring
> no longer has exactly the same centre, *the origin has played*. Something is missing that
> would make the circle perfect.[13]

Repetition is based on the ellipsis because the repeated must remain "invisible
and undeterminable." In Derrida, repetition is symbolised by the ellipsis rather
than by the circle to emphasise that, in repetition, the beginning of the circle
must be displaced. The imageries used by Jabès and Derrida differ only ostensibly. Admittedly, Jabès adheres to the image of concentric circles in order to
institute at their middle a point, a centre of presence/absence, God that every
circle refers to. Nonetheless, such a relation could solely be visible in the inaccessible space of the Book. Because we have only the script, which in its continuity
passes from one circle to another, in our actually experienced reality we indeed

---

10 *Ibid.*, p. 117.
11 *Ibid.*
12 Jacques Derrida, *Writing*, p. 374.
13 *Ibid.*, p. 373.

encounter the ellipsis, as suggested by Derrida.[14] The image of concentric circles and God's point would only be its representation. Finally, repetition has an unignorable ethical dimension to it. Unlike any form of the identity principle, repetition discriminates rather than uniformises, and it indicates loss instead of replacing the lost with a mock-up of the past. Repetition helps think something without abolishing the difference between the "object" and the thinker. It establishes their community and, in doing so, gives elementary justice to that which is. Jabès' ethics is oriented on things rather than on people alone, and repetition unites in protest against the unstoppable disaster of creation.

Resemblance

The idea of resemblance is a recurrent theme in Jabès, particularly in his middle and late periods, serving as the overarching concept of *The Book of Resemblances* series. Rather than a fixed concept, resemblance accumulates findings of ongoing explorations around a certain primary idea. Apparently, resemblance is a notion that serves to *examine the relationship of beings in a repetition-based reality*. As it is difficult to distinguish resemblance from repetition, I would draw the following line between them: while repetition is an act, an event, *resemblance designates relationships between the repeated and the repeating*. Jabès talks of resemblance only after he has shown in his previous books that similarity, in its colloquial sense, is impossible as it stumbles over ontological obstacles.[15] Having developed

---

14 It is difficult to ascertain in how far the opposition of Jabès' circle and Derrida's ellipsis actually separates the two concepts. In my reading, a conflict between them can be avoided. However, Derrida insists on eliminating the concept of the "centre" and on going beyond absence and presence. At the same time, Jabès, as frequently emphasised, believes that thinking, be it only imaginary thinking, of the centre of absence is necessary. In *Yaël* he writes: "Even absence needs a centre" (BQ II, p. 83). As this is the centre of nothing, and hence an empty, inaccessible point of permanent displacement, this concept produces similar effects to the consistent elimination of the idea of the centre. Derrida himself is anyway also haunted by the spectre of the centre. The centre disappears only where reality is entirely aleatory, as in Deleuze's thought. That is why the differences between Jabès and Derrida are certainly less significant than their difference from Deleuze.

15 Jabès seems to address similarity as colloquially understood in the following passage: "Nothing does not resemble nothing: the likeness of the world and God is the likeness of All and Nothing" (LR I, p. 114). And further: "God is dissimilarity at the heart of everything similar to Him" (*Ibid.*, p. 115). The separateness of fragmented things excludes their similarity in the first place; each thing is autonomous and

the idea of repetition and an awareness of discontinuity that divides beings, he revisits the concept of resemblance the meaning of which differs totally from the colloquial one. Discussing resemblance in Jabès, we must remember that resemblance is a wish, a hope for repeating something radically different in order make contact with it:

[…] every time I am similar to the other [à un autre].
[…] Likeness operates on the level of faith.
[…] There is no [il n'y a point] book outside its likeness to the book when faith is lacking.
[…] Any book is but a dim likeness of the lost book.
[…] In the beginning was the word that wanted to resemble.
[…] All creation is an achievement of likeness, is the act through which it risks asserting itself.[16]

To understand these passages, we could usefully recall Jabès' observation that "repetition is the power of resemblance."[17] Thus, though resemblance is based on repetition, it is also something more than just repetition. This seems to be associated with the fact that *resemblance is the only mechanism of establishing bonds between beings in fragmented reality*. Because repetition can be neither shown nor proven – after all, it is grounded in the impossible – resemblance is a form of faith. Resemblance means believing that there is indeed a repetition-based connection, for example, between two books. What is more, this faith not so much concerns relationships between the already existing beings as rather underpins the coming-into-being of that which is repeated, providing, so to speak, a protective horizon for the emergence of beings.

Resemblance is a wish to make repetition a reality, a wish that enables repetition to take place. "All creation is an achievement of likeness," claims Jabès, adding that there is no book outside its likeness and faith. It was in this way,

---

non-comparable. Ignorance of this and insistence on the common notion of similarity are as dangerous as ignorance of the role of Nothing discussed in the previous Chapter. Jabès mentions that people's faces are evaluated only in terms of similarity: it is the only possible, and simultaneously mistaken, approach. Polemicising in a way with Lévinas' idea of the Other's unique face which triggers ethical responsibility, Jabès views the face rather as the source of hurtful inferences made by people who fail to notice that similarity is a meagre basis of conclusion-drawing. The Jews, he adds, have suffered much because of this (DEJ, pp. 307–308).

16 LR I, pp. 9, 29, 30, 49, 50 (except the first line, in Jabès, "From *The Book of Resemblances*," pp. 15, 20, 21).

17 *Ibid.*, p. 75.

as Jabès himself asserts, that *The Book of Resemblances* came into being out of its conscious similarity to *The Book of Questions*.[18] Celan might have had the same thing in mind when he spoke of the poem which "attempts to gain a direction"[19] toward an object, without fusing with it. In Jabès, however, it is not only about making a new book[20]: since all being means "being-continually-created" ("keeping alive the fire of creation"), resemblance forms the horizon of everything that happens in its being.

Though there is no connectedness among beings, each of them in its solitude can direct itself towards another one, and this faith-underpinned direction-taking can be referred to as resemblance. Resemblance, thus, wrests a being out of its solitude (though only in an imaginary way, perhaps) and is the only bond that has survived the catastrophe. Because beings, in their solitude, direct themselves towards each other, their peculiar solidarity is produced as they establish relationships through resemblance.

> To resemble . . . does not mean to become the other but to let the other be you, to some extent. It means to perish doubly within him and doubly live his death through one subjective bond.[21]

Resembling, taking shape as somebody that resembles, does not entail "becoming the other" because repetition precludes retaining or copying identity in time. Rather, it makes it possible to shape one's being as a repetition of the other's being towards which one turns. In this sense, resembling enables the other to become me. Admittedly, I perish and survive once only, but directing myself in resemblance to another being, I can – *through a subjective bond* – embody two deaths and two survivals.

---

18 DB, p. 113.

19 Paul Celan, "Speech on the Occasion of Receiving the Literature of the Free Hanseatic City of Bremen," in *Selected Poems and Prose of Paul Celan*, trans. John Felstiner (New York and London: W.W. Norton, 2001), p. 396.

20 In writing, resemblance is, however, very strongly visible. In Jabès, it is additionally associated with the fact that the writer does not have his "own" words or letters but uses the already existing ones. As such, although he creates his books anew, he must constantly refer to what has been written before. The drive to create his own book, which severs him from the past, produces a discontinuity through which resemblance can take place. Jabès emphasises this reasoning by a play on words: the writer is a gatherer – a re-assembler – of words (*rassembleur*), and as such, he is doomed to resemblance (*ressemblance*). Cf. PHD, p. 120.

21 BR II, p. 14.

Unmistakably, Jabès merges the ontological and the ethical in his concept of resemblance. It is a far more radical step than Lévinas' gesture of replacing ontology with ethics as first philosophy, which was, in a degree, just a reversal of the previous order. *In Jabès, ethics is not an injunction but rather a pursuit of beings which is formed alongside their ontological coming-into-being within dispersed reality.* Jabès seems to dismantle the established hierarchies of ontological and ethical argumentation in order to show the primordial level of happening/enowning, where ontology is entirely inseparable from ethics. If Lévinas endeavoured to respond to Heidegger by giving ethics precedence over ontology, Jabès – who thinks at the same level as Heidegger – finds ethical components in Heidegger's thought. Clearly, an ethical command is missing here, even in the form demanded by Lévinas. Jabès was always sceptical about the Lévinasian idea of responsibility for the other[22] though, basically speaking, he should have shared the vision of an ethical impulse produced by the other's existence alone. Yet Jabès' ontologised ethics focuses rather on underscoring resemblance to the other, in solitude that nonetheless endures. This vision is closer to Blanchot's *communauté inavouable*, a community in which the dying other is accompanied, but his loneliness, rather than reduced, is just repeated in the bystander's loneliness:

"You will resemble the dead in the moment of dying," said reb Maalad. "In the end, you will take on a likeness to all exhausted likenesses."[23]

But, in Jabès, resemblance is not limited to the community of the dying (or community with the dying other, as in Blanchot), which is only a particular case of the ontological relationship among beings. Awarded no distinguished position, the human is simply one of the things that arise, repeat and resemble just as other ones do. It is not a coincidence that the sentence which opens the analysis of Creation in Chapter Three – "We are all equal before language" – is to be found nowhere else than in *The Book of Resemblances*. This language, taken to be the fundamental structure of reality, determines relationships of all things, including the human being. What is more, Jabès apparently presupposes that it is the recognition of one's resemblance to and equality with things that produces a truly ethical community. Resemblance is what "is at the same time identical,"

---

22 Also this issue fell victim to the academic, philosophical and literary fight between Judaism and (Greek) Christianity. In his conversations with Marcel Cohen, Jabès doubts whether the idea of total responsibility for the other was not more Christian than Jewish (EEJ, p. 73). Jabès himself was sceptical about this kind of responsibility as an unviable illusion. His ethics is far more anti-humanistic and a-humanistic.

23 LR I, p. 118.

"something unknown laid over the known,"[24] he observes. In resemblance, we are most ourselves and, at the same time, transcend ourselves most. Even though the structure of fragmented reality prevents us from giving an account of the "unknown," by *distancing ourselves from the known in the representation*, we can turn towards the unknown. In this way, resemblance seems to guarantee respect for all beings in their separateness and ensure elimination of violence. Emphatically, this must be a resemblance that is aware of the solitude of beings, which it ventures to override, rather than a blind resemblance that takes itself to be the basis of sameness.

Having elucidated the ethical dimension of resemblance, let us focus on its structure. According to Jabès, resemblance is possible where separate beings exist, and that means in time. Time pushes things similar apart and, consequently, "future guarantees resemblance."[25] Because there is no continuity in time, nothing is identical with itself. Resemblance is possible where identity is precluded:

> Where resemblance appears everything is shifted apart [*décalé*]: being is not being, things are not things, the book is not the book.[26]

However, while in the real time beings are disjoined, resemblance – like Benjamin's "flash of recognition" – produces an unexpected connection across time that has passed. As resemblance itself is a matter of faith, it does not remove the real time but, instead, breeds a subjective feeling of reproducing the moment when the similar existed. This feeling is called by Jabès "the time of resemblance":

> Resemblance is a brief harmony [*accord*] of the infinite. You resemble him that resembles you, the time of resemblance.
> There is no eternal image.
> The eternity of God is the absence of image.[27]

Resemblance seems to suspend for a moment the fragmentation of reality and the discontinuity of time, binding two moments and two beings. Their separateness is not abolished, and they cannot be said to be *one and the same thing*. Resemblance presupposes that A is similar to B, and B to A and, as such, *in the*

---

24 DB, p. 113.
25 LR I, p. 88.
26 *Ibid.*, p. 104.
27 *Ibid.*, p. 95.

very structure of this depiction it presupposes two separate beings. Besides, it is not a reciprocal relationship.[28]

In this respect, Jabès endorses Wittgenstein's idea of "family resemblances."[29] In this concept, resemblance is not derivable from the common features several beings share but is a relation that precedes them: A is in a degree similar to B, B in another degree to C, and so forth. It is not the plane of properties that produces resemblances of beings; if it were so, they would be derivative constructs. Resemblance can be seen only in a concrete juxtaposition of beings whose autonomy is not reducible to a set of properties. Similarly, Jabès states:

> "The Jew is the Jew," he said, "because he is similar to the Jew. He is because he resembles...; but the one he resembles does not exist by himself but because he resembles... He is only his resemblance to another [un autre], to the other [l'autre]."[30]

In Jabès, Wittgenstein's insight is bolstered by the ontological assumption that there is no available plane on which to juxtapose beings in the first place. Resemblance does not follow from commonly shared features; more than that, *resemblance cannot be even perceived in the comparison of beings, and it is revealed only in one of them choosing direction towards other ones.* Resemblance is an ungraspable, residual bond of discrete beings.

In this way, the elusive "time of resemblance" comes into being. While Jabès contrasts its fleeting nature with the "eternity of the image," he underscores that there is no eternal image. This can be construed as ruling out the possibility of stable and comparable features which guarantee similarity in the colloquial sense of the term. "The eternity of is the absence of image," adds Jabès, which is understandable if we remember that God is a point in which repetition and contentlessness reach their pinnacle. Unlike identity in the metaphysics of presence, resemblance cannot thus be permanent. Instead, it is a momentary "harmony of the infinite." Celan seems to have expressed the same insight when he wrote about the poem which "lays claim to infinity" and "seeks to reach through time."[31] This is just a small step away from Benjamin's idea of "the time of the now":

> History is the subject of a structure whose site is not homogeneous, empty time, but time filled by the presence of the now [*Jetztzeit*]. Thus, to Robespierre ancient Rome

---

28 Cf. *Ibid.*, p. 115. "You can be similar to God, but God is not similar to anything" and, as such, he is again the centre of "non-reciprocity" of the relation.

29 Ludwig Wittgenstein, *Philosophical Investigations*, trans. G.E.M. Anscombe (Oxford: Basil Blackwell, 1986), § 65–67.

30 LR I, p. 106.

31 Celan, "Speech," p. 396.

was a past charged with the time of the now which he blasted out of the continuum of history. The French Revolution viewed itself as Rome reincarnated. It evoked ancient Rome the way fashion evokes costumes of the past. Fashion has a flair for the topical, no matter where it stirs in the thickets of long ago; it is a tiger's leap into the past. This jump, however, takes place in an arena where the ruling class gives the commands. The same leap in the open air of history is the dialectical one, which is how Marx understood revolution.[32]

To Benjamin, time is discontinuous, which is obscured by the structure of history. There are moments, however, when the continuum of history is "blasted," and the past moments, no longer positioned in "empty, homogeneous time," are manifest in their "now-time." The present performs a dialectical "tiger's leap" into the past to reproduce it as the present.

Jabèsian repetition is underpinned by the same structural principle. His starting point is discontinuity in time, from which hollowness of all constructions of history results. What follows is that beings have neither identities nor a plane on which to be compared. Nevertheless, a being can direct itself towards another one, analogously to the French Revolution, which – in Benjamin's account – turned to ancient Rome. While in Benjamin, the past appears as the present in the moment of "the dialectical leap," in Jabès, the moment of recognition of resemblance is "the time of resemblance" – "harmony of the infinite" – and a fusion of two separated moments. Paradoxically, only one of the beings recognises its resemblance to another one; there is no "objective" resemblance. But only in this way is connectedness possible between beings set apart by discontinuous time.

Concluding our analysis of resemblance, we should add that the search for resemblance amounts, in Jabès, to wandering, which is inseparably bound up with exile in the desert of reality:

"Our resemblances [*ressemblances*] are gathered remnants [*rassembles*] of infinite, arid memory," he said.
The city humiliates the face, obliterates resemblances.
The desert gives us back our forgotten traits.
[…] Wandering is a restless search for resemblance within the impossible resemblance to God, to self.
"Wandering," he said "were nothing else than an attempt to re-create the face cut into pieces by absence."[33]

---

32 Benjamin, "Theses," p. 261.
33 LR I, p. 63.

Resemblance can be seen where one recognises discontinuity separating entities, not where they are treated as beings: that is why the desert is a privilege place of recognising resemblances. All resemblances converge in the endpoint of absence:

> There are degrees – sometimes imperceptible – in resemblance.
> Look at the resemblance of white to white, likewise of white to ideally white, and of the absent book to the book of all our absences.[34]
> All paths lead into the night, a place where all resemblance is abandoned [...].[35]

Resemblances, thus, have their degrees and head towards the central point of absence, which is devoid of content and, as such, demarcates the limit to resemblances. For it can be said that everything is similar there (no longer differing in content) and, at the same time, dissimilar in the highest degree (being a pure repetition). In this sense, Jabès talks in the passage quoted above of God's utter dissimilarity from himself.

There is a terrifying equivalent of this divine point in the human world:

> "In the Nazi camps [...] the resemblance of barely living beings reached – o daylight of crime! – its zenith."[36]

In the camp, the human is his bare form to which he has been reduced by uttermost violence. Nowhere else is he more degraded and, simultaneously, more equal with other people and closer, in his condition, to God. The idea of resemblance meets its *ne plus ultra* here. The ultimate community has been established in the most ruthless way imaginable. Resemblance is here the movement of extreme simplification, which haunts Jabès' writing in so many equivalent forms. It can be the worst of evils, as it is in the just described context, or it can be a voluntary community of the equal – of equal people and equal things – in the ultimate renunciation of violence. Can the ultimate depletion bear a positive ethical value? The answer to this question is associated with the last of the poet's three ethico-ontological concepts, a notion to which he devoted his last book.

Hospitality

It is no coincidence that Jabès erects his last book upon the concept of hospitality. Each book ending is, in him, a play with the end and with the community

---

34 PHD, p. 121.
35 LR I, p. 79.
36 *Ibid.*, p. 65.

of equal things – that is, with the void of the whiteness of the Book. In *The Book of Hospitality*, which was meant to be his last work, Jabès summons the lustre of everything he has written so far in order to fashion a space of the white for his books and for himself. Motte writes:

> *Le Livre de l'hospitalité* as a whole displays a recapitulative strategy embracing a broad variety of the preoccupations that impelled Edmond Jabès' work over the years. Meditations on death, cast in the light of its imminence, color the volume from first page to last. […] Yet despite its elegiac tone and retrospective stance, *Le Livre de l'hospitalité* also testifies to a powerful and ongoing engagement in the world, one that is far more explicit than anything to be found in the texts that precede it.
>
> […] *Le Livre de l'hospitalité*, I believe, attempts to perform the same connective gesture [As • (*El*) with regard to *The Book of Questions*] with regard to Jabès' work as a whole, adumbrating dialogical relations between his books and the cycles in which they figure, suturing various thematics together in compelling ways, as the poet takes stock of his writings as an oeuvre […].It is a powerfully potential moment for him, one where speech and silence, desire and duty, thought and deed might be reconciled, however tenuously […].[37]

Thus, *The Book of Hospitality* is a book of hospitality in the double sense of the term: it studies the notion of hospitality and, simultaneously, itself seeks to practice hospitality towards everything it calls upon and binds together. Similarly to any other Jabèsian book ending, the content converges here with its conditions of utterability – an utterance is possible only because it performatively practices what it utters. Hence the weight of the unique moment in which the content and the conditions of sayability unite and approximate the power of the whiteness of the Book closer than ever before. As Motte aptly notices, *Le Livre de l'Hospitalité* – written in the shadow of actual death – offers the most specific of these moments Jabès had ever chanced upon. It is his ultimate, least-staged vanishing, marked only by the frailest, liminal form of writing, which balances between still-describing and already-non-existing:

> The words are put together […] not by me but by the man I was, once, who wrote for himself.
>
> As if what his pen still wrote were written in the past, which was my present once, before a sudden and final rupture, whose date I cannot tell; for I am without memories and words, and where I try to move, with difficulty, time is overthrown.[38]

---

37 Motte, "Hospitable Poetry," pp. 35–8.
38 LH, p. 93.

The Book of Hospitality is, thus, not only a text which uses the notion of hospitality to explore the community of things but also *a place*[39] where everything that aspires to a separate or strong existence – the author including – abdicates its claims. The idea of place has distinct connotations in Jabès: the place designates a field of reality which not so much exists as affords others an opportunity to exist. The desert is the model of the place. Its images recur in *The Book of Hospitality*, where it is a locus of ultimate, present absence:

"The desert is the place of all presence," he said, "a real place.
Neither past. Nor future.
Where am I?
My past has enchanted my future."
The nomad said: "You are in your memory, which isn't [*n'est…point*], as could be thought, bound to the past, but chained to the present it makes."
"I remember nothing," I answered him, "so I don't exist."
"You exist in the Nothing," the nomad replied.[40]

Having wrestled with memory and forgetfulness, Jabès returns to the desert, the metaphor for the place of ultimate non/presence, where nothing is remembered anymore and, as such, dissolves in the community of things. Memory stops making sense and crafting the past for him. The time of language fades away. In this way, he approaches the goal he sensed as early as in *Yaël*: "I must go, go, go till the All dissolves into Nothing [*se résout en Rien*]."[41] However, the point lingers on, resists being absorbed and leaves a trace of this wandering in writing.

The desert helps Jabès re-examine the idea of *hospitalité* because, after all, it has its permanent dwellers – the nomads. Their behaviour represents a paradigmatic example of hospitality to Jabès. In *The Book of Hospitality*, he recounts a car trip across the desert he went on with his friend when still in Egypt.[42] Equipped with a car and furnished with provisions, they set off assured of being well prepared and running no risk. However, when they had already been far away from human dwellings, the car broke down, tumbling down a dune. Aware that they would not be able to return on foot, they started to prepare for death. It is only in his last book that Jabès revisits the experience and, in doing this, strips the desert of all its literary and mythical aura, showing it as a place where death is a patent

---

39   Cf. Motte, "Hospitable Poetry," p. 40.
40   LH, p. 96.
41   BQ II, p. 109. The phrase Jabès uses – *se résoudre* – means also deciding and resolving to do something. In the light of the idea of hospitality, this connotation is certainly deliberate.
42   LH, pp. 84–5.

and immediate possibility. When, entirely exhausted, they had already lost all hope, a nomad unexpectedly appeared. He rescued them without saying a word and helped them get back to town.

What Jabès found most fascinating about the nomad was that when some time later the poet coincidentally met him again, the nomad did not remember anything. He remembered neither the faces of the people he had rescued nor the event as such. This was not due to frail memory or indifference. As Jabès concludes, this is simply the way the nomad lives and this is what the behaviour of the human formed by the desert is like: one helps anonymous wanderers only to remember nothing of it later. One does not rescue particular people because of their exceptionality or familiarity with them. One helps wanderers as such; one helps those in need of help. According to Motte, the nomad treats the other as an undifferentiated representative of the whole.[43] He helps unfailingly, but he goes away and forgets equally unfailingly. He does not use words, yet his entire behaviour anyway expresses a mute rapport with those he helps. In this, no one crosses the barrier of their solitude, nor uses language to communicate. Help does not involve names, meanings, social relations as they do not exist in the desert. What exists is only a bare relationship of lonely things which do not overcome their seclusion though they can help each other. This is what Jabès calls hospitality.

This story serves Jabès as a starting point for re-considering the generalised idea of hospitality, in which ethics dovetails with negative ontology. As the desert is the precondition for the nomad's hospitality, so this generalised hospitality presupposes prior ontological desertification. In other words, hospitality is a response to the fragmentation of reality, a response which does not seek to negate the desert, instead accepting it as its inevitable condition. In one of his late interviews, Jabès explains his notion of the desert in the following way:

> Surely there is no more faithful emblem of the infinite. In the mountains the sense of infinitude is disciplined by heights and depths and by the sheer density of what you confront; thus you yourself are limited, defined as an object among other objects. At sea there is always more than just water and sky; there is the boat to define your difference from both, giving you a human place to stand. But in the desert the sense of the infinite is unconditional and therefore truest. In the desert you're left utterly to yourself. And in that unbroken sameness of sky and sand, you're nothing, absolutely nothing. The appalling silence tells you so. It abolishes you. Enter the desert and you broach a new grammar of being. It's a grammar of death. In the desert you are divested of everything.– even language, which counts for nothing, makes no more sense, in a world from which

43 Motte, "Hospitable Poetry," p. 42.

man has been erased. [In the desert] language balks, comes to an end; the grammar of the living is overcome by a more potent grammar of death.[44]

Jabès infers ultimate conclusions from the image of the desert used to depict modern reality. The separateness of being is ultimately overthrown in it. The universe is an infinite whole in relation to which language wields no power. The "grammar of being" mutates completely. In this way, Jabès relies on Jewish tradition to draw final conclusions from modern thinking, joining Nietzsche, Kafka, Benjamin and Heidegger in this enterprise. Facing the desert that reality has become, he proposes a fitting solution in hospitality that originates in the nomad's life, which is closest to the desert and persist against it. In the desert, ethics means as much as language – nothing. *Hospitality is the last lifeline, which requires recognising the realness of the desert.*

Hospitality can appear where the guest comes from nowhere and has only his wandering for the name and the goal:

"I bless you, my visitor [*mon hôte*], my guest [*mon invité*]," said the holy rabbi, "because your name is: *The one who wanders* [*chemine*].
The road [*le chemin*] is in your name.
Hospitality is a crossroads."[45]

Hospitality can be extended to those who, having no permanent place, are on the road all the time. They are not designated by any meaningful words, names, attributes, backgrounds or places of residence: *they are only those who wander across them.* They are a thing as such because no appellation holds them, traversed and transcended by them as it is. But those who offer hospitality live in the same manner. It is not just a fortuitous word choice that Jabès relies on a peculiarity of the French language, in which the same word – *hôte* – denotes the guest and the host. Hospitality is not a unilateral gesture the settled one makes towards the wandering one; rather, it is a symmetrical relationship of two migrants whose paths intersect, making them *hôtes*: guests and hosts in one.

This shows the ultimate difference between Jabès' hospitality and Lévinas' responsibility. In Lévinas, responsibility for the other is not a relationship, but an ethical injunction placed on every human being and sustaining his subjectivity.[46] It is not symmetrical in the least; on the contrary, it is an expression of utmost asymmetry in which I must take full responsibility for the other, no matter how

---

44 QJQW, p. 16.
45 LH, p. 13.
46 Cf. Maurice-Ruben Hayoun, *Petite histoire de la philosophie juive* (Paris: Editions Ellipses, 2008), p. 144.

he responds. I am obligated before I undertake any action, prior to my intentionality and prior to freedom.[47] In Jabès, in turn, *hospitality is not an ethical injunction placed on the individual but a mutual relationship of two wanderers in the desert*. Instead of fostering subjectivity, it overthrows subjectivity.

Lévinas emphasises that responsibility persists regardless of the Other's behaviour and, in doing that, he in fact still measures one action against another in terms of the exchange of gifts to conclude that no matter what the result of such measurement is, responsibility cannot cease. Jabès does not reason in such categories at all, for he assumes they are not adequate to the desert. In the desert, there are neither signposts nor injunctions, and the words in which one could wish to convey them are lost in the unmeasurable vastness of the void. Lévinas is to Jabès what Nietzsche was to Heidegger: the last representative of a centuries-long tradition of thinking who, admittedly, radicalises and reverses this tradition, but fails to step beyond it. His critique of morality notwithstanding, Lévinas puts his ethics in verbal prescripts. Jabès' ethics, *if it can be called ethics in the first place, is an ontological relationship of things as such*:

> "My responsibility for you," he wrote, "is comparable to the sky's for birds and the ocean's for its fauna and flora.
> Who could hold the earth responsible for the day being born and dying?" he wrote.[48]

This is Jabès' implicit criticism of two issues in Lévinas. First, he criticises Lévinas for focusing his ethics on the human being, which alienates him from the community of things and hurls him back into the dominion of language. Second, he denounces Lévinas' failure to perceive the paradoxes of total ethics and unconditional responsibility. Responsibility for everything and everybody easily leads to a lack of responsibility for anything at all. This is the fact Lévinas refuses to consider, while Jabès accepts it as an inevitable consequence. This is what his hospitality is like: *it is a responsibility for everything – therein things – equal to a responsibility for nothing*. As part of reality, each thing is defined by everything it is not. In this sense, it responsible for reality through its very form. But in this regard, it cannot change anything, for it always belongs to reality. The ethical injunction in Jabès could make sense only if it helped go beyond reality. In this, Jabès is again in tune with Wittgenstein's reasoning in the *Tractatus*.[49] For

---

47 Cf. Lévinas, *Beyond the Verse*, pp. 127–8.
48 LH, p. 18.
49 *The Tractatus* offers a vision of transcendental ethics which cannot take place in the world, but only in its inaccessible outside (ct. theses 6.42, 6.421 – 6.423); Ludwig Wittgenstein, *Tractatus Logico-Philosophicus*, trans. John Ogden, with an Introduction by Bertrand Russel (London: Kegan Paul, Trench, Trubner and Co. Ltd., 1922), p. 88.

this reason, the only form of such a behest is, as already mentioned, *continuing to mark, in the scream or in the point, the discontinuity between reality and that which – as the impossible – is its beyond. Within reality, ethics* de facto *does not exist, being only the outermost point of the community of things.*

Therefore, hospitality is not based on obligation or mutuality:

> "I don't deserve hospitality I owe you."
> "Accept it. I will know you have forgiven me," said a sage.[50]

Hospitality unhinges the notions of debt, guilt and forgiveness. Jabès does not try to find either justifications or total responsibility for everything. On the contrary, following, as it were, the course of desertification, he strives after the community of all things, in which *guilt, debt and forgiveness stop making sense.* It is responsibility that lays guilt while hospitality liberates:

> Always within the reach of what comes up against it [*se présente*], hospitality can be thought only through what it offers.
> Responsibility alienates [*aliène*]. Hospitality relieves [*allège*].
> To give welcome to the neighbour for his presence alone, in the name of his being, only for what it represents.
> Because he is.
> "Responsibility is a daughter of dialogue it naively leans on.
> Hospitality is a silent understanding. That's its property."[51]

To put it in Derridean terms, responsibility – with Lévinas as its chief advocate – is still all too logocentric for Jabès. It is based on dialogue, and its focus on the human being is coupled with the capacity to speak. Yet Jabès regards abiding by a meaningful utterance as violence and, consequently, seeks the "silent understanding" of hospitality. Responsibility is human while hospitality is Divine rather:

> To man, excessive power of speech.
> To God, excessive power of silence.[52]

Hospitality is not definable, for a definition would entail "narrowing while hospitality suffers no limitation."[53] It means respect for the other, without any moralising raptures but wary all the time lest the other should bring death.[54] For it is

---

50 LH, p. 18.
51 *Ibid.*, p. 21.
52 *Ibid.*, p. 55.
53 *Ibid.*, p. 57.
54 *Ibid.*, p. 60.

impossible to know who stealthily readies themselves to finish you off, observes Jabès. *His notion of hospitality combines peculiar austerity and ostensible indifference with boundless understanding of and succor for another thing.* Cherishing no illusions about hazards, hospitality does not idealise the other, as Lévinas-inspired thinking tends to do. Undoubtedly, Jabès tries, in this way, to draw conclusions from what the Shoah disclosed to be possible. He endeavours to accept reality as a given instead of denying it in and through the idea of total responsibility. Hospitality is an idea adjusted to the modern condition, sharing its anti-humanism, and yet salvaging the ethical impulse despite all the experiences of history. Ronnie Scharfman explains:

> Jabès' concept of hospitality [...] functions as the crucial link between himself as referential, autobiographical subject of the enunciation which he reveals so openly in this text [*Le Livre de l'Hospitalité*] and that postmodern, post-Auschwitz, decentered, fragmented subject of the depersonalized statement which we have come to identify as Jabès' text. I would suggest that hospitality is posited in this text as the ultimate virtue, the polar opposite of exclusion, the unique and supreme weapon against the nihilism of intolerance whose name is Auschwitz.

Hospitality means, as Scharfman enumerates, "respect for the other, and for the alterity of the other," "patience," "mutual recognition of solitude, anonymity, wandering" and, finally, "in practical, referential terms survival."[55] Scharfman aptly links hospitality to sur-viving. Hospitality extended by another helps one survive, without providing any explanations, without either entering the relations of indebtedness and payback or getting entangled in purposiveness.

> [...] desolate [*désolé*] land of sand where hospitality guarantees survival.[56]

Hospitality corresponds to the way of being in the desert. It does not offer any meaning and boils down only to sustaining the thing in its being. "Hospitality is no gift [...]; it is given even before requested."[57] Things connected by hospitality do not interfere with each other's solitude but *show themselves to themselves as a part of the only reality in which they are all co-dependent*:

> The foreigner allows you to be yourself by making a foreigner of you.[58]

55 Ronnie Scharfman, "Welcoming the Stranger: Edmond Jabès' *Le Livre de l'hospitalité*," in Antoine Régis (ed.), *Carrefour des cultures: Mélanges offerts à Jacqualine Leiner* (Tübingen: Gunter Narr Verlag, 1993), pp. 237–42, on pp. 239, 241.
56 LH, p. 90.
57 *Ibid.*, p. 76.
58 F, p. 1.

You are a foreigner. And I? [*Et moi?*]
For you I am the foreigner. And you? [*Et toi?*]
Star [*étoile*] remains forever separate from star; what brings them close is but their will to shine together.[59]
To obey the unexpressed demands of hospitality means to learn about our dependence on the other.[60]

Hospitality is not kindness; it has nothing, colloquially speaking, human to it. This is highlighted in *Le Livre de l'Hospitalité* in a hypothetical dialogue of God with characters of the Torah. Asked by Eve if we are free and have our own place, God replies:

"You are here, with God. […] I am all your freedom and your place."
And Abraham would doubtless say:
"Loneliness is a place."
Then, Moses would no doubt say:
"Lord, are you so ungenerous that I'll have to die separated from my people and myself? Without a tomb?"
And then a sage would say logically:
"Open the place, Lord, which I keep ajar with so much effort.
I grow weaker and my heart's ardour abates."
And everybody asked to speak would certainly say:
"Lord, where is my homestead? Hostile land and inhospitable sky. Nowhere did I feel sheltered.
Am I of so little interest to you?"
And God would undoubtedly reply:
"Ungrateful creatures. You accuse me of not doing the duty of the host/guest [*hôte*]. Boundless is the hospitality of the Book. But you have no idea of that."[61]

Hospitality does not consist in offering care, interest, accommodation or protection, as people would be inclined reproachfully to point out to God. Instead, hospitality consists in *providing a place* where a thing can endure and survive. God is not hospitable because he does not provide the place. Instead, the Book, which came into being as a result of creation, does, and God is only a guest in it. Therefore, God cannot be blamed for failing to do the host's duty, for he is himself a visitor in the Book. Hospitality, in general, eludes the opposition of care and indifference. It guarantees survival, but, as we remember, survival in Jabès is tantamount to experiencing inhuman suffering.

---

59 *Ibid.*, p. 7.
60 LH, p. 70.
61 *Ibid.*, pp. 65–7.

> Harsh hospitality.
> Of the desert.
> Of the race.
> Of oblivion.[62]
> [...] desolate [*désolé*] land of sand where hospitality guarantees survival. [...] The
> Book is this land.[63]

Hospitality provides a place and allows abiding in it. It offers survival and dooms to survival. It makes no sense and defies interpretation.[64] It discloses reality in its nakedness. Austere and ascetic, it takes in everybody on equal terms and without exception, just like death and oblivion host the living. As such, it is "the last voice."[65] In the same way, the writer hosts, in his book, those who have passed, without even calling them by their names, and offers them the same blank place within which he is himself engulfed.

The End in Whiteness: A Possibility of Modern Ethics

The messianic equality of things, as discussed in Chapter Six, is an illusion – a convergence point out there on the horizon, but never actually present here and now. Of course, Jabès' hospitality refers to this illusion in an effort to place the messianic equality within the ultimate ethical command. But in this way Jabès arrives at a breaking point and reaches the dark origin of his thinking, where all the themes of his work coalesce. Hospitality is not "merely" an ethical notion: it is the same ideal of equality outside language that has recurred in this volume from its beginning, as the centre of *tzimtzum*, or the moment of salvation, or the pivot of created reality. Nowhere else is Jabès closer to modern philosophy; nowhere else must he more effortfully distance himself from Heideggerian *Gelassenheit*, which is governed by the same mechanism, without however exploring its own inner impossibility or cultivating a robust ethical investment. In Jabès, the

---

62 *Ibid.*, p. 29.
63 *Ibid.*, p. 90.
64 In this sense, hospitality has little to do with quasi-materialist insights that appealed to late Derrida. Like *khōra* – in Derrida's reading of Plato, the non-place which only takes in and gives place without ever being occupied – Jabès' hospitality predates those whom it "helps," refuses to be explained or exhausted and does not take on any denotations. Both concepts attempt to reach the non-binary infrastructure of all oppositions, the non-sense that is the precondition of sense. Cf. Jacques Derrida, *Khōra* (Paris: Galilée, 1993), pp. 15–37, 58–62, 92–97. See also, Jacques Derrida, *"Khōra,"* trans. Ian McLeod, in *On the Name*, ed. Thomas Dutoit (Stanford, CA: Stanford UP, 1995), pp. 89–130.
65 LH, p. 87.

equality of things is both an ethical ideal, an expectation of messianic salvation and the most dreadful of all modern conditions. Positive and negative appraisals unite in its midpoint. Jabès' hospitality implies that *modern thinking, to whose mechanisms it is subject, comes forth as a result of enveloping the unchangeable structure of the remnant with sundry kinds of content.*

This structure nurtures both utter nihilism and the ethical ideal. Jabès' thought is a testament to desperate attempts at giving an ethical vector to this structure's illusory centre. Can such an enterprise at all succeed? At any rate, this vector belongs to the field that has been damaged by the very movement of simplification, leading to the disclosure of the dark point of unity. Jabès walks here a tangled, dialectical path. On the one hand, he accepts the way simplification eradicates ethical notions; more than that, he joins this movement in the desire to see desolation finally completed. But on the other hand, he wants to harness this inexorable tendency with ethical reins, no matter how feeble they could be. As such, he must combine two incompatible pursuits in his thinking. Is it even possible? That it is not is not a foregone conclusion. *For both tendencies do not reach their consummation, bound and, at the same time, deferred by the central point of tzimtzum.* Simplification never comes to its end and, consequently, never leaves the territory where an ethical vector can be formulated. Jabès' ethics stands a chance of success because it is inconclusive; exactly because it is a sheer impossibility to reach the point where hospitality and radical evil are indistinguishable, the difference between them can still be marked. If, like Jabès, one presupposes the simplification movement to be inevitable, *sustaining adamantly the difference between hospitality and radical evil – a difference which arises due to the very structure of tzimtzum one heads towards – would be the only salvaged ethical injunction.*

Along these lines, we may infer that the age of mature modernity knows only one categorical imperative: *the irremovable modern difference that appears on the horizon of the movement towards simplification must be used for the sake of ethics and in order to save it.* Simplification is unavoidable, but it is our call how we use the fact that it cannot reach completion and must halt in the last difference. This difference must be erected into the last ethical rampart.

Ultimately, the vision of hospitality does not lead to anything except to the repetition of the same dark point which has fed modern philosophy for over two centuries. The careful work on sensitivity which would correspond to thus-conceived *hospitalité* – descending the rungs of the quietness of sound down to the almost-lowest silence – re-enacts Heidegger's path in *Contributions to Philosophy* but tries to keep to the ethical side. However, the goal of this journey contradicts the way in which it is supposed to proceed. Each step, though seemingly a unique achievement on the road towards the community of things as such, may be just one step further in the closed circle of depletion. Between all and nothing there is a breaking point, a point of ultimate indeterminacy, and nothing more seems to be there for philosophy now. Maintaining ethics in this point may be philosophy's final task until the logic of modernity eventually passes.

Le Livre de l'Hospitalité is a book for which a writer like Jabès cannot possibly fail to be grateful. That which has eluded him all the time – the moment of the fleeting accord of life and meaning – seems to have been given to him just before death. The book's conclusion echoes Wittgenstein's words at the end of the Foreword to his *Tractatus*: "the problems have in essentials been finally solved. And if I am not mistaken in this, then the value of this work […] consists in the fact that it shows how little has been done when these problems have been solved"[66]:

> You'll manage to express it [the thing that has eluded you] once in your lifetime; it will be in your final encounter with death.
> You'll have to speak with discretion, and all you'll say will be just a few brief sentences.
> You'll be astonished that you've needed your whole life to collect so few words.
> And you'll have yourself only for the interlocutor.
> Don't return anymore to this one thing to say [*chose à dire*]. It is a thing in becoming and thus irrevocably doomed.
> Like the moment.[67]

Ultimately, to say this thing would take an eternity of all individual eternities that open up in their moments. That is why it deserves to be preserved for saying out loud in that lone moment – encounter with death – when words are no more and hospitality flings its gate open. It is there that Jabès' thought relegates its ultimate illusion, looking for the messianic consummation in the moment where nothing is anymore.

> "The word of our origin is a word of the desert. O desert of our words," wrote Reb Aslan.
> "There is no possible return if you have gone deep into the desert."
> […] "Sand, the asking. Sand, the reply. Out desert has no limits," wrote Reb Semama.

He held a bit of sand in each hand: "On the one hand, questions, to the other, answers. Same weight of dust," he also said.[68]

> I write the desert.
> So strong is the light

---

66 Wittgenstein, *Tractatus*, p. 24.
67 LH, pp. 89–90.
68 BR II, p. 103.

that the rain has evaporated.
Face of the present. Face of the past.
A veil between them. A damp curtain.
The eye blurred again with a tear from ages ago.
Melancholy. Melancholy.
He had – it seemed to him – a thousand
things to say
in words that said nothing;
waiting, in a row;
in underground words
with neither past nor destiny.
This haunted him to no end;
up to the point where he
had nothing more to say,
that's it, that's it.[69]

Victorious, the day like the point of flash on the horizon.[70]

No bounds for the unknown
nor frontiers to the infinite.

Horizon. Horizon. Horizon.[71]

Nulles bornes, à l'inconnu
ni frontières, à l'infini.
L'horizon. L'Horizon. L'Horizon

---

69 LSLS, pp. 384, 395, 396.
70 A, p. 293. The passage comes from a posthumously published text which Jabès wrote
    when he was 18 years old.
71 BS, p. 59.

11 Theology of the Point: Jabès as a Modern Kabbalist

It seems that the account of Jabès' work as epitomising Jewish philosophy of modernity is now complete. The structure of his thinking has been shown to be closely bound up with the modern conjuncture and its modes. Let us now apply the insights compiled so far to one particular theme reiterated across Jabès' body of writing. Specifically, let us see how the double bind of Jewish philosophy of modernity is involved in Jabès' Kabbalism.

What is his Kabbalism exactly? References to the Kabbalah – in terms of its cosmology and (a)theology – are abundant in z Jabès' works,[1] but they will not be my focal point in this Chapter. Instead, I will address one special aspect of his Kabbalah-derived inspirations exemplified in speculations on words, wordplay and permutations of letters. Jabès employs them time and again in strictly purposive, rather than autotelic, gestures. As a matter of fact, operations at the basic level of language help him establish and express new, unexpected conceptual links.[2] Yet, if such engagement can be called "Kabbalism," it is only in a highly metaphorical sense of the term, for Jabès does not work on Hebrew, the only language that would give such pursuits a theological validation. Instead, he relies on the thoroughly secular French language.

How is such Kabbalism related to Jewish philosophy of modernity? In this Chapter, I will argue two points. One of them – a simpler one resulting from explorations in the previous Chapters – is that Jabès' Kabbalism is strictly

---

1 David Mendelson observes that, in Jabès, the translated key-words of Judaism, such as "law" and "writing," form, as they did in the kabbalists, a hidden, inner language through which the "Upper" manifests itself in the "Lower." David Mendelson, "La science, l'exil et les sources du desért" in Écrire le livre, p. 251. However, in this Judaism after God, the "Upper" is no longer God's message but the concealed laws of fragmented reality themselves.

2 In this, Jabès is part of the rich tradition of Jewish thought in which the Kabbalah and philosophy tended to intertwine while theosophical speculations were philosophically studied. For example, in the 13th and 14th centuries, thinkers such as Abraham ibn Latif and Josef ibn Wakar endeavoured to reconcile the developing Kabbalah and the Maimonidean tradition founded on medieval Aristotelianism (Hayoun, *Petite histoire*, p. 74). Importantly, two movements – mystical symbolism and philosophical speculation – historically developed in parallel in the Kabbalah (Gershom Scholem, *Kabbale*, p. 119).

modern, structurally conditioned by modernity and post-Theistic.[3] His linguistic manipulations have the same origin as Hegel's wordplays, Surrealists'
experimentations and the psychoanalytic model of language mechanisms. At
the same time, Jabès introduces references to the Kabbalah and other Jewish
traditions into this modern framework of thinking by, for example, permutating God's names. His detachment from the Jewish past surfaces in his choice of
French instead of Hebrew, which the kabbalists of old viewed as the only sacred
language and, consequently as the only one suitable for this purpose.

My other point, a bolder one, is that in his Kabbalism Jabès does not simply
depend on the structure of modern thinking but also comes to realise how this
structure functions. The utter simplification attained by the poet reveals perhaps
the fundamental line of forces generative of the patterns that organise modern
philosophy.

I will explore this point in conclusion to this Chapter. But first, I will attempt to
define the sources of Jabès' Kabbalism and show its two essential versions: associations of letters and meditations on the point. I will discuss the role of the point in
Jabès' texts by juxtaposing it with Derrida's *différance*. To finish with, I will describe
the movement of simplification and erasure, which permeates the last two parts of
The Book of Questions, and examine its meanings within the framework of Jewish
philosophy of modernity.

Introduction: Linguistic Kabbalism in Jabès' Thinking

The first question is why Jabès needs linguistic Kabbalism in the first place. His
interpreters have rarely, if at all, inquired into this. Addressing the issue indirectly, they have tended to emphasise the irreducible dual embedment of such
language practices in the Kabbalah and in modern literature. "As an heir to Jewish
tradition, Jabès subjects French words to the same tests that exegetes and the
kabbalists applied to the text of the sacred Book," states Shillony.[4] Shillony argues
that Jabès follows the mystics of language in "refusing to believe in a coincident"
behind the affinities of words.[5] Motte compares Jabès' letter-juggling to the practices of Abraham Abulafia, one of the most eminent mediaeval kabbalists, and

---

3   Matthew Del Nevo calls Jabès a "kabbalist after God." Matthew Del Nevo, "Edmond
    Jabès and Kabbalism after God," p. 404.
4   Shillony, *Edmond Jabès*, p. 68.
5   *Ibid.*, p. 18.

to the literary devices used by Jabès' contemporaries, such as John Barth, Walter Abish, Georges Perec and other members of the Oulipo group.[6]

Clearly, on these accounts, Jabès' Kabbalism is not definable fully either as a continuation of techniques developed and perfected by generations of mystics or as a literary game. His Kabbalism is dissociated from the Kabbalah by a modern distance which the poet takes from the legacy of Judaism, to the point of discarding Hebrew. Admittedly, Abraham Abulafia himself used texts in other languages as well, but he considered those languages to be adulterated versions of the Hebrew ur-language.[7] This idea is by no means upheld in Jabès. At the same time, his Kabbalism differs from the literary game in not being autotelic. It distinctly serves as a tool for thinking and, more than that, it is an immanent, *requisite element* of the thinking process, without which, like in the kabbalists,[8] thinking could not go on. Jabès' Kabbalism is both modern and severed from its sources as well as indispensable as a result of the laws governing modern thinking.

What particular features does Jabès attribute to this thinking? He presupposes its incompletion because thinking which follows the principles of inference fails to render truly relevant conclusions. Thinking thus has a certain external dimension to it, which cannot be directly grasped. This is where Kabbalism enters the stage. Permutations of letters and plays on words are moments when thinking veers into the dimension external to it: it abandons the realm in which thoughts are combined based on their meaningful content and comes to rely on seemingly contingent and meaningless linkages. Subsequently, these external associations help thinking find a new course and meaningfully organise its conclusions. *Linguistic Kabbalism is, therefore, the moment when thinking confronts its own outside.* It is a direct consequence of the fact that this outside is there, embodied in writing.

If it is indeed the case, Jabès' works should contain traces of quasi-dualism of the utterance's meaningful content and its material outside – its written form. Let us have a look at the following passage:

> As far back as I can remember and as much as I can be sure, I believe the spelling errors I made as a child and adolescent were the origin from which my questioning grew. I had trouble understanding that a word copied a little differently, with a letter too many or

---

6   Warren F. Motte, "Récit/Écrit," in *Écrire le livre*, pp. 161–70, on p. 167.

7   Scholem, *Major Trends*, pp. 134–5.

8   Ouaknin, *Concerto*, p. 321.

too few, suddenly did not represent anything, that my teacher could angrily cross it out with red ink and claim the arbitrary right to punish me for inventing it, as it were. So a word did not exist unless spelled correctly, as someone – but who? God perhaps? – had chosen, had decreed it should be spelled. And how had the letters come to have such power over man that they could lay down the law? What mystery dwelled in them?[9] Sometimes I also thought if I spelled a word my way I could be the only one to live with it, to love it. [...] Among my challenged *vocables*, I felt both free and a slave to their freedom.[10]

Both these childhood memories and Jabès' later linguistic Kabbalism are founded on the experience of a fundamental discord between the utterance's meaning and its rendering in writing. The script is the utterance's condition of possibility, yet changes in it are not translatable into changes in meaning in any straightforward, readily comprehensible way. On the contrary, an ostensibly minor modification – adding or removing one letter – can entirely change the word's meaning. This effect resembles Wittgenstein's "dawning of an aspect,"[11] that is, a situation in which one and the same graphic form (or drawing) can be perceived in various ways, but because at a given moment only one of these ways is discernible, a sudden realisation that another perception is also possible is surprising and unexpected.

Nevertheless, like Wittgenstein, Jabès views this incommensurability as too weighty to approach merely as an interesting, but marginal, side-effect of writing. Rather, it seems to him to embody the elementary difference between meaning and the outside in which it is inscribed and which conditions it. If so, Kabbalism in Jabès can be expected to hinge on the central tension of the perspectival world. In other words, a seemingly trifling difference between adding one letter in writing and the alteration in the utterance's meaning can represent *the same structure that causes the difference and connection between the imaginary and the real.*

Let us look into this idea, revisiting the passage quoted above: "I had trouble understanding that a word copied a little differently, with a letter too many or too few, suddenly did not represent anything, that my teacher could angrily cross it out with red ink and claim the arbitrary right to punish me for inventing it, as it were. So a word did not exist unless spelled correctly, as someone – but who?

---

9   In the original: *la mystère… dans ses lettres*, which seems to allude to Mallarmé's "La Musique et les Lettres" (Eng. translation 'Music and Letters' or "Music and Literature") and, perhaps, also to Blanchot's essay on Mallarmé in *The Work of Fire*.

10 BR II, p. 46.

11 Wittgenstein, *Investigations*, pp. 192–214.

God perhaps? – had chosen, had decreed it should be spelled. What mystery dwelled in them [letters]?" Clearly, Jabès presupposes that the meaning works correctly only if its graphic form abides by the rules whose origin is difficult to establish. If the word is "incorrect" on the plane of letters, it *ceases to exist at all* on the plane of meaning. An ensemble of arbitrary rules is imposed on writing, determining when and on what conditions it yields meaning.

What follows is that meaning is conditional, and its conditionality is revealed only in confrontation with writing – similarly to the imaginary discussed in Chapter Three. On this model, writing is analogous to the real: it reveals the fact that a set of letters which are meaningless in one order can be meaningful in another order; therefore, *particular symbolic orders co-exist within writing*. That the same structure which I described before as the principle of Jabès' negative ontology is at work here is confirmed by the fact that writing, which is the condition, is not autonomous either but is in itself entangled in meaning: seeing letters, we cannot but consider their potential meaning-making character. Writing and meaning are, thus, inter-connected and divided by *a discontinuity, an inexplicable gap*. We know its name: it is Jabès' *tzimtzum*. Jabès' linguistic Kabbalism explores how the immanently limited meaning meets its outside. As such, it is a practice that constantly revolves around *tzimtzum*.

It is easier to understand now why language operations in Jabès' texts are sus-pended between references to the Kabbalah and the legacy of Hegel, Mallarmé and the Surrealists. His Kabbalism germinates in its own soil and solves its own problem, one that has a modern structure.[12] But, at the same time, while

---

12 William Franke explains that in Jabès' Kabbalism "[t]he common noun for book, *livre*, turns out like the adjective for free, *libre*, to be subject to voiding at the center: by sup-pressing their central letter, *li(v)re* (book) and *li(b)re* (free) are pared down equally to *li re* (the infinitive "to read"), and then, by further hollowing out, eliminating all but the first and the last letter in each word, to *le*, the singular, masculine, definite article for generically designating whatever is anything at all. But *le* reversed is also the Hebrew name of God, namely, El. In this manner, the Hebrew name of God, which is in prin-ciple unpronounceable, silent, is found at the core of the book, and of reading and of naming in general, and so of language itself.
Jabès works with French the way the kabbalah writers worked with the Hebrew language, finding presumable mystical truths of the universe inscribed within it. Mere contingencies of the French language are presented as miraculously revealing the mys-tery of Creation by the Name of God, the empty and unpronounceable divine Name that creates all from Nothing. But whereas the kabbalists supposed Hebrew to have been the language of Creation itself, Jabès uses French to show how the self-subversive forms and fictive powers of a human language can be seen to mirror an undelimited

producing a complex re-construction of Judaism, Jabès could not possibly over-look the tradition in which permutation techniques had a theological and cos-mological relevance ascribed to them. He could not possibly fail to draw on the uniqueness of the Hebraic text, the reading of which automatically entails a reduced interpretation, for it requires adding vowels to the scripted text.[13] The Kabbalah is for Jabès a model of the connection between an ostensibly trifling difference in meaning and the graphic form on the one hand and a fundamental ontological difference on the other. For this reason, in his linguistic practices Jabès adopts the Kabbalah's forms and vocabulary.[14] Nevertheless, the difference they serve to explore is not the difference that the Kabbalah studies. First of all, the former is not the difference between the world and transcendent God, that is, between the literal meaning of the text and its hidden, full meaning, respec-tively.[15] Fullness is supplanted here with the central void of *tzimtzum*, which can never be reached because it is revealed only in a displacement between two inter-twined dimensions.

---

power of creativity from Nothing. Such power of creation from nothing was tradition-ally attributed to divine Word and Name alone." Franke, "Singular," p. 630.

Franke aptly grasps the modern nature of Jabès' Kabbalism, which is practised in another language and is atheistic. However, it is difficult to share his view that the poet's aim is to show the "fictive powers of a human language." I think that something far more important is at stake: Kabbalism does not investigate how fiction comes into being but rather how the basic structure of modern reality functions.

13 The Hebraic script, like other Semitic scripts, basically does not include vowels, with the unique exception of what are referred to as *matres lectionis*. Vowels tend to be noted in a special way wherever writing a word unambiguously is crucial, which is the case, for example, with some editions of the Torah (though its proper text is not dotted, which opens up multiple interpretive possibilities). Vowels are written by means of a special system based first of all on points (נקודות). Hence the idea Jabès is eager to pick up that even one point can entirely change the meaning of the word, and, as such, whether it is present or absent determines the shape of the world. The (Babylonian) Talmud's book of *Eruvin* contains a famous parable in which rabbi Akiba talks to a scribe copying the Torah and exhorts him to be particularly careful neither to omit nor to add any single letter lest he should destroy the entire universe. Ouaknin, *Concerto*, p. 343.

14 According to Del Nevo, "Kabbalah offers a structural model and helps him [Jabès] organize his metaphysical premises, as well as being a means of giving specific, sensible coherence to universal problems." Del Nevo, "Edmond Jabès and Kabbalism after God," p. 405.

15 Idel voices similar insights when he compares the Kabbalistic and Derridean ideas of the text. See Idel, *Absorbing Perfections*, pp. 78–9.

From Letters to the Point

After this introduction, let us have a closer look at Jabès' linguistic Kabbalism. I will focus on two types of it.

I have already mentioned one of the techniques Jabès applies as he uses the affinities in the graphic forms of various words. As, in Gematria, the same numeric value of two words with entirely different meanings made the kabbalists think their interrelationship, so Jabès builds on similarities in the written form to discover the "encrypted" relationships. What relationships are they? Here are a handful of examples. In the seventh part of *The Book of Questions*, the word "silence" is shown to comprises the particle "*Il*" – "He." What follows is that the sentence "God – He – *is*" contains another one: "*silence exists [silence est]*."[16] This is supposed to mean that God's existence is identical with his withdrawal, speechlessness and silence. The far-fetched link on the plane of lettering harbours a trace of truth about *tzimtzum*.

As the kabbalists speculated about God's Name, so Jabès often manipulates the word "*Dieu*." One of these manoeuvres involves re-ordering its letters and adding one more, which re-makes "*Dieu*" – God – into "*deuil*," mourning.[17] The association of God and mourning ushers in the ideas we are already familiar with in Jabès: God is the central void, the great "Absent" one, whose being is mourning because it involves erasure of positive being. A yet another connection, which is based not only on the similar graphic form but also on the homophony of parts of words, is: *Dieu = vide = vie d'yeux* (God = Emptiness = Life of the eyes).[18] This sentence also associates God with the void but identifies him with "life of the eyes" as well, which invites various interpretations. The image may evoke the life of man gazing into the central void, but it may as well convey the gaze that the void itself turns to man, which is what happens with the onset of the Book, as discussed in Chapter Seven. The latter interpretation is consistent with another association: "*cieux = yeux + ciel*" (the heavens = eyes + heaven).[19] The heavens turn out to be a gaze from heaven: a gaze of the Nothing that was brought in by Creation. The same overtones pervade passages of *Intimations The Desert*:

> the word SOLEIL, which contains, how could we doubt it, the words ŒIL and LOI in mysterious order, gigantic pupil, heavenly eye with lashes of fire.[20]

---

16 BQ II, p. 374.
17 *Ibid.*, p. 411.
18 *Ibid.*, p. 410.
19 *Ibid.*, p. 410.
20 BR II, p. 73.

The sun is here the centre of the gaze from the heavens which, at the same time, constitutes the Law. All these images play with the Kabbalah motifs (God as fire), yet they revolve around the radically atheist thought that God, as the centre of non-being, is a negative organisation principle of the world. Still another association conveys the mechanism of the Book:

> "If it is true that within every word another word trembles to be born, look, listen how inside the word SEUIL, 'threshold,' there struggles the word SEUL, 'alone.'"
> "Thus you are alone at the deserted threshold of the Book [au seuil désert du Livre]."[21]

French is perfect for such verbal games, some of which are hardly translatable into any other language. The passage above links solitude to the threshold. In doing this, it parallels Kafka's parable "Before the Law," where radical singularisation is combined with abiding just before the impassable boundary. Besides, the passage captures our inscription in the Book: as SEUL is inscribed and hidden in SEUIL, so man finds himself at the deserted threshold of the Book: *before* it and, yet, also *in it*, which he cannot see for himself.

Each of the examples is closely interwoven with Jabès' respective thoughts. However, their functions can differ. Some of them just illustrate thoughts as catchphrases which pithily convey the poet's central idea (e.g. *Dieu = vide*). Yet, even in such cases, they are ontologically justified: a simple relationship on the plane of the written form corresponds to a link which ordered reasoning can reach only by a detour. Other examples give a "grounding" to more risky correlations and suggest a direction for thinking to follow (e.g. *SOLEIL – LOI – ŒIL*). Still other ones, finally, *play on the very structure of association in order to convey a thought*, as the last quotation does. Jabès' Kabbalism becomes essentially relevant at this point. An idea is no longer separable from the link through which it manifests itself in writing. In other words, to grasp the idea, it is necessary to resort to the utterance overdetermined by inner associations.

This brief survey of examples of letter permutations shows that their functions form a continuum. There are passages in which associations at the level of the graphic form only complement directly conveyable ideas; there are passages in which external connections blaze the trail for thinking; and, finally, there are passages in which permutations are central as they *help thoughts organise around the structure of association*. It seems that this continuum is ordered by the principle of the growing relevance of the external link in writing to the meaningful content. At each consecutive stage, the material connection of letters grows more

---

21 *Ibid.*, p. 1.

and more essential to the meaningful content. In other words, this continuum develops asymptotically towards *the very outside of meaning*. The further position a passage occupies in it, the greater the role of the structure in relation to the content.

Having mapped this continuum, we can proceed to meditations on the point – the other set of Jabès' techniques, which should as a matter of fact be considered crucial to his work.

Kabbalism of the point results from the evolution of *The Book of Questions*. Such Kabbalism hardly appears in the cycle's initial parts, arising only as a consequence of the progressing movement of simplification and condensation. The title of the seventh part is •, the point as such, which provides at the same time the axis of inquiries in the volume. This prolonged movement towards reflection on the point seems consistent with the direction of the continuum described above? If it is indeed the case, this kind of Kabbalism can be regarded as its ultimate form. *For, in the point, the meaningful content is most reduced while the structure to which the point belongs is most visible.*

In this sense, Kabbalism of the point is the opposite of the technique in which connection in the written form only complements the thought. In reflection on the point, the written form has the central role, and thought is only auxiliary to it. This is clear in Jabès' choice of • – of something that is no longer a verbal sign – for the title of the last and nodal part of *The Book of Questions*. Its parenthesised subtitle only supplements this point. In this, Jabès sets out to search for the structure that is the condition of possibility of Kabbalistic techniques in the first place. The force which so far has just combined words of different meanings in their "external" written form and then withdrawn to make room for interpretation becomes here the object of exploration in and by itself.

Below, I will therefore focus on Kabbalism of the point. First, I will provide its theoretical underpinnings, examining the meanings of the point in Jabès, and then I will study its use to establish what it is that Jabès grasps in his Kabbalism.

Introduction to Kabbalism of the Point, or on Jabès' Materialistic *Différance*

As already stated, the point results from simplification and condensation of Jabès' other Kabbalistic techniques. Consequently, to examine its complex nature, let us first ask simply how it differs from these techniques.

Among the examples above, the association of "*Dieu*" and "*deuil*" brings together words which differ only little in writing but greatly in meaning. But for Jabès' atheological thought, they would hardly collocate with each other. The role of association lies therefore in bringing together words whose meanings are wide apart, relying on a far *smaller* difference they display in writing.

How does this change if "*Dieu*" and "*deuil*" are replaced by two points: • and •? The difference on the plane of the graphic form ostensibly disappears, for these are *the same* two points. And yet, they are different for, after all, they are separate and do not overlap. This is, obviously, the old Leibnizian problem of the identity of indiscernibles. Putting two points side by side reveals a deeper and more elusive difference than the one between "*Dieu*" and "*deuil*": this is the difference behind *individualisation*.[22] How about the plane of meanings? The point has no permanent meaning: it can represent the singular, "being" in its individuality and All as well. It is an utterly simplified sign which means simply "something" rather than anything definite. Therefore, juxtaposing two points serves *to make visible the fundamental, incomprehensible difference disclosed on the plane of writing when meaning is reduced to the utmost.*

This is the source of the paradoxical nature of Jabès' point. This point is first and foremost a *sign* of this basic difference, which has a lot in common with Derrida's *différance*. It is a sign, for it is the only way of referring to a difference which is itself ungraspable. Between two points there can be no difference in meaning; there is only the most basic difference due to which there can be any separate beings at all. This is the reason why the point serves here as a sign of difference as such. But it is certainly not a sign of classic semiology Derrida speaks about,[23] for it does not refer to anything present. The only thing it does is simply referring without ever resting in any stable referent. For difference is not a referent that can be referred to. But paradoxically, the very movement of referring is an operation of *that which it is to refer to*, that is, of difference! This is the most intriguing conclusion of reflection on Jabès' point: *this point is a sign of difference, it refers to difference which it cannot reach, but this referring itself is differential.* In other words, the point is a sign of difference because difference makes it a sign.

---

22 Already Moses Cordovero explored the point as the smallest unit dividing being from non-being. See Draï, *Pensee juive*, p. 145.

23 As Derrida argues in "Différance," "this structure presupposes that the sign, which defers presence, is conceivable only on the *basis* of the presence that it defers and *moving toward* the deferred presence that it aims to reappropriate. According to this classical semiology, the substitution of the sign for the thing itself is both *secondary* and *provisional*: secondary due to an original and lost presence from which the sign thus derives; provisional as concerns this final and missing presence toward which the sign in this sense is a movement of mediation." Jacques Derrida, "Différance," in *Margins of Philosophy*, trans. Alan Bass (Chicago: Chicago UP, 1984), pp. 1–28, on p. 9.

Consequently, *the point is both a sign of difference and the "embodiment" of difference's operation as such.* In this fundamental paradox, separating the sign and the signified is pointless. Let us explore this peculiarity in more detail. The point is a site of self-differentiation. Each attempt to interpret it triggers another difference and separates it from itself: that is why no stable description of the point can be provided. Yet, despite all this, it seems to be located at a certain *place*. Admittedly, we cannot "offer an account" of the point because of its self-differentiation, but we can *refer* to the place it occupies in space and regard *this place as sustaining – for us – the totality of its movement.* As such, this place would be a place where the point works but also where the point *is*, without going beyond it. Thus, by assuming that there is a certain space *distinct* from our interpretation, we can refer to the point without triggering differentiation within our own thinking.

Jabès presupposes such a space in his specific materialism, and the point, as I will show below, is for him first of all a dot of ink on paper. Paradoxical though this may sound, *if the point is to convey the abstract difference, it must be identified with a material object.*[24] Ultimately, a purely material difference between

---

24 How important this assumption is suggested by the fact that the only mainstream philosophical text explicitly quoted in the *Books* is a passage from Wittgenstein's *Tractatus Logico-Philosophicus* in which the idea of the point is related to matter (thesis 4.063 appears in *El*; BQ II, p. 345): "An illustration of the concept of truth. A black spot on white paper; the form of the spot can be described by saying of each point of the plane whether it is white or black. To a fact that the point is black corresponds a positive fact; to the fact that a point is white (not black), a negative fact. [...] But to be able to say that a point is black or white, I must first know under what condition a point is called white or black [...]. The point at which this simile breaks down is this: we can indicate a point on the paper without knowing what white and black are.

... The verb of a proposition is not "is true" or "is false"... That which "is true" must, on the contrary, already contain the verb." (The first paragraph from Ludwig Wittgenstein, *Tractatus*, p.43, the second – altered – from BQ II, p. 345).

In 4.063 Wittgenstein seeks to show that the assertion can be understood as ascribing to a point in space – symbolising any proposition – either of two colours: black or white, which corresponds to ascribing truth-value or false-value to a proposition. A problem with this comparison is that it does not account for propositions without a sense, which cannot be defined as either true or false. In 4.064 Wittgenstein adds that the assertion does not give a proposition a sense, "for what it asserts is the sense itself." Therefore, he views the spot image as inadequate in that it seems to suggest that, first, the spot corresponds to every sentence (i.e. it is true or false but cannot have no sense), and that, second, whiteness and blackness obtain before the procedure of verifying logical comes into being and is applied. This explains, I believe, why Jabès quotes this passage.

ourselves and a fragment of matter before our eyes is necessary to prevent the reference to the difference embodied in the point from being absorbed in the difference itself. Materialism consists here in presupposing a special plane – let us call in the plane of inscription – which is in and by itself separate from the movement of difference. As such, this plane is entrusted with the role of sustaining difference based on the distance produced by ostension between the looker and the object.

This leads to more general conclusions. Jabès needs materialism in order to think a framework external to thinking, a certain space in which thinking is inscribed. *As a result, thought can refer to itself through mediation of this space.* The concept of such space has already surfaced in this volume. It is, of course, the Book, which – though an abstract concept – is by no means randomly material in Jabès. *The Book is "material" because it is the ultimate barrier to the working of difference, which must unfold within the Book and, consequently, cannot subsume the difference between the Book and itself.* Matter comes to embody the ineffaceable, that which resists thinking and persists as the "point," "remnant," "waste" (to use any of the notions cherished in modern philosophy). *Therefore, materialism is here a product of thinking itself, which breeds within itself an obstacle and then links it to the representation of matter in order to avoid the engulfing power of difference.* In crafting such an obstacle, thinking stabilises itself by presupposing a plane of scrutiny from which it is visible as bound to a certain place.

That materialism and the Book are closely interconnected is not a coincidence. Both concepts presuppose that thought cannot grasp a certain field directly but needs to be looked at itself. As discussed in Chapter Seven, this necessity is a paradoxical consequence of perspectivism: the premise of multitude and fragmentation of symbolic orders makes it necessary to think a radical space of discontinuity which holds the orders and from which they are scrutinised. Jabès' meditations on the point yield the same conclusion as, ultimately, they must presuppose a bare materiality in which difference is preserved for us so that we can refer to it. The sign does not guarantee such stability because it works based on difference itself; hence, a bare, non-referential materiality is necessary. It turns

---

"We can indicate a point on the paper without knowing what white and black are" – in Jabès, the point (Wittgenstein's spot), *as the primary difference,* can be indicated only as prior, predating any procedure analogous to Wittgenstein's establishment of logical value. What in Wittgenstein is only a partly adequate simile would be exceptionally adequate in Jabès, and for the same reason, too. Ultimately, a point can be indicated *before* telling the difference between white and black because the point embodies difference, which precedes and makes possible any distinction.

out that *the split between materiality and thinking is deeper than the power of difference, which cannot surmount it.* By postulating this modern materialism, we essentially turn difference against itself; we make difference separate itself from thinking through difference. Crucially, while so far difference has worked within language or at its limit (as is the case with the point), locating difference in materiality generally seeks to break linguistic communication and transfer thought to the level of ostensive indication of a thing. In the same gesture, we attribute to the thing indicated the possibility to gaze at our own position. Hence, it is not about the Aristotelian primacy of an "at-hand," subjected to the power of the human gaze. In Jabès' materialism, which is so closely implicated in the principles of modern thinking, *gazing at materiality means, at the same time, being looked at by matter.* The power of difference turns here also against thinking itself and disrupts its subjectifying scrutiny, making it particular and inscribed. Therefore *modern materialism can be a way in which perspectivism apprehends itself, a way in which the fragmented scrutinises the fragmented.* Whatever cannot be expressed in language remains in the awed gaze reciprocated by the silent stare of matter. On this model, to take the position of bare materiality means to experience perspectivism. Consequently, it is no wonder that modern thinking can no longer utter what it considers true and, instead, delves off into the gaze of matter, trying – to no avail – comprehensively to render this effect in thousands upon thousands of written pages.

Insights about thus-conceived materiality are substantiated by Derrida. It is hardly a coincidence that, treading similar paths to Jabès, Derrida referred to *différance* by means of the material difference between "e" and "a." He also used the quasi-concept of "infrastructure" (developed later by Rodolphe Gasché), which "relegates" the conditions of possibility of discourse into its "outside" in a quasi-materialistic manner. Nevertheless, Jabès seems to be more consistent than Derrida. He elaborates a single reference to matter into fully-fledged "materialism," with the Book – a space of ultimate emplacement – as its major quasi-concept.[25]

---

25 As explained in Chapter One, I will not compare Derrida and Jabès comprehensively even though the affinity of the former's *différance* and the latter's point is so conspicuous that it actually calls for charting their similarities and divergences. I will offer one observation only. I believe that the basic hiatus between the two concepts lies in that Derrida's trace "properly has no site," being a simulacrum of presence which constantly shifts, refers to itself and erases itself (Derrida, "Différance," p. 24). This assertion stands in contrast to locating difference in the graphic form of *différance*. Jabès, in turn, apportions his point a place and, even, acknowledges its special space,

To conclude this part of my argument, the reasoning above suggests that Jabès' point essentially involves three inseparable properties. First of all, the point is a sign of basic ontological difference which, when meaning is reduced to the utmost, is the backbone of reality. Second, the point is, at the same time, this very difference because thinking about it absorbs the sign's referential movement. Third, the point must be identified with a material "dot," for only then can it be emplaced, thereby halting difference's engulfing movement. Consequently, the point is a material foothold around which difference continues to oscillate.

Thus-conceived, the point embodies all the paradoxes of Jabès' universe. Their traces were revealed in the examination of letter permutations: the power of the external, graphic link blazed a trail for constructing new meanings. Yet, the "idea" of the point is not about traces; this "outside" is not imprinted onto meaningful utterances anymore. On the contrary, the point in Jabès is no longer an element in a meaningful inquiry; instead, the point is *the movement of the forces of difference themselves around an empty centre*. It is a nomen omen anchorage point from which to start exploring the underlying ontological structure. The triple definition of the point – as a sign of difference, difference itself and its material anchoring – represents the same relationship that binds (1) the perspectival world that refers to the inaccessible beginning; (2) this very beginning, that is, *tzimtzum*; and (3) the Book, in which particular *tzimtzums* are inscribed.

This theoretical framework will support our analysis of Jabès' texts devoted specifically to the point. They can be divided into two groups. In the "static"

---

i.e. the Book. His "impossible materialism," as noted earlier, makes him continue to refer to the outside of matter. So while the "*a*" in Derrida's *différance* marks that which falls silent, built into the "pyramid" of the word (*Ibid.*, p. 23), Jabès' point appears as a crystallised embodiment of this muffling and takes its place.

The difference between Derrida and Jabès results from the messianic structure of Jabès' writing, which, though not aiming at utter silence, uses silence as the key moment of its structure. As such, it enforces the materialistic concept of the Book. This messianic mobilisation and fall are missing in Derrida (at least in his early thought), as a result of which he can rely on the concepts of game and event as well as draw on Nietzsche's concepts of "dance" and affirmation. Perhaps it also helps Derrida think more radically about deconstruction of presence. In this respect, Jabès is more entangled in the tension generated by metaphysical concepts. For example, he uses the notions of origin, the primordial, finitude and fall, which Derrida criticises as metaphysical, for example, in Heidegger. Cf. Jacques Derrida, "Ousia and gramme," in *Margins of Philosophy*, pp. 29–68, on p. 63–64. Nevertheless, it is this tension that fosters Jabès' vision of radical materialism. In this way, metaphysical concepts, rather than being discarded, are harnessed against traditional metaphysics.

group, Jabès depicts the ontological role of the point and reflects on the point as a constitutive "element" of reality. The "dynamic" group approaches the point as an asymptote of the simplification movement, where the point is the accomplishment of the goal pursued by writing. Let me begin from the "static" texts.

The Point as the Basis of Creation

In many passages, Jabès describes the point as a presupposed, basic element of ontology. Let us focus on the following passage:

> In the beginning was the point and the point hid a garden.
> Guided by their past, the Jews noticed, in their daily practice of the text, that the word had roots. They made the trunk of consonant and a life-giving branch of vowel, like God had made a day star of the flaring point and a night star of the burnt-out [ébloui] point.[26]

The passage explicitly evokes the Kabbalistic garden motif.[27] Like the kabbalists, Jabès employs the garden image to express the idea of *the multiplicity of*

---

26 P, p. 28.

27 The "garden" obviously invites associations both with the Garden of Eden, man's first place after Creation, and with the traditional Kabbalistic symbol of the orchard – a פרדס, *pardes* – which appears, for example in the title of Cordovero's chief work *Pardes Rimonim* (*Orchard of Pomegranates*). The orchard symbol – *pardes* – serves as the anagram of four manners of text interpretation, applicable to the Torah in particular. According to Scholem, this reading dates back to Josef ibn' Aqnin, Maimonides' disciple, though it was fully elaborated in *Pardes* by Moses of Leon (who probably authored also a major part of the *Zohar*). According to this work, the four interpretation levels include: *Peshat* (literal meaning), *Remez* (allegorical meaning), *Drash* (Talmudic and Haggadic meaning) and, finally, *Sod* ("mystery," i.e. the hidden mystical meaning accessible only to the chosen few). The first letters of these words make up the word *pardes*. The orchard symbolism was disseminated as a shorthand for the interpretive levels by students of Moses of Leon in two popular Kabbalistic works: *Ra'ja Mehemna* and *Sefer ha-Tikkunim*, and became a common Kabbalistic topos even though authors tended to disagree on what particular levels precisely meant. The idea actually reminds of the mediaeval Christian motif of four levels of interpretation. Who inspired whom is unclear, as noted already by Pico della Mirandola. Gershom Scholem, "Signification," pp. 117–124. Moses of Leon combined his reading of the four interpretive levels with the old Midrash story about four rabbis who entered paradise (that is, *pardes*). In the story, three of the rabbis fail while one – Akiba – is successful. Each of them reaches a particular level of interpretation, with Akiba being the only one to attain *Sod*, the mystical meaning, which enables him to leave the garden. The mystical meaning involves perceiving the internal split of reality and various forms of divine presence, but does not stop at that. Reb Azai, who stopped at *Peshat*, loses himself in the dualism of

ontological layers. With the idea of *pardes*, the kabbalists could claim that the sensory world and the literal interpretation harbour other, deeper layers, which can be reached through mystical reflection. In the passage, Jabès states that "the point hid the garden." The point appears at the beginning, holding the garden within itself. If the garden is construed as the entire developed world, the idea the image conveys is that *the world is not just everything there is but an entity that is in itself a unit of a deeper structure*. The garden-world lies within the point which delimits it from the outside and emplaces it in a peculiar space. If this reading is correct, Jabès uses the Kabbalistic image of the garden to show that there is a level where the internally opulent world can be reduced down to a simple unit. The statement "The point hides the book it contains"[28] can be interpreted in the same way. In other words, the book – with all the manifold elements it encompasses – is only a point within a certain dimension. Its parts are not autonomous because they all depend on their position in this point.

Consequently, *to see the point means, at the same time, to proceed to a level viewed from which the previously simple "all" turns out to be a limited entity.* The point reveals the world, "book," or "garden" as incomplete and placed in a broader space. For this reason, in the passage above, Jabès identifies the point with stars, which make the world *visible*. Without the point, the world is but a simple, immediate "all" while, with the point, it becomes properly a world, that is, something delimited and singular.

Creation. Akiba, however, goes beyond the fragmentation of reality in search of secret coherence. According to tradition, God revealed himself to Akiba exactly as the God of coherence in ultimate silence. "Wind came. But God was not in the wind. And after wind, an earthquake, but God was not in the earthquake. And after the earthquake, a fire, but God was not in it. And after the fire, the voice of supreme silence, in which God passed." Draï explains that "the last lesson shows the level reached by Reb Akiba, one comparable with the level of prophet Elijah, who was able not to try to see God in material elements but beyond humanly graspable and expressible symbolism […], in the climax [*le fin du fin*] of epistemic perception, in the subtlety [*finesse*] of the silence of matter." Draï, *Pensee juive*, p. 127.

Jabès' association of the point with the "garden" displays multiple analogies with the Kabbalah. As will be shown in below, coming to know the point means, in Jabès, immersing in an ever-deeper silence. The epistemic order is opposite to the order of Creation, in which the garden represents the development from the point of a world, determined by this point, with its entire opulence. The point is at the beginning as "the root" of the garden of Creation, and also at the end as the goal of mystical meditation on Creation and approximation of silence.

28 BQ II, p. 393.

To sum up, in Jabès' thought the point has two fundamental aspects to it. First, it is the place of rootedness, that is, of inscribing a world or a book within a broader space. Second, it makes a world or a book singular and visible as individual entities. The latter aspect is very directly evoked in Jabès' texts in which the point is identified with the vowel in an obvious play on the peculiarities of the Hebrew language:

> *("God was the first to break the silence," he said. "It is this breakage we try to translate into human languages."*
> *"Vowels make us see, make us hear. Vowels are image and song. In our ancestors' script, vowels are points."*
> *"God refused image and language in order to be Himself the point. He is image in the absence of images, language in the absence of language, point in the absence of points," he said).*[29]

The passage posits the equivalency of (1) the point, (2) vowel, (3) break and (4) the gap between the split fragments, that is, consonants. What follows is that *the point is the distance which connects and, at the same time, separates shards of reality.* This distance only makes them visible. The point is to reality what the vowel is to consonants: it destroys their simple unity and weaves the resulting pieces into a broader plane, where they only become discernible. Furthermore, Jabès associates the point with God, whereby he asserts that the gap left in the world by God's absence makes it possible to look at this world from outside and spot its limitedness. The point as an elementary form of discontinuity is, thus, the *condition of possibility of the world's perceivability.*

> You need space to read the world. Readability depends on distance.[30]
> All splits from All to allow us conceive of the All, which otherwise would be unthinkable. Nothing is separate from Nothing so that they might mirror each other and thus be named by Nothing.[31]

Consequently, thinking about the world is possible only because of disjunction embodied in the point. But this means also that the world which we know through the point must be in advance marked by a split that makes it readable. Even though Jabès follows here in the footsteps of German idealism, such notion of the point does not allow any Hegelian sublation in absolute knowledge. The point must endure for the world to remain readable. The point is, therefore, the condition of possibility of knowledge and, also, the condition of impossibility of

---

29 BQ II, p. 353.
30 BQ I, p. 381.
31 BR II, p. 72.

knowledge (making knowledge always incomplete and dependent on the ultimate remnant it cannot subsume).

> Jabès reflects in the same way on human life:
> "'The road of life is straight as an 'i' topped by a point it cannot ever join, which makes it legible to us," he said.[32]
> He made this absurd statement that each letter of our name was a phase of our life, and if death haunted us day and night, it was because the last letter, drawn like the others by our hand, fascinates us with its singular visibility.
> He also said, the fact that the last letter of his first name was unpronounced rather confirmed that this letter was, not dead, but a letter of death.
> And added: Sometimes the letter of death divides the flourishing letters of a name.
> Against the time of life granted, it silently opposes the eternity of time that is its own.
> [...] Could it be that man is a book [un livre] that he can read only in the book [le livre] he will write? And if the very act of writing made it possible?
> My life is in the book, and the book is my life.[33]

Human life must contain an inner split, a negative remnant that resists understanding. This place, at the same time, directs thoughts to a space into which entire life is inscribed and from whose point of view it is a singular entity. "The last letter" of life forms the point which does not belong to life anymore but makes life perceivable: it is "exceptionally visible." Unpronounceable, it demarcates the destination that life heads towards. Therefore, life cannot be seen – "read" in Jabès' vocabulary – from within: it will show itself only in the last dot of its final book, where it will no longer be. As long as there is readability, reality continues fragmented, and, consequently, life cannot achieve total coherence.

"Let us make the point. Let us see,"[34] exhorts Jabès. Making the point is like a lightning discharge that splits and simultaneously illumines the whole. Consequently, the point can be conceived not only in static terms, as an element of ontology, but also dynamically. The point is the goal of the movement of thinking. Let us focus on this goal now.

The Point as the End of God's Erasure and Withdrawal

As already mentioned, for Jabès, writing is the movement of simplification. Each consecutive writing act strives to reduce the meaningful content and to focus on the structure behind its cycle. It is in this context that Jabès explores the point's

---

32 *Ibid.*, p. 28.
33 *Ibid.*, pp. 65, 67.
34 Let us take our bearings, BQ II, p. 105 (quotation altered).

dynamic function. *The point is, namely, an asymptote of the simplification move-ment* – a goal this movement pursues but never attains. This simplification could be deemed only a formal experiment. But those familiar with Jabès' thought know that he does not even take such notion into account. If not experimentation, what is the aim of simplification? First, it serves to unveil fundamental ontological difference. In the previous section, this difference was discussed as a presupposed element of ontology; here, however, simplification serves to show that as an utterance's meaning is gradually reduced, the point-difference will remain as an irreducible remnant. Second, the simplification movement involves, in parallel, *reproducing the process of God's withdrawal, which results in God's reduction down to the point, an interval and minimal absence.*

As discussed in the previous section, Jabès identifies the point – elementary difference – with God after *tzimtzum*. Here, however, he ventures much further. Namely, he suggests that the simplification movement effected by the writer is, mysteriously, co-extensive with God's withdrawal. Even more intriguingly, the order of ontology is, in this, indistinguishable from the order of epistemology. Namely, the writer discovers the event which *has already come to pass* and made the negativity of difference the foundation of ontology; and, at the same time, he simultaneously, provokes this event himself in his drive towards simplification. As already suggested, this paradoxical action is *a repetition* of God's withdrawal rather than just coming to know God's withdrawal. The writer destroys the abundance of writing and causes its desertification in order to know the parallel desertification unfolding in the world.

It is easy to notice that, in this way, he falls into a historical pitfall. The process of "desertification" seems, theoretically, to reach into the future: it seeks to unveil the point on the horizon. But this point is, at the same time, the origin. To pursue the beginning means is to enter the future.[35] Hence, the idea of the point compromises any concept of both the origin and the goal in which these notions serve to locate inquiry in the stable order of past, present and future. As already mentioned, the essence of the point, as Jabès sees it, lies in *separation itself* which precedes distinguishing moments in time and makes such distinguishing possible in the first place.[36] This is why the way of destruction, which Jabès follows in

---

35 Cf. BR III, p. 32.
36 This property of the point, which is always not-here, always deferred, is compellingly grasped by Alberto Folin: "[In Jabès], the *point* condenses negativity most radically because Difference between Being and Nothing, and one parallel to it – between voice and silence – do not form either an ontological opposition (man vs. animal,

writing, both reveals that which precedes reality and pursues the goal of desertifying it, in doing which God's withdrawal is repeated. Reality is based on a nothere – whether the past or the future – which it cannot reach. Hence, meditation ultimately focuses on the point itself[37] as the centre of discontinuity, no matter where it is located.[38] "In the utterances of the book, past and future cannot be distinguished,"[39] writes Jabès.

I will return to this paradox in the conclusion because it is a tell-tale aspect of Jewish philosophy of modernity. For now, I will attend to Jabès' texts to investigate how the movement of simplifying writing down to the point dovetails in them with God's withdrawal.

Importantly, across the successive parts of *The Book of Questions* the text is incrementally stripped of protagonists, dialogues and narratives; passages are utterly compressed and stories are getting increasingly skeletal to disappear completely. These processes are accompanied by linguistic Kabbalism, which involves erasing letters. The written words are partly crossed, which reduction yields shorter words, dismantled down to individual syllables. Most of these words contain the particle *El*, one of the Hebraic names of God.[40] As early as in

---

animal vs. nature, and so forth) or a temporal opposition (past vs. present). On the contrary, Difference lies in the mutual attachment turned toward the future: it *is* not [*il y a*], but it *will* be [*il y aura*]. In the *point*, voice and silence co-exist in such a radically negative way that we cannot state anything about the present because as soon as we break silence by saying a present thing, we have already crossed the limit which made difference possible – we have stepped into future, into death." Alberto Folin, "La figure du silence dans l'imaginaire moderne: Leopardi et Jabès," in *Écrire le livre*, pp. 147–56, on p. 153. Thus difference does not lie within being itself but is prior to it (like Derrida's *différance*), though not temporally. Any attempt to utter it immediately severs from it, differentiates and defers. Difference embodied in the point is where it is no more immediate: in the future. In this optics, time is only an attempt to stabilise difference – which is based on not-being-here – by inscribing it in the register of the past or the future.

37 "Questioning the point meant unflagging questioning of the question that had come up with it. Unassailable point, favorable and fatal to all thought – fighting with its own excess – for which it is crest and base" (BQ II, p. 440).

38 "As in a plane or solid system of reference, ordinate abscissa and cure, so the unreasonable, the extravagant and the unexpected help define the position of the vibrant point of any quest" (*Ibid.*, p. 356).

39 BR III, p. 24.

40 Jabès evokes here two main names of God in Jewish tradition: to *Elohim* (*El* in an older and shorter version; *El* appears in the *Tanakh* mainly in poetic texts and less frequently than *Elohim*, but as a matter of fact *Elohim* is the plural form while *El*

the first *Book of Questions*, Jabès states that the Name of God is what remains after writings have been erased multiple times.[41] In the last part of the series, *El* emerges from the names of the protagonists introduced and removed in the previous volumes:

~~Y A~~ E L
E L ~~Y A~~
~~A~~ E L ~~Y~~
E L[42]

Jabès gives his protagonists names that heed the logic of Hebrew names, which contained *El* as their component, for example Micha-el ("who is like God?"), Rapha-el ("God is healer") and Dani-el ("God is my judge").[43] Three names of the eponymous protagonists of the fourth, fifth and sixth *Book of Questions* contain *El* interwoven with the particle *Ya*, God's ancient name and an element of the Tetragrammaton.[44] In this way, the divine Name is demonstrated to engender all other names.

---

underscores God's singularity) and to the Tetragrammaton. The Tetragramaton figures in Jabès' writings as multiple allusions to the unpronounceable name, to the four (unnamed) letters which, having vanished, are the pinnacle of God's absence (see BQ II, p. 437). As regards crossing out and permutating letters (chiefly in *The Last Book*), these procedures involve predominantly *El*. Likely, Jabès employs the name *El* in such contexts because it is shorter and, as such, more easily amenable to the Kabbalistic operation. Nonetheless, both names of God crucially connote different things in Jewish tradition. According to the Talmud, God adopts different names in his different involvements. *Elohim* is the name of the Judge who judges the creation (*ha-beriot*) while the Tetragrammaton designates God "of mercy" (Draï, *Pensée juive*, p. 356). It is not clear whether Jabès observes this distinction, but given his knowledge of Jewish mysticism and the Talmud, it is certainly possible, to say the least. That he uses the Tetragrammaton to describe God's absence may thus imply that post-*tzimtzum* reality is devoid of mercy. At the same time, erasure of letters to arrive at *El* may indicate that God's withdrawal is, at the same time, an enactment of judgment.

41 BQ I, p. 95.
42 BQ II, p. 376.
43 In *Yaël*, Jabès himself points out that the eponymous protagonist's name is similar to such names as Nuriel, Uriel, Rasiel, Raphael, and so forth (cf. BQ II, p. 67).
44 In Debrauwere-Miller's original interpretation, Yaël – the protagonist whose name serves as the title of the fourth *Book of Questions* – personifies the Shekhinah (God's Presence in exile, which is the last, tenth sefirah and also, according to the *Zohar*, God's feminine aspect). In Jabès' text, Yaël is the narrator's love – a mysterious, changeable and elusive character that tends to be described as the "female half of being." Like the Shekhinah, she is erotically charged. Her name (as prophet Elijah's too) seems to be

In another permutation, Jabès applies this procedure to reading, in which the book [*LIVRE*] and being free [*LIBRE*] are erased first and then reading itself [*LIRE*] is crossed out to yield LE: the definite article denoting "He" and, at the same time, "it," that is, simply, All:

L I ~~V~~ R E
L I ~~B~~ R E
L I R E
L I R E
L E[45]

"EL" and its reverse "LE" are both erected upon the void which enters – or, more precisely, *reveals itself as already existing* – within the words it destroys. Consequently, they bear the trace of absence. This encapsulates Jabès' premise that God is the pinnacle of absence, being both the "only One" and "the One" whose indeterminacy encompasses All. The degradation of God's Name ends with the restitution of pure *EL*, as Shillony observes.[46] This *EL* is no longer the

---

a direct compound of two Names of God: *Ya* and *El*, given also to one of Biblical figures. As Debrauwere-Miller concludes, in the *Zohar*, *Ya* corresponds to the Shekhinah while *El* to the sefirah of *Tiferet*, the centre of God's consciousness. Both these sefirot were divided before Creation. According to Debrauwere-Miller, Jabès may deliberately use these rather than any other syllables to show God's inner split in the name of Yaël. *Ya* and *El* form two disjoined elements in God, who, as a result, cannot achieve a stable identity. Like the Biblical Jacob, the narrator of the fourth part of *The Book of Questions* has a revelatory dream of God's Presence, which visits him as Yaël. Marked with this experience, the narrator wishes to reproduce Yaël's presence in the book, attesting also to the primary unity of the Shekhinah and *Tiferet*, revealed to him in Yaël. Undoubtedly, in Jabès, it is the metaphor for the primordial, perfect and complete language. The narrator's intent is, however, disastrous as he breaks the mystical unity in the act of writing. The properties of writing discussed above are here interwoven with references to the Kabbalah tradition, where the Shekhinah and *Tiferet* are divided as voice and articulation. The narrator is exiled into *Sitra Achra*, the demonic "other side," where he wanders in search of fragmented Yaël, who embodies the originary unity of language. Cf. Nathalie Debrauwere-Miller, "Tree of Consciousness: The Shekhinah in Edmond Jabès' *Yaël*," *Literature & Theology*, 17/4 (December 2003), pp. 388–406. There is, however, an interesting twist to this reasoning, which sheds light on Jabès' Jewish philosophy of modernity, for the Biblical name Jael, in fact, *is not* the compound of two Divine Names and has a different etymology. Thus, Jabès' speculation is his own invention.

45   *Ibid.*, p. 91.
46   Shillony, *Edmond Jabès*, p. 18.

erstwhile Name, but a form of primordial absence. The death of God is not a singular event but a process of slow and endless withdrawal.

But God's withdrawal does not stop at disclosing *EL* as the basis of words; it progresses to reduce also this already transformed Name.[47] When the words "God" (*Dieu*) and "mourning" (*Deuil*) are erased, L alone remains. As Jabès insists, all mourning is above all the mourning of God (in both senses of the genitive: God's mourning and mourning for God):

D I
E U
D E
U I
L[48]

"L" as such is the last stage on the way to the point, on which the rest of the text focuses. In this way, it turns out that "all efforts to write are polarization of the point,"[49] arranging it in various combinations. Ultimately, the point appears on the horizon of writing, as its goal, basis and sole object: its condition of (im)possibility.[50] "Everything is washed away. Only the point is left, arbiter of obliteration."[51]

In her insightful interpretation of the last four parts of *The Book of Questions*, Brown calls their progression "tracking of the advancement towards the absolute by means of reaching beyond appearances and imaginary representations."[52] Three characters – Yaël, Elya and Aely – are metaphors for the stages of this gradual erasure.[53] Aely is, basically, only a remnant left over after the fall of

---

47 Also here Jabès draws on the Kabbalah. Two eminent mediaeval kabbalists Judah Halevi and Abraham ibn Ezra observed that both Divine Names – יהוה and אלוהים – consist almost only of *matres lectionis*. As such, they do not designate anything in the world itself but embody the divine spirit within the universe sustained by this spirit. See Scholem, "Name of God" 2, p. 172. In Jabès, similarly, the names are finally reduced to the point only, which is not a word even, but the material cornerstone of reality, the elementary difference.

48 BQ II, p. 411.

49 *Ibid.*, p. 412.

50 Cf. Josh Cohen, "Desertions," p. 97.

51 BQ II, p. 392.

52 Llewellyn Brown, "Les metamorphoses du point: • (*El, ou le dernier livre*) d'Edmond Jabès," *Litteratures*, 38 (1998), pp. 145–55, on p. 145.

53 As Bounoure observes, while Sarah and Yukel, the protagonists of the initial parts of *The Book of Questions*, are annihilated by the spasm of history, the three more peculiar characters in the last parts of *The Book* – Yaël, Elya and Aely – are destroyed by 'an

representation – an eye, the Law.[54] But this name, too, will be erased to have only the point for the title of the last book. In the course of the four books, a certain "active force" comes to the fore, operating from outside of the writer and his characters – a "charged alterity," which strives to reveal itself *through* the writer and his characters.[55] Its movement erases the characters and demands to speak itself. In this process, Brown goes on, the writer realises that he is not the source of his words, that another force steps in and out, emptying the writing process of meanings. This force intercepts writing to express itself. Writing reaches its "zero level" and turns into the cut-off point [*point de butoir*] for meaning.[56]

Brown posits also an interesting theory of the erasure process which is consistent with the conclusions of the previous Chapters. Namely, as she suggests,[57] the consecutive forms of writing in the last parts of *The Book of Questions* are pairings of two dimensions: representation and God. Representation brings about the internal plenitude of passages while God is their empty core and inner movement. In this perspective, the erasure process is nothing else than the disclosure of the empty centre.[58] This is the key paradox of Jabès' Kabbalah: *God reveals himself where his ultimate withdrawal from representation comes to pass.* In other words, God's revelation is God's death conceived in Nietzsche's fashion. The force which in Brown's reasoning manifests in and through erasure is thus God's revelation through his withdrawal from representations. The writer, who is himself erased in the process, gives this revelation writing.[59]

---

abyss hiding in the deepest corner of interiority rather than by any readily locatable force" (Bounoure, *Edmond Jabès*, pp. 79–80).

54 Brown, "Metamorphoses," p. 145.

55 *Ibid.*, p. 146.

56 *Ibid.*, p. 147.

57 *Ibid.*, pp. 148–9.

58 Also Guglielmi reads the last part of *The Book of Questions* as the fall of representation and erasure of God's image. He writes: "As the books progress, Jabès' movement destroys ever more radically the form and properties, the established harmony of the dominant transcendental model and pushes further and further away the divine image in order to, on its behalf and in its place, institute henceforth the *point*, which marks the shifting place where distance, abandonment, distortion and negativity appear and interrogate." Joseph Guglielmi, "Le dernier état des questions," *Change*, 22 (février 1975), pp. 177–8.

59 For this reason, Jabès frames the writer both as the agent and a victim of "God's death": "The meandering word dies by the pen, the writer by the same weapon turned back against him. 'What murder are you accused of?' Reb Achor asked Zilliech, the writer. 'The murder of God,' he replied. 'I will however add in my defense that I die along with Him.'" (BQ I, p. 338).

Summing up these insights, Jabès follows the Kabbalah to assert that "When God, *El*, wanted to reveal Himself, He appeared as a point."[60] In doing this, he suggests that *the ultimate path towards desertification is, at the same time, the path of revelation.* The wiping-out of the meaningful world down to a simple point is to reveal its ultimate basis, which, being eternally displaced into not-here, is the absent God himself. Therefore, reduction to the point is a way of finding the community of God and Creation:

> "I'm inclined to believe that our nothingness and God's do not at all have [ne sont point] the same scope. One envelops the other. We must see them in this perspective," wrote Reb Hamouna.
>
> And added, in order to illustrate his remark: "Imagine day engulfing the night, then night engulfing the day. All we shall ever be is nothing within nothing, a circle within a circle."
> And if God were the smallest circle?[61]
>
> If God, as we know Him, has chosen to manifest Himself in a point, is it not to proclaim His likeness to a point?
> [...] "The point reveals God outside resemblance."[62]
> He tried to read the book within the book and thereby destroyed it in each of its words. But the book also destroyed him, so that nothing was left either of him or of the book except for two small points, one black, one white, which soon fused.
> [...] "A point so small, and yet it holds the ashes of all other points," he said.[63]

Concluding: the point is ultimately *pure difference* abstracted from its contentful iterations – an asymptote of the movement of simplification. At the same time, the point comprises all these iterations, the way that the kabbalists believed it did.[64] It is the smallest, central circle whence all forms of the world develop and which they encompass. This pattern is unveiled and, simultaneously, repeated in writing.

The final point contains all the remaining ones turned into "ashes."[65]

---

60 BQ II, p. 341.

61 BR II, p. 28.

62 LR I, p. 31 (in *From the Book to the Book*, p. 155).

63 BQ II, pp. 341–2.

64 For the kabbalists, the point is a locus of contradictory forces. See Marc-Alain Ouaknin, *Tsimtsoum* (Paris: Albin Michel, 1992), p. 154.

65 Of course, the image of ashes evokes also the Shoah as another iteration of God's withdrawal.

Conclusion: What the Theology of the Point Actually Describes

Let us first recapitulate our argument in this Chapter. First, I showed that Jabès' linguistic Kabbalism begins from the insight that meaningful utterances can be analysed from the perspective external to them, i.e. writing. This means that there is more to language than only content relations. Jabès generalises this insight and views meaning itself as limited and inscribed in another dimension embodied in writing. In this way, an ostensibly simple difference between the content of an utterance and its graphic rendering becomes a form of basic ontological difference which, in the world of perspectivism, divides the finite symbolic order from its outside. This premise causes Jabès' linguistic Kabbalism to evolve and focus on the point. Jabès' point is a sign of difference, difference itself and its material emplacement in one. I presented also two functions that the point performs in Jabès' texts. First, the point is a presupposed, basic element of ontology as it embodies distance that both separates things and makes them visible. It breaks their unity, but, *as a void*, it forms a new plane of continuity where they become visible. Second, the point is the ultimate goal of the simplification movement that Jabès' texts undergo. In this function, the point is a negative remnant which is disclosed when meaning is reduced to a minimum. At the same time, this process rehearses the act of God's withdrawal from the Creation.

I believe that the identification of the point with God and of the erasure movement with God's *tzimtzum* is a key to Jabès' Jewish philosophy of modernity. Let us explore this correlation in more detail. Throughout this Chapter, I have attempted to show that speculation on the point is not actually a religious meditation in Jabès, who does not reflect on the Revelation as the Revelation does not exist for him. Consequently, he cannot be said to continue the Kabbalah. Radical though the kabbalists always were in their speculations to the point of identifying God with nothing, they always found the Revelation essential and viewed their extreme mystical insights as mysteries available to the chosen few and *invariably rooted directly in the Torah's injunctions*. As Idel underscores, the kabbalists speculated on the mystical meanings of the Scripture but always regarded it as a message from the divine Author himself.[66] To fathom those mysteries meant to rise to the level that transcended reality. Consequently, the most radical conclusion about the nature of God could not possibly breed the idea of his non-existence, for the speculation did not abolish the Torah's lower meanings.

---

66   Idel, *Absorbing Perfections*, pp. 103–104.

Jabès sees things entirely differently. He discards the God of Theism as a construct of human thinking. The Torah does not matter to him as the God-given Law. What serves as the material of his speculation is *any text*. For the speculation discovers the relationships which found reality as such and are reflected in every utterance. Like Kant and Hegel, Jabès does not rely on the Revelation as the source proper of knowledge, instead *perceiving this source everywhere around him*. Reality no longer has a transcendent dimension, but each of its elements reflects the same pattern and principle: the structure of the excess remnant. As such, it can be disclosed in the movement of simplification, which, rather than on the Torah, works on any text whatsoever. This movement results in the Kabbalism of the point, where speculation is brought down to its basic level: to relations constituted around the irreducible trace. This final trace, interval, discontinuity – or whatever else we choose to call it – is identified by Jabès with the "new," contemporary God.

But why with God actually? The reason is that the role of this basic difference seems so immense to Jabès that it is comparable solely with the position God takes in the world of Theism. "Theology of the point," which features in the title of this Chapter, shows the movement *which elevates the effect of simplification's philosophical work – difference – to the position of God*. The point is here the central place of radically atheistic reality and, at the same time, turns out so vital that it calls for the former Theistic language. In this way, Jabès reproduces the Kabbalah's mystical speculation, investing it with entirely new meanings.

Does this choice have anything "specifically Jewish" to it? The answer is no, it does not, insofar that before and after Jabès a similar gesture was applied to other traditions. When Kant supplants the Christian notion of God with the idea of pure reason, he follows the same path; when Hegel finds his "proper understanding" of Christianity, filling it with the dialectics of his own philosophy, he also erects the radically atheistic *concept* to the position of God. And after Jabès, for example, Jacques Lacan states in his Seminar XX:

> The Other, the Other as the locus of truth, is the only place, albeit an irreducible place, that we can give to the term "divine being," God, to call him by his name. God (*Dieu*) is the locus where, if you will allow me this wordplay, the *dieu* – the *dieur* – the *dire*, is produced. With a trifling change the *dire* constitutes *Dieu*. And as long as things are said, the God hypothesis will persist. [...] in the end only theologians can be truly atheistic, namely those who speak of God.[67]

---

67 Jacques Lacan, *On Feminine Sexuality*, p. 45.

Following in the footsteps of Hegel and Lacan, Žižek links God to the minimum, irreducible *quantum* of negativity, a split that activates reality's inner movement and, also, makes it excessive.[68] A simple comparison implies that both Jabès' thought and these examples deal with *the same base difference*. But the issue is far more captivating because whatever differences there are between, for example, Lacan, Žižek and Jabès – and they are by no means negligible – they *are all diminished by the very act of questing for a minimum difference*. The simplification movement, which unfolds in all of them (perhaps even enforced by the logic of modern thinking), heads towards its ultimate point, invalidating content differences underway. At the same time, each of these separate, albeit parallel, paths, if looked at from the perspective of their end-point, *seems to employ these secondary, invalidated differences to cloak itself as radically different from the other ones*.

Is it not how Christianity is "employed" by Hegel, Lacan and Žižek, and Judaism by Jabès? They list "proper readings" of each of these religions, arguing how aptly they describe the modern mechanisms of atheistic reality. But, in fact, they comb these respective traditions for meticulously selected resources which are already organised around the structure of the remnant in order to discover in them, in the movement of simplification, an irreducible distance, a split, and so forth, and identify it with God. Does the identical logic behind these gestures not cancel out the fundamental differences between Christianity and Judaism, which served to make these gestures? And if these differences are cancelled out, what drives this obsessive pursuit of *self-distinction*, this obsessive emphasis that the thus-discovered thought is "essentially" Jewish or Christian? In this movement of dissolution, which after all abolishes all grounding, what is it that produces and propels the need for the ultimate, inexplicable grounding of the "truly" Jewish or Christian difference?

My take on this issue is that all the thinkers listed above, including Jabès, *discover one and the same logic of difference that can be regarded as the logic of modern reality*. That the same difference is at stake *is warranted by this difference itself* as the ultimate goal of the simplification movement. To pursue it, one must first choose "the positive content," to use Hegel's coinage; there can be no simplification movement without this initial multiplicity which resists it. Simplification consists in "discovering" the workings of basic difference within this multiplicity. It is a double and inevitably overdetermined gesture: *simplification "places" this difference in the positive content, claiming at the same time to discover it*. This is

---

68 Cf., e.g. Žižek, *Less Than Nothing*, p. 110 ff.

not the end, however. Reduction leads to the implosion of the initial content, in which nothing is left except basic difference, with the inner variety becoming its function. The final point is utter simplification. This is where, I believe, the thinkers catalogued above make their breakthrough gesture: *protecting themselves against the logic of ultimate simplification, they turn back just before its end and reach for an ostensibly external difference to stop this destructive movement.* This external difference is not analysed but kept as the last shield against perishment. In this sense, it is material. What kind of difference is meant here? A viable answer is: the difference between Judaism and Christianity.

A very similar movement has already surfaced in this Chapter. Namely, when, following Jabès, I examined the point as a sign of difference and difference itself that engulfs it, I found that this difference had to be *emplaced*, to be anchored in matter. To stabilise the movement of thinking, an external difference was needed between difference and the characters on the paper, *which simply are before us.* If used at the beginning of the simplification movement, such an ostensive example would inevitably be deconstructed as a reference to the "logic of presence." *And yet, at the end of this movement, the "present," looking-and-looked-at materiality is requisite as a barrier against the engulfing force of difference.*

I believe that insisting on the rigorous distinction between one's own path of philosophical simplification and those of others – by arguing that it is "truly" Jewish or Christian, materialist or idealist, leftist or rightist, and so forth – is to serve as the same quasi-"presence" that mounts up a blockade to ultimate difference. *The positive content, which served initially as material to be simplified, turns into a barrier against the final act of simplification.* The starting point becomes an irreducible anchorage point for difference, making it at all visible. On this account, Jabès' "materialism" represents the same logic that underpins his "Judaism" and Hegel's, Lacan's or Žižek's "Christianity." Indication of the differences that are prior to the enacted simplification performs the same function as making an ink stain on paper: it emplaces and retains base difference. It gives respite from the labour of differing on particular issues as it is enough to point to this base difference to make separation from other positions definitive and self-evident. Furthermore, it helps perceive one's own position as well. In this stoppage that modern thought finds so alluring – in this silent reciprocation of gazes between thought and difference which it has instituted, which it gazes at and by which it is ultimately gazed at – one arrives at self-recognition as a piece on the map of perspectivism.

Hence, it can be said that the self-depiction of one's philosophy as Jewish or Christian *finally inscribes the entire force of base difference within the "contingent" difference of positive content and helps perceive this philosophy as looked at by a fixed gaze*. There is nothing behind "true" philosophical Judaism or Christianity except one fundamental difference which constructs modern thinking. However, this difference is not directly graspable or describable. "Just before" it is arrived at, "just before" the simplification movement achieves its end, it must come to a halt to avoid being absorbed: *in this act of stoppage, base difference is projected on the material that has been annihilated and distinguishes this material radically from all other ones.* This explains why history is so essential to modern philosophy. History is, first of all, a dead lump of a broken narrative about events which modern thought revives and saturates with its own difference so as to subordinate to present thinking the past that has led to it. But the same historical material that is so bluntly reorganised provides the last possible point that enables self-distinction. Therefore, it is as much organised by modern thinking as it supports modern thinking as a certain "at-hand" lying before us and having a gaze. Were it not for the historical distinctions, which as such are contingent in the light of base difference, all modern paths would merge into one. A barrier to the ultimate simplification is, thus, put up by drawing a contingent, historical dividing line and attributing an organising power to it, which comes from basic difference. In this way, for example, the difference between philosophical Judaism and Christianity is raised to the status of the fundamental division that has informed the entire Western philosophy. At the same time, our own position is looked at by the fixed gaze of split history.

It is only by renewing this delimitation over and over again, which requires a meticulous separation of Athens from Jerusalem and of Christianity from Judaism, that base difference can be fixed in one place. In other words, the radical self-distinction of one's way is an ultimate embodiment of fundamental modern difference. Adhering to a clearly demarcated philosophical "position," to unambiguous identification with "Judaism," "Christianity," "materialism" and their likes, indicates thus that *the movement of simplification has approached its end and, unable to actually reach this end, it has had to turn back and settle on a compromise difference which blocks thought in confrontation with materiality.* As Jabès' reflection on the point implies, "pure" difference is not available: when approaching it, thinking must flinch and halt at an external fulcrum. In this perspective, the modern humanistic disputes of "truly" Jewish or "truly" Christian philosophical positions are a double sign: a sign of success, that is, of arriving at the common structure of base difference; and a sign of inevitable failure as this difference is projected onto the positive content, which produces positions sustained only by resistance to the force of negativity.

This resistance is highly symptomatic and betrays the tension of modern thinking. For exploring dispassionately an illustrative historical difference between Judaism and Christianity would take a painstaking study of differences between particular texts, an accurate examination of how both traditions have evolved and a methodical scrutiny of how they have come closer to and moved away from each other in the process. This is not how Jewish philosophy of modernity spins its narrative: admittedly, it employs historical material, but it does so only to "discover" in it a difference it has presupposed and heads to. It aims to purify, universalise and, then, extend this difference onto issues which seem to have little to do with it. Characteristically, negligible differences can in this way be inflated into absolutely fundamental divisions. Any common measure for more or less significant distinctions disappears as the basic separation is fundamentally relevant while all other differences are entirely overridden by it. In this way, the outcome is settled in advance, and the closure is ostensibly embedded in the already existing historical material, whose stone-hard look suffers no remonstration.

This implies yet another consequence. If, this is indeed how the positive content, simplification movement and base difference are interrelated, discourses informed by this configuration can be expected to have a specific relationship to history. Namely, the past of the tradition on which they draw will not be directly available to them. They will not perceive themselves as located within and determined by its continuity. Rather, I believe, their relationship to this past will be based on the structure of *inscription* in history, which inscription is an act of re-interpretation consisting in severance. In their perception of history, the discourses will consciously consider themselves to be "a foreign body" which, though apparently discovering the "true" meaning of the old, insufficiently reflexive tradition, is itself based on another speculative mechanism. This pattern is glaringly visible in Hegel's notion of Christianity. If these insights are correct, *an inexplicable discontinuity should arise in the continuum of history as framed by the new discourses – a trace of the projection of base modern difference onto the "historical material."* This trace in history should be closely associated with difference as the goal of the simplification movement.

Jabès' meditations on the point help notice this association. He states, namely, that "our sources precede us" and that, searching for the ultimately purified point, we are actually searching for the event that gave rise to all our thinking, for *tzimtzum*. Therefore, Jabès presupposes a discontinuity in history, a discontinuity which is responsible for the end of simplification.

If this reasoning is correct, Jabès' "theology of the point" tells us more and, at the same time, less than it would like to. It tells us less because, instead of reviving the Kabbalah, it turns the Kabbalah into a material for the movement of modern difference. In doing so, it drags the Kabbalah, and entire Judaism with it, into endless wars over what is actually Jewish and what is not. Yet it also tells us more because the white flame of purely modern difference appears from behind the Kabbalistic curtain. Jabès' writings provide one of the most accurate, radical and consistent accounts of how this difference works.

Conclusion: Edmond Jabès and Jewish Philosophy of Modernity

If it still makes any sense draw a disciplinary dividing line between literary studies and philosophy, this line should perhaps be demarcated by their different ways of reading. Literary studies have long struggled to define its object of research. The transgressiveness of literature has seen one definitional attempt after another fail. Hence perhaps the ancillary status of literary studies, where the text is both the point of departure and the endpoint – a space only momentarily illumined by interpretation, which cannot fathom the material bulk of writing. Philosophy has for ages chased the chimera of a transparent text that, arguably, resists interpretation but must eventually surrender if read with the belief that it harbours *thoughts*. Has the erstwhile way of reading philosophical texts (even those that belied the illusion of a purely communicative function) not impressed itself indelibly on philosophy? Does it not still impact the habits of reading in which a conceptual scaffolding is immediately extracted from a text and, also immediately, seen as the world?

If it were indeed the case and if philosophy still focused not so much on reading as on *the questioning* which the text just prompts, such a residuum would offer an immense interpretive opportunity. For philosophy lacks that elementary distance to the text which may curb the interpretive drive but holds interpretation firmly within the bounds of writing. Hence philosophy boldly ventures to interpret in a, so to speak, blinded manner. If Nietzsche chided philosophy for its neglect of philological accuracy and for mistaking a hastily and once only understood text for reality itself, might we say that today, when deconstruction has become part of the academic doxa, philosophy offers us a remedy to reducing the effects of writing to the text as such? Might we say that it is in philosophy that we can find a counterbalance to an all too easy equation of the world with the text and an a-priori acknowledgement that reality is our construct? Perhaps philosophical reading, with its nuisance of seriousness and finding the world in a text rather than the other way round, can lead us back to the abandoned path that deconstruction once walked. Taking the effect of the text for "reality" itself made philosophy a laughing stock once, but today the same gesture can embarrass those who see the effect of the text as merely the effect of the text.

Throughout this book, I have attempted to read Edmond Jabès' writings philosophically, that is, to look for a reality rather than a text in them, as a result of a trifling, half-inadvertent mistake. The outcome of such reading is Jabès' philosophy, an effect of radical perspectivism. This philosophy, as an added value, sheds light on the modern construct of Judaism in the humanities. It also helps think the genesis and the role of modern simplification as well as to give it an ethical vector.

Let us now compile the conclusions from the argument in this book. My first intent was to determine whether Jabès' philosophy could be described as Jewish philosophy of modernity and, if so, whether it augmented this philosophy in any way. To settle that, we should best revisit the ideal type of Jewish philosophy of modernity defined in Chapter One and compare it with the aspects of Jabès' thinking discussed across this volume. As listed at the beginning, the distinctive features of Jewish philosophy of modernity include:

Traces of the modern turn. This is a vivid feature of Jabès' radicalised and simplified thinking. It surfaces, for example, in (a) the idea of an inaccessible originary disaster associated with Luria's *tzimtzum*; (b) the notion that absence is the foundation of reality marked by the trauma of God's withdrawal;[1] (c) insistence that a thinking based on stability, presence, being, and so forth, *has become* a dangerous illusion which a "nomadic thinking" must ultimately expose; (d) the belief that Judaism is in crisis and calls for an essential re-interpretation; (e) the utter separation between the structure and the content of thinking: Jabès is searching for a pattern of forces that affect the consecutive "books," whereby their content is secondary to the movement in which they are generated; (f) repeated foregrounding of historicity and attempts to understand the modern condition against the former ages. Consequently, Jabès' writings are stamped by the originary catastrophic event that resists being revealed while enforcing repeated attempts to unveil it. The modern shift produces the need for radical simplification which ostensibly aims to show the sources of the crisis though, essentially, it completes this crisis.

Endorsement of modern (post-)Kantian premises. As shown in the foregoing, basically every element of Jabès' thinking reflects the structure of the remnant, which I defined as a relationship between finite, limited perspectives and a lack, an empty centre that delimits them and is their inaccessible goal. Philosophically speaking, this structure is the legacy of the Kantian "thing in itself" and the aporia of the continuity of the series. The structure of the remnant appears in the following of Jabès' fundamental concepts: (a) in the idea of *tzimtzum* as an "empty" place of separation and connection between the imaginary and the real; (b) in the concept of the *vocable*, whose "core" is the very distance of *tzimtzum*;

---

1   See Guglielmi, *Ressemblance*, pp. 18–19.

(c) in the movement of messianism triggered by the attempt to unite reality fragmented by the void of *tzimtzum*; messianism vainly endeavours to remove this excessive remnant and achieve the Unity of things; (d) in the relationship between the Book and a book: the Book is, in Lacanian parlance, a *pas-tout*, a "not-Whole," i.e. a Whole with a hole produced each time by a partial book; that is why a book makes it possible to see the Book, but always in displacement; (e) in the position of the Jew/writer, who is always separated from a place from which he could properly interpret himself; (f) in meditations on the point, which are the final and ultimate form of thinking on the structure of the remnant, where this structure is reduced to elementary and material relationships. Besides the structure of the remnant, Jabès' work amasses also other modern assumptions: (a) perspectivism, described by the poet as a structurally necessary existence of many finite forms of knowledge, which he calls "books"; (b) discarding the notion of transcendent God. Jabès' God is subject to the laws of the reality he "created"; (c) identification of God with the void, negativity and remnant (d) presupposing an external agency that "gazes at" the fragmented perspectives and confers continuity on them – though this agency cannot be directly known.

Dependence of thinking on the structure of the remnant. Admittedly, Jabès does not consider himself a philosopher and does not delve into the crisis of 20th-century philosophy, but his thought seems to enact the same structures that have affected philosophy ever since Kant. Thinking, namely, does not entail taking a neutral account of the object; rather, thinking makes up part of the object. Thinking is particularly subjected to the structure of the remnant and, as such, it depends on a dimension it cannot grasp.[2] For this reason, thinking constantly turns towards its own conditionality and seeks to go beyond its own forms in order to, finally, take hold of the unknown territory. Therefore, even though Jabès does not tackle the self-overcoming of philosophy, his thought is anyway based on the structure of constant transgression and endeavours to go beyond itself. Jabès himself believed that he crossed beyond no-longer adequate literature. Besides relying on this inner structure of self-overcoming, Jabès' thinking (alongside Heidegger's *Denken* and Lacan's *enseignement*) can be treated as an

---

2   In his interesting article, Guy-Felix Duportail sets out to show how Jabès' concepts can be explained in the logic of the remnant which is the stitch (*point de suture*) of the Whole. According to Duportail, the position of God – particularly of God's Name – in Jabès is such a stitch. For the name is unpronounceable and, as such, does not belong to the symbolic order, yet marks the trace of its constitution. See Guy-Felix Duportail, "Le degré 451 de l'écriture." *Les Cahiers Obsidiane*, no. 5 – *Edmond Jabès* (Paris: Capitales/Obsidiane, 1982), pp. 83–9.

outcome of transgression of traditional forms of discourse, specifically of philosophy and literature. As his writings defy generic classifications, they reflect the movement of abolishing the existing forms of reflection. *Judaism as a "non-philosophy."* Jabès may not get explicitly involved in the 20th-century debate on surmounting philosophy, but he does discern in Judaism a knowledge about the structure of the remnant that underlies thinking.

Throughout this volume, Jabès has been quoted time and again as insisting that Judaism means self-awareness of the condition in which ultimate truth can never be known, for it is separated from cognition by a minimal, yet irremovable boundary. I have shown that, according to Jabès, Judaism "knows" that that truth as such is inaccessible and, for this reason, continues to wander through partial and perspectival truths. Judaism's knowledge is not a knowledge of dogmas and theorems, but a knowledge of the intuitive art of reading forged in years upon years of suffering, hope and messianic mobilisations.

Connection between the "discovery" of Judaism and the transformation in Western thought. Jabès sees Judaism as a knowledge that the Jews have had for centuries and Western culture acquires only in the 20th century, when submerging in a deep crisis. According to Jabès, Judaism has known for long that the concept of truth is problematic, that interpretation must be continually practised, that time is discontinuous, that language has a creative power, that the author is lost in the message, and that one must hold out messianic hope; Judaism had known it long before Western thought chanced upon these insights. As such, Judaism is, to Jabès, a "hidden truth" of this thought, which is revealed only when the erstwhile certainties have been recognised as illusory. Importantly, Jabès views the Shoah as a key event in this re-appraisal. Produced by the vicious power founded on the illusion of truth and certainty, the Shoah is supposed to bring this illusion to an end and expose it with full clarity.

"Acquisition" of Judaism as a practical act. In this book's Chapters, I have shown many times that Jabès' thinking, which seeks to re-invent Judaism in the modern space, is not a purely theoretical enterprise. On the contrary, it entails a profound existential change. The writer's condition is the condition of an exile who turns his life into a space of continual exploration of the Book. Jabès' thinking is neither a distanced contemplation nor even a philosophy that "opens into life," as in Rosenzweig; Jabès' thinking simply crosses the pre-modern boundary between life and theory. Besides, Jabès' messianism – an effect of the structure of the remnant and framed in the notions of Judaism – is based on the vision of acts which can be called *praxis* since understanding of reality goes hand in hand with a sweeping re-making of reality. Finally, Jabès makes a gesture similar to Lévinas', yet far more radical than his. Namely, the Jabèsian concept of "hospitality," as

depicted in *Le Livre de l'Hospitalité*, represents an attempt to project an elementary ethical act that predates language, in the silent community. To Jabès, this is, however, not a new "first philosophy" underpinning further reflection, but rather a goal that thinking is supposed to pursue, heading towards its own expiry. We can say thus that "self-overcoming of thinking" is here brought to the point where thinking is to be replaced by an extralinguistic, silent act of "pure" action.

Establishment of oppositions that cut through entire history. Although Jabès does not refer explicitly to the Athens-vs.-Jerusalem opposition, he frequently contrasts Jewish (anti-idolatrous, monotheistic, focused on the central void of reality) thought with thinking that upholds truth, stability and permanent being. Jabès extends this opposition, formative of his reasoning, onto entire history. For example, he references the astonishment of Titus' troops on entering the Holy Temple in Jerusalem, when they found its most sacred place empty. This event, as Jabès sees it, stands for the clash between the Romans and a people that erected Nothing into divinity, making it the centre of the world and the essence of the holy Book.[3] By the same token, Jabès emphatically makes a gesture that recurs throughout Jewish philosophy of modernity, albeit in more disguised forms. Namely, he projects the shift from a thinking he seeks to surmount (i.e. "idolatrous" thinking) to an apophatic and anti-idolatrous thinking (i.e. "Jewish" thinking) onto the same opposition that has purportedly been there throughout the ages. In this way, he attributes to ancient Judaism the identification of God with Nothing and, in this way, blurs the difference between the onetime and the present cult of the Lord. The ease with which Jabès alternates between the "current" argumentation and such historical examples implies how "universal oppositions" of the Athens-vs.-Jerusalem type are constructed.

Construction of a selective vision of Judaism accommodating modern philosophical tenets. This has been shown throughout the volume. As I have attempted to demonstrate, Jabès re-interprets Judaism as a radically atheistic tradition which embraced the void and absence as God. In his view, Jewish monotheism essentially does not involve faith in a personal deity but recognises that the entire world depends on the inaccessible remnant of *tzimtzum*. Jabès sieves the extraordinary and internally contradictory plenitude of the Judaic legacy for elements that fit into his modern thinking and can be employed to convey modern paradoxes. Of course, he does not negate that his vision of Judaism is idiosyncratic and unorthodox, but though admitting that his is a radical re-interpretation of Judaism, he anyway projects it onto Judaism's past. Like Scholem, Jabès is attached to the

---

3   F, p. 72.

most antinomic movements within Jewish tradition and regards continuity in rupture as Judaism's key feature.

Construction of a selective vision of Judaism in which the basic tenets are those that conform with modern philosophy. Such tenets include radical monotheism,[4] anti-idolatry, the primacy of word over image, intertextuality, dismissal of one dogmatic truth for the sake of multiple interpretations, desacralisation of the world, positive appreciation of "life as such," messianism, precedence of a practical act (ethics) over ontology, acceptance of uncertainty intrinsic to happening/ enowning and the nomad's condition. Jabès' vision of Judaism seems to utterly radicalise 20th-century re-workings of Jewish tradition. Given its extremity, some commentators contend that it has little to do with "true" Judaism.[5] However, this radicalism sheds light on Jewish philosophy of modernity as such because it shows that the movement which directs philosophy towards Jewish tradition is informed less by Judaism itself and more by the patterns of modern thinking.

Re-constructed Judaism as underpinning re-interpretation and re-appraisal of previous philosophical insights. This is perhaps the least visible trait of Jewish philosophy of modernity in Jabès' work, the main reason being that he rarely refers to philosophy's past and, thus, does not feel urged to re-interpret it. It is only in the "Letter to Jacques Derrida" that he suggests philosophy should take into account

---

4   Why should radical monotheism tie in with modern philosophy if I claimed earlier that this philosophy perceived reality as one, continuous, atheistic space devoid of transcendence? The reason is that, unlike "Greek" idolatrous monotheism, radical monotheism offers a structure that depicts an uncrossable and ubiquitous transcendental boundary between reality and its "thing in itself." It is enough to identify God with the position of the remnant– as Jabès does – for radical monotheism to become an atheistic doctrine, paradoxical though it may sound.

5   The Shoah researcher and Jabès' interpreter Berel Lang disagrees with his refashioning of Judaism, stating: "It is difficult for modern consciousness to admit that the idea of the divided self, of a spirit alienated from itself, is itself a recent artifact – that the image of the Jew as congenitally alien is not *itself* congenital, but rather an historical contrivance, nourished conscientiously in the romantic notion of alienation by volunteer poets and philosophers from nineteenth-century Germany, France and England." The careful reading of Judaism's key writings, the Bible in particular, shows that they are not exclusively a description of an alienated consciousness; on the contrary, they are rife with evocations of God's presence and plenitude. That is why Lang concludes that "we learn from *The Book of Questions* more about Jabès than we do about the Jew, more about Jabès' life as a Jew than about the Jew's life as Jew." Lang, "Writing-the-Holocaust," pp. 201, 205.

"the question of the Book" it has so far eschewed.[6] Yet Jabès makes a structurally similar gesture in relation to literature. As discussed in Chapter Eight, he replaces literature with "writing" governed by the same mechanisms as his Judaism. Jewish tradition seems to him an un-literary basis for e-assessing literature. Besides, Jabès frames Judaism time and again as an agency capable of restoring memory to Western thought, which takes pains to avoid memory. By the same token, Judaism becomes a footing that helps Western culture perceive its own suppressed content. Finally, Judaism is to Jabès the experience of exile and because, in his view, this experience has become common in the 20th century, Jewish tradition affords an opportunity to understand the now-universal wandering.

The survey above shows that Jabès' writings paradigmatically enact characteristic features of Jewish philosophy of modernity, without however relying directly on philosophical discourse (with a few rare exceptions). Yet, as I have tried to show in this volume, this is exactly why Jabès' work tells us more about Jewish philosophy of modernity than it would were it engaged in strictly philosophical debates. As it stands now, Jabès' work is a testament to the workings of forces that transcend the limits of philosophical discourse – of forces that determine the specific mechanisms of modern thinking and can be traced in literature, psychoanalysis and historical research as well. In Jabès' writings, these forces are vividly inscribed in Jewish tradition. Resulting from the inner dynamics of writing, Jabès' own path to re-constructing Judaism shows the distance between the simplification movement and the positive content it uses.

Before finishing, we should ask how Jabès' philosophy as described in this book can augment the very concept of Jewish philosophy of modernity. In this respect, I find four elements crucial.

One element concerns the status of historical narrative in Jewish philosophy of modernity. We can ask whether, if historical material serves this philosophy as "the positive content" in which the movement of modern difference unfolds, it *really* refers to the past events in the first place. In other words, is the past accessible to it at all? These questions are particularly pertinent in case of the Shoah, an event that post-war Jewish philosophy of modernity had to re-think thoroughly. As already mentioned, Jabès has been accused of making a pretence of describing the Shoah while in fact subordinating it to *the idea of a discontinuous and traumatic event which anyway results from his thinking.* Put differently, he does not address the Shoah as a real historical fact – with all its ineffaceable

---

6   BM, pp. 36–48 ("Letter to Jacques Derrida on the Question of the Book "). See also
    Cahen, *Edmond Jabès*, p. 78.

particularity – but frames it as just one of the many ways in which the universal mechanism of modern difference expresses itself.[7] This accusation could, in fact, be levelled against all kinds of Jewish philosophy of modernity that have referred to the Shoah.

How can the charge be rebutted? First, it is part of a broader, aporetic situation. On the one hand, when depicting the Shoah accurately as a chain of particular events, we acquire historical knowledge, but we risk reducing it to just an objective fact that evacuates radical discontinuity completely. On the other hand, the narrative employed, for example, by Jabès, a sketchy and fractured one as it is, implies admittedly that the very possibility of a historical narrative about the Shoah has become problematic because of the nature of its object yet, at the same time, surrenders detailed knowledge of the past. Particular events – and human actions, which have an ethical aspect to them, after all – are then consigned to the background by an impersonal and non-subjective trauma of discontinuity. Patently, this aporia is an offshoot of the modern disintegration into the content of "historical material" (which is radically separated from the present) and the structure of thinking (which enables us to render the discontinuity of the historical event here and now, yet at the price of reducing it to one, repeated difference stripped of any historical particularity). This aporia seems irremovable, as does the impact of the modern turn.

If it is indeed the case, *Jewish philosophy of modernity is severed from historical events by the very movement of interpretation.* Asking whether they are "really" accessible to it is pointless. Similarly, it is impossible to determine how Judaism re-counted in this philosophy is related to "true" Judaism. The only viable conclusion is that Jewish philosophy of modernity has been shaped in a specific space produced by the modern turn. Consequently, it is organised around the structure of the remnant, a minimal, irreducible difference. Jewish philosophy of modernity brings this remnant into any "positive material" that it processes, particularly into the legacy of Judaism. Tradition, which Jewish philosophy of modernity considers external, is thus in fact informed by its own structures.

As far as the memory of the Shoah is concerned, we should bear in mind that Jabès never put forward his narrative of the Shoah as the only legitimate one, repeatedly insisting that since he had not gone through Auschwitz, his testimony was less potent than testimonies of such survivors as, for example, Primo Levi. The point is that to authorise any of these ways as appropriate and dismiss other ones as groundless makes no sense. The corpus of 20th-century texts about the

---

7   Cf. Cahen, *Edmond Jabès*, p. 53.

Shoah must accommodate both Levi's analysis of crystalline precision and Jabès' chaotic, riven writing focused on radical discontinuity. It is a sheer impossibility to grasp the horror of the Shoah with any tolerable exactness without realising that the inhuman power of inexplicable evil merges in it with the utterly mundane pragmatism of mass killing. The fissure between a dispassionate, analytical account of events and the repetition of the trauma which obliterates historical particularity is perhaps an unavoidable aporia of thinking about the Shoah – an aporia that revolves around the central point where the universal trauma takes on a most concrete and most monstrously real shape.

Another aspect of Jabès' thought which sheds light on the concept of Jewish philosophy of modernity is the radical simplification movement. Jabès' writings are an example of gradual purification in which the content of thinking is reduced to the point where only the bare structure of thought remains. As shown in Chapter Nine, this movement is characteristic of modern thinking. Yet Jabès not only succumbs to it but also makes it into the object of his writings. He pursues radical simplification himself in order to explore the mechanism that determines his thinking. This is achieved at the price of stripping his texts of content. As we remember, the end of *The Book of Questions* is marked by meditations on the point as such. As a result of this reduction, Jabès' writings are emptied out of content differences and focus on base difference which approximates the Derridean *différance* but is embedded in materiality. In this simplification, Jabès' texts begin to describe the same structures that were dwelled on by other thinkers, not only by Derrida, who was, after all, an assiduous reader of, Jabès, so their affinities are hardly surprising. Jacques Lacan, particularly in his later work, explored the same logic of not-Whole and the remnant resisting reduction. Though it would be very far-fetched to ascribe any directly Lacanian inspirations to Jabès, a bulk of his insights is immensely redolent of Lacan's findings.[8]

---

8 Affinities between Jabès and Lacan deserve a separate study. Here I will limit myself only to a handful of examples. First, Jabès and Lacan often insist that whatever is available to cognition or consciousness depends on an ungraspable grounding, on a primary condition which leaves a trace in the symbolic order (*tzimtzum* in Jabès and symbolic castration in Lacan). "For origin […] knowledge has the no of ignorance it grew out of, a denial, likewise, of all origin" (BS, p. 72), states Jabès. Second, in both, this structure makes it possible and impossible at the same time to apprehend the Whole, for (1) only the trace indicates the Whole, but (2) the Whole cannot be apprehended otherwise than in a displacement which produces the trace. Jabès observes: "Then knowledge would be but a hole within a hole" (F, p. 95). Third, Jabès' vision of the Jew/writer as a silent remnant corresponds to Lacan's notion of the subject as a remnant produced by

What is more, as I have shown throughout this book, many of Jabès' thoughts resemble ideas of other modern philosophers, such as Kant, Hegel, Nietzsche, Wittgenstein and Heidegger. In all these cases, Jabès is closest to them when he seeks to dismantle his thought down to the pure structure between singularity and multiplicity – the whole and the remnant. This suggests that in his pursuit of ultimate reduction Jabès blurs differences that set him apart from philosophers remote from him, even those he firmly opposes (e.g. Heidegger).

This observation sheds light on the concept of Jewish philosophy of modernity. Namely, this philosophy is subject to the negative force of simplification, which eclipses the distinction between Jewish philosophy of modernity and other frameworks within modern thinking. If this conclusion holds, Jewish philosophy of modernity would be based on an inner aporia. Its internal movement would lead it to ultimate depletion, where the very differentia specifica of this philosophy evaporated. Of course, Jabès' thought is an extreme example of this process, matched in the depth of reduction perhaps only by the Derridean *différance* even though, instead of being an aim in and by itself, *différance* is just a by-product of deconstruction's work. Therefore, we cannot aver that each and every form of Jewish philosophy of modernity seeks utter simplification where it ceases to differ from other modern forms of thinking. However, such a pitfall seems to be structurally inscribed in its discourse. This helps explain why it is so vital to this philosophy to continue to differ from other frameworks which are so similar to it in many respects. Especially telling is the attitude to Heidegger, who serves as a permanent – and often negative – point of reference for Lévinas and Derrida.

Consequently, we can say that Jewish philosophy of modernity is stretched between the modern structure of simplification and the necessity to preserve distinction from other frameworks of thought it could encounter in the ultimate reduction. This explains the eagerness to keep drawing a dividing line between

---

inscription in the symbolic order. This similarity is so strong that Jabès pronounces in a highly Lacanian fashion: "The *I* is not the *Me* […] What comes newly into the world is perhaps the I. What first feels the impact of this event, the Me" (F, p. 34). Fourth, Jabès and Lacan share the same materialism brought forth when the Kantian "thing in itself" is linked to materiality. Matter in Jabès (for example stones, sand, eand so forth) and the real in Lacan are based on the same structure. The fact that both thinkers understand the *réel* not as something that "simply" is but as an inaccessible field where the symbolic order and possibility of description break down is not only the legacy of Kant, but also of the Surrealists, who used the notion in this exact way. It should be remembered also that Jabès and Lacan were associated with the Surrealists in their youth.

the "Greek" and the "Jewish," the "pagan" and the "monotheistic." This line does not run along the real lines of influence of Athens and Jerusalem. Instead, it is demarcated within the historical material by an a-priori difference which *elevates trifling details into key distinctions between poles of transhistorical oppositions.* Characteristically of modern thinking, its envisioned distribution of relevance among particular diverges from that offered by the historical context. An utterly trivial trait can be exaggerated into the cornerstone of that which is "Greek" or "Jewish." This attests that a completely different force which seeks self-distinction operates within the positive material turned dead after the modern shift.

This leads us to the third aspect of Jabès' work that augments the concept of Jewish philosophy of modernity. In Chapter Eleven, I sought to show that thinking which undergoes the movement of simplification must halt before the ultimate difference and project it into the "positive content" from which it started. I propose to call the thus-used material *the dimension of inscription.* As shown in this book, this dimension of inscription is an indispensable correlate of modern difference. If Jabès' thought is viewed as an extreme enhancement of this mechanism, it can be said that *in Jewish philosophy of modernity the movement of negativity takes Judaism for its dimension of inscription.*

Jabèsian Judaism is strictly modern even though it is shrouded in the *content* of Jewish tradition. Entire philosophy of identity may actually be based on this principle. Judaism serves in it to ultimately stabilise the workings of difference. I believe that it is not a coincidence that this philosophy also displays materialist leanings and relies on historical research. Both matter "at-hand" and the "objectively existing historical material" function here as a "non-philosophy," to apply Derrida's expression again. They produce a semblance of knowledge free from the movement of difference because they are "external" to philosophy. Paradoxically enough, *the severance of Jewish philosophy of modernity from Judaism of old braces it against its own movement of negativity.* Jewish philosophy of modernity can at will refer to the "obvious," past Jewish thinking and mask, at the same time, its own interpretation imposed on this thinking. In this strategy, philosophical reflection is suspended and the historical material is called upon directly, without inquiring whether its selection and theorisation are not always-already determined by the structures of this philosophy. Referencing historians rather than philosophers cuts off the movement of difference and guarantees inscription. In this sense, the ready historical account has a material status.

It is, as a matter of fact, no coincidence that Jewish philosophy of modernity (particularly in the first half of the 20th century) has been prominently affected by Gershom Scholem, who considered himself a historian rather than a philosopher. He studied and discussed the source material which is still a starting point in research on Jewish mysticism. Yet Scholem's study is enormously charged with his own preferences, premises and philosophical theses, which has been amply shown over recent decades by, for example, Idel.[9] And yet, many Jewish philosophers of modernity – form Benjamin to Derrida, to Jabès himself – have drawn on Scholem, heedless of the risk that what they find in Jewish tradition is no longer Jewish tradition "as such," but rather modern structures. However, the gesture of referring to an external source, that is, an objective historian, guaranteed inscription. The status of Scholem's work in Jewish philosophy of modernity shows how much it is entangled, at its origin, in the modern movement of organising the past content through the modern structure.

There are reasons to believe that Judaism's triumphant march into Western philosophy in the 20th century had less to do with discovering the formerly marginalised tradition and more with using its "positive content" in the play of modern difference. Jewish tradition which appears in these philosophical interpretations is thoroughly re-worked and ordered around the structure of modern philosophy. Pursuing complete simplification, Jabès' thought seems to expose these patterns. For, in heading towards the ultimate difference, it got reduced so much that the border dividing it from other ostensibly remote forms of modern thinking became purely formal. The movement of simplification in Jabès shows, in this way, that the founding difference of Jewish philosophy of modernity can indeed be a projection of the base difference of modernity onto the historical material. If so, Judaism would only be an object of modern philosophical play, providing the dimension of inscription and helping one framework of modern philosophy set itself off from other ones. Yet the content of Judaism would be re-interpreted to the point where the former religious thinking became merely a form for the radically atheistic and apophatic structure of the remnant.[10] The

---

9   Cf. Idel, *Old Worlds*, pp. 245–7.

10 This pattern explains the problem raised by Elliot R. Wolfson. In his study *Language, Eros, Being: Kabbalistic Hermeneutics and Poetic Imagination*, Wolfson uses ideas of 19th- and 20th-century philosophers to interpret the Kabbalah, observing how surprisingly similar they are to Kabbalistic thinking. Wolfson explained it by citing a long chain of the Kabbalah's influence on Western philosophy, stretching from Jacob Böhme to Schelling and Hegel, to Heidegger. Cf. Elliot R. Wolfson, *Language, Eros, Being: Kabbalistic Hermeneutics and Poetic Imagination* (New York: Fordham UP, 2005), p. xv. Of course, such influences should not be overlooked, but they do not really explain the issue away as we can further inquire why these and not any other inspirations proved so resonant. The concept of Jewish philosophy of modernity explains this affinity in more thorough terms than a simple "influence."

"truly Jewish" concepts would turn into functions of modern thinking in this way. Monotheism would serve as a name for the relationship between continuous reality and its ungraspable limit; messianism would be a function of modern perspectivism; and *tzimtzum* would designate the primary reduction in which the symbolic order arose.

Jewish philosophy of modernity would thus differ from other, similar strategies of interpreting past traditions – for example, from Hegel's, Lacan's and Žižek's "Christianity" – *only in selecting the content on which it projected base difference in order to split off from the ultimate simplification.*

To conclude about Jewish philosophy of modernity on the basis of Jabès' work is a risky venture. His thinking pursues radical simplification, and, consequently, my conclusion must bear its mark. It is unclear whether this reduction indeed reveals the structure inherent to Jewish philosophy of modernity or whether it implants this structure there and only feigns discovery. One thing is obvious: discussing Jewish philosophy of modernity, one is entangled in a double bind one has ascribed to this philosophy.

To finish with, it is important to remember that the way the thus-constructed concept of Jewish philosophy of modernity is applicable to individual thinkers must be studied separately. It would be difficult to formulate any general conclusions here because authors who re-interpret Judaism to use it in philosophy (more broadly, in the humanities) are far too diverse. On the one pole, there are "typical" representatives of Jewish philosophy of modernity, shaped primarily by Western thought and acquainted with Judaism via mediation, such as Benjamin, Bloch, Kafka, Derrida. On the other pole of the continuum, there are thinkers who moved in the opposite direction, using religious engagement in Judaism to bring its ideas into Western philosophy, such as Joseph Soloveitchik, Yeshayahu Leibowitz and Abraham Joshua Heschel. The difference of the latter's vision of Judaism from the former's – in particular the latter's scepticism about radical messianism – vividly shows how much more "modern" than "Jewish" Jewish philosophy of modernity is. Their concepts seem to be, in themselves, *a trace* of Judaism from before it was irrevocably lured into the desert of modernity – of Judaism which has not gone through utter depletion as it has in Jabès.

The last aspect that Jabès' writings add to Jewish philosophy of modernity is the ethical dimension of the simplification movement. If modern thinking is indeed threatened to be voided by its pursuit of pure difference, the imperative left over from post-Jerusalem philosophical Jerusalem should be to curb this pursuit with ethical reins. The case of Heidegger shows how easy it is to sacrifice ethics for the movement of purification. Thus, shouldn't the Jewish tradition, which poses itself as a dimension of inscription, offer – as its ultimate legacy – an ethical assessment of the consequences of simplification? Only a thin line divides messianic equality and justice from *Gelassenheit*, and Jewish philosophy can and should preserve this line as an expression of its distinction. Persisting where the structural difference has completed its work, this difference helps turn simplification towards ethics: against extreme violence and *for justice*.

It is pointless to seek bounds to the boundless, but it is on us that the position of the boundless depends.

References

I. Primary Literature

I A. Edmond Jabès' Poetry

"L'attente." *Europe*, 954, Octobre 2008. **[A]**

Je bâtis ma demeure. Poèmes 1943–1957. Paris: Gallimard, 1959. **[JBMD]**

Le Seuil Le Sable. Poésies complètes 1943–1988. Paris: Gallimard, 1990. **[LSLS]**

I B. Edmond Jabès' Prose

Le Livre des Questions

The Book of Questions. Volume I: The Book of Questions; The Book of Yukel; Return to the Book, trans. Rosmarie Waldrop. Middletown, CT: Wesleyan University Press, 1991. **[BQ I]**

The Book of Questions. Volume II: Yaël; Elya; Aely; El, or the Last Book, trans Rosmarie Waldrop. Middletown, CT: Wesleyan University Press, 1991. **[BQ II]**

Le Livre des Ressemblances

Le Livre des Ressemblances. Paris: Gallimard, 1976. **[LR I]**

The Book of Resemblances. 2: Intimations The Desert, trans. Rosmarie Waldrop. Hanover and London: Wesleyan University Press, 1991. **[BR II]**

The Book of Resemblances. 3: The Ineffaceable The Unperceived, trans. Rosmarie Waldrop. Hanover and London: Wesleyan University Press, 1991. **[BR III]**

Le Livre des Limites

Le Parcours. Paris: Gallimard, 1985. **[P]**

The Book of Shares, trans. Rosmarie Waldrop. Chicago, IL and London: University of Chicago Press, 1989. **[BS]**

The Book of Dialogue, trans. Rosmarie Waldrop. Middletown, CT: Wesleyan University Press, 1991. **[BD]**

The Little Book of Unsuspected Subversion, trans. Rosmarie Waldrop. Stanford, CA: Stanford University Press, 1996. **[BUS]**

Le Livre de l'Hospitalité. Paris: Gallimard, 1991. **[LH]**

The Book of Margins, trans. Rosmarie Waldrop. Chicago, IL and London: Chicago University Press, 1993. **[BM]**

The Foreigner Carrying in the Crook of His Arm a Tiny Book, trans. Rosmarie Waldrop. Hanover and London: Wesleyan University Press, 1993. **[F]**

"From *The Book of Resemblances.*" *Studies in 20th Century Literature*, 12/1, Special Issue on Edmond Jabès, 1987. pp. 13–25.

From the Book to the Book: An Edmond Jabès Reader, trans. Rosmarie Waldrop. Hanover and London: Wesleyan University Press, 1991.

I C. Edmond Jabès' Articles

"Enlarging the Horizon of the Word", trans. Rosmarie Waldrop. In Eric Gould (Ed.), *The Sin of the Book: Edmond Jabès*, Lincoln and London: University of Nebraska Press, 1985. pp. 32–7. **[EHW]**

"Le plus haut défi." *Change*, 22, février 1975. **[PHD]**

"Qu'est-ce qu'un livre sacré?" In Adélie Rassial and Jean-Jacques Rassial (Eds.), *L'Interdit de la représentation. Colloque de Montpellier 1981*. Paris: Seuil, 1984. pp **[QQLS]**

"The Question of Displacement into the Lawfulness of the Book," trans. Rosmarie Waldrop. In Eric Gould (Ed.), *The Sin of the Book: Edmond Jabès*. Lincoln and London: University of Nebraska Press, 1985. pp. 227–44. **[QDLB]**

"There is such a thing as Jewish writing…," trans. Rosmarie Waldrop. In Eric Gould (Ed.), *The Sin of the Book: Edmond Jabès*. Lincoln and London: University of Nebraska Press, 1985. pp. 26–31. **[JW]**

I D. Interviews with Edmond Jabès

Auster, Paul. "Interview with Edmond Jabès." In Eric Gould (Ed.), *The Sin of the Book: Edmond Jabès*. Lincoln and London: University of Nebraska Press, 1985. pp. 3–25. **[IEJ]**

"Dialogue avec Edmond Jabès." In Richard Stamelman and Mary Ann Caws (Eds.), *Écrire le livre autour d'Edmond Jabès. Colloque de Cerisy*. Seyssel: Champ Vallon, 1989. **[DEJ]**

From the Désert to the Book: Dialogues with Marcel Cohen, trans. Peter Joris. Barrytown, NY: Station Hill Press, 1992. **[DB]**

Saint Cheron, Philippe de. "Entretien avec Edmond Jabès."*La Nouvelle Revue Française*, 464, septembre 1991. **[EEJ]**

Taylor, Benjamin. "The Question of Jewishness and The Question of Writing: An Exchange with Edmond Jabès." *The Threepenny Review*, 21, Spring 1985. pp. 16–8. **[QJQW]**

II. Secondary Literature on Edmond Jabès

Alcalay, Ammiel. "Désert Solitaire: On Edmond Jabès." In Ammiel Alcalay (Ed.), *Memories of Our Future: Selected Essays 1982–1999*. San Francisco: City Light Books, 1999. pp. 55–9.

Altizer, Thomas J. J. "The Apocalyptic Identity of the Jew." *Journal of the American Academy of Religion*, 45/3, September 1977.

Amir, Eshel. "Cosmopolitanism and Searching for the Sacred Space in Jewish Literature." *Jewish Social Studies*, 9/3, Spring/Summer 2003.

Anidjar, Gil. "Literary History and Hebrew Modernity." *Comparative Literature Studies*, 42/2, 2005. pp. 277–96.

Auclair, Georges. "Convergences?" *Les Cahiers Obsidiane*, no. 5 – *Edmond Jabès*. Paris: Capitales/Obsidiane, 1982.

Auclair, Georges. "Déchanger." In Richard Stamelman and Mary Ann Caws (Eds.), *Écrire le livre autour d'Edmond Jabès. Colloque de Cerisy*. Seyssel: Champ Vallon, 1989.

Barsacq, Stéphane. "Dans la double dépendance du nom." *Europe*, 954, Octobre 2008. pp. 276–9.

Baumgarten, Jean. "Trois contes de Rabbi Nahman de Bratslaw." *Les Cahiers Obsidiane*, no. 5 – *Edmond Jabès*. Paris: Capitales/Obsidiane, 1982.

Bavčar, Evgen. "Mots pour Jabès." *Change*, 22, février 1975.

Benedetti, Riccardo de. "Dans l'incondition de l'écriture: Jabès et Blanchot." In Richard Stamelman and Mary Ann Caws (Eds.), *Écrire le livre autour d'Edmond Jabès. Colloque de Cerisy*. Seyssel: Champ Vallon, 1989. pp. 171–80.

Benhamou, Maurice. "maintenant que quelqu'un vienne." *Les Cahiers Obsidiane*, no. 5 – *Edmond Jabès*, Paris: Capitales/Obsidiane, 1982.

Bilen, Max. "Edmond Jabès: du déchirement à l'unité." In Richard Stamelman and Mary Ann Caws (Eds.), *Écrire le livre autour d'Edmond Jabès. Colloque de Cerisy*. Seyssel: Champ Vallon, 1989. pp. 253–70.

Blanchot, Maurice. "Edmond Jabès' *Book of Questions*," *European Judaism: A Journal for the New Europe*, 6/2, Summer 1972, pp. 34–7.

Blanchot, Maurice. "Interruptions," trans. Rosmarie Waldrop and Paul Auster. In Eric Gould (Ed.), *The Sin of the Book: Edmond Jabès*. Lincoln and London: University of Nebraska Press, 1985. pp. 43–54.

Bounoure, Gabriel. *Edmond Jabès. La demeure et le livre*. Montpellier: Fata Morgana, 1984.

Boyer, Philippe. "Point d'amure," *SubStance*, 2/5–6, Winter 1972– Spring 1973.

Boyle, Peter, *Museum of space*. St. Lucia: University of Queensland Press, 2004.

Brandt, Joan. *Geopoetics: The Politics of Mimesis in Poststructuralist French Poetry and Theory*. Stanford, CA: Stanford University Press, 1997.

Brown, Llewellyn. "Le rythme et le chiffre: *Le Livre des questions* d'Edmond Jabès." *Littérature*, 103/3, 1996. pp. 52–62.

Brown, Llewellyn. "Les métamorphoses du point: • *(El, ou le dernier livre)* d'Edmond Jabès." *Littératures*, 38, 1998. pp. 145–55.

Cahen, Didier. *Edmond Jabès*. Paris: Éditions Pierre Belfond, 1991.

Cahen, Didier. "En marge de la délivrance." *Les Cahiers Obsidiane*, no. 5 – *Edmond Jabès*. Paris: Capitales/Obsidiane, 1982.

Cahen, Didier. "Jalons." *Europe*, 954, Octobre 2008. pp. 263–7.

Cahen, Didier. "Le corps nomade." *Change*, 22, février 1975.

Cahen, Didier. "Les réponses du livre." In Richard Stamelman and Mary Ann Caws (Eds.), *Écrire le livre autour d'Edmond Jabès. Colloque de Cerisy*. Seyssel: Champ Vallon, 1989.p. 57.

Cahen, Didier. "Simplicite de Jabès. Entretien," *Europe*, 954, Octobre 2008.

Caws, Mary Ann. *Edmond Jabès*, Amsterdam: Rodopi, 1988.

Caws, Mary Ann. "Edmond Jabès. Sill and Sand." *L'esprit créateur*, 32/2, Summer 1992. pp. 11–8.

Caws, Mary Ann. "*Livre des Marges, Livre du Partage*: réflexions sur deux textes d'Edmond Jabès." In Richard Stamelman and Mary Ann Caws (Eds.), *Écrire le livre autour d'Edmond Jabès. Colloque de Cerisy*. Seyssel: Champ Vallon, 1989.

Caws, Mary Ann. "Signe et encadrement: Edmond Jabès ou *Le Livre en Question (I)*." *Les Cahiers Obsidiane*, no. 5 – *Edmond Jabès*. Paris: Capitales/Obsidiane, 1982. pp. 291–3.

Chalier, Agnès. "Le chant de l'absence." *Les Cahiers Obsidiane*, no. 5 – *Edmond Jabès*. Paris: Capitales/Obsidiane, 1982.

Chalier, Agnès. "Le désert jabèsien et la notion de vide dans la philosophie classique chinoise." In Richard Stamelman and Mary Ann Caws (Eds.), *Écrire le livre autour d'Edmond Jabès. Colloque de Cerisy*. Seyssel: Champ Vallon, 1989.

Chaouat, Bruno. "Forty Years of Suffering." *L'esprit créateur*, 45/3, Fall 2005. pp. 49–62.

Cohen, Josh. "Désertions: Paul Auster, Edmond Jabès, and the Writing of Auschwitz." *The Journal of the Midwest Modern Language Association*, 33/3 and 34/1, Autumn 2000 – Winter 2001. pp. 95–102.

Cohen, Josh. "To Preserve the Question." In *Interrupting Auschwitz: Art, Religion, Philosophy*. London and New York: Continuum, 2005.

Cohen, Marcel. "A propos de Sara et de Yukel." In Richard Stamelman and Mary Ann Caws (Eds.), *Écrire le livre autour d'Edmond Jabès. Colloque de Cerisy.* Seyssel: Champ Vallon, 1989. pp. 253–62.

Cohen, Marcel. "Anamnezy," trans. Adam Wodnicki. In Edmond Jabès (Ed.), *Aeli.* Kraków: Austeria, 2006.

Cohen, Marcel. "Dix anamnèses." *Europe*, no. 954, Octobre 2008.

Cohen, Marcel. "Lorsqu'une oeuvre..." *Les Cahiers Obsidiane*, no. 5 – *Edmond Jabès.* Paris: Capitales/Obsidiane, 1982.

Dacan, Édith. "Le corps et l'écriture dans le *Livre des Questions*." *Les Cahiers Obsidiane*, no. 5 – *Edmond Jabès.* Paris: Capitales/Obsidiane, 1982.

Debrauwere-Miller, Nathalie. "La 'Conscience d'un Cri' dans la poétique d'Edmond Jabès." *French Forum*, 30/2, Spring 2005. pp. 97–119.

Debrauwere-Miller, Nathalie. "Tree of Consciousness: The Shekhinah in Edmond Jabès' *Yael.*" *Literature & Theology*, 17/4, December 2003. pp. 388–406.

Del Nevo, Matthew. "Edmond Jabès and Kabbalism after God?" *Journal of the American Academy of Religion*, 65/2, 1997. pp. 403–42.

Del Nevo, Matthew. "Edmond Jabès and the Question of Death." In Tod Linafelt (Ed.), *Strange Fire. Reading the Bible after the Holocaust.* New York: New York University Press, 2000. pp. 121–34.

Del Nevo, Matthew. "Edmond Jabès and the Question of the Book." *Literature & Theology*, 10/4, December 1996. pp. 301–6.

Derrida, Jacques. "Edmond Jabès (1912–1991): Letter to Didier Cahen," trans. Pascale-Anne Brault and Michael Naas. In Pascale-Anne Brault and Michael Naas (Eds.), *The Work of Mourning.* Chicago: University of Chicago Press, 2003. pp. 119–25.

Derrida, Jacques. "Edmond Jabès and the Question of the Book," trans. Alan Bass. In *Writing and Difference*, London and New York: Routledge, 2005. pp. 77–96.

Derrida, Jacques. "Ellipsis." In *Writing and Difference*. pp. 371–8.

Duncan, Robert. "The Delirium of Meaning." In Eric Gould (Ed.), *The Sin of the Book: Edmond Jabès.* Lincoln and London: University of Nebraska Press, 1985. pp. 207–26.

Duportail, Guy-Felix. "Le degré 451 de l'écriture." *Les Cahiers Obsidiane*, no. 5 – *Edmond Jabès.* Paris: Capitales/Obsidiane, 1982.

Erbertz, Carola. *Zur Poetik des Buches bei Edmond Jabès: exiliertes Schreiben im Zeichen von Auschwitz.* Tübingen: Gunter Narr Verlag, 2000.

Fernandez- Zoïla, Adolfo. "Écriture en-temps et dialogue dans le livre, selon Edmond Jabès." In Richard Stamelman and Mary Ann Caws (Eds.), *Écrire le livre autour d'Edmond Jabès. Colloque de Cerisy.* Seyssel: Champ Vallon, 1989.

Fernandez- Zoïla, Adolfo. "Edmond Jabès et les structures éclatées." *Change*, no. 22, février 1975.

Fernandez- Zoïla, Adolfo. *Le Livre, recherche autre d'Edmond Jabès.* Paris: Jean-Michel Place Editeur, 1978.

Fernandez- Zoïla, Adolfo. "Le neutre en devenir chez Edmond Jabès." *Les Cahiers Obsidiane*, no. 5 – Edmond Jabès. Paris: Capitales/Obsidiane, 1982.

Folin, Alberto. "La figure du silence dans l'imaginaire moderne: Leopardi et Jabès." In Richard Stamelman and Mary Ann Caws (Eds.), *Écrire le livre autour d'Edmond Jabès. Colloque de Cerisy.* Seyssel: Champ Vallon, 1989. pp. 147–56.

Franke, William. "Edmond Jabès, or the Endless Self-Emptying of Language in the Name of God." *Literature & Theology*, 22/1, March 2008. pp. 102–17.

Franke, William. "The Singular and the Other at the Limits of Language in the Apophatic Poetics of Edmond Jabès and Paul Celan." *New Literary History*, 36/4, Autumn 2005. pp. 621–38.

Frémon, Jean, "Ainsi toujours désignant ce qui manqué." *Les Cahiers Obsidiane*, no. 5 – Edmond Jabès. Paris: Capitales/Obsidiane, 1982.

Gardaz, Elizabeth. "Rhétorique et figures du silence dans l'oeuvre de Jabès." In Richard Stamelman and Mary Ann Caws (Eds.), *Écrire le livre autour d'Edmond Jabès. Colloque de Cerisy.* Seyssel: Champ Vallon, 1989.

Gould, Eric. "Godtalk." In Eric Gould (Ed.), *The Sin of the Book: Edmond Jabès.* Lincoln and London: University of Nebraska Press, 1985. pp. 160–70.

Gould, Eric. "Introduction." In Eric Gould (Ed.), *The Sin of the Book: Edmond Jabès.* Lincoln and London: University of Nebraska Press, 1985. pp. xii–xxv.

Goujat, Olivier. "Ça suit son cours d'encre." *Europe*, 954, Octobre 2008.

Gubar, Susan. "The Long and the Short of the Holocaust Verse." *New Literary History*, 35/3, Summer 2004. pp. 44–68.

Guglielmi, Joseph. "Edmond Jabès et la question du livre." *SubStance*, 2/5–6, Winter 1972–Spring 1973.

Guglielmi, Joseph. "Edmond Jabès ou la fascination du désert." *Critique*, 28/296, Janvier 1972. pp. 32–52.

Guglielmi, Joseph. "Journal de lecture d'Edmond Jabès." In Richard Stamelman and Mary Ann Caws (Eds.), *Écrire le livre autour d'Edmond Jabès. Colloque de Cerisy.* Seyssel: Champ Vallon, 1989. pp. 87–105.

Guglielmi, Joseph. *La ressemblance impossible: Edmond Jabès.* Paris: Les éditeurs français réunis, 1978.

Guglielmi, Joseph. "Le dernier état des questions." *Change*, 22, février 1975.

Gunnars, Kristjana. *Stranger at the Door: Writers and the Act of Writing.* Waterloo, Ontario: Wilfried Laurier University Press, 2004.

Handelman, Susan. "'Torments of an Ancient Word': Edmond Jabès and the Rabbinic Tradition." In Eric Gould (Ed.), *The Sin of the Book: Edmond Jabès.* Lincoln and London: University of Nebraska Press, 1985. pp. 55–91.

Harris, Paul. "Nothing: A User's Manual." *SubStance*, 35/2, 2006.

Hawkins, Beth. *Reluctant Theologians: Franz Kafka, Paul Celan, Edmond Jabès.* New York: Fordham University Press, 2003.

Israel-Pelletier, Aimée. "Edmond Jabès, Jacques Hassoun, and Melancholy: The Second Exodus in the Shadow of the Holocaust." *MLN*, 123/4, September 2008 (French issue). pp. 797–818.

Jabès-Cresson, Viviane. "A l'écoute du livre." In Richard Stamelman and Mary Ann Caws (Eds.), *Écrire le livre autour d'Edmond Jabès. Colloque de Cerisy.* Seyssel: Champ Vallon, 1989. pp. 277–84.

Janin, Pierre-Philippe. "Un sang d'encre." *Les Cahiers Obsidiane*, no. 5 – *Edmond Jabès.* Paris: Capitales/Obsidiane, 1982.

Jaron, Steven. *Edmond Jabès: The Hazard of Exile.* Oxford: Legenda, 2003.

Jasper, David. "*The Sacred Désert: Religion, Literature, Art, and Culture.* Oxford: Wiley-Blackwell, 2004.

Kania, Ireneusz. "Jabès, czyli o składaniu rozsypanego Tekstu," trans. Zbigniew Wodziński. In Edmond Jabès (Ed.), *Powrót do Księgi.* Kraków: Austeria, 2005.

Kaplan, Brett Ashley. "Pleasure, Memory, and Time Suspension in Holocaust Literature: Celan and Delbo." *Comparative Literature Studies*, 38/4, 2001. pp. 310–29.

Kaplan, Edward. "The Atheistic Theology of Edmond Jabès." *Studies in 20th Century Literature*, 12/1, 1987, pp. 43–63.

Kaplan, Edward. "Edmond Jabès: un prophétisme sans Dieu." In Richard Stamelman and Mary Ann Caws (Eds.), *Écrire le livre autour d'Edmond Jabès. Colloque de Cerisy.* Seyssel: Champ Vallon, 1989.

Kaplan, Edward A. "The Problematic Humanism of Edmond Jabès." In Eric Gould (Ed.), *The Sin of the Book: Edmond Jabès.* Lincoln and London: University of Nebraska Press, 1985. pp. 115–30.

Kinczewski, Kathryn. "Reading Disfigured." In Eric Gould (Ed.), *The Sin of the Book: Edmond Jabès.* Lincoln and London: University of Nebraska Press, 1985. pp. 179–87.

Kluback, William. *Edmond Jabès, The Poetry of the Nomad.* New York: Peter Lang Publishing, 1998.

Kronick, Joseph G. "Edmond Jabès and the Poetry of the Jewish Unhappy Consciousness." *MLN*, 106/5, December 1991. pp. 967–96.

Kronick, Joseph G. "Philosophy as Autobiography: The Confessions of Jacques Derrida." *MLN*, 115/5, December 2000. pp. 997–1018.

Laifer, Miryam. *Edmond Jabès. Un judaïsme après Dieu.* New York, Berne & Frankfurt am Main: Peter Lang, 1986.

Lang, Berel. "Writing-the-Holocaust: Jabès and the Measure of History." In Eric Gould (Ed.), *The Sin of the Book: Edmond Jabès.* Lincoln and London: University of Nebraska Press, 1985. pp. 191–206.

Laruelle, François. "Le point sur l'Un." In Richard Stamelman and Mary Ann Caws (Eds.), *Écrire le livre autour d'Edmond Jabès. Colloque de Cerisy.* Seyssel: Champ Vallon, 1989. pp. 121–32.

Laruelle, François, "Projet d'une philosophie du livre." *Les Cahiers Obsidiane,* no. 5 – *Edmond Jabès.* Paris: Capitales/Obsidiane, 1982.

Lazer, Hank. "Is There a Distinctive Jewish Poetics? Several? Many? Is There Any Question?" *Shofar: An Interdisciplinary Journal of Jewish Studies,* 27/3, Spring 2009.

Lévy, Sydney. "The Question of Absence." In Eric Gould (Ed.), *The Sin of the Book: Edmond Jabès.* Lincoln and London: University of Nebraska Press, 1985. pp. 147–59.

Listoe, Daniel B. "Seeing Nothing: Allegory and the Holocaust's Absent Dead." *SubStance,* 35/2 (110), 2006. pp. 51–70.

Major, René. "Jabès et l'écriture du nom proper." In Richard Stamelman and Mary Ann Caws (Eds.), *Écrire le livre autour d'Edmond Jabès. Colloque de Cerisy.* Seyssel: Champ Vallon, 1989.

Malaprade, Anne. "La voix secrète," *Europe,* no. 954, Octobre 2008.

Meitinger, Serge. "Mallarmé et Jabès devant le livre: Analyse d'une divergence culturelle." In Richard Stamelman and Mary Ann Caws (Eds.), *Écrire le livre autour d'Edmond Jabès. Colloque de Cerisy.* Seyssel: Champ Vallon, 1989. pp. 133–43.

Mendelson, David. "La science, l'exil et les sources du désert." In Richard Stamelman and Mary Ann Caws (Eds.), *Écrire le livre autour d'Edmond Jabès. Colloque de Cerisy.* Seyssel: Champ Vallon, 1989.

Missac, Pierre. "Eloge de la citation ou de la citation conçue comme instrument de critique: une étude issue des idées de Walter Benjamin et appuyée sur des textes d'Edmond Jabès." *Change,* 22, février 1975.

Missac, Pierre. "Marge pour deux regards." *Les Cahiers Obsidiane,* no. 5 – *Edmond Jabès.* Paris: Capitales/Obsidiane, 1982.

Mole, Gary D. *Lévinas, Blanchot, Jabès: Figures of Estrangement*. Gainesville, FL: University Press of Florida, Gainesville 1997.

Mosès, Stéphane. "Edmond Jabès: d'un passage à l'autre," In Richard Stamelman and Mary Ann Caws (Eds.), *Écrire le livre autour d'Edmond Jabès*. *Colloque de Cerisy*. Seyssel: Champ Vallon, 1989.

Motte, Warren F. "Hospitable Poetry." *L'esprit créateur*, 49/2, Summer 2009. pp. 34–45.

Motte, Warren F. "Jabès' Words." *Symposium*, XLI/2, Summer 1987. pp. 140–56.

Motte, Warren F. *Questioning Edmond Jabès*. Lincoln and London: University of Nebraska Press, 1990.

Motte, Warren F. "Récit/Écrit." In Richard Stamelman and Mary Ann Caws (Eds.), *Écrire le livre autour d'Edmond Jabès*. *Colloque de Cerisy*. Seyssel: Champ Vallon, 1989. pp, 161–70.

Nahon, Claude. "La question de l'origine et l'oeuvre d'Edmond Jabès." In *La Question de l'Origine*. Nice: Z'éditions, 1987.

Patterson, David. "Through the Eyes of Those Who Were There." *Holocaust and Genocide Studies*, 18/2, Fall 2004. pp. 274–90.

Petitdommage, Guy. "Edmond Jabès ou le devenir-écriture." *Les Cahiers Obsidiane*, no. 5 – *Edmond Jabès*. Paris: Capitales/Obsidiane, 1982.

Pfeiffer, Jean. "Le dialogue d'Edmond Jabès." *Les Cahiers Obsidiane*, no. 5 – *Edmond Jabès*. Paris: Capitales/Obsidiane, 1982.

Pinhas-Delpeuch, Rosy. "Dans la double dépendence du désert." In Richard Stamelman and Mary Ann Caws (Eds.), *Écrire le livre autour d'Edmond Jabès*. *Colloque de Cerisy*. Seyssel: Champ Vallon, 1989. pp. 181–90.

Raczymow, Henri. "Qui est Edmond Jabès?" *Les Cahiers Obsidiane*, no. 5 – *Edmond Jabès*. Paris: Capitales/Obsidiane, 1982.

Rebellato-Ribondi, Chiara. "Rien ne se crée, rien ne se perd." *Les Cahiers Obsidiane*, no. 5 – *Edmond Jabès*. Paris: Capitales/Obsidiane, 1982.

Rolland, Jacques. "Hors du jeu, au plus fort de l'enjeu." *Les Cahiers Obsidiane*, no. 5 – *Edmond Jabès*. Paris: Capitales/Obsidiane, 1982.

Schaffer, Carl. "Chaos and Void: Presencing Absence in Edmond Jabès' *The Book Of Questions* and Juan Rulfo's *Pedro Paramo*." *History of European Ideas*, 20/4–6, 1995. pp. 859–64.

Scharfman, Ronnie. "Mort-né: itinéraire d'un vocable." In Richard Stamelman and Mary Ann Caws (Eds.), *Écrire le livre autour d'Edmond Jabès*. *Colloque de Cerisy*. Seyssel: Champ Vallon, 1989.

Scharfman, Ronnie. "Welcoming the Stranger: Edmond Jabès' *Le Livre de l'hospitalité*." In Antoine Régis (Ed.), *Carrefour des cultures: Mélanges offerts à Jacqualine Leiner.* Tübingen: Gunter Narr Verlag, 1993. pp. 237–42.

Schneider, Ulrike. *Der poetische Aphorismus bei Edmond Jabès, Henri Michaux und Rene Char: zu Grundfragen einer Poetik.* Stuttgart: Franz Steiner Verlag, 1998.

Shillony, Helena. *Edmond Jabès: une rhétorique de la subversion.* Paris: Lettres Modernes, 1991.

Shillony, Helena. "Edmond Jabès: une rhétorique de la subversion et de l'harmonie." *Romance Notes,* XXVI/1, 1985. pp. 3–11.

Shillony, Helena. "Métaphores de la négation." In Richard Stamelman and Mary Ann Caws (Eds.), *Écrire le livre autour d'Edmond Jabès. Colloque de Cerisy.* Seyssel: Champ Vallon, 1989.

Silverman, Maxim. *Facing Postmodernity: Contemporary French Thought on Culture and Society.* London and New York: Routledge, 1999.

Stamelman, Richard. "La parole partagée dans la nuit de l'être." In Richard Stamelman and Mary Ann Caws (Eds.), *Écrire le livre autour d'Edmond Jabès. Colloque de Cerisy.* Seyssel: Champ Vallon, 1989.

Stamelman, Richard. "Le dialogue de l'absence." In Richard Stamelman and Mary Ann Caws (Eds.), *Écrire le livre autour d'Edmond Jabès. Colloque de Cerisy.* Seyssel: Champ Vallon, 1989.

Stamelman, Richard. "Nomadic Writing: The Poetics of Exile." In Eric Gould (Ed.), *The Sin of the Book: Edmond Jabès.* Lincoln and London: University of Nebraska Press, 1985. pp. 92–114.

Stamelman, Richard. "The Strangeness of the Other and the Otherness of the Stranger: Edmond Jabès." *Yale French Studies,* 82/1, 1993. pp. 118–34.

Starobinski, Jean. "Out of this violated mineral night…," trans. Rosmarie Waldrop. In Eric Gould (Ed.), *The Sin of the Book: Edmond Jabès.* Lincoln and London: University of Nebraska Press, 1985. pp. 41–2.

Stoddard, Roger Eliot. *Edmond Jabès in Bibliography: "Du blanc des mots et du noir des signes" – A Record of the Printed Books.* Paris and Caen: Lettres modernes minard, 2001.

Strauss, Walter A. "*Le Livre des questions* de Jabès et la question du livre." In Richard Stamelman and Mary Ann Caws (Eds.), *Écrire le livre autour d'Edmond Jabès. Colloque de Cerisy.* Seyssel: Champ Vallon, 1989.

Sussman, Henry. "Pulsations of Respect, or Winged Impossibility Literature with Deconstruction." *diacritics,* 38/1–2, Spring-Summer 2008. pp. 44–63.

Teboul, Jean-Pierre. "La coupure de la trace." *Les Cahiers Obsidiane,* no. 5 – *Edmond Jabès.* Paris: Capitales/Obsidiane, 1982.

Trivouss-Haïk, Hélène. "Désirer lire la mise en acte de l'écrit." In Richard Stamelman and Mary Ann Caws (Eds.), *Écrire le livre autour d'Edmond Jabès. Colloque de Cerisy*. Seyssel: Champ Vallon, 1989. pp. 271–6.

Valavanidis-Wybrands, Harita. "Passer outre." *Les Cahiers Obsidiane*, no. 5 – *Edmond Jabès*. Paris: Capitales/Obsidiane, 1982.

Valente, José Angel. "Edmond Jabès: la mémoire du feu." In Richard Stamelman and Mary Ann Caws (Eds.), *Écrire le livre autour d'Edmond Jabès. Colloque de Cerisy*. Seyssel: Champ Vallon, 1989. p. 157.

Waldrop, Rosmarie. "Edmond Jabès and the Impossible Circle." *SubStance*, 2/5–6, Winter 1972–Spring 1973. pp. 183–94.

Waldrop, Rosmarie. *Lavish Absence: Recalling and Rereading Edmond Jabès*. Middletown CT: Wesleyan University Press, 2002.

Waldrop, Rosmarie. "Miroirs et paradoxes." *Change*, no. 22, février 1975. pp. 193–204.

Wall-Romana, Christophe. "Dure poésie générale." *L'Esprit Créateur*, 49/2, Summer 2009. pp. 1–8.

Walter, Guy. "La spiritualité du silence après la Choah dans *Le Livre des questions*." In Richard Stamelman and Mary Ann Caws (Eds.), *Écrire le livre autour d'Edmond Jabès. Colloque de Cerisy*. Seyssel: Champ Vallon, 1989.

Wellhoff, Jean-Pierre. "Une stratégie de la distraction." *Les Cahiers Obsidiane*, no. 5 – *Edmond Jabès*. Paris: Capitales/Obsidiane, 1982.

Wybrands, Francis. "La rumeur, le désastre." *Les Cahiers Obsidiane*, no. 5 – *Edmond Jabès*. Paris: Capitales/Obsidiane, 1982.

III. Other Secondary Literature

Agamben, Giorgio. *Homo Sacer: Sovereign Power and Bare Life*, trans. Daniel Heller-Roazen. Stanford, CA: Stanford University Press, 1998.

Agamben, Giorgio. *Remnants of Auschwitz: The Witness and the Archive (Homo Sacer III)*, trans. Daniel Heller-Roazen. New York: Zone Books, 1991.

Améry, Jean. *At the Mind's Limits: Contemplations by a Survivor on Auschwitz and Its Realities*, trans. Sidney Rosenfeld and Stella P. Rosenfeld. Bloomington: Indiana University Press, 1980.

Arendt, Hannah. *Eichmann in Jerusalem: A Report on the Banality of Evil*. New York et al.: Penguin Books, 2006

Aristotle. *Metaphysics*, Books VII and XII, trans. William D. Ross. Oxford: Oxford University Press Reprints, 1924.

Atlan, Henri. "Niveaux de signification et athéisme de l'écriture." *La Bible au present*. Paris: Gallimard, 1982.

Bataille, Georges, "Base Materialism and Gnosticism," trans. Allan Stoekl, Carl R. Lovitt and Donald M. Leslie, Jr. In Fred Botting and Scott Wilson (Eds.), *The Bataille Reader*. Oxford and Malden, MA: Blackwell, 1997. pp. 160–164.

Bauman, Zygmunt. *Modernity and the Holocaust*. Ithaca: Cornell University Press, Polity, 1989.

Jean, Baumgarten. "Mystique et messianisme chez Rabbi Nachman de Bratslav." *Critique*, 728–729, Paris, I–II 2008.

Bellet, Roger. *Stephané Mallarmé. L'encre et le ciel*. Seyssel: Champ Villon, 1987.

Bencheikh, Jamel Eddine, *Poétique arabe*. Paris: Gallimard, 1989.

Benjamin, Walter. "Theses on the Philosophy of History." trans. Harry Zohn. In Hannah Arendt (Ed.), *Illuminations: Essays and Reflections,*. New York: Schocken Books, 1969.

Berlin, Isaiah. *The Magus of the North: J. G. Hamann and the Origins of Modern Irrationalism*, H. Hardy (Ed.). Farrar, Straus and Giroux, 1994.

Bielik-Robson, Agata. *Erros. Mesjański witalizm i filozofia*. Kraków: Universitas, 2012.

Bielik-Robson, Agata. *Na pustyni. Kryptoteologie późnej nowoczesności*. Kraków: Universitas, 2008.

Blanchot, Maurice. "Being Jewish," trans. Susan Hanson. In *The Infinite Conversation*. Minneapolis: University of Minnesota Press, 2003. pp 123–9.

Blanchot, Maurice. *Le dernier à parler*. Montpellier: Fata Morgana, 1984.

Blanchot, Maurice. *L'Espace Littéraire*. Paris: Gallimard, 1955.

Blanchot, Maurice. *Faux pas*. Paris: Gallimard, 1975.

Blanchot, Maurice. "Literature and the Right to Death," trans. Lydia Davis. In *The Work of Fire*. Stanford, CA: Stanford University Press, 1995. pp. 300–344.

Blanchot, Maurice. "Reflections on Surrealism," trans. Charlotte Mandell. In *The Work of Fire*. Stanford, CA: Stanford University Press, 1995. pp. 85–97.

Blanchot, Maurice. *The Step Not Beyond*, trans. Lycette Nelson. Albany: State University of New York Press, 1992.

Blanchot, Maurice. *The Unavowable Community*, trans. Pierre Joris. Barrytown, NY: Station Hill Press, 1998.

Blanchot, Maurice. *The Writing of the Disaster*, trans. Ann Smock. Lincoln and London: Nebraska University Press, 1986.

Bloom, Harold. *A Map of Misreading*. New York: Oxford University Press, 1975.

Bloom, Harold. *Kabbalah and Criticism. A Continuum Book*. New York: The Seabury Press, 1975.

Bloom, Harold. *Paul Auster*. Broomall, PA: Chelsea House Publishers, 2004.

Boyer, Philippe. "Le point de la question." *Change*, 22, février 1975. pp. 41–73.

Celan, Paul. "Speech on the Occasion of Receiving the Literature of the Free Hanseatic City of Bremen," trans. John Felstiner. In *Selected Poems and Prose of Paul Celan*. New York and London: W.W. Norton, 2001.

Cohen, Abraham. *Everyman's Talmud: The Major Teachings of Rabbinic Sages*. New York: Schocken Books, 1995.

Derrida, Jacques. *D'un ton apocalyptique adopté naguère en philosophie*. Paris: Galilée, 1983.

Derrida, Jacques. *Khôra*. Paris: Galilée, 1993.

Derrida, Jacques. "*Khōra*," trans. Ian McLeod. In Thomas Dutoit (Ed.), *On the Name*. Stanford, CA: Stanford University Press, 1995. pp. 89 –130.

Derrida, Jacques. *Of Grammatology*, trans. Gayatri Chakravorty Spivak. Baltimore: Johns Hopkins UP, 1997.

Derrida, Jacques. *Margins of Philosophy*, trans. Alan Bass. Chicago, IL: Chicago University Press.

Derrida, Jacques. *Parages*. Paris: Galilée, 2003.

Derrida, Jacques. *Positions. Entretiens avec Henri Ronse, Julia Kristeva, Jean-- Louis Houdebine, Guy Scarpetta*. Paris: Éditions de Minuit, .

Derrida, Jacques. *Sovereignties in Question: The Poetics of Paul Celan*, Thomas Dutoit and Outi Pasanen (Eds.). New York: Fordham University Press, 2005.

Derrida, Jacques. *Writing and Difference*, trans. Alan Bass. London and New York: Routledge, 2005.

Draï, Raphaël. *La penseé juive et l'interrogation divine. Exegèse et epistemologye*. Paris: PUF, 1996.

Elior, Rachel. *Mistyczne źródła chasydyzmu*, trans. M. Tomal. Kraków and Budapest: Austeria, 2009.

Eliraz, Izrael. "Dans le plein champ de la langue." *Europe*, 902–903, 2004. pp. 298–307.

Fackenheim, Emil L. *To Mend the World: Foundations of Post-Holocaust Jewish Thought*. Bloomington and Indianapolis: Indiana University Press, 1994.

Felstiner, John. *Paul Celan: Poet. Survivor. Jew*. New Haven, CT: Yale University Press, 2001.

Fichte, Johann Gottlieb. *The Science of Knowledge: With the First and the Second Introductions*, trans. Peter Heath and John Lachs. Cambridge et al.: Cambridge University Press, 2013.

Fine, Lawrence. *Physician of the Soul, Dealer of the Cosmos: Isaac Luria and His Kabbalistic Fellowship*. Stanford, CA: Stanford University Press, 2003.

Foucault, Michel. *Dits et écrits I. 1954–1975*. Paris: Quarto Gallimard, 2001.

Foucault, Michel. *The Order of Things: An Archaeology of Human Sciences*, London and New York: Routledge, 2005.

Frank, Daniel H., and Leaman Oliver (Eds.). *History of Jewish Philosophy*. London and New York: Routledge, 1997.

Freud, Sigmund. "Mourning and Melancholia." In *The Standard Edition of the Complete Psychological Works of Sigmund Freud*, James Strachey (Ed.), *Volume XIV (1914–1916): On the History of Psycho-Analytic Movement, Papers on Metapsychology and Other Works*. London: The Hogarth Press and The Institute of Psycho-Analysis. pp. 243–58.

Gadamer, Hans-Georg. *Gadamer on Celan: "Who Am I and Who Are You" and Other Essays*, trans. and ed. Richard Heinemann and Bruce Krajewski. Albany, NY: State University of New York Press, 1997.

Gasché, Rodolphe. *The Tain of the Mirror: Derrida and the Philosophy of Reflection*. Cambridge, MA: Harvard University Press, 1986.

Gasché, Rodolphe. *Of Minimal Things. Studies on the Notion of Relation*. Stanford, CA: Stanford University Press, 1999.

Gross, Benjamin. *L'aventure du langage. L'alliance de la parole dans la pensée juive*. Paris: Albin Michel, 2003.

Grozinger, Karl Erich. *Kafka a Kabała*, trans. J. Guntner. Kraków: Austeria, 2006.

Habermas, Jürgen, *Filozoficzny dyskurs nowoczesności*, trans. M. Łukasiewicz. Kraków: Universitas, 2007.

Habermas, Jürgen. *Theory of Communicative Action*, trans. Thomas MacCarthy. Boston, Mass: Beacon Press, 1981.

Hayoun, Maurice-Ruben. *Petite histoire de la philosophie juive*. Paris: Éditions Ellipses, 2008.

Handelman, Susan A. *The Slayers of Moses: The Emergence of Rabbinic Interpretation in Modern Literary Theory*. Albany, NY: State University of New York Press, 1982.

Hegel, Georg Wilhelm Friedrich. *Enzyklopadie der philosophischen Wissenschaften im Grundrisse*. http://www.hegel.de/werke_frei/hw108174.htm.

Hegel, Georg Wilhelm Friedrich. *Hegel's Science of Logic*, trans. Arnold V. Miller. New York: Humanity Books, 1998.

Hegel, Georg Wilhelm Friedrich. *Lectures on the Philosophy of Religion. Together with a Work on the Proofs of the Existence of God: Volume I*, trans. E. B. Speirs, B.D., and J. Burdon Sanderson. London: Kegan Paul, Trench, Trübnner & Co. 1895.

Hegel, Georg Wilhelm Friedrich. *Lectures on the Philosophy of Religion: Volume III. Consummate Religion*, trans. R. F. Brown, P. C. Hodgson and J. M. Stewart, Peter C. Hodgson (Ed.). Oxford: Clarendon Press, 2006.

Hegel, Georg Wilhelm Friedrich. *The Phenomenology of Mind*, trans. J. B. Baillie Mineola, NY: Dover Publications, 2003.

Heidegger, Martin. *Being and Time*, trans. J. Stambaugh. Albany: State University of New York Press, 2010.

Heidegger, Martin. *Discourse on Thinking: A Translation of Gelassenheit*, trans. John M. Anderson and E. Hans Freund, with an Introduction by John M. Anderson. New York, Evanston and London: Harper and Row, 1966.

Heidegger, Martin. *Kant and the Problem of Metaphysics. Fifth Edition, Enlarged*, trans. Richard Taft. Bloomington and Indianapolis Indiana University Press, 1997.

Heidegger, Martin. *Contributions to Philosophy: From Enowning*, trans. Parvis Emad and Kenneth Maly. Bloomington: Indiana University Press, 1999.

Heidegger, Martin. *The Question Concerning the Thing: On Kant's Doctrine of the Transcendental Principles*, trans. James D. Reid and Benjamin D. Crowe. Rowman & Littlefield International, 2018.

Hume, David. *An Enquiry Concerning Human Understanding*, Charles W. Hendel (Ed.). Pearson, 1995.

Heidegger, Martin. *A Treatise of Human Nature*. Mineola, NY: Dover Publications, 2003.

Idel, Moshe. *Absorbing Perfections: Kabbalah and Interpretation*. New Haven, CT and London: Yale University Press, 2002.

Idel, Moshe. *Old Worlds, New Mirrors: On Jewish Mysticism and Twentieth-Century Thought*. Philadelphia: University of Pennsylvania Press, 2000.

Idel, Mosze. *Kabała. Nowe perspektywy*, trans. M. Krawczyk. Kraków: NOMOS, 2006.

Jacob, Max. *Hesitant Fire: Selected Prose of Max Jacob*, trans. and ed. Moishe Black and Maria Green. Lincoln and London: University of Nebraska Press, 1991.

Jonas, Hans. "The Concept of God after Auschwitz: A Jewish Voice." *The Journal of Religion*, 67/1, January 1987. pp. 1–13.

Kafka, Franz. *The Blue Octavo Notebooks*, trans. Ernst Keiser and Eithne Wilkins, Max Brod (Ed.). Cambridge, MA: Exact Change, 1991.

Kafka, Franz. *Proces*, trans. Bruno Schulz. Warszawa: PIW, 1974.

Kant, Immanuel. *Critique of Pure Reason*, trans. Paul Guyer and Allen W. Wood. Cambridge: Cambridge University Press, 1998.

Kant, Immanuel. *Krytyka władzy sądzenia*, trans. J. Gałecki. Warszawa: PWN, 1986.

Kant, Immanuel. *Religion within the Boundaries of Mere Reason and Other Writings*, trans. Allen Wood and George di Giovanni. Cambridge: Cambridge University Press, 2003.

Kofman, Sarah. *Nietzsche et la métaphore*. Paris: Payot, 1972.

Kojève, Alexandre. *Introduction to the Reading of Hegel: Lectures on the Phenomenology of Spirit*, trans. James H. Nichols, Jr. New York: Basic Books, 1969.

Kristeva, Julia. *La revolution du langage poetique*. Paris: Seuil, 1974. English translation: *Revolution in Poetic Language*, trans. Margaret Waller. New York: Columbia University Press, 1984.

Lacan, Jacques. *The Seminar, Book X: Anxiety* (1962–63), trans. Cormac Galligher, http://www.lacaninireland.com/web/published-works/seminars/.

Lacan, Jacques. *The Seminar of Jacques Lacan, Book XX: On Feminine Sexuality: The Limits of Love and Knowledge (Encore 1972-1973)*, trans. Bruce Fink, Jacques-Alain Miller (Ed.). New York and London: W.W. Norton & Company, 1999.

Lacan, Jacques. *The Seminar, Book XXIII: Joyce and the Sinthome* (1975–76), trans. Cormac Galligher. http://www.lacaninireland.com/web/published-works/seminars/.

Lévinas, Emmanuel. *Beyond the Verse: Talmudic Readings and Lectures*, trans. Gary D. Mole. Bloomington and Indianapolis: Indiana University Press, 1994.

Lévinas, Emmanuel. *Difficult Freedom: Essays on Judaism*, trans. Seán Hand. Baltimore: Johns Hopkins University Press, 1997.

Lévinas, Emmanuel. "Exercices sur la *Folie du jour*. Approche de Blanchot" *Change*, 22, février 1975. pp. 14–25.

Lipszyc, Adam. *Sprawiedliwość na końcu języka. Czytanie Waltera Benjamina*. Kraków: Universitas, 2012.

Lipszyc, Adam. *Ślad judaizmu w filozofii XX wieku*. Warszawa: Fundacja im. Mojżesza Schorra, 2009.

Mallarmé, Stéphane. *OEuvres complètes*. Paris: Gallimard, 1945.

Markowski, Michał Paweł. *Nietzsche. Filozofia interpretacji*. Kraków: Universitas, 2001.

Milchman, Alan, and Alan Rosenberg. *Eksperymenty w myśleniu o Holocauście. Auschwitz, nowoczesność i filozofia*, trans. L. Krowicki and J. Szacki. Warszawa: Scholar, 2003.

Morgan, Michael L., and Peter Eli Gordon (Eds.). *The Cambridge Companion to Modern Jewish Philosophy*. Cambridge: Cambridge University Press, 2007.

Mosès, Stéphane. *The Angel of History: Rosenzweig, Benjamin, Scholem*, trans. Barbara Harshav. Stanford, CA: Stanford University Press, 2009.

Nancy, Jean-Luc. *The Inoperative Community*, trans. Peter Connor et al., Peter Connor (Ed.). University of Minnesota Press, 1991.

Neher, Andre. *L'exil de la parole. Du silence biblique au silence d'Auschwitz*. Paris: Seuil, 1970.

Nehamas, Alexandre. *Nietzsche. La vie comme Littérature*, trans. V. Beghein. Paris: Presses Universitaires de France, 1994.

Newton, Adam Zachary. "Versions of Ethics: Or, The SARL of Criticism: Sonority, Arrogation, Letting-Be." *American Literary History*, 13/3, Fall 2001. pp. 603–37.

Nietzsche, Friedrich. *Beyond Good and Evil: Prelude to a Philosophy of the Future*, trans. Judith Norman, Rolf-Peter Horstmann and Judith Norman (Eds.). Cambridge et al.: Cambridge University Press, 2003.

Nietzsche, Friedrich. *Daybreak: Thoughts on the Prejudices of Morality*, trans. R. J. Hollingdale, Maudemarie Clark and Brian Leiter (Eds.). Cambridge: Cambridge University Press, 2003.

Nietzsche, Friedrich. *Ecce homo*, trans. A. Ludovici. Mineona, NY: Dover Publications, 2012.

Nietzsche, Friedrich. *Untimely Meditations*, trans. R. J. Hollingdale, Cambridge: Cambridge University Press, 1997.

Nietzsche, Friedrich. *On Truth and Lies in a Nonmoral Sense*, trans. Daniel Brazeale. Create Space Independent Publishing Platform, 2005.

Nietzsche, Friedrich. *Thus Spoke Zarathustra*, trans. G. Pakes. Oxford: Oxford University Press, 2005.

Nietzsche, Friedrich. "The Antichrist," trans. H. L. Mencken. In Anthony Uyl (Ed.), *Writings of Nietzsche. Volume I*. Woodstock, ON: Devoted Publishing, 2016.

Nietzsche, Friedrich. *Twilight of the Idols*. In *The Portable Nietzsche*, trans. W. Kaufmann. New York: Viking Penguin Press, 1977.

Nietzsche, Friedrich. *Selected Letters*. Ibid., pp. 29–30, 73, 440–442, 456–457, 684–688.

Nietzsche, Friedrich. *The Will to Power*, trans. W. Kaufmann and R. J. Hollingdale. New York: Vintage Books, 1968.

Nietzsche, Friedrich. *The Gay Science*, trans. W. Kaufmann. New York: Vintage Books, 1974.

Nietzsche, Friedrich. *On the Genealogy of Morals*, trans. D. Smith. Oxford: Oxford University Press, 1996.

Nordholt, Annelies. *L'expérience de l'écriture dans l'oeuvre de Maurice Blanchot*. Amsterdam: Centrale Drukkerij Universiteit van Amsterdam, 1993.

Ouaknin, Marc-Alain. *Concerto pour quatre consonnes sans voyelles. Au-delà du principe d'identite*. Paris: Payot, 2003.

Ouaknin, Marc-Alain. *The Burnt Book: Reading the Talmud*, trans. Llewellyn Brown. Princeton: Princeton University Press, Lieu Commun, 1995.

Ouaknin, Marc-Alain. *Tsimtsoum*. Paris: Albin Michel, 1992.

Patai, Raphael. *The Messiah Texts*. New York: Avon Books, 1979.

Pieniążek, Paweł. *Suwerenność a nowoczesność. Z dziejow poststrukturalistycznej recepcji myśli Nietzschego*. Łódź: Wyd. UŁ, 2006.

Quinzio, Sergio. *Hebrajskie korzenie nowożytności* (Radici ebraiche del moderno), trans. M. Bielawski. Kraków: homini, 2005.

Roditi, Edouard. "Paul Celan and the Cult of Personality." *World Literature Today*, 66/1, Winter 1992. pp. 11–20.

Rosenzweig, Franz. *The Star of Redemption*, trans. Barbara E. Galli. Madison: Wisconsin University Press, 2005.

Roudinesco, Elisabeth. *Retour sur la question juive*. Paris: Albin Michel, 2009.

Schelling, Friedrich Wilhelm Joseph. *Philosophical Inquiries into the Nature of Human Freedom*, trans. James Gutmann, La Salle, IL: Open Court, 1992 (1936).

Shestov, Lev. *Athens and Jerusalem*, trans. Bernard Martin. Athens, OH: Ohio University Press, 1966.

Scholem, Gershom. *Another Thing: Chapters in History and Revival II*, Avraham Shapira (Ed.). Tel Aviv: Am Oved, 1990.

Scholem, Gershom. *La Kabbale*. Paris: Gallimard, 2011.

Scholem, Gershom. *Le Nom et les symboles de Dieu dans la mystique juive*. trans. M. R. Hayoun and G. Vajda. Paris: Les Éditions du Cerf, 1983.

Scholem, Gershom. *Major Trends in Jewish Mysticism*. New York: Schocken Books, 1949.

Scholem, Gershom. "Name of God and the Linguistic Theory of the Kabbalah," parts 1 and 2. *Diogenes* 79, 1972, pp. 59–80 and *Diogenes* 80, 1972, pp. 164–94.

Scholem, Gershom. *On the Mystical Shape of the Godhead: Basic Concepts in the Kabbalah*, trans. J. Neugroschel. New York: Schocken Books Inc., 1991.

Scholem, Gershom. "On Lament and Lamentation," trans. Lina Barouch and Paula Schwebel. *Jewish Study Quarterly*, 21, 2014, pp. 4–12.

Scholem, Gershom. *On the Kabbalah and Its Symbolism*, trans. Ralph Manheim. New York: Schocken Books, 1996.

Scholem, Gershom. *On the Possibility of Jewish Mysticism in Our Time & Other Essays*, trans. J. Chipman, A. Shapira (Ed.). Philadelphia and Jerusalem: The Jewish Publication Society, 1997–5758.

Scholem, Gershom. "Reflections on Jewish Theology," trans. Gabriela Shalit. In *On Jews and Judaism in Crisis: Selected Essays*, Werner J. Dannhauser (Ed.). Philadelphia, PA: Paul Dry Books, 2012. pp. 261–297.

Scholem, Gershom. *The Messianic Idea in Judaism*. New York: Schocken Books, 1995.

Simon, Heinrich, and Marie Simon. *Filozofia żydowska*, trans. T. Pszczołkowski. Warszawa: Wiedza Powszechna, 1990.

Taubes, Jacob. *From Cult to Culture: Fragments Toward a Critique of Historical Reason*, Charlotte E. Fonrobert and Amir Engel (Eds.). Stanford, CA: Stanford University Press, 2010.

Tora, trans. Izaak Cylkow. Kraków: Austeria, 2010.

Wittgenstein, Ludwig. *Philosophical Investigations*, trans. G. E. M. Anscombe. Oxford: Basil Blackwell, 1986.

Wittgenstein, Ludwig. *Tractatus Logico-Philosophicus*, trans. John Ogden, with an Introduction by Bertrand Russel. London: Kegan Paul, Trench, Trubner and Co. Ltd., 1922.

Wodziński, Cezary. *Kairos. Konferencja w Todtnaubergu. Celan – Heidegger*. Gdańsk: słowo/obraz terytoria, 2010.

Wolfson, Elliot R. *Language, Eros, Being. Kabbalistic Hermeneutics and Poetic Imagination*. New York: Fordham University Press, 2005.

Wyschogrod, Edith. *Spirit in Ashes: Hegel, Heidegger, and Man-Made Mass Death*. New Haven, CT and London: Yale University Press, 1985.

Žižek, Slavoj. *The Sublime Object of Ideology*. New York and London: Verso, 1989.

Žižek, Slavoj. *On Belief*. London and New York: Verso, 2001.

Žižek, Slavoj. *Puppet and Dwarf. The Perverse Core of Christianity*. Cambridge: MIT Press, 2003.

Žižek, Slavoj. *The Ticklish Subject: The Absent Centre of Political Ontology*. New York and London: Verso, 2008.

Žižek, Slavoj. *Less Than Nothing. Hegel and the Shadow of Dialectical Materialism*. London and New York: Verso, 2012.

Index

Studies in Jewish History and Memory

Edited by Lucyna Aleksandrowicz-Pędich

www.peterlang.com

Printed in Great Britain
by Amazon